EISENHOWER
at Columbia

EISENHOWER
at Columbia

Travis Beal Jacobs

With an introduction by
Eli Ginzberg

Transaction Publishers
New Brunswick (U.S.A.) and London (U.K.)

Library of Congress Catalog Number:
ISBN: 0-7658-0036-5
Printed in the United States of America

Library of Congress Cataloging-in-Publication Data

Jacobs, Travis Beal.
    Eisenhower at Columbia / Travis Beal Jacobs.
        p. cm.
    Includes bibliographical references (p.) and index.
    ISBN 0-7658-0036-5 (acid-free paper)
    1. Eisenhower, Dwight D. (Dwight David), 1890-1969—Career in education.
2. Presidents—United States—Biography.   3. College presidents—New York
(State)—New York—Biography   4. Columbia University—Biography.
I. Title.

E836 .J26 2000
378. 747'1'092—dc21   00-062884
[B]

To
Beal and Holmes

In memory of my dear sister Sarah, 1932–1997

Contents

Preface

Two years after World War II, General Dwight David Eisenhower, the leader of the victorious Allied Armed Forces in Europe and the Chief of Staff of the United States Army, accepted the Presidency of Columbia University in the City of New York. General Eisenhower—America's most popular war hero and one of the most famous people in the world—in his first civilian position was to succeed Nicholas Murray Butler, perhaps the greatest university president of the century, and he would lead a world renowned, but recently troubled, university. Five years later Eisenhower would be elected President of the United States, and the associations he had made as President of Columbia University played a significant role in his defeat of Senator Robert A. Taft for the Republican Party nomination in 1952. His experience at Columbia contributed to his education as a civilian and helped to prepare him for the Presidency; it also would contribute to the critical historical assessment of him that dominated for many years.

For two decades Dwight Eisenhower, from the beginning of World War II until he left the White House in early 1961, played a leadership role on the world stage longer than any American since George Washington, Thomas Jefferson, and John Adams, and his Columbia tenure came at the middle of this period, between the two signal events of his career. Yet, the story of Eisenhower at Columbia has not been told; scholars briefly have repeated critical contemporary assessments and largely dismissed or ignored that part of his career and have focused, instead, on his World War II record and his performance in the White House.

Soon after Eisenhower arrived on Morningside Heights journalists began describing his Presidency as a sorry scene. In 1950 Richard H. Rovere critically commented on the "intense hostility" toward Eisenhower "on the part of the majority of both faculty and student body." Max Frankel, who entered Columbia College "at the same time" the General arrived on campus, started writing for the *Columbia Spectator* and within a year was reporting on Eisenhower and campus activities for *The New*

York Times. Frankel quickly "suspected" that the University's Trustees had White House ambitions for the General, and he has recalled that the President's absences "made a mockery of Eisenhower's academic pretensions....Like most Columbia teachers and students," he added, *Spectator* reporters "were openly contemptuous of Ike's campus caper." By the spring of 1952, after Eisenhower had announced his candidacy for the Republican Party nomination, Rovere asserted, "His tour of duty at Columbia was disappointing to almost everyone, including, apparently, himself....He accepted the job only because it gave him a forum....As we are now seeing, his use of Columbia as a forum was quite successful." A few weeks later writer William V. Shannon, emphasizing "Eisenhower's disastrous failure as president of Columbia University," concluded, "This experience is important. It was his only civilian job."[1]

Eisenhower scholars often have not moved beyond these early judgments. For example, two decades after the General left Columbia University, Herbert S. Parmet briefly concluded in *Eisenhower and the American Crusades*, "Eisenhower and the super-intellectual climate of Columbia were not compatible." Peter Lyon, in his biography *Eisenhower: Portrait of the Hero*, wrote: "It was all wrong all around." In *Eisenhower: Soldier, General of the Army, President-Elect, 1890–1952* Stephen E. Ambrose, Eisenhower's foremost biographer, decided that the Columbia presidency did not warrant inclusion in the subtitle. Ambrose spent only a few pages on the subject, asserting that "Eisenhower intended to do a good job at Columbia, retire after a few years, then perhaps do a bit of writing on national and international affairs." Although Blanche Wiesen Cook devoted nearly one-half of *The Declassified Eisenhower* to his pre-White House years, she described Columbia as "a political stopgap." Thus, in 1984 Louis Galambos, editor of *The Papers of Dwight David Eisenhower*, stated in the "Introduction" to volumes X and XI, *Columbia University*, that Eisenhower's "activities as President of Columbia University seem to have received far less attention than they deserve." Yet, even the Eisenhower Centennial Celebrations in October, 1990, paid very little attention to his Presidency of the University; moreover, in 1993 *American Experience's* "Eisenhower," a two and a-half hour PBS Video program narrated by historian David McCullough, did not even mention the subject. And the dust-jacket for Geoffrey Perret's recent biography, *Eisenhower*, promises a "new, in-depth life"; yet, after only several pages Perret concluded that Columbia "was an episode he seemed almost happy to forget."[2]

The Columbia period occupied roughly four years of Dwight Eisenhower's life, and it played a vital role on his road to the White House. It was far more than an interlude. He had accepted the Columbia position in June, 1947, and was installed as the University's thirteenth President on October 12, 1948, two days before his fifty-eighth birthday. His Presidency of Columbia can be broken into four periods: (1) the long presidential search and the interregnum between his appointment and his arrival on campus on May 2, 1948; (2) his first year, from his arrival and installation through his temporary return to Washington and the Pentagon in early 1949 and his illness that spring; (3) his major period at Columbia without interruption from September, 1949, through December, 1950; and (4) his leave of absence to become NATO Commander through the 1952 presidential campaign and his resignation on the eve of his Inauguration as President of the United States on January 20, 1953.

Columbia had been searching unsuccessfully for a President since the retirement of Nicholas Murray Butler in 1945. Under Butler's brilliant leadership it had become one of the world's most prestigious universities, but the last years of his forty-three year tenure were tragic and detrimental to the University on Morningside Heights. General Eisenhower's term as Chief of Staff, from December, 1945, to February, 1948, has been told thoroughly by his biographers; no understanding— and no assessment—of his Presidency of Columbia is possible, however, without an examination of the University during the protracted search. That story needs to be told and, though Eisenhower was not central to it, several Trustees had been interested in the war hero from the start. Columbia faced major problems during this period, and two prominent educators declined the Presidency and several others expressed no interest in the position.

Why, then, did General Eisenhower even consider the Columbia Presidency, when he had other opportunities? What interests and educational philosophy did he bring to Columbia? He had demonstrated his administrative skills in the Army, but would they work at a large, complex, urban university? How did the General view his role as President, and what were his goals and accomplishments? What led, moreover, to the bitter political disputes on the Morningside Heights campus during the 1952 presidential campaign, when the General ran as the Republican Party nominee against Governor Adlai E. Stevenson?

Dwight Eisenhower was one of the dominant figures of his age, and the answers to these and other questions show that Columbia represented an important and influential part of his career and that it cannot be dismissed as merely wrong, irrelevant, or absurd, as several writers have suggested. He brought to the University proven leadership qualities, his managerial and organizational skills, and his enormous popularity and ability to work with others; moreover, his charisma, energy, and commitment infused a vitality into everything he did. Through his presidency he had the opportunity to develop and articulate in the nation's foremost city his views on a variety of subjects from democratic citizenship to federal aid to education and academic freedom in the growing anti-communist atmosphere of the Cold War, and his speeches and activities received extensive media coverage throughout the country.

President Eisenhower, after writing his White House *Memoirs,* embarked on his *"Reminiscences,"* with the assistance of Kevin McCann, whose association with Eisenhower began in 1946 as a speech writer. McCann, who quickly had become a confidant of the General's, was "delighted" about the new project and was particularly interested in "a comprehensive memoir on the Columbia years." He knew the General's memory needed "jogging" for this personal account, and he wrote a long letter to a colleague from the Columbia period "for a clearer idea of what is needed." He wrote: "Those were terribly crowded years; in some respects...they were for [Eisenhower] much more hectic than the White House tour." McCann added: "If the Columbia years were to be given the fall treatment...the product might easily be in bulkage the equivalent of the *Mandate* volume in *The White House Years*—particularly if it covered all the months—omitting only the actual conduct of SHAPE [Supreme Headquarters, Allied Powers Europe]—from the arrival at 60 Morningside Heights until the acceptance of his resignation by the Trustees....He did have a world eminence there."

McCann continued: "The Presidency of the United States was an inevitable corollary to the Presidency of Columbia, joined with the Supreme Command in Paris [NATO]...and, of course, the Wartime years Command. Consequently, if God gives him time and energy, the Columbia years should not be scanted in his Reminiscences." The General, McCann reported, already had dictated some twenty thousand words on his Abilene boyhood.

Within a year, however, Eisenhower suffered his second major heart attack, and his personal account of his Columbia years received only two short chapters in *At Ease: Stories I Tell to Friends*, published in 1967. The General never presented, as McCann had hoped, "the Eisenhower record at Columbia clearly and fully and warmly."[3]

Neither Eisenhower nor his biographers have attempted to address fully his Presidency of Columbia. The story could fill, as McCann suggested in 1964, a larger volume than this. Eisenhower's civilian and political education can no longer be told without considering the significance of his Columbia tenure.

Notes

1.　Richard H. Rovere, "The Second Eisenhower Boom," *Harper's Magazine* (May, 1950), p. 33; Rovere, "The Eisenhower Story," *Progressive* (May, 1952), p. 5; Max Frankel, *The Times of My Life and My Life with the Times* (New York, 1999), pp. 93–95, 104; William V. Shannon, *New Republic,* June 9, 1952, p. 20.

2.　Herbert S. Parmet, *Eisenhower and the American Crusades* (New York, 1972), p. 15; Peter Lyon, *Eisenhower: Portrait of the Hero* (Boston, 1974), p. 382; Stephen E. Ambrose, *Eisenhower. Soldier, General of the Army, President-Elect*, 1890–1952 (New York, 1983), pp. 480, 478; Blanche Wiesen Cook, *The Declassified Eisenhower* (New York, 1981), p. 82; *The* Papers of *Dwight David Eisenhower*, Vol. X, *Columbia University,* ed. Louis Galambos (Baltimore, 1984), p. xxiii; "Eisenhower," *American Experience*, PBS Video (1993); Geoffrey Perret, *Eisenhower (New* York, 1999), p. 384. The History Channel's five-hour program, "Eisenhower: Warrior and President," on June 6, 2000, contained little reference to Columbia.

3.　Kevin McCann to Robert C. Harron, December 16, 1964 (copy given to author by McCann).

Acknowledgements

I have lived with this project for many years. The study began as a senior history thesis for Professor F. Wilson Smith at Princeton University on Eisenhower and the 1952 presidential campaign, and I quickly learned that the hostility to Eisenhower and the bitterness of that campaign still existed on the Morningside Heights campus. Robert C. Harron, a close family friend and the Director of Public Relations at Columbia, offered valuable suggestions and arranged for me interviews with prominent individuals at the University. They shared with me many thoughts and recollections, which contributed enormously to my senior thesis. A few of the professors had worked closely with Eisenhower at Columbia and were willing to talk with me at length because of their association with my father, Albert Charles Jacobs, who had joined the Columbia School of Law Faculty in 1927 and served as Provost of the University from 1947 to 1949. Soon after writing the thesis, I decided to attend graduate school in American history at Columbia, instead of entering the School of Law. While studying for my doctorate I hardly had time to think about the Eisenhower manuscript, although a number of persons with whom I had talked, from Allan Nevins, Harry J. Carman, and John A. Krout to Kevin McCann, Joseph Campbell, and Robert C. Harron read that thesis and encouraged me to revise and expand it after I completed my doctoral studies.

Over the years my questions have changed and, even during the writing of the thesis, the focus had shifted from the 1952 controversy on Morningside Heights to include the entire Eisenhower period at Columbia. And, over the years, intervals of neglect have been frequent and long, whether for the demands of teaching at a small, liberal arts college, other projects, or department administrative duties. I have, though, occasionally conducted additional interviews, most of which are recorded and are better described as long conversations. These interviews have helped to clarify my views and, also, have prompted me to ask more questions; I regret that I lacked the knowledge and perspective to take better advantage of most of the earlier interviews. I am particularly grateful for the recollections, either during interviews or in letters, of Carl W. Ackerman, Jacques Barzun, Douglas M. Black, Joseph Campbell, Harry J. Carman, James Dohr, David Herbert Donald, Mamie D. Eisenhower, Milton S. Eisenhower, Barbara Foltz, Peter Gay, Eli Ginzberg, Henry F. Graff, Louis Hacker, W. Averell Harriman, Robert C. Harron, R. Gordon Hoxie, Albert C. Jacobs, Philip C. Jessup, Robert L. Johnson, Grayson L. Kirk, John A. Krout, William E. Leuchtenburg, Kevin McCann, Clifford C. Nelson, Allan Nevins, Raymond J. Saulnier, Robert L. Schulz, Ellis D. Slater, Young B. Smith, Arthur Hays Sulzberger, Adrienne Swift, Lionel Trilling, David B. Truman, Bruce Wonnacott, and Philip Young. Ellan Robinson Reynes gave me permission to use the William E. Robinson Papers at the Dwight D. Eisenhower Library; Helen L. King to use her oral history interview; John G. Kirk to use Grayson L. Kirk's oral history interview; and Ken Roberts to use the Clifford Roberts oral history interview. I am also grateful to Jessica Silver and the Vestry of Trinity Church in the City of New York for consulting Vestry Minutes, and to David L. Stebenne for sending me his forthcoming article, "Thomas J. Watson and the Business-Government Relationship, 1933–1956."

I am particularly thankful for the encouragement, suggestions, and criticisms from Joseph Campbell, Harry J. Carman, Eli Ginzberg, Louis Galambos, Henry F. Graff, Robert C. Harron, R. Gordon Hoxie, Elizabeth S. Hughes, Albert C. Jacobs, John A. Krout, Clifford C. Nelson, Allan Nevins, Raymond J. Saulnier, Philip Young, and Samuel Vaughan (the General's publisher at Doubleday) after they read the manuscript in its various stages. President Emeritus Grayson L. Kirk read the first six chapters, which included his first year as Provost, and sent me several long letters with comments. Professor Herbert S. Parmet generously read the manuscript in its final stages.

At Columbia University I am indebted to William Theodore DeBary, Marion Jemmott, and Corinne Rieder for granting me permission to use essential material in the Central Archives of Columbia University in Low Memorial Library and to Sarah Vos, who assisted me in locating files; to the Directors of the Oral History Research Office from Louis Starr to Ronald J. Grele and its staff who have been most helpful; to David Mortimer, who generously provided me with valuable material on Eisenhower and the American Assembly, the General's favorite project at Columbia; to M. Halsey Thomas, Curator of Columbiana when I wrote my thesis; and to Meg Dooley, Senior Staff Officer, Columbia University Development and Alumni Relations, for her interest and encouragement.

John E. Wickman, former Director, and Daniel D. Holt, Director, Dwight David Eisenhower Library, Abilene, Kansas, and the staff, especially Dwight E. Strandberg, have been most generous with their assistance during my visits to the Library and in answering letters and telephone calls. In the fall of 1998 Dan Holt organized a joint conference on "The Presidents Eisenhower" with the Eisenhower Library, Eisenhower Foundation, and Kansas State University to mark the 50th anniversary of Eisenhower's Installation at Columbia University. I delivered the main talk, "Ike's Columbia Crusade," and Professor Sue Zschoche offered thoughtful comments.

The thoroughness of the *Eisenhower Papers* project at Johns Hopkins University under the editorship of Louis Galambos is impressive, and on more than a few occasions I have marveled at the informative footnotes; I have tried to cite the *Eisenhower Papers* when those volumes published material from Columbia's Central Archives or the Eisenhower Library. I am very thankful for this assistance from Columbia University, the Eisenhower Library, and the editors of the *Eisenhower Papers* in my efforts to understand Eisenhower at Columbia, a story both complex and controversial.

"Eisenhower, the American Assembly, and 1952," a paper presented at Gettysburg College's "The Eisenhower Legacy: A Centennial Symposium," in October, 1990, appeared in *Presidential Studies Quarterly* (Summer, 1992); in a slightly revised form it was included in a collection of symposium papers, *Reexamining the Eisenhower Presidency,* edited by Shirley Anne Warshaw and Foreword by Louis Galambos (Westport, 1993). I delivered a paper at the University of Kansas' "Ike's America," also an Eisenhower Centennial Conference, and participated that fall at Columbia University's "Reminiscences" of his presidency. A paper presented for a University Seminar at Columbia in January, 1997, appeared, in revised form, as "Eisenhower Comes to Columbia" in *Columbia Columns* (Autumn, 1997).

Throughout the project I have received generous support from the Middlebury College Faculty Research Fund and from the Earhart Foundation. I have had, moreover, encouragement from colleagues and students at the College. I am particularly grateful to William B.

Catton, John M. McCardell, Robert L. Ferm, James R. Ralph, Jr., Barbara L. Bellows, and William B. Hart. Jim somehow found time to read the manuscript, in spite of his demanding teaching schedule and committee assignments. Ronald E. Rucker and the staff at the Egbert Starr Library responded to numerous inter-library loan requests. Sara M. Gregg, a Middlebury graduate studying for her doctorate in American history at Columbia, commented on the manuscript, did some last minute research for me in New York and assisted with the proofreading. She also reminded me about the portrait of Eisenhower in Butler Library. Mary E. Curtis and Irving Horowitz were most understanding when I missed several deadlines because of my commitment to finish a major project in time for Middlebury College's Bicentennial, and Laurence Mintz did not allow those delays to interfere with his fine copy editing. My sons Beal and Holmes, as well as Connie Carroll, undoubtedly are as glad as anyone that I have finally finished the manuscript.

One final but important comment. My mother and father gave me many opportunities, and I wish that they could have seen this manuscript. When I returned to Morningside Heights for research on my senior thesis, I had the privilege of talking with some of Columbia's eminent teachers and scholars. That marvelous opportunity, as well as a growing appreciation for the world of books and learning, which I had been so fortunate to experience, without doubt prompted me to pursue a career in history.

Travis Beal Jacobs
Bridport, Vermont

Introduction

It is with much pleasure that I respond to the author's request that I write an introduction to his illuminating, informative, and interesting volume entitled *Eisenhower at Columbia.*

I have long been flattered that General Eisenhower arranged, through his personal physician and my World War II friend, Major General Howard Snyder to have me to lunch while he was Chief of Staff early in 1947 to explore two issues: If the Columbia trustees offered him the presidency should he accept it; and if he came to Columbia, what were my ideas about initiating a multi-year research project on *The Ineffective Soldier: Lessons for Management and the Nation,* 3 volumes (1959), that at the time was still an aspiration, not even an outline.

A few words about each of the foregoing, together with a few observations on relevant Columbia matters; and a few long distant appraisals about the two years plus that Eisenhower served as the active president of Columbia.

During the three-hour luncheon during which General Snyder said not one word after introducing me, Eisenhower wondered out loud whether he should accept any type of university position; whether he (and Mamie) would be happier if he became the head of a small liberal arts college in a suburban or rural location; and whether the Columbia trustees appreciated his decision if they made him an offer that he accepted that he would not devote much time or effort raising funds for the university.

I saw no point in misleading Eisenhower and I told him not to trust any assurances that one or all of the trustees would give him about his not being expected to become a fund-raiser. I stressed that the Columbia financial outlook had deteriorated greatly and that the university urgently needed to improve its much weakened finances.

Eisenhower asked me a few additional questions about Columbia, but I concluded that while he heard what I said he was considering accepting a Columbia offer if it were forthcoming without reference to his aversion to money-raising. In point of fact during his brief and frequently interrupted period as Columbia's president before relocating to his new assignment in early 1951 as head of the Supreme Headquarters, Allied Powers, Europe in Paris, he raised some money for Columbia but in total relatively little.

I knew from earlier discussions with General Snyder that Eisenhower had been seriously disturbed by the successful counter-attacks that the Germans had launched on the Western Front in December 1944 which reduced the U.S. reserves to a dangerously low point. When Eisenhower was subsequently informed that about 2.5 million Americans of military age had been rejected for service or prematurely separated while the war was still underway, he decided that the explanations for this serious waste of military manpower should be studied and remedial action taken to avoid its repetition. And Snyder had informed Eisenhower that I had identified the same issue for my research agenda just as soon as I returned to Columbia campus.

By far the larger part of our extended luncheon conversation focused in and around questions that General Eisenhower put to me about what such a research agenda would comprise; what skills the research team required; and how a multi-year project could be funded.

I drafted and redrafted based on Eisenhower's subsequent discussions with me many successive versions of our project that originally was entitled "Adjustment to Work" until Walter Reuther who had been asked by Eisenhower to comment on an early version pointed out that "adjustment" carried with it a manipulative implication and suggested that we find a more appropriate title which we did—"The Conservation of Human Resources"—a phrase of Teddy Roosevelt's!

Eisenhower asked the senior academic administrators at Columbia to review our plan and assured them that if they approved it he would seek funding off campus. Eisenhower talked to Secretary Forrestal of the Department of Defense about our project and he asked me to call on the Secretary to explore in more detail the Department of Defense's interest. I spent an hour with the Secretary who offered to have the Department of Defense defray all of the costs. I thanked him for his offer; expressed appreciation for his willingness to make all relevant military records available to us but pointed out that he would hear from General Eisenhower presently whether Columbia would look to the Department of Defense for the financing of what was initially planned as a five-year or longer research project. On my return to the campus, I recommended to Eisenhower that he thank the Secretary for his offer of broad-scale cooperation but decline the Department's willingness to fund the research. I was uneasy about how the Defense Department might respond to our findings and policy recommendations. Eisenhower agreed and obtained the requisite funding from about ten leading corporations including Coca Cola, General Dynamics, Dupont, General Electric, Exxon, CBS, Consolidated Edison and several others.

It took the Conservation of Human Resources research team nine years to complete its major three volume work on *The Ineffective Soldier: Lessons for Management and the Nation,* Columbia University Press, 1959. However, the research team completed earlier two important studies of military manpower in World War II—*The Uneducated* (1953) dedicated to Maj. Gen. Snyder which elicited special praise from President Eisenhower. In 1956 I forwarded a draft of *The Negro Potential* to General Snyder with the request that if the President's schedule permitted I would welcome his reactions. I heard from General Snyder very shortly thereafter that President Eisenhower found the draft manuscript "too apologetic" and I promised General Snyder to do what I could to provide a more balanced account of the interactions between black troops and a thoroughly segregated Armed Forces that prevailed during World War II. I made a large number of stylistic but no substantive changes in redrafting *The Negro Potential* and on my next visit to the White House the President told me that he had read my new draft and found it acceptable, observing that poor style can on occasion be as misleading as faulty analysis.

In early 1946 when I was still living in Washington working for the War Department a Columbia faculty advisory committee on the search for a new president asked me to call on Senator James William Fulbright of Arkansas to learn whether he would entertain an offer to become the next president of Columbia. I had a pleasant tea at his home during which the Senator explained that I had come both too late and too early. He definitely would have been interested if he were still a member of the House of Representatives; but the inquiry came too early in his Senatorial career.

As a student, researcher, and junior faculty member I had witnessed the steady decline of Columbia University during the fif-

teen year period of President Butler's physical decline and the ensuing turmoil of the Great Depression and World War II and the inability
of the Columbia trustees to speed Butler's resignation which was
finally forthcoming in 1945. By that time Butler had lost his eye-
sight, his hearing, and had to be supported by an aide in walking
from his campus home to his campus office.

Professor Jacobs' revealing and insightful account of Eisenhower's
two years plus as Columbia's president is focused on illuminating a
period in the General's post World War II experience, a period during which Governor Thomas Dewey of New York was expected to
win the presidency in 1948 in which case he would have run for
re-election in 1952, a strategically different scenario than the one
that developed as a result of Truman's upset electoral victory in 1948.

Professor Jacobs' book also contributes to a deepened understanding of another major twentieth-century U.S. happening—how
one of the nation's foremost universities was speeded on a down-
ward spiral by an enfeebled president and incompetent trustees
but took a first step toward recovery with the appointment of General Eisenhower in 1947, a recovery that was not completed until
1980 with the appointment of President Michael Sovern, a half
century after the University's initial decline. There are not many
books based on source materials, well researched and well written,
that can claim the distinction of adding new knowledge and understanding of the U.S.'s leading mid-century's national personality
and at the same time providing new understanding of how a leading university in fast fall eventually took a first step towards stabi-
lization and recovery.

1

Searching for an Eisenhower

Great personalities make great universities.
—Nicholas Murray Butler
Inaugural Address, 1902

When a Committee from the Board of Trustees of Columbia University
asked me to consider becoming President of that great institution, I said
(as I did later when other people had ideas about another Presidency)
that they were talking to the wrong Eisenhower.
—Dwight D. Eisenhower, *At Ease* (1967)

Amid the pomp and splendor of a medieval pageant, General of
the Army Dwight D. Eisenhower, the leader of the victorious Allied
crusade against Nazi Germany, became the thirteenth President of
Columbia University in the City of New York on October 12, 1948.
Nearly twenty thousand persons had assembled in front of Low
Memorial Library and Alma Mater to witness Eisenhower's Installation and the beginning of his second crusade, this one for youth and
democratic citizenship. Never had there been such a gathering of
American college and university presidents to pay tribute to a new
colleague, and they were joined in the colorful procession by representatives of thirty-eight foreign universities, including ancient Bologna, Paris, Oxford, and Cambridge, delegates from thirty learned
societies, and Columbia's Trustees. Forty-six years earlier Nicholas
Murray Butler, in his Inaugural Address in front of Low Memorial,
had declared, "Great personalities make great universities," and he
went on to become the greatest university president of the twentieth
century, fulfilling his own prophecy.[1] And, now, Columbia's Trustees had another great personality assuming the presidency.

The dignitaries marched under overcast skies from Nicholas Murray
Butler Library across South Field and 116th Street to the platform,

1

and that afternoon Columbia's prominence was unchallenged in an awesome display of academic brilliance and media attention. Eisenhower, World War II's most popular and widely acclaimed general, had an infectious grin and his expressive blue eyes conveyed his intensity and vitality; on the day of his Installation, however, he was grim and without any trace of his famous smile as he walked in the solemn and slow procession with the University's Provost through the center of the campus and the huge crowd.

After the national anthem and invocation came the welcoming speeches. Student and alumni leaders spoke first, and then Robert Livingston Schuyler, Gouverneur Morris Professor of History and former President of the American Historical Association, asserted on behalf of the University's faculties that the new President's career "gives us solid ground for hope in Columbia's future under his leadership." Finally, Eisenhower, in academic gown and wearing the honorary Doctor of Laws hood awarded him in 1947 at the Special Columbia University Convocation for the nation's wartime military leaders, received the University's Charter and symbolic keys from Frederick Coykendall, Chairman of the Board of Trustees.

As Coykendall presented Eisenhower "the chair of the presiding officer"—a black haircloth armchair which had been Benjamin Franklin's—the sun burst through the clouds and the new President began his Installation Address under blue skies. The former Supreme Commander and Chief of Staff of the United States Army quickly stated that if America were "a land where the military profession is a weapon of tyranny or aggression . . . a life-long soldier could hardly assume my present role." In the United States, though, he could become an educator without altering "his fundamental life purposes—the protection and perpetuation of basic human freedoms." He could see, indeed, a parallel in the pursuit of these goals. At a time when Soviet Russia's blockade of Berlin was intensifying the Cold War and the Allies were airlifting supplies to Berliners, the fear of communism was growing in America. The General promised, however, that there would be "no administrative suppression or distortion of any subject," no "intellectual 'iron curtain,'" at Columbia. Further, "The facts of communism, for example, shall be taught here. . . . Ignorance of communism, fascism, or any other police-state philosophy is far more dangerous than ignorance of the most virulent disease."

Eisenhower then expressed what would be one of his major themes at Columbia, "democratic citizenship." At every institution "general education for citizenship must be the common and first purpose." Commenting on "a growing doubt among our people that democracy is able to cope with the social and economic trials that lie ahead," he saw that some Americans had a "stark fear that our way of life may succumb to the combined effects of creeping paralysis from within and aggressive assault from without." Only education could combat "doubt and fear," and institutions like Columbia had a "heavy obligation" to prevent democracy from collapsing into "tyrannical regimentation" or "social anarchy." Enlarging on this opinion, he stated, "To assign the university the mission of ever strengthening the foundations of our culture is to ennoble the institution and confirm the vital importance of its service."

Columbia University would be "a dynamic institution," one "dedicated to learning and research and to effective cooperation with all other free institutions which will aid in the preservation and strengthening of human dignity and happiness." The General asserted that his energies would be devoted "to the support of Columbia's able and distinguished faculty, in the service of all humanity." The sun was still shining as the procession left the platform; Mamie Eisenhower, who later recalled the Installation ceremonies as "touching" and "inspiring," considered the sun's appearance a "very good omen."[2]

*   *   *

After V-E Day, May 8, 1945, General Eisenhower commanded the United States occupation forces in Germany, and he returned home from Europe in late 1945 to become Chief of Staff, an appointment which President Harry Truman had assured him would last no more than two years; Columbia's search for a successor to Nicholas Murray Butler coincidentally had started the day Germany surrendered in 1945 and by 1947 it had become desperate. Eisenhower's biographers have critically assessed his career during this period; a brief discussion, nonetheless, provides a reminder of his amazing worldwide popularity and a glimpse into his interests and activities as he pondered what he would do when he retired from the Army after his Chief of Staff tour. The story of Columbia's inability to appoint a new president, however, has never been told, and it is essential for understanding Eisenhower's Presidency of the University. Though Eisenhower's name had suggested itself in

1945—it was, after all, on everyone's lips—not until the spring of 1947 did the two paths become interwoven.

On May 7, 1945, Eisenhower accepted the surrender of Hitler's Germany in Reims and cabled the Combined Chiefs of Staff: "The mission of this Allied force was fulfilled." The European war had ended, and General George C. Marshall, the Chief of Staff, told him, "You have completed your mission with the greatest victory in the history of warfare. . . . Since the day of your arrival in England three years ago, you have been selfless in your actions, always sound and tolerant in your judgments and altogether admirable in the courage and wisdom of your military decisions." Marshall, who did not give praise lightly and had placed his fullest confidence in Eisenhower throughout the war, concluded, "You have made history, great history for the good of mankind and you have stood for all we hope for and admire in an officer of the United States Army. These are my tributes and my personal thanks." On May 8 Eisenhower in his "Victory Order of the Day" to the "Men and Women of the Allied Expeditionary Force" asserted, "The crusade on which we embarked in the early summer of nineteen forty-four" with D-Day "has reached its glorious conclusion. . . . Full victory in Europe has been attained."[3]

While victory celebrations erupted with the defeat of Hitler's forces, Eisenhower recalled years later in *At Ease*, "Like so many other men and women who had been at war physically or emotionally, exhaustion rather than exultation was my first reaction to victory in Europe." During the next two months, while he set up his occupation headquarters in Frankfurt, he became the center of a whirlwind of attention, from the European capitals of London, Prague, and Paris to Washington, New York, West Point, Kansas City, and Abilene. Even before the parades began, Marshal Georgi Zhukov, who had led the Red Army's onslaught on Berlin, traveled to Frankfurt and presented him with the Order of Victory, Russia's highest award.[4]

Prime Minister Winston Churchill invited Eisenhower to London for the Guildhall Ceremony on June 12, and the occasion required him to deliver the principal speech in the historic hall. It was, the General later wrote, "the first formal address of any length that I had to give on my own. . . . I labored at it mightily, never satisfied with a single paragraph." One evening, when a friend visited his headquarters in Frankfurt, "I began to quote from memory and to my astonishment was able to go through the entire talk without pause." London gave General Eisenhower, biographer Kenneth Davis emphasized, "one of the greatest triumphs ever accorded any man, and by far the greatest ever accorded by that ancient capital to one who was not an Englishman." He arrived for the impressive Guildhall occasion in a horse-drawn carriage, and the huge, solemn audience included the United Kingdom's distinguished military and civil officials. Eisenhower was made a Freeman of the City of London and received the Duke of Wellington's sword, "as a symbol of the sword I was to receive" but which was not ready.

"The high sense of distinction," he began, was "mingled with feelings of profound sadness. . . . Humility must always be the portion of any man who receives acclaim earned in the blood of his followers and sacrifices of his friends." Insisting that "this august body is really honoring . . . all Allied men and women that have served with me in this war," he declared "that when two peoples will face the tragedies of war to defend the same spiritual values, the same treasured rights, then in the deepest sense those two are truly related. So even as I proclaim my undying Americanism, I am bold enough and exceedingly proud to claim the basis of kinship to you of London." Continuing, he emphasized, "No man alone could have brought about this result. Had I possessed the military skill of a Marlborough, the wisdom of Solomon, the understanding of Lincoln, I still would have been helpless without the loyalty, vision, and generosity of thousands upon thousands of British and Americans." Concluding with his "most cherished hope . . . that after Japan joins the Nazis in utter defeat, neither my country nor yours need ever again summon its sons and daughters . . . to face the tragedies of battle," he stressed the importance of remembering that "neither London nor Abilene, sisters under the skin, will sell her birthright for physical safety, her liberty for mere existence." London newspapers printed the Guildhall speech on the front page, along with Lincoln's Gettysburg Address, and Eisenhower, standing on a balcony with Churchill, told the large crowd, "I'm a citizen of London now, too." Later at Buckingham Palace King George VI conferred on him the Order of Merit.[5]

His triumphant return to the United States began on June 18. Fighter planes and bombers accompanied his plane into Washington's National Airport where Mamie Eisenhower and General Marshall were among the thirty thousand Americans and dozens of photographers welcoming him back. Over a million persons watched the General, waving and smiling, in an open car parade proceeding down Constitution Avenue to the Capitol. "My imagination," he told a Joint

Session of Congress, "cannot picture a more dramatic moment than this in the life of an American." He paid tribute to three million Americans who "resolutely faced every terror the ruthless Nazi could devise" and to President Franklin D. Roosevelt "who, until his tragic death, led America in war." Eisenhower concluded: "I will say nothing other than that from his strength and indomitable spirit I drew constant support and confidence in the solution of my own problems." He received a long standing ovation; afterward, President Harry Truman presented him with the Distinguished Service Cross at the White House. He held an afternoon press conference, and that evening he returned to the White House for a stag dinner.

The next morning the Eisenhowers went to New York by train and a cheering crowd of possibly four million persons enthusiastically greeted him. "Hour upon hour," he wrote in *At Ease*, "we traveled avenues jammed with people, with incalculable others hanging out the windows of towering office and apartment buildings." Mayor Fiorello LaGuardia accompanied him on the thirty-seven-mile ride and at City Hall made him an honorary citizen of the City. Eisenhower claimed in his speech that "New York simply cannot do this to a Kansas farmer boy and keep its reputation for sophistication." He attended at his request a baseball game and watched the Boston Braves defeat the New York Giants at the Polo Grounds. That evening at a Waldorf Astoria dinner he emphasized that "peace is an absolute necessity to this world. . . . I believe that we should let no specious argument of any kind deter us from exploring every direction in which peace can be maintained." The next day he went up the Hudson River to West Point and reviewed the corps of cadets at the United States Military Academy, from which he had graduated and received his commission in 1915.[6]

On June 21 Eisenhower flew to Kansas City and joined Mamie, who had taken the train, his mother, and four brothers for a huge celebration. That evening a special train proceeded through eastern Kansas. He was greeted by large crowds at Lawrence, Topeka, and Manhattan, and in Abilene thousands of "citizens who had been waiting for hours surged forward in an uncontrollable mass when the supreme commander at last appeared." During the war he had been unable to return home to attend his father's funeral, and that night the five Eisenhower brothers stayed with their mother in their home. The next day people from all over the area—quadrupling the town's population of 5,000—celebrated. "Through this world it has been my fortune, or misfortune, to wander at considerable distances," the General, speaking without notes, declared. "Never has this town been outside my heart and memory." As he said "thanks to Kansas, to Dickinson County, and to Abilene for a reception that so far exceeds anything any of us could imagine," his voice cracked. The writer Steve Neal has emphasized that "the crowd roared in thunderous applause and cheers, overwhelming Ike" and, putting the hero's welcome home in perspective, added, "His series of triumphant personal appearances were without precedent in American history, but the return to Abilene had been the most satisfying of all." In late June Mamie and Ike Eisenhower went to White Sulphur Springs, West Virginia, for ten days and were accompanied by their son John, who had graduated from West Point in 1944, and Mamie's parents.[7]

On July 10 the General flew back to his headquarters in Frankfurt, where the complex problems as Commander of the American occupation forces were far different than those during wartime. Initially, his command had to decide which troops would be redeployed to the Pacific to fight Japan, which would remain with the occupation forces, and which would be sent home. In Europe the Jewish survivors of the Nazi concentration camps and the millions of displaced persons required immediate attention and, as the editors of Eisenhower's *Papers,* emphasized, "There was too little food, too little fuel, too little of everything in those first prewar months." This shortage affected plans for reparations, and the need for economic recovery, in turn, confronted the issue of fraternization with the Germans as well as Eisenhower's vigorous efforts to remove Nazis from positions of influence. The American public, moreover, wanted rapid demobilization, especially after the dropping of the atomic bombs on Hiroshima and Nagasaki in August and the end of World War II with the defeat of Japan.[8]

In the later part of July, 1945, Churchill, Stalin, and Truman had met at Potsdam, near Berlin, but failed to solve the growing problems between the Americans and Soviets over Germany. Eisenhower, nonetheless, remained confident and in August wrote to former Vice President Henry A. Wallace, "So far as a soldier should have opinions about such things, I am convinced that friendship—which means an honest desire on both sides to strive for mutual understanding—between Russia and the United States is absolutely essential to world tranquility." During the conference the President, riding in a car with the General and General Omar Bradley, turned to Eisenhower and said, "General, there is nothing that you may want that I won't try to help you get. That definitely and specifically includes the presidency in 1948." Recalling in *Crusade in Europe* that he doubted "any soldier of our country was ever so suddenly struck in his emotional vitals," Eisenhower wrote that he laughed and replied: "Mr. President, I don't know who will be your opponent for the presidency, but it will not be I."[9]

Shortly after the Potsdam Conference Eisenhower, who had declined an earlier invitation to the Russian victory parade because of his return to the United States, flew to Moscow with Marshal Zhukov. Stalin, in an unprecedented gesture, invited the General to view with him the big National Sports Parade in Red Square, and Eisenhower wrote that "no other foreigner had ever been invited to set foot on top on Lenin's tomb." He and Stalin watched the performers for five hours and, "through an interpreter, we conversed intermittently during the entire period of the show." It was during Ambassador W. Averrell Harriman's dinner for Eisenhower at the Embassy in Moscow on August 14 that news came of Japan's surrender.[10]

Eisenhower returned to Washington for consultations on November 11: "The main tasks ahead, as I understood them, would be appearances before congressional committees who wanted my testimony on unification of the armed services and on various proposals, particularly universal military training. My personal objectives were limited—to do some Christmas shopping that couldn't be finished in an overseas PX." Truman, though, had accepted General Marshall's request for relief from duty, and he decided to appoint Eisenhower as Chief of Staff. During a break in Washington he and Mamie went to Iowa by train, visiting her relatives; almost immediately after their arrival Mamie, alarmed by her shortness of breath, entered a hospital with bronchial pneumonia. Eisenhower called Major General Howard Snyder, M.D., in Washington. At General Marshall's request, Snyder had been her doctor during World War II, and Eisenhower told him "I will have a plane set up for you in the early morning" to fly to Des Moines. A couple of days later Eisenhower, assured by Dr. Snyder that his wife was "on the road to recovery," left for Chicago for a speech on November 20 at the American Legion convention; he was coming down with a bad cold, and Snyder accompanied him on the train.[11]

Eisenhower's cold was not helped by a parade on a brisk and windy November morning in Chicago and, against Snyder's advice, he removed his hat and overcoat; "bare head in the automobile with arms widely extended," he responded to the greetings of the immense crowd. He rested in the afternoon; held a press conference, following Truman's announcement of Eisenhower's promotion; and, after a couple of scotches, left for the American Legion banquet and speech. That night he returned to Washington with bronchial pneumonia himself. Thanksgiving morning, again in spite of his doctor's orders, he testified at a specially scheduled House Committee on Foreign Affairs hearing and was subjected to lengthy questioning; Snyder, meanwhile, "made arrangements for him to be transferred" to the hospital in White Sulphur Springs. He left the hospital on December 2 and, already confirmed as Chief of Staff, assumed his duties on the 3rd; Mrs. Eisenhower was discharged from the Iowa hospital on December 5 and returned to their residence at the Wardman-Park Hotel in Washington.[12]

As Chief of Staff, the Eisenhowers were assigned Quarters No. One at Fort Myer, outside Washington. Marshall had lived there, as had General Douglas MacArthur. Eisenhower, according to Snyder, had "a hard time getting Mrs. Eisenhower even interested to go out to inspect the Chief of Staff's quarters. . . . She seemed to be in a complete 'punk.'" Snyder, who had agreed to be the family physician and was treating her with a "moderate sedative," emphasized that she "resisted all the persuasive efforts . . . to change her residence of World War II," the Wardman-Park. "We had almost to take her physically and transport her to Fort Myer before we could persuade her that she could be happy in the home"; Eisenhower could not understand the difficulty, since Quarters No. One offered a very pleasant environment, generous living accommodations with rooms for guests, and "a complete staff of experienced household employees."[13]

"No personal enthusiasm," Eisenhower wrote, "marked my promotion to Chief of Staff, the highest military post a professional soldier in the United States Army can reach. . . . The job ahead was not pleasant." According to his memoirs, he had told Truman that he would rather retire, but the President replied that he needed him and that "my tour could be brief if I chose"; when the President found a replacement for General Bradley at the Veterans Bureau, Bradley would succeed him. From the hospital Eisenhower wrote his close boyhood friend, "Swede" Hazlett, that "there is nothing I want so much as opportunity to retire." If he and Mamie "could start out roaming the United States looking for the home we would like to live in the rest of our lives, I would be up and on the go within twenty minutes." He added: "The job I am now taking represents nothing but straight duty." He would preside over the demobilization of the Army, "a dreary business. The taste of it I had during World War I at a far lower level did nothing to whet my appetite for the task now to be performed at the top." He knew, moreover, that there would be endless battles on the Joint Chiefs of Staff, where each member had equal power. It was a far cry from his wartime position as Supreme Commander, and he soon wrote his son that his new position "was a sorry place to light after having commanded a theater of war."[14]

His lack of enthusiasm did not, however, diminish the commitment and energy he took to the Pentagon. He entered office at a time when the atomic bomb and tensions with the Soviet Union were rapidly determining American foreign policy. He firmly believed in the necessity of a peacetime military establishment that could meet the nation's new worldwide requirements and obligations, in the unification of the armed forces, and in the importance of Soviet-American cooperation. Yet, as his *Papers* show, "each of these basic ideas was severely challenged. . . . Slowly and grudgingly, he was forced to give way on all three fronts." The demand to bring the troops home produced "Bring Back Daddy" clubs and enormous pressure on Congress and the War Department; "for a time," Eisenhower recalled, "the Army let its heart run away with its head." He argued for a unified command, with a strong civilian secretary, but the National Security Act of 1947 essentially reflected the Navy's determination to keep the Joint Chief of Staffs with a weak Secretary of Defense; moreover, the Joint Chiefs could never agree on a war plan. Finally, Eisenhower, while "realistic about Russia's great power," during crises "patiently asked what hard evidence indicated that the Russians intended suddenly to sweep across western Europe"; the Administration, nonetheless, moved towards a tough foreign policy with the Truman Doctrine and Marshall Plan.[15]

Other demands on his time, meanwhile, illustrated his enormous popularity. The paperwork and mail were overwhelming, and each week he often signed over a thousand letters. He faced a "total lack of privacy. . . . I had to live with the knowledge that every phone call I made or received was monitored from beginning to end," and his mail, "unless from my wife or a close relative or friend," was read by a staff member. Stephen Ambrose has calculated that during his first year in the Pentagon Eisenhower delivered forty-six major speeches and testified thirteen times before Congress; the second year there were thirty speeches and twelve Congressional appearances. The General declined forty invitations for every one he accepted; "some of them," nonetheless, were "difficult to refuse." Continuing his *Diary* entry, he asserted: "I so firmly believe we should all do our part to reawaken in our country a realization of our own blessings and what we have to do to protect them. . . . that when any organization that has a similar purpose asks me to appear, I feel a sense of guilt when I decline."[16]

During 1946 he traveled widely and Mamie often accompanied him; before his term was over he had visited every state. After a trip to Canada, he left for the Far East in May. He talked with MacArthur, who commanded the occupation forces in Japan, and met with Marshall, who had accepted from President Truman the frustrating assignment of trying to bring an end to the civil war in China. Truman had told Eisenhower that he wanted either Marshall or Eisenhower to become Secretary of State; the Chief of Staff offered to ask General Marshall who, no matter how much he wanted to retire, would never decline a Presidential request. The Eisenhowers went to Central and South America, where huge crowds greeted him, and she went with him on an inspection trip of Europe and England. They saw John Eisenhower, who was stationed in Vienna, and in October they spent a week at Culzean Castle, where Scotland had given him an apartment for life residence. During that stay the British royal family entertained them overnight at Balmoral Castle.[17]

That December Mamie and Dwight Eisenhower entered a hospital at Coral Gables, Florida, for "a combination of rest, outdoor recreation and various kinds of therapy." The doctors, he informed his son, wanted "to see if they can find the source of infection inside me," and he had "painful but not disabling" bursitis-arthritis in his left arm. The General played golf every morning on the hospital course and, according to Dr. Snyder, soon "included the full 18 holes." After physical therapy, he went fishing either in the Everglades or at Lake Okachobee for large mouth bass. "Placing a bass plug in the water exactly where he wanted it was always a complete entertainment for the General. If not dissuaded, he would continue for twelve hours a day." Mamie Eisenhower, meanwhile, entertained herself, and with "an inexhaustible supply of quarters" she enjoyed hours with the "one-armed bandits"—slot machines—still present at military installations. The General flourished and after one week, according to an aide, "the General has shown signs which are sufficient reward to those who are devoted to him. He looks rested, is clear-eyed and tanned, and if the treatment prescribed for his bursitis proves successful, we can say—'Mission Accomplished.'" The month-long stay provided his first extended vacation since the mid-1930s, and Eisenhower was, Snyder emphasized, once again "an active, vital, dynamically functioning individual."[18]

The speeches and public appearances, the travels throughout the United States, and the trips to Europe, Latin America, and the Far East kept Eisenhower in the limelight during 1946 and into 1947; meanwhile, he was besieged by lucrative offers to publish his wartime memoirs. "To all of these proposals," he wrote in At Ease, "I turned a deaf ear. For one thing, I was really tired; I wanted nothing so much as the opportunity to loaf a while and then try to find out what to do with the rest of my life." The various proposals, he continued, "annoyed me, because I was also preoccupied with official duties."

While postponing any decision on writing his own account, he fully supported a professional, historical account of the Army's role during World War II and especially of his European command, SHAEF. After his education at West Point, Eisenhower had "little or no interest left in military history." Then, while on assignment to the Canal Zone in Panama in the 1920s with General Fox Connor, he profited from "a sort of graduate school in military affairs and the humanities." The reading assignments in the evenings and his conversations with Connor—as well as the General's constant questioning—were a valuable educational experience for the young officer during his three years in Panama. Later, under General John J. "Black Jack" Pershing, Commander of the American Expeditionary Force in World War I, Eisenhower prepared a battlefield guide "to the actions of Americans in the war," and the research took him through France, "following the lines of trench warfare that had stabilized almost rigidly between late 1914 and the weeks preceding the Armistice in 1918." This training and, in particular, Connor's influence, contributed to Eisenhower's decision to support the Army's history of World War II, and his "clear grasp of the importance of carefully researched history" impressed Forrest Pogue, author of the excellent volume, The Supreme Command.[19]

In early 1947, with his immense popularity undiminished and his Chief of Staff assignment scheduled to last only into 1948, Eisenhower was in his fifty-seventh year. No American had been so warmly cheered in so many different parts of the world, and few Americans in those postwar years had traveled and spoken so extensively throughout the United States and testified so often before Congress. He was far too active and energetic to retire; in spite of attractive financial offers, however, he had not decided what he would do and where he and Mamie would live.

* * *

In the spring of 1945 Columbia's Nicholas Murray Butler, eighty-three years old, blind, and almost totally deaf, received a visit from Marcellus Hartley Dodge; Thomas J. Watson probably accompanied Dodge. Life Trustees of the University and old friends of the President, they informed Butler that the Trustees thought he should resign. Reluctantly, he accepted the facts. A Special Meeting of the Trustees was held and the announcement came in late April: Butler would retire on October 1, 1945, the forty-fourth anniversary of his election to the Presidency, and become President Emeritus.[20]

For years Butler had refused to consider retirement, even though his recent Commencement performances had been "pretty tragic," according to Carlton J. H. Hayes, Professor of History and America's wartime Ambassador to Spain. In 1942 Chairman Coykendall, a few days before Commencement, had taken the rare precaution of talking with the Chairman of the Committee of Public Ceremonies, Professor of Law Albert C. Jacobs. Coykendall asked Jacobs, because of Butler's infirm condition and failing sight, to take over the Commencement ceremonies if the President faltered during his address. It was an extremely windy and cold day; Butler, as he began his talk, shuffled his notes in the wind and became confused. Jacobs had memorized the President's address, and he debated for what seemed to him hours whether to step up to the microphone and have the President sit down. Finally, Dr. Butler "completely abandoned his notes and in an amazing fashion launched forth on an entirely different subject, delivering a brilliant address."[21]

President Butler's last Commencement address in June, 1945, evoked deep emotions. A colleague movingly described the "noble figure, rising from his chair, thrusting aside the proffered arm of a friend, stepping forward for the previously calculated number of steps and delivering his speech, erect and confident as ever." The thousands of graduates, families, and spectators could glance in every direction and see the University he had created, physically and intellectually, over four decades. In Butler's day, Dean Young B. Smith of the School of Law recalled, he had been a great, able leader who raised money, attracted outstanding persons to the faculty, built buildings, and had "the dream."[22]

Butler had missed the opportunity to retire in 1932—his seventieth year, his fiftieth reunion at Columbia College, and his thirtieth anniversary as President. All provided a unique occasion for him to close his remarkable career. By that time, as Columbia's Pulitzer-Prize winning historian Allan Nevins wrote, Butler had made the University "the largest and richest seat of learning in the largest and richest city on the globe." His predecessor Seth Low, who had resigned to run successfully for the mayoralty of New York City, had given Columbia a national reputation, and Butler built upon it. The School of Law became famous under the distinguished leadership of Harlan Fiske Stone, a future Justice and Chief Justice of the Supreme Court of the United States. Butler had been instrumental in making Teachers College part of Columbia in 1901; he had appointed Virginia Gildersleeve Dean of Barnard College, and under her strong leadership from 1911 to 1947 Barnard became a highly reputable women's college; and—no small accomplishment—he had received from Joseph Pulitzer a million dollars for a School of Journalism. He had obtained millions of dollars from the Rockefeller Foundation, the General Education Board, and the Carnegie Corporation, and then land and money from Edward S. Harkness to bring into reality the Medical Center with the College of Physicians and Surgeons and an agreement with Presbyterian Hospital. A gift from Marcy Dodge, a member of the Class of 1903 and a Trustee from 1907 through the Eisenhower years, had enabled Butler to build Hartley Hall, the first dormitory on the Morningside Heights campus. In effect, the gift inaugurated an extensive construction program. The Columbia campus grew rapidly: over a dozen additional buildings appeared between then and 1934 when South Hall opened—financed by a four million dollar gift from Harkness and renamed Butler Library in 1946. "Few institutions," biographer Michael Rosenthal has written, had depended "for their development on the energies of one man" as had Columbia on Butler. [23]

With Columbia University as a focus, Morningside Heights became, for Butler, the Acropolis of America. The Union Theological

Seminary, the Jewish Theological Seminary, the Juilliard School of Music, Riverside Church, the Cathedral of St. John the Divine, St. Luke's Hospital, and International House contributed to the creation of a great intellectual center. Butler, himself, gave the University an international reputation. An inveterate traveler and also President of the Carnegie Endowment for International Peace, he received honorary degrees from thirty-seven foreign universities and decorations from fifteen countries. Foreign dignitaries, when they arrived by ocean liner in New York, regularly dined at the President's House at 60 Morningside Drive. He had written more than a dozen books on education, international relations, and politics; in 1912 he had been the Vice Presidential candidate on the Republican ticket; and in 1931 he had shared the Nobel Peace Prize with Jane Addams. Butler's influence pervaded every phase of higher education and his achievements transcended the physical development of the campus. He was, according to the scholar Lindsay Rogers, in the foreword of an unfinished biography, "a great university president—the greatest of the twentieth century."[24]

He had his detractors. Some called him Czar Nicholas and others Nicholas Miraculous, a name coined by Theodore Roosevelt, who as President of the United States had attended Butler's inauguration. Seth Low had remained on the Board of Trustees but resigned in 1914 because of Butler's anti-Semitic policies for Columbia. Three years later, as historian Richard Hofstadter noted, "the vain and imperious" Butler's opinions led to the dismissal of several faculty members who opposed conscription when the country entered World War I. The progressive historian Charles A. Beard, protesting in a letter to the autocratic Butler, resigned in defense of academic freedom.[25]

During the 1930s Butler, with his eyes and ears failing, found it more and more difficult to lead the University and raise money. He had allowed, according to historian Jacques Barzun, "various people, four or five of them whom we called the Archbishops, to run the place as they wanted and that had brought about a certain disunity, incoherence in administrative affairs." Professor Jacobs recalled that Butler had been "amazingly adept getting his wealthy New York friends to support the University. But he had genuinely resented anyone else taking part in this endeavor." No longer, though, was he able to ride the subway downtown to Wall Street by himself and, as his friends who had contributed so generously to Columbia over the years died and the Great Depression depleted other fortunes, his fund-raising ability deteriorated. Still, "he felt only he could" do the job, but during his last years the Trustees realized how "undependable were his assurances of money coming into the University." In an effort to meet the administrative needs, in 1937 the Trustees named Frank D. Fackenthal Provost of the University. A graduate of Columbia College in 1906, Fackenthal had become Secretary of the University in 1910, and for all practical purposes had been chief executive officer for several years.[26]

Butler, nonetheless, had created the structure of the University's administration and, when he ceased to be effective, it did not operate as well. Trustee Douglas Black, who became the President of Doubleday in 1946, had graduated from Columbia College and the School of Law, and he recalled that during World War II with Butler "getting to be pretty ill" one Trustees Meeting had only "lasted nineteen minutes" and "we didn't have the parade ... just came out and took our places at Commencement." He added that the Board finally had given Provost Fackenthal authority, by Statute, "to take action on all matters relating to the academic administration of the University except as such required Trustee action." Fackenthal, nonetheless, remained in Butler's shadow, and President Butler remained ever so conscious of his prerogatives. Black reflected that when faculty members Enrico Fermi and H. C. Urey, pioneers in atomic physics, received other offers, there was "nobody who was the boss man" with whom they could negotiate, and they left for the University of Chicago and took the Manhattan Project with them. Physicist I. I. Rabi, who had been instrumental in bringing Fermi to Morningside Heights, recalled that Robert Hutchins "came in and raided Columbia," taking Harold Urey and his crowd and Fermi and his crowd, who left Columbia denuded." Lamenting the University's loss, Rabi stressed that Butler "was quite advanced in age and had never been very close to the science departments"; moreover, "Fackenthal, of course, was not in a position to take action, independent action." Rabi added that Butler, nearly blind, presented him with the Nobel Prize for Physics in 1944, and "he did the honor of calling me 'Fermi.'"[27]

Finally, difficult as it was, the Trustees requested Butler's retirement in 1945; the Board, however, had lacked the strength and leadership to address the problem for over a decade. Butler, of course, had appointed every Trustee; he had dominated the Board; it had become, in effect, "little more than a rubber stamp" for him. At the end of his Presidency he was determined that Fackenthal, his former Secretary, would not succeed him, and he reminded the Trustees in his resignation comments that, according to the University's Statutes, the Dean of the Graduate Faculties, George B. Pegram, would become Acting President on October 1.[28]

In 1932 it would have been daunting for anyone to have succeeded Nicholas Murray Butler at Columbia. His achievements had been monumental. By 1945 the lack of strong leadership and fundraising for over a decade meant that Butler's successor would face a challenge far greater than Butler's formidable shadow. There had been no building projects on campus and, worse, the University had deferred badly needed maintenance on existing buildings. When Fackenthal undertook the long overdue rehabilitation, a "quite sizable debt" accrued. At the close of World War II Columbia was in dire financial condition, and there had been little time for the presidential search as October 1 and Butler's resignation approached. The Trustees, consequently, turned once again to Fackenthal, who was sixty-two, and elected him Acting President.[29] At a time when thousands of veterans with the G.I. Bill were flocking to colleges and universities and were overwhelming housing facilities and faculty staffing, Columbia faced the postwar challenges and inflation with an Acting President, an administration badly in need of reorganization, a search for a new president, and grave financial strains. Moreover, Butler, still "hanging on," maintained his powerful influence with the Trustees and faithfully attended Board Meetings; since the mid-1930s he had nearly destroyed the great University he had created.

Any assessment of Dwight D. Eisenhower's Presidency of Columbia University must emphasize this formidable legacy of Nicholas Murray Butler and his sad final years at the helm, and it must also include the impact of the long, drawn out search to find a successor. During that period Butler's presence at the Trustees Meetings severely hampered Fackenthal's leadership of the University; meanwhile, the financial situation grew worse. Furthermore, the course of the futile presidential search from the spring of 1945 until June, 1947, sowed deep seeds of discontent on the Morningside Heights campus and contributed to the subsequent opposition to General Eisenhower among many members of the Columbia community.

The story of the search leading to Eisenhower's appointment has never been told in detail; as the story unfolds, it explains much about Columbia, the University's problems, and the difficulties Eisenhower would face. If the tale is complicated, so was Columbia—an extremely large, variegated urban institution with some 25,000 to 30,000 students in over two dozen different schools with different faculties. Perhaps the Trustee Search Committee assumed that Eisenhower's immense popularity and prestige would solve easily the financial and leadership problems; perhaps, as Eisenhower's successor Grayson Kirk suggested, "The Search Committee may actually have been unaware of the horrendous financial and other problems that had accumulated during Butler's last years."[30]

On May 7, 1945, the Board appointed a Special Trustee Committee under the Chairmanship of Thomas I. Parkinson to recommend names to be considered for final action by the Trustees. Parkinson, Chairman of the large Equitable Life Assurance Society, knew the University well and was an influential member of the Board; he had been a Professor of Legislation at the School of Law and had acted briefly as Dean following Harlan Fiske Stone's resignation in the mid-1920s. Marcellus Hartley Dodge, Chairman of the Remington Arms Company, served on the Committee; in 1905, when the insurance industry in New York was under investigation, the owner of the *New York Times*, which supported the investigation, "felt it incumbent on this newspaper to pay off at once a loan from the Equitable Life Assurance Society." Dodge anonymously "came to the rescue" and enabled the *Times* to do so. As loyal as any alumnus, he served as Clerk of the Board and attended to much of the Committee's correspondence; he played an increasingly active role in the search. Other members included the Reverend Dr. Frederick S. Fleming, Rector of historic Trinity Church in lower Manhattan (Columbia's first home, as King's College, had been on land given by Trinity Church on Park Place); George E. Warren, a retired banker and director of a number of firms; and Coykendall (ex officio), President of the Cornell Steamboat Company and Director of the Columbia University Press. The Committee's charge: the formidable task of recommending Nicholas Murray Butler's successor. The selection proceedings would be dominated, ultimately, by Parkinson and a Trustee not on the Committee, Thomas J. Watson, President of International Business Machines.[31]

At the Committee's first meeting in June, only a few weeks after V-E Day and as the country was preparing for General Eisenhower's triumphant return to the United States, "his name spontaneously suggested itself." It seemed "wishful thinking" for, among other things, the Battle of Okinawa still raged in the Pacific and the proposed invasion of Japan was months off. Journalist Alden Hatch, who during World War II had written *General Ike,* reported, however, that his name kept reappearing before the Committee. In early 1946, according to Hatch, the Trustees approached Chief of Staff Eisenhower through a friend in the War Department. The General had replied to the Columbia inquiry that he had an obligation to fulfill at the Pentagon. Hatch's article, "The Prexy Plan of General Ike," appeared shortly after Eisenhower accepted the position, and he asserted that Mamie Eisenhower and the General's brother, President Milton S. Eisenhower of Kansas State University, had read "every word" of the article before publication. Trustees Dodge and Parkinson had talked with Hatch, and Dodge complimented Hatch on the article, declaring in a letter to Eisenhower that it was "a very fine piece of work and he hoped that the General was "happy about it." Both Ike and Mamie Eisenhower, indeed, were "pleased."[32]

In mid-March, 1946, Tom Watson traveled to the Pentagon to ask Chief of Staff Eisenhower to speak at the Diamond Jubilee opening at the Metropolitan Museum of Art in New York City. The General accepted, later observing "it does seem a bit ridiculous that they should want a soldier in such surroundings." During the meeting he had mentioned his brother's efforts in establishing a "Citizenship" course at Kansas State, and Watson replied that he knew that and planned to see Milton Eisenhower in Kansas soon. When the General and Mamie went to New York on April 2, 1946, for the Jubilee, the IBM President had more opportunities to talk with him.[33]

The Trustees, meanwhile, had authorized the University Council, an advisory group comprising delegates from all the faculties, to appoint a special search committee. The Committee would consist of a member from each faculty and would suggest to Parkinson's Committee, not to the Board, "the names of persons eligible to fill the position of President of the University." The Executive Committee of the University Council received nominations from the various faculties and even before Commencement, 1945, had named seventeen persons to serve on it.

This Committee commanded widespread respect throughout the University, and its members included prominent academic leaders during Eisenhower's Presidency and some of his closest associates. The Chairman was the soft-spoken Dean George B. Pegram of the Graduate Faculties. The senior Dean and a renowned physicist, Pegram had brought to Columbia Nobel Prize winners I. I. Rabi and Enrico Fermi; he had been instrumental in the early development of the atomic bomb, but he dissolved into tears upon hearing the news of Hiroshima. Within a year of Eisenhower's arrival Pegram would become Vice President of the University. Dean Young B. Smith, as teacher and scholar, had continued building on the foundation left by Harlan Fiske Stone to make the School of Law one of the foremost in the country. Harry J. Carman, the Dean of Columbia College and a prominent American historian, never forgot his rural, upstate New York roots; tall, gangling, vigorous, and enthusiastic, Carman for years had been the most popular professor at the College. Provost Fackenthal, who became Acting President in October, served as Secretary; during the summer he tried to persuade the Trustees to make Pegram the Acting President. Visiting Professor Floyd Taylor, who contributed editorials to the *New York Herald-Tribune* and within the year would become Director of the University's new American Press Institute, represented the School of Journalism and did much of the Committee's research and writing. Pegram, Fackenthal, and Smith, as well as Professor of Geology Leslie C. Dunn and Professor of Surgery Allen O. Whipple, were chosen for the Committee's Executive Committee of Five.[34]

Final exams were hardly over in 1945 when the Faculty Committee began its arduous task. The deliberations would be confidential, but members were "free to discuss possible candidates with those who might be able to make helpful comment." The Committee soon received 174 suggestions, forty-three of whom were associated with Columbia; on August 6 it reduced its list from sixty-four candidates to eleven and began considering eight additional names. Although the Trustees originally had not set a deadline for the Committee's recommendations, Pegram informed his colleagues that a report by the end of August would be "very desirable." Consequently, throughout August sub-committees prepared reports on the nineteen individuals. On August 25, ten days after Japan's surrender to end the Pacific War, the Committee retained eleven names and, after extensive discussions and voting, reduced the number to eight.[35]

Over Labor Day weekend, 1945, the Committee completed its report on "the most promising" candidates and, as Dean Carman recalled, submitted it "with the memorandum that any one of the eight would be agreeable to the Committee." Within a span of three months the Pegram Committee diligently had prepared an extremely thoughtful and detailed study with perceptive comments concerning the "qualifications and the doubts" about the candidates. The list clearly illustrated what the University's faculties expected of a new president. Fackenthal specifically commented that "the faculty pretty much preferred somebody with an academic background and in my opinion rightly so." The field of education, he believed, should produce its own leaders. The Committee did not, according to Carman, "try to single out any one of the eight," although he acknowledged that at least one suggestion did not have majority support. "I don't think that any of us was enthusiastic for everyone." Finally, the Committee stressed that it would "welcome the opportunity of investigating" persons suggested by the Trustees.[36]

Seven prominent educators and one United States Senator appeared on the faculty list, and each of the eight would continue to enjoy a long, successful, and distinguished professional career. Four came from the Columbia community, and among them was Jacques Barzun, the brilliant intellectual historian, scholar of the English language, and gifted writer and teacher. "His judgments," the report stated, "are unhesitating and decisive," and he "quickly detects and dislikes mediocrity in others." Barzun had come to the United States from Paris in 1919 and to Columbia in 1927; in 1955 he became Dean of the Graduate Faculties and, later, Provost. Another candidate, economist Robert DeBlois Calkins, had been Dean of the College of Commerce at the University of California before joining Columbia in 1941 as Dean of the Business School. The Committee concluded that his writings "reveal competent though not brilliant and comprehensive scholarship." In 1947 he became vice president and director of the Rockefellers' General Education Board and in 1952 President of the Brookings Institute. Philip C. Jessup, Hamilton Fish Professor of International Law and Diplomacy, had taught at Columbia since 1925 and had served as legal adviser to the federal government officials at the Bretton Woods and San Francisco Conferences; in 1947 several Trustees asked for a Special Meeting of the Board and expected the selection of Jessup. In 1948 President Truman appointed him the United States Representative to the United Nations General Assembly and the following year he became Ambassador-at-Large. Three times as many faculty members had suggested him as any one else, but the Committee was concerned about his health and had several reservations. Although Dean Smith recalled that the majority of the Committee did not endorse Jessup, he had strong support. The last Columbia candidate was the dynamic John A. Krout, whose "scholarly distinction is unquestioned." He had joined the Department of History in 1922 and, at the time of the presidential search, served as the department's chief executive officer. The Committee did not view him as "an impressive or colorful figure in public," but it acknowledged that he was "an excellent public speaker." In 1949 he succeeded Pegram as Dean of the Graduate Faculties, and he later became Provost and Vice President.[37]

Four distinguished non-Columbia candidates completed the list. Vannevar Bush, eminent scientist and electrical engineer, had been at the Massachusetts Institute of Technology as Vice President and Dean of Engineering before assuming in 1939 his current position, President of the Carnegie Institution. A skilled administrator, he had directed during World War II the important Office of Strategic Research and Development, where he had been responsible for the assignment of civilian scientists to military affairs. The Committee wondered whether "he would like to devote his next efforts to the presidency of a large university," and observed that his age, fifty-five, was "not in his favor." Bush was, in fact, the only one of the eight over fifty. Another prominent scientist recommended was Lee Alvin DuBridge, a physicist and "highly esteemed administrator." Former Investigator for the National Defense Research Commission and Director of the Radiation Laboratory at M.I.T., which had played a crucial role in developing radar technology for the military during the war, DuBridge in 1946 became the President of the California Institute of Technology; Eisenhower, after he became President of the United States, named DuBridge Chairman of the President's Science Advisory Committee. The Honorable James William Fulbright, the third non-Columbia suggestion, had been a lecturer in law at the University of Arkansas and, from 1939-1941, its President; in 1944 he had been elected to the United States Senate, and he later would serve with distinction as Chairman of the Foreign Relations Committee. Professor George Mullins, representing the Barnard College faculty, had so persuasively presented Fulbright's candidacy that at the time of the report he ranked "highest among the eight persons."

The Committee, nonetheless, worried that his "experience in the world of academic scholarship and in the sphere of university administration is more limited that we would wish." A Committee member, without authorization, asked Fulbright if he might be interested in the position and, when this appeared in the newspapers in October, it badly hurt whatever chance he might have had. Finally, the name of Chancellor William Pearson Tolley of Syracuse University concluded the list. "A vigorous, dynamic person," a Columbia Ph.D. and an ordained minister of the Methodist Episcopal Church, he had been a Professor of Philosophy and President of Allegheny College before going to Syracuse in 1942, where he had had much "success in revitalizing" the University. During the next two decades under his impressive leadership Syracuse became one of the nation's largest private universities.[38]

It was an extremely impressive list. The Faculty Committee believed that any one of the eight candidates could provide the leadership Columbia required in the postwar world. Each, with the possible exception of Fulbright, was an eminent scholar and educator and had an established reputation in the academic world. After a while, in mid-November, Pegram and Fackenthal were told at a meeting with the Trustees' Committee "to re-examine the campus group to be sure that no interesting name had been omitted from the preferred list," to consider New York lawyer and Under Secretary of War John J. McCloy, and to make any pertinent additional suggestions. Or, as Dean Carman ruefully recalled, "In due time the Trustees advised us that no one of the eight seemed satisfactory. . . . Would we please look further?" Specifically, Parkinson told Pegram to provide "as soon as possible" the faculty's "final attitude toward one or two of the names" discussed.[39]

While the Trustees remained ambivalent about the faculty suggestions and had mentioned McCloy, their major problem was Nicholas Murray Butler's adamant insistence that Dean Willard Rappleye of Columbia's College of Physicians and Surgeons succeed him. The medical school, under Rappleye's leadership since 1931, had moved to the forefront of medical training, and he was "acclaimed nationally for his initiative in adapting the medical curriculum to the rigid advances of medical science." Rappleye had aspirations to be the next president of Columbia, but he had little support, even from the medical school; he knew, though, that Butler wanted the Trustees to elect him.[40]

In December the Faculty's Executive Committee expressed its opposition to Rappleye at a dinner with Parkinson's Committee. When Chairman Coykendall subsequently questioned Rappleye's scholarship during a telephone conversation with Butler in January, 1946, the President Emeritus called the comment "not only false but grotesque." He insisted that Rappleye was "the only one who ought to be considered" and "action ought to be taken at once. The University," he added, "is being very much criticized for its apparent lack of capacity to deal promptly with this vital question." He claimed, moreover, that the Trustees' delay was harming his fund-raising activities. Two days later Parkinson's Committee met, and afterwards he promptly informed Butler that "further consideration of all possibilities is desirable." Butler, nonetheless, remained adamant in his support of Rappleye, and Watson tactfully tried to persuade him that the Trustees had a "duty" to consider several other names before presenting a final report.[41]

The Trustees did have other names, as Watson informed Butler, but the Committee did not seem to know what to do. Specifically, they could not decide whether they should interview Fulbright. They may have doubted that the Senator would consider the position and have feared another embarrassing newspaper leak; they may, also, have worried about his lack of academic stature. Whatever the reason, the Parkinson Committee evidently had little enthusiasm for Fulbright. They held an informal dinner for DuBridge who, according to Rector Fleming, "did not prove quite the sort we are looking for." They were advised to consider "seriously" Milton Eisenhower of Kansas State University, and Watson recommended "very serious consideration" for Chancellor Tolley of Syracuse and two other college presidents. Tolley, though, told Watson that he was "not available at this particular time." Watson believed that these three were the best educators from the outside and, the IBM President concluded, if we decide to take an outside man who is not an educator, I would put General Eisenhower at the top."[42]

Watson's recommendation of General Eisenhower came shortly after the Chief of Staff had appeared at the Metropolitan Museum of Art's Diamond Jubilee celebration. A few days later Dodge, who had seen Watson's suggestion, stopped by Dean Carl Ackerman's office in the School of Journalism to talk about the presidency. Ackerman had declined to serve on the Faculty Committee; a prominent *New York Times* correspondent and successful public relations expert, he had become Dean in 1931 and during the 1930's had made the Journalism School a graduate institution. Although he had informed Coykendall that he personally supported Fackenthal to succeed Butler, he told Dodge that he did not want to discuss the selection process. Trustee Dodge, however, persisted and soon mentioned General Eisenhower. Ackerman replied that, if the University wanted an army officer, he preferred General Marshall. He mentioned that he had seen Eisenhower at a number of newspaper conferences during the war and doubted that the General had "the understanding of either the fundamentals or the philosophy of world politics or national politics." The Dean, moreover, viewed Eisenhower primarily as "an operating man who functioned under the direction of men" like President Franklin D. Roosevelt or Prime Minister Winston Churchill. He added that when Eisenhower appeared before newspaper editors, he "gave the impression of having only a superficial knowledge or interest in anything outside of his immediate problems of operation and personnel." When Dodge asked about Dr. Rappleye, Ackerman asserted that the president should not be a M.D. and suggested, instead, Professor Jessup. Dodge then inquired "at much greater length in regard to specific experiences in press conferences with General Eisenhower"; as Dodge left, he asked that the conversation be kept confidential.[43]

The Columbia community, meanwhile, became increasingly concerned about the lack of progress in the presidential search and looked more and more to Fackenthal, in spite of his age. "As we recognize the apparent futility of our present search" and no "dominant individual" claimed attention, Trustee Committee member Fleming suggested in February, 1946, that Fackenthal be named President for a specific term. The Rector argued, moreover, that Fackenthal then "would be able to make a much greater contribution." As the Faculty Committee prepared to respond in the spring of 1946 to the Trustees' "request for further information," it considered Fackenthal, and the Acting President promptly excused himself from further meetings. As Dean Carman reflected, Fackenthal was on the job and had been "a great administrator of a tough place." The Committee knew that it would be "honoring him and not doing any damage to the institution." True, Carman admitted, Fackenthal would have "only a short time to serve" before retiring, but it would "give us opportunity to look further."[44] Fackenthal's awkward position and the pressing demands on his office worried many at Columbia. A year had expired since the announcement of Butler's retirement and, in spite of the Acting President's abilities, a void had been created. Douglas Black, who Jacques Barzun thought "had a very fine sense of what a university was," had urged Fackenthal's appointment at a dinner for younger Trustees at the University Club in June, 1946. Black could appreciate the Acting President's difficult position, because for several years at Doubleday he, himself, had been in the position of chief responsibility, as first vice president, without the title of president; years later he commented that the Trustees never had given Fackenthal the real "authority." Fackenthal, meanwhile, was "very much aware that I was not Dr. Butler's—nor Mrs. Butler's—candidate for Acting President." While many considered Fackenthal a sentimental choice, he had devoted himself to Columbia University. Professor Jacobs, who had become Assistant to the President for Veterans Affairs upon his return from the war, believed that Fackenthal deserved to be President after Butler's retirement.[45]

Jacobs based his argument on his experience working with Fackenthal in Low Memorial after the war. A Rhodes Scholar from the University of Michigan, at the age of twenty-four Jacobs had been the first American to become a don at Oxford University, and three years later in 1927 he had taken a year's leave of absence from Oxford to teach at the Columbia School of Law. He had decided to stay in New York and, under a grant from the Laura Spelman Rockefeller Foundation, he began some pioneering research in the field of family law. During World War II Jacobs served as Director of the Navy's Dependents Welfare Division and administered the Navy's allotments, dependents, and welfare programs for three million persons. Even before he returned to Columbia in 1946, Fackenthal had asked him to be Assistant to the President for Veterans Affairs—veterans were constituting some 80 percent of the new students at the University—and he would be relieved of teaching responsibilities at the School of Law. Jacobs, however, turned down the offer. Far behind in his professional career after over three years in the Navy, he wanted to bring out a new edition of his casebook on *Domestic Relations*; moreover, after his intense administrative activity in the Navy, he "wanted no more."[46]

Yet, "within ten days" of his arrival back at the Law School, Acting President Fackenthal in effect drafted Jacobs for the position, even though he was saddled with a full teaching schedule for the spring semester. Nearly 8,000 veterans were on campus, many of whom were married and needed a place to live, and the figure would reach over 14,000 veterans in the fall. Then that spring the retiring Treasurer of the University, with the approval of Parkinson and several other Trustees, asked Jacobs to be the next Treasurer. Jacobs discussed the proposition with Fackenthal and wrote his close friend, Dean Smith. After due consideration he decided not to pursue the matter; meanwhile, the Parkinson Committee instructed the Faculty Committee to prepare a report on Jacobs.[47]

On May 17, 1946, with the academic year drawing to a close, the Faculty Committee submitted to the Parkinson Committee its second report. Although General Eisenhower's name had been suggested to it by Trustee Committee member George Warren in 1945, and Watson and Dodge had been mentioning him during the spring of 1946, there is no evidence that the Pegram Committee ever considered the General or was asked to do so by the Trustee Committee; indeed, his name does not appear in either faculty report.[48]

The May report contained the statements and recommendations it had approved on Rappleye, Jacobs, Fackenthal, and Professor William Robbins, the Director of the New York Botanical Gardens and a Columbia professor. The Pegram Committee had dropped Vannevar Bush, since it preferred a candidate under fifty, and removed four more from its original list of eight; it added Jacobs, ranking him second to Fulbright and ahead of Calkins and Krout. It explicitly expressed, moreover, its conviction that Dean Rappleye "would not be in the best interests of the University." Ironically, this "strong negative report" was the only Committee action that had any impact, and the Trustees dropped Rappleye from any further consideration. The Committee also rejected John J. McCloy; Robbins, it added, was in his mid-fifties and too old. Frank Fackenthal, it emphasized, would be "preferable" to anyone that age. Indeed, the Committee declared that "the appointment of Mr. Fackenthal . . . if only for a brief term, would insure the progress of the University and give opportunity for the selection or development of a successor."[49]

The candidacies of Fackenthal and Fulbright continued to pose serious problems for the Trustees. President Emeritus Butler, upon hearing of Fackenthal's recommendation by the faculty, exploded. He could not and would not tolerate the idea. "Oh, for heaven's sake," Parkinson later quoted Butler as saying, "don't name my Clerk as President." As for Fulbright, the Trustee Committee still hesitated.

One Trustee believed that at a dinner meeting of eighteen Trustees in May they had "definitely made a choice" and that the Special Committee would present Fulbright's name at a Special Meeting of the Board. This Trustee was "disappointed" and "very surprised" to learn that the Senator had not been "approached," and he wanted to know from Dodge "what has happened apparently to side-track our choice." It was probably a letter Dodge received from United States Senator Alexander Smith that prompted the decision to wait. Fulbright had talked with the New Jersey Senator about the position, and Dodge inferred from Smith's letter that his Arkansas colleague probably would not accept an offer. Dodge told Parkinson he would talk with Smith, "if it becomes important to know definitely whether" Fulbright will "accept or not" and if Parkinson, himself, did not want to ask Smith. When Dodge's suggestion was rejected, he admitted to Smith that it was a question whether Fulbright should give up his important work in Washington "at this serious time in our history."[50]

By Commencement, 1946, one year had elapsed without a recommendation to the Board by the Parkinson Committee, and the implications were becoming more and more apparent to Columbia and the larger academic community; indeed, the situation was becoming a public embarrassment. The Pegram Committee, meanwhile, in May had appointed a subcommittee to discuss further its report with the Trustees, but by mid-June the Trustee Committee had not bothered even to reply to the offer. After the Trustees dropped Fackenthal's name—Lindsay Rogers called the Trustee's decision "outrageous"—and made no move to approach Fulbright, the Pegram Committee concluded that additional suggestions would be futile. Parkinson and Coykendall even ignored Dodge's suggestion that Dean Pegram should at least receive "an answer." In effect, they announced to the Columbia community that the Faculty Committee's role had come to an end and that they were summarily dismissing the thoughtful work and advice of some of the University's most distinguished leaders. The decision hurt morale on campus, and the presidential search would thereafter lose support. The faculty, as Dean Carman sadly recalled, had been "disregarded completely."[51] All this made Fackenthal's position awkward.

The Trustees, refusing to give Fackenthal the proper title for his responsibilities, as Black had suggested, finally admitted that the Acting President and the University needed a Provost. That title, however, remained Fackenthal's official one, and he might need it "for a brief term of active service following the appointment or inauguration of a permanent President." Thus, Fackenthal asked Professor Jacobs to become Assistant to the President for the general administration of the University and to resign his Professorship of Law. "This would cast your lot into administration, " he wrote, "but I am sure you need have no concern in that regard no matter who becomes permanent President." Jacobs had been preparing to turn over the veterans program to his assistant, so that he could return that fall to teaching and writing at the School of Law. He agreed to stay in Low Memorial, though "the atmosphere at Columbia was very unstable." Knowing that the presidential decision probably would not be made very soon and assuming that, in any case, the new President would want his own assistant, Jacobs believed that "I just could not quit at that time" on Fackenthal, "a splendid person who had dedicated his whole life to Columbia." Nor, he wrote, could he turn his back on the University "I had served so long and loved so well." He refused, however, to resign his Professorship.[52]

The Acting President's Office needed assistance, and the Trustees recognized it. In effect, they were asking Fackenthal and Jacobs to serve as President and Provost without the titles; moreover, Fackenthal's comment that Jacobs need not worry about "who becomes permanent President" carried an implication. Undoubtedly, it expressed a Trustee decision to address more than the current problem: the University needed continuity in leadership and the Trustees saw Jacobs continuing as Provost in the new administration. President Emeritus Butler endorsed Jacobs' appointment, but he regretted the title. He preferred "a title similar to that of Provost"; while his refusal to retire earlier had contributed to the awkward situation, he sensed intuitively the problem with titles. Though the Trustees knew that changes were necessary, after their decision on Fackenthal they could do nothing about titles. Dodge, who regretted opposing Butler on the issue, talked with several Trustees and informed the Acting President: "This is the logical and necessary action to take," and he hoped there would be no delay. Chairman Coykendall concurred, and he told Fackenthal that Butler did not understand the appointment was "not necessarily a permanent title."[53] Still, it would have been better if the Trustees had defined clearly the new position; this failure to state specifically responsibilities would be repeated after Eisenhower's appointment and lead to serious misunderstandings and problems.

Not surprisingly, during the summer of 1946 Parkinson's Committee and the University's administrative and academic leaders began traveling different roads. Little leadership came from Board Chairman and Committee member Coykendall, who was in his mid-seventies. "Since we have not found a man we apparently can all agree on through the suggestions of the Faculty," Marcy Dodge told Parkinson, "let us do a systematic job of our own in trying to locate our man." Fackenthal, meanwhile, gave every indication that he wanted some time to guide the University. With his Assistant Jacobs and strong faculty support, he started planning for the coming academic year. When several prominent faculty members, including Jacques Barzun, were tempted by attractive offers from other universities, he had confidence that Jacobs and the Deans would work closely together to keep Columbia's best teachers and scholars.[54]

Individual Trustees during the summer of 1946 began separate searches, but Trustee Committee files contain no reference to any discussions about General Eisenhower that summer or fall. Trustees invited possible candidates to meet for lunch or dinner in New York, and Dodge, probably the hardest working and most devoted Trustee, traveled "all around the country interviewing people." He would seek someone's advice about the Columbia plight when he was, actually, interviewing him informally. For example, he visited James Phinney Baxter, III, President of Williams College since 1937. A former Professor of History at Harvard, Baxter had just completed a term as President of the Association of American Colleges. During the war he had been Deputy Director, Office of Strategic Services, and thereafter had served as historian in Vannevar Bush's Office of Scientific Research and Development. He recently had finished his study of that organization, *Scientists Against Time,* and in 1947 the book received the Pulitzer Prize in History.[55]

When the Trustee Committee considered offering Baxter the Columbia Presidency, Dean Pegram strongly urged that the faculty be taken into confidence, so "the faculty would say that they had been told the fact." Parkinson ignored the advice, and at the Trustees Meeting on October 7 he reviewed his Committee's activities. Either before or after the Board Meeting the Committee authorized offering the position to Baxter who, after deliberating for a month and visiting three of his Trustees in Chicago, decided that he would stay in Williamstown. "There is no disguising the fact," Dodge sadly wrote, "it is very disappointing."[56]

The Parkinson Committee did not report officially at the December 2, 1946, Board Meeting, even though it had important information. Perhaps it informally mentioned that Baxter recently had declined the presidency and that Parkinson was planning to offer it on the 6th to President Robert G. Sproul of the University of California at Berkeley. Earlier, Sproul had met for luncheon with Trustees at the Downtown Association, and soon Watson was calling and writing him. In an enthusiastic letter he emphasized the combination of Columbia and the United Nations in New York. "I visualize an organization, headed by the President of Columbia University and recognized by our State Department as its official representative, which would take an active part in the development not only of educational policies but plans and procedure in connection with the big role that the United States must play in the United Nations."

The IBM President added that the Board, of course, was "unanimous in wanting you." After waiting six weeks, Sproul wrote that the California Board of Regents had learned about the offer and asked him to take no action until their meeting on January 24, 1947. "It now seems likely," he wrote, "that my decision will be negative." After the meeting Sproul avoided the telephone calls from Watson and officially declined the offer in a letter on the 27th.[57]

Sproul then delivered a severe blow to Columbia's prestige. In a speech to the Berkeley students, with Governor Earl Warren present, he said: "In terms of the work done on this campus, I believe this a straight furrow in educational philosophy and, therefore, I have decided that I shall not take my hand from the plow to which it has been set for the past seventeen years." The *New York Times* article reported that Sproul "had been offered a $25,000 a year post as president of Columbia University, New York." Columbia's Director of Public Relations, Robert C. Harron, later commented: "I'll never forgive him." Harron realized immediately how much the bad publicity would hurt the presidential search; an outstanding newspaper reporter with unquestioned integrity, he had served as a Lieutenant Commander in the Navy's Amphibious Force on the beach in the Okinawa invasion and he deeply resented the way Sproul had used the University. Doug Black, not disagreeing, merely assumed that the California educator had known what a strenuous challenge Columbia would be and, therefore, had gone to the Regents and used Parkinson's offer to obtain a better contract. In any event, the California Regents did increase his salary and retirement benefits.[58]

Columbia's interest in General Eisenhower resurfaced during the Sproul episode. On January 23, 1947, a few days after Sproul had informed the Trustee Committee that his acceptance was unlikely but before his formal refusal, Eisenhower came to New York for a speech and stayed at the Waldorf-Astoria. Watson undoubtedly talked with him about the Columbia presidency that evening. Such a conversation would explain why Watson tried unsuccessfully several times to reach Sproul the next day, when there was very little likelihood of a positive answer from the California educator; moreover, after Eisenhower's Installation at Columbia, Watson fondly recalled an evening at the hotel: "My mind went back to the night when, in your apartment at the Waldorf-Astoria, I first talked with you about Columbia."[59]

On February 21, 1947, Eisenhower attended Columbia's Special Convocation for America's World War II heroes. The Convocation, organized largely by Jacobs, also honored, in his words, millions of young Americans and "upwards of 15,000 students and alumni of Columbia, some hundreds of whom did not return." Among those attending the ceremonies in the Rotunda of Low Memorial, including Eisenhower, were Generals Marshall, Henry "Hap" Arnold, and Alexander A. Vandergrift, and Admirals Ernest J. King, William F. Halsey, and Chester W. Nimitz. Trustee Black, Deans Pegram and Carman, and Jacobs met Eisenhower for the first time; Trustee Watson also had another opportunity to talk with the General.[60]

A conversation during the reception illustrated the General's remarkable memory. During the war Dean Bion East's only son had joined the Army Air Corps. While training in Florida he and a friend acquired a cocker spaniel from a dog pound, and they renamed him James Stuart Dunnington, III. "In the North African campaign where they were bomber pilots and later as fighters in Sicily the spaniel was their constant and devoted companion. Finally, the inevitable happened—the Dean's son failed to return from a mission." Dean East, who had "heard frequently about James Stuart Dunnington, III, wrote General Eisenhower, asking that the dog be sent home—it would mean so much to his wife and himself." Eisenhower prepared the order, but then General Carl Spaatz, Commander of the Air Forces in the N. W. Africa and Sicily Theatre, argued that "this would be a very heavy blow to the morale of the squadron which had suffered extremely heavy losses." Eisenhower "with his great human understanding by letter explained the situation" to the Dean. When the unit, one of the oldest in European service, returned home, the friend delivered James Stuart Dunnington, III, to Dean and Mrs. East. Nearly four years later at the Convocation Dean East, who had never met Eisenhower, "thanked him for his kindness. The General at once said: 'You must be Dean East. And how is James Stuart Dunnington, III? And where is he? I would like to see that dog.'"[61] The story soon became well known on Morningside Heights.

The Trustees also approached another Eisenhower during this period, the General's brother Milton. The General recalled in his memoirs, *At Ease*, "When a Committee from the Board of Trustees of Columbia University asked me to consider becoming President of that great institution, I said (as I did later when other people had ideas about another Presidency) that they were talking to the wrong Eisenhower." Trustee Dodge, indeed, had been urged to interview Milton Eisenhower in Kansas, and soon after the Sproul episode in January, 1947, he wrote Parkinson that the Kansas State University President would be in Washington and Philadelphia in late March. Years later Milton Eisenhower remembered telling Dodge that, since several Trustees already had mentioned Columbia to his brother, he himself had no interest in the position.[62]

For years a favorite story on campus was that the Trustees, meaning Watson and Parkinson, chose the wrong Eisenhower. The legend, as Philip Jessup recounted, held that the Trustees were discussing candidates and someone suggested a call to Robert M. Hutchins, the precocious educator who had become Chancellor of the University of Chicago at the age of thirty. "He in his usual abrupt way said that Eisenhower was the best man, meaning Milton Eisenhower, of course, and this was immediately picked on by Tom Watson, who thought this was marvelous and forthwith went and asked Ike." While Jessup jocularly added: "I think that the great fallacy in my version is that I don't think any of the Columbia Trustees would have asked Bob Hutchins' opinion," a Trustee, indeed, had called Hutchins who said: "Get Eisenhower."[63]

The General's name kept reappearing that spring, but the Trustee Committee could point to little progress as the end of the second year of the search approached. At a luncheon John D. Rockefeller, III, told Marcy Dodge that Columbia "would be very fortunate" to have Dwight Eisenhower; John D. Rockefeller, Jr., added his belief that Eisenhower was "more cut out" for a university presidency "than possibly for the Presidency of a Foundation." By this time the General, after "months" of pressure, had agreed that "if and when I left the military service, I would at least confer with the Board of Trustees before I made any move." While General Eisenhower had been worrying about his post-Chief of Staff career far more than his recollection in *At Ease* implied, pressure also was mounting on Morningside Heights for Parkinson's Committee to act.[64]

The search gave many indications of disintegrating that spring. Committee members were meeting often for luncheon at the Downtown Association; whenever rumors circulated around the campus about another candidate, Chairman Coykendall invariably said: "No selection has been made." The Committee became "not very communicative," even from Trustee Black's point of view. "They had the authority and they didn't want anybody getting into their act."[65] Columbia's failure to name Butler's successor was publicly embarrassing and graphically illustrated the University's plight. Trustees had talked with and considered prominent leaders but, unfortunately, the University was no closer to having a new President than it had been on the day Nicholas Murray Butler retired.

Two prominent educators had declined the presidency, and the search for an Eisenhower seemed to be at an end. Parkinson's Committee knew that Milton Eisenhower had refused to be considered and General Eisenhower had said that he would not meet with them until after he had decided to retire from the Army. The Committee could not know when that would be and could not wait. Even a casual inquiry on the Morningside Heights campus revealed the disaffection with the Trustee Committee. Helen Reid, President of the New York Tribune, Inc., and a Trustee of Barnard College, saw the University "drifting," and she wrote Marcy Dodge, "You must be badly worried about the Presidential problem." In spite of Butler's aversion, Fackenthal "should have been appointed President until a permanent selection was made, "according to Jacobs, and the situation for Columbia University "would have been much better."[66]

Notes

1.   *New York Times,* October 13, 1948.
2.   Ibid.; Mamie D. Eisenhower, personal interview, December 17, 1975, Gettysburg, Pa.
3.   Dwight D. Eisenhower to Combined Chiefs of Staff, May 7, 1945, *The Papers of Dwight David Eisenhower: The War Years,* vol. IV (Baltimore, Md., 1970), ed. Alfred D. Chandler, p. 2696; and Eisenhower to Men and Women of the Allied Expeditionary Force, May 8, 1945, *Occupation, 1945,* vol. VI (Baltimore, Md.,

1978), eds. Chandler and Louis Galambos, pp. 16-17 (*PDDE*); George C. Marshall to Eisenhower, May 8, 1945, cited by Stephen E. Ambrose, *Eisenhower: Soldier, General of the Army, President-Elect, 1890-1952* (New York, 1983), p. 408.

4. Dwight D. Eisenhower, *At Ease: Stories I Tell to Friends* (New York, 1967), p. 297; *PDDE*, VI, 155; Kenneth S. Davis, *Soldier of Democracy: A Biography of Dwight Eisenhower* (New York, 1945), p. 543.

5. Eisenhower, *At Ease,* pp. 298-300, 388-90; Eisenhower to King George VI, June 13, 1945, *PDDE*, VI, 161; Ambrose, *Eisenhower*, 410-12.

6. *New York Times*, June 19-20, 1945; *PDDE*, VI, 163, fn. #3; Davis, *Soldier of Democracy*, pp. 544-47; Ambrose, *Eisenhower*, pp. 412-13.

7. *New York Times*, June 22-23, 1945; *PDDE*, VI, 163, fn. #3; Davis, *Soldier of Democracy*, pp. 548-52; Steve Neal, *The Eisenhowers* (Lawrence, Kans. 1984), pp. 223-24.

8. "Introduction," *PDDE*, VI, xi.

9. Eisenhower to Wallace, August 8, 1945, in Ambrose, *Eisenhower*, p. 427; Dwight D. Eisenhower, *Crusade in Europe: A Personal Account of World War II* (New York, 1948), p. 444.

10. Ibid., pp. 459-65; Eisenhower to Marshall, August 16, 1945, *PDDE*, VI, 284-85; Ambrose, *Eisenhower*, pp. 429-30.

11. Eisenhower, *At Ease*, p. 314; Clarence G. Lasby, *Eisenhower's Heart Attack: How Ike Beat Heart Disease and Held on to the Presidency* (Lawrence, Kans., 1997), p. 29; Howard M. Snyder, "Draft of DDE: Summary of 1945," Howard M. Snyder MSS., Dwight D. Eisenhower Library, Abilene, Kans. (DDEL).

12. Snyder, "Draft of DDE, 1945" Snyder MSS., DDEL; Eisenhower to Sol Bloom, November 15, 1945, and to John Eisenhower, November 22, 1945, *PDDE*, VI, 536-40; Ambrose, *Eisenhower*, p. 432.

13. Snyder, "Draft of DDE," Snyder MSS., DDEL.

14. Eisenhower, *At Ease*, p. 316; Eisenhower to Edward Everett Hazlett, Jr., November 27, 1945, and to John Eisenhower, December 15, 1945, *PDDE*, VI, 552-57, and *Chief of Staff* VII, 636-37.

15. "Introduction," *PDDE*, VII, xv-xix; Eisenhower, *At Ease*, p. 317.

16. Ambrose, *Eisenhower*, pp. 433-35; Eisenhower, *At Ease*, p. 321; Robert H. Ferrell, ed., *The Eisenhower Diaries* (New York, 1981), March 8, 1947, p. 140.

17. "Chronology," *PDDE*, IX, 2312-2397, and VI, 496, fn. #1; Ambrose, *Eisenhower*, pp. 440-43.

18. Eisenhower to John Eisenhower, November 14, 1946; Eisenhower to Walter Beedle Smith, December 7, 1946, *PDDE*, VIII, 1380-82, 1427-29; Ferrell, ed., *Eisenhower Diaries*, December 2 and 7, 1946, p. 139; Snyder, "Summary of Year 1946," Snyder MSS., DDEL.

19. Eisenhower, *At Ease*, pp. 185-87, 204-205, 324; Ambrose, *Eisenhower*, pp. 76-77, 456; Forrest C. Pogue, "Genesis of *The Supreme Command*," in Gunter Bischof & Stephen E. Ambrose, ed., *Eisenhower: A Centenary Assessment* (Baton Rouge, La. 1995), p. 23.

20. Douglas H. Black, 1967, Oral History Project (COHP), Butler Library, Columbia University; The Trustees of Columbia University in the City of New York, *Minutes*, Special Meeting, April 23, 1945, Central Archives, Low Memorial Library, Columbia University (CACU).

21. Albert Marrin, *Nicholas Murray Butler* (New York, 1976), p. 51; Albert C. Jacobs, "Memoirs," Unpublished, 1974.

22. Marrin, *Butler*, p. 52; Young B. Smith, personal interview, April 26, 1959, New York, N.Y.

23. Allan Nevins, "University City Within the City," *New York Times Magazine*, June 6, 1948; Michael Rosenthal, "Nicholas Murray Butler: Captain of Erudition," Columbia Library Columns XLIV (Autumn, 1995), 8.
24. Lindsay Rogers, "Reflections on Writing Biography of Public Men," *Political Science Quarterly* 88 (December, 1973), p. 733.
25. Andrew S. Dolkart, *Morningside Heights: A History of Its Architecture & Development* (New York, 1998), pp. 159, 408; Richard Hofstadter, *The Progressive Historians: Turner, Beard, Parrington* (New York, 1970), pp. 285-86.
26. Jacques Barzun, personal interview, April 5, 1979, New York, N. Y.; Jacobs, "Memoirs," 1974; Rexford G. Tugwell, *To the Lesser Heights of Morningside: A Memoir* (Philadelphia, 1982), pp. 241-42; Kevin McCann, personal interview, July 25, 1972, Gettysburg, Pa.,
27. Douglas Black, personal interview, June 6, 1973, N. Y., New York; I. I. Rabi, 1983, COHP.
28. Black, interview, June 6, 1973; Smith, interview, April 26, 1959; Grayson Kirk to author, March 13, 1992; Trustees, *Minutes*, April 23, 1945, CACU.
29. Frank D. Fackenthal, 1956, COHP; McCann, interview, July 25, 1972; Trustees, *Minutes*, October 1, 1945, CACU.
30. For years it was understood that the *Minutes* and records of the Faculty Committee, which Dean Pegram had requested be returned to Fackenthal's office, had been destroyed. See Carl W. Ackerman MSS., August 5, 1947, Library of Congress (LC); Carl W.Ackerman, personal interview, March 24, 1958, New York, N. Y.; Harry J. Carman, personal interview, January 30, 1958, New York, N.Y. During research for this manuscript, the records of the Faculty Committee and correspondence of the Trustees Special Committee were located in Columbia's Central Archives in Low Memorial. Kirk to author, March 13, 1992.
31. Trustees, *Minutes*, May 7, 1945, CACU. On Dodge's death, the Editorial, "An Outstanding Citizen," disclosed Dodge's "rescue." *New York Times*, December 28, 1963. Susan E. Tifft and Alex S. Jones, *The Trust: The Private and Powerful Family Behind The New York Times* (New York, 1999), pp. 75-76, 800.
32. Alden Hatch, "The Prexy Plan of General Ike," *Collier's*, September 23, 1947, p. 11. Hatch also talked to Parkinson. Dodge to Parkinson, July 14, 1947, and Parkinson to Coykendall, July 17, 1947, unmarked folder containing correspondence of the Trustees Special Committee (TSC folder), CACU; Dodge to Eisenhower, September 8, 1947, and Craig Cannon to Hatch, September 13, 1947, Eisenhower MSS., DDEL; Eisenhower, *At Ease*, p. 316.
33. Eisenhower to Milton Eisenhower, March 15, 1946, *PDDE*, VII, 942-44.
34. For the composition of the Committee, see "Report of the Special Committee," September 5, 1945, CACU; Fackenthal, 1956, COHP; Carman, interview, January 30, 1958; Ackerman, interview, March 24, 1958.
35. Special Committee of the Faculty, *Minutes*, June 4, June 28, August 6, August 7, August 28, and August 29, 1945, CACU.
36. "Report of the Special Committee," September 5, 1945, CACU; Carman, interviews, January 30, 1958, and December 1, 1961; Fackenthal, 1956, COHP.
37. "Report of the Special Committee," September 5, 1945, CACU; Carman, interview, January 30, 1958; Young B. Smith, interview, February 4, 1958, and April 26, 1959.
38. "Report of the Special Committee," September 5, 1945, CACU; Carman, interview, January 30, 1958, and December 1, 1961. "I am tempted," Fulbright replied to Mullins on September 10, 1945, "to accept your offer to come to Washington to discuss details. I should like very much to have an opportunity to visit with you." Unmarked letter folder with Search Committee material, TSC folder, CACU.

39. Special Committee of the Faculty, *Minutes*, November 21, 1945; and Parkinson to Pegram, November 16, 1945, TSC folder, CACU.

40. Carman, interview, January 30, 1958; Ackerman MSS, August 5, 1947, LC; *New York Times*, August 20, 1976.

41. Parkinson to Coykendall, December 17, 1945; Dodge to Parkinson, December 31, 1945, and January 13, 1946; Butler to Coykendall, January 14, 1946; Parkinson to Butler, January 17, 1946; Butler to Parkinson, January 13, 1946; Watson to Butler, January 22, 1946, TSC folder, CACU.

42. George Zook to Dodge, tel. March 10, 1946; Dodge to Parkinson, February 26, 1946; Fleming to Dodge, March 6, 1946; Watson to Parkinson, April 18, 1946; Watson to Tolley, April 25, 1946; Tolley to Watson, April 27, 1946, TSC folder, CACU.

43. "The Story of General Eisenhower," August 5, 1947, Ackerman MSS., LC.

44. Frederick S. Fleming to Parkinson, February 13, 1946, and to Dodge, March 6, 1946, TSC folder, CACU; Carman, interview, January 30, 1958, and December 1, 1961.

45. Albert C. Jacobs, 1968, COHP; Black, interview, June 6, 1973; Jacques Barzun, personal interview, April 5, 1979, New York, N. Y.; Fackenthal, 1956, COHP; Albert C. Jacobs, personal interview, February 5, 1965, Hartford, Ct.

46. Fackenthal to Jacobs, November 24 and December 7, 1945; Jacobs to Fackenthal, December 4, 1945, CACU; Young B. Smith to Jacobs, November 26, 1945; Jacobs to Smith, December 11, 1945, Albert C. Jacobs MSS., Bentley Library, Michigan Historical Collections (MHC), University of Michigan; Jacobs, "Memoirs," 1974.

47. Fackenthal to Jacobs, January 18, 1946, CACU; Trustees, *Minutes*, October 7, 1946, ibid.; Jacobs, WNYC Broadcast, February 20, 1946; Jacobs to Smith, April 29, 1946, and Smith to Jacobs, May 4, 1946, Jacobs MSS., MHC; Jacobs, "Memoirs," 1974; George Mullins to Smith, May 9, 1946, CACU.

48. Alden Hatch, who had written "The Prexy Plan of General Ike" after talking with Dodge and Parkinson in 1947, later asserted: "There may have been inquiries by individual trustees. . . . I do not believe that there was any serious move on the part of the Trustees to select Ike in April, 1946." Hatch to Ackerman, April 5, 1957, Ackerman Mss. (LC).

49. Pegram Committee Report to Parkinson, May 17, 1946, TSC folder, CACU; Ackerman, interview, March 24, 1958; Carman, interview, December 1, 1961. Professor Eli Ginzberg was asked by the committee "to elicit" Fulbright's availability, and the Senator told him: "You are, regrettably, a year too late or several years too early. I would have taken this most seriously under consideration had I not been just elected to the Senate. Ginzberg, 1975, Oral History Interview, Dwight D. Eisenhower Library (OHDDEL).

50. Black, 1967, COHP; Carman, interview, January 30, 1958; Ackerman, interview, March 24, 1958; Dodge to Parkinson, May 27, 1946, and Dodge to H. Alexander Smith, TSC folder, CACU.

51. Pegram to Parkinson, May 17, 1946; Dodge to Coykendall, June 11, 1946, TSC folder, CACU; Lindsay Rogers, 1958, COHP; Carman, interview, December 1, 1961.

52. Fackenthal to Jacobs, June 24 and 27, 1946; Jacobs to Fackenthal, July 2 and August 3, 1946; Fackenthal to Trustees, July 20, 1946, CACU; Jacobs, "Memoirs," 1974.

53. Fackenthal to Butler, July 23, 29, 31, 1946; Butler to Fackenthal July 24 and 31, 1946; Coykendall notation, July 27, 1946; Dodge to Fackenthal, July 27, 1946, CACU; *New York Times*, August 6, 1946.

54. Dodge to Parkinson, June 15 and October 6, 1946, TSC folder, CACU.

55. Black, interview, June 6, 1973; Albert C. Jacobs, personal interview, December 28, 1973, Ann Arbor, Mi. Dodge to Parkinson, August 20 and n.d. (August), 1946, TSC

folder, CACU; Carman, interview, December 1, 1961.

56. Dodge to Parkinson, October 5 and November 11, 1946; Baxter to Dodge and to Parkinson, November 8, 1946, TSC folder, CACU; Trustees, *Minutes*, October 7, 1946, ibid.; Memo, "Dr. James P. Baxter," in Trustee Willard King MSS., "undated, miscellany," in Ackerman MSS., LC; Black, interview, June 6, 1973.

57. Trustees, *Minutes*, December 2, 1946, CACU; Watson to Sproul, December 19, 1946, Sproul to Mrs. Ogden Reid, December 24, 1946; Dodge to Parkinson, January 26, 1947; Sproul to Parkinson, January 15 and 27, 1947, TSC folder, CACU.

58. *New York Times*, February 9, 1947; Robert C. Harron, personal interview, February 5, 1965, Hartford, Ct.; Black, interview, June 6, 1973; Carman, interview, December 1, 1961; *New York Times*, December 16, 1969; *Oakland Tribune*, March 1, 1947, TSC folder, CACU.

59. According to Eisenhower's appointment book, he did not stay at the Waldorf between January and May and, by then, according to him and Milton Eisenhower, discussions about Columbia were well underway. *PDDE*, IX, 2358-70.

60. During the convocation the film in a motion picture camera burst into flame and caused considerable consternation in the packed rotunda. Jacobs, "Memoirs," 1974; Black, interview, June 6, 1973; Carman, interview, December 1, 1961.

61. Jacobs, "Memoirs," 1974; Jacobs, "Address Before the Denver Chamber of Commerce," March 21, 1952, Jacobs MSS., MHC.

62. Eisenhower, *At Ease,* p. 336; Milton Eisenhower, personal interview, July 26, 1972, Baltimore, Md.

63. Philip Jessup, personal interview, June 17, 1977, Norfolk, Ct.; Sue Zschoche, "The Making of Presidents: Who Have Universities Sought as Leaders and Why?" The Presidents Eisenhower Conference, October 2, 1998, Kansas State University.

64. Dodge to Parkinson, April 28, 1947, TSC folder, CACU; Eisenhower, *At Ease*, p. 336.

65. Harron, interview, February 5, 1965; Black, interview, June 6, 1973.

66. Helen Reid to Dodge, May 5, 1947, TSC folder, CACU; Jacobs, interview, February 5, 1965.

2

Waiting for Ike to Arrive

The great leader of American youth in the days when our very existence depended on the decisions he made will have to decide at Columbia matters of far-reaching importance. We welcome him because of his
vibrant personality; because he is a true patriot . . . because he is not an
educator in the narrow sense of the term. He is much more.
—Provost Albert C. Jacobs
World-Wide Broadcast
June 29, 1947

He was not too enthusiastic about the decision he had made.
—William E. Robinson
October 17, 1947

I saw in Columbia, because of its standing among American educational institutions and its influence on the educational process, opportunities as large and rewarding as the environment might be strange and
difficult.
—Dwight D. Eisenhower, *At Ease*, 1967

"A group of the Trustees, apparently spearheaded by Mr. Tom
Watson, began pressuring me to accept" the Columbia Presidency
late in the spring of 1947, General Eisenhower recalled in his *Diary*. The pressures had been "worthy of most super salesmen." Other
groups were offering him positions, including "the head of the Boy
Scouts (a most appealing offer), while a group of Midwesterners
said they had a senatorship ready . . . . Another group was anxious
that I consider a commercial venture, but this type of thing was
easy to refuse." He had agreed he would talk with Columbia's Trustees before making any decision, but he did not indicate when that
might be.[1]

In the spring of 1947, however, Parkinson's Search Committee,
which had the responsibility of recommending a candidate to the

Board, was in no position to wait, and its efforts for a new President were in disarray. Perhaps the Committee members began to perceive, as had others, the depth of their problem. President James Conant of Harvard, according to Dodge, recognized that the Columbia position "is a difficult job to handle on account of Dr. Butler really not handling it for ten years." Committee members knew, moreover, that within the Columbia community support for Acting President Fackenthal was growing daily.[2]

Trustees not on the Parkinson Committee, meanwhile, had received little information. John G. Jackson, increasingly impatient, finally asked for an informal discussion following the Board Meeting on April 7. If Dwight Eisenhower were not available, the prominent New York City lawyer told Parkinson, "we should give most serious consideration to the permanent appointment" of Fackenthal. "A strong feeling among the faculty" endorsed the Acting President; moreover, Jackson knew that the idea had "a good deal of support" among Trustees. During the informal session the Parkinson Committee presumably expressed its interest in two men: Vannevar Bush, who had been suggested by the Faculty Committee eighteen months earlier, and Arthur Compton, the President of Washington University in St. Louis. Compton, the recipient of the Nobel Prize for Physics in 1927, during the war had been the Director of the Metallurgical Atomic Laboratory, and Dodge recently had had dinner with him and Mrs. Compton in St. Louis. Bush, meanwhile, had agreed to come to New York, "ostensibly at least" because of his recommendation of Secretary of War Robert Patterson for the position. It is doubtful, though, that the Committee that afternoon gave the Trustees the opportunity to wrestle with the problem posed by Dodge a few days later: "If we . . . make an effort to find out" if Compton were available, "before we talk seriously to Dr. Bush," could the Committee go to Compton without being willing to "recommend his name to the Trustees."[3]

Nor did Committee members themselves pause to think about the problem of approaching candidates simultaneously; instead, during the next few weeks they considered at least six individuals, excluding Fackenthal. Parkinson, apparently, talked with Bush, who declined to be considered for the Presidency of Columbia; a senior Trustee argued strongly against the recommendation of Secretary Patterson; Dodge talked several times with President John William Nason of Swarthmore, who had just missed being included on the Faculty Committee's original list of eight names; Watson urged that

President Everett Case of Colgate University be considered again and mentioned another person; and President James Conant suggested a candidate. Meanwhile, the Student Board of Columbia College unanimously requested Fackenthal's election. With Trustees moving in different directions, the search verged on veering out of control.[4]

As the May Meeting of the Board approached—two years after Butler had agreed to retire—other Trustees put more and more pressure on the Parkinson Committee. Although the Committee, once again, did not present a formal report, during another informal session afterwards Trustees extracted from the Committee a promise to call a Special Meeting before Commencement. It was agreed, moreover, that the Committee would "report on the one name finally discussed" on May 7. That person was Philip Jessup, the Professor of International Law whose name had been on the original Faculty list. Watson immediately began "making further inquiries," and Jessup, who recently had been ill, authorized his physician to release his medical records.[5]

It is difficult to reconstruct the sequence of events between the agreement on May 7 to call a Special Meeting, which soon would be scheduled for Tuesday, May 27, and the decision of the Board on June 2 to offer the presidency to General Eisenhower. Most of the decisions came during informal conversations or over the telephone, and there are few written records. It is extremely unlikely that the Parkinson Committee itself had mentioned Jessup. Indeed, the possibility of a formal discussion of Jessup's candidacy worried Dodge. He informed Parkinson that "a quarter of the Board . . . are not ready to vote definitely for Dr. Jessup at this time"; furthermore, he added Watson's concern that whatever they did about Jessup, it should "not be embarrassing."[6]

Parkinson, Watson, and Dodge, consequently, decided not to present Jessup's name for a formal vote on May 27 and to propose that there be no formal discussion of any candidates. The positive medical report on Jessup, ironically, may have entered into their decision, since it would have strengthened the arguments of his supporters; Jessup thereafter enjoyed an extremely active career and lived to the age of eighty-nine. In any event, Dodge soon scheduled a meeting with Swarthmore's Nason at the Century Association on May 13, and on the eve of the Special Meeting of the Board he sent a long letter to a Trustee colleague, in which he discussed his preference for the Board to concentrate on Nason. He arranged, meanwhile, for Arthur Compton to travel to New York for a luncheon with a few Trustees at the Downtown Association on May 28, the day after the Special Meeting.[7] For the Search Committee to schedule an interview with an eminent educator, the day after many Trustees thought that Jessup would be presented for a formal vote, illustrates the search's disarray; meanwhile, Watson was arranging a meeting with General Eisenhower.

Twenty Trustees, nearly the entire Board, gathered in Low Memorial on May 27. The Committee "presented orally an interim report," and neither the report nor the discussion was recorded in the *Minutes*. Since two candidates were being seen in the next twenty-four hours, the Committee had to avoid a Trustee vote on Jessup and, for that matter, the possibility of a vote on Fackenthal. Watson, who had gone "out of his way to know" Eisenhower after the war, indicated that he would see the General that evening—Eisenhower was taking President Truman's place and speaking at a dinner at the Hotel Commodore. The IBM President knew that would be his last chance to persuade Eisenhower, and he would urge him to give "an early answer." Second, the Committee was meeting with Compton the next noon. The Committee had put itself in a position where either a "yes" or a "no" vote on Jessup would be awkward and embarrassing and the Trustees agreed, resolving "that further formal consideration of candidates for the Presidency be deferred."[8]

After the luncheon for Compton a Trustee leaving the Downtown Association told Joseph Campbell, the University's Assistant Treasurer, that they had a new candidate. Campbell, a Columbia College alumnus, during World War II had supervised the University's government contracts, including the arrangements for the atomic energy project, and in 1949 he became Treasurer and Vice President for Business Affairs. Some years later Eisenhower, as President of the United States, appointed him to the Atomic Energy Commission and then Comptroller General of the United States. Campbell "saw several Trustees that day of the 'historic' Compton discussion," and he understood that the scientist was about to be offered, and would have accepted, the Presidency, Watson, however, called during the meeting and told Parkinson that Eisenhower might agree. Since Parkinson's Committee had "tried for a long time to get" Compton to New York and the Trustees, even before the call, had known that Watson had pressed Eisenhower the previous evening about the Presidency, they must have been terribly uneasy throughout the luncheon for Compton.[9]

The General had taken the night train back to Washington, and he described his conversation with the IBM President in a letter to Milton Eisenhower. "Watson came to see me and this time seemed to be speaking with somewhat more authority." Eisenhower gained the impression that Watson had been "talking to a number of other Trustees, or directors or whatever they are called," and, to his chagrin, Watson pressed him seriously "to take over the job once I have been relieved as Chief of Staff." The IBM President emphasized "the importance of public service," and "built up the rosiest picture of what I would be offered in the way of conveniences, expenses, remuneration and so on." While Eisenhower insisted that he himself "was *not* the one in the family best qualified" and that he lacked experience and doubted that he would be "either efficient or happy," he gathered that the Trustees hoped to draw more foreign students to the University and that Eisenhower's worldwide fame would assist the program.[10]

Watson's hopes and the Chief of Staff's comments sufficiently encouraged the Trustee to proceed. When he learned that the General and Mrs. Eisenhower were going to West Point on June 1 to celebrate the Class of 1915 Reunion and deliver the Commencement Address on June 3, he informed the General's office at the Pentagon that he would drive to West Point on June 2. Parkinson, meanwhile, agreed to call a Special Meeting of the Board for the morning of June 2 in his office at the Equitable Building.

Sixteen Trustees met and "counted noses and voted" to authorize Parkinson and Watson to go to West Point and offer the presidency to Eisenhower. Five members of the Board, according to Black, expressed their opinion that the General should not be the next President of Columbia University; three of them, significantly, served on Parkinson's five member Search Committee. The Trustees not supporting the selection of Eisenhower included the Chairman of the Board, Coykendall; the Clerk of the Board, Dodge; and Rector Fleming of Trinity Church; the other two Trustees were Doubleday's Black and Albert G. Redpath, a long-time director of the *Columbia Law Review* and founding partner of a New York stock brokerage firm. Ultimately, Watson, who did not have the authority of a Search Committee member, probably had made too many commitments on behalf of the Board for the Trustees to say "No." Thus, Watson and

Parkinson, in spite of the opinion of some of the Board's most influential members, received the authority they coveted, and they left immediately for West Point. The Board did attach one condition: If Eisenhower accepted, he would have to assume office within twelve months, so that he would be at Columbia University in time for the start of the 1948 academic year.[11]

"Frankly," Eisenhower had added in his letter to Milton after talking with Watson on the 27th, "I do not want to tie myself down—at this time—to any promise." He reflected on his interest in accepting an executive position with the Boy Scouts, which "appeals to me very much but again my resentment at having to promise *now*" probably means "No." He was, therefore, "disappointed" that Columbia had come back to him, and he suggested, "I think it would be most helpful if your particular friend on the Board would begin an intensive campaign to make these birds see not only that you are the best qualified man for the position but that entirely aside from your own standing and your own high reputation in the academic and administrative world you would inescapably carry with you a very definite part of whatever prestige they may hope to gain by naming me." Milton's "particular friend" was Marcy Dodge.[12]

During the winter and spring the brothers had begun a series of discussions about the Columbia proposal. Milton Eisenhower might have recalled that in 1939 he had asked his brother's advice on accepting a deanship at Pennsylvania State College or remaining in the Department of Agriculture under the New Deal in Washington. Eisenhower was in the Philippines, serving as General Douglas MacArthur's assistant, and his reply contains remarkable insights and is fascinating in light of the decision he faced in 1947. "My conception of a worth-while college dean is a man that, as the years go by, becomes a guide and inspiration to our youth, not through feverish activity and solution of involved administrative problems, but through the ripened viewpoint from which he sees youth's questions, and the high average of wisdom he uses in helping them solve their problems." The dean's "value derives from character, knowledge and personality—not from ceaseless expenditure of nervous energy." Milton, though, decided to stay in Washington. When he was offered the presidency of Kansas State in 1943, the General replied during the Allied campaign in North Africa. He urged Milton to accept: "I regard the position . . . as one of public trust and offering opportunities for public service to challenge the talents of any man. . . . It would allow you to be a real factor toward influencing a healthy development of young America."[13]

The rosy picture Watson had painted about Columbia for Eisenhower in New York City became even more beautiful at West Point, when he and Parkinson talked with the General at the home of the Academy's Superintendent, General Maxwell D. Taylor. "In a moment of weakness," Eisenhower later confided to Dean Harry Carman, "I listened to the blandishments of a couple of your Trustees." When the Chief of Staff told them that "the President of Columbia should be a scholar of renown, one who knows his way around the academic world," the Trustees replied that they sought "a leader. . . . We have many fine scholars on campus." Watson and Parkinson informed him that he "wouldn't have anything to do with curriculum, or faculty, or any of that sort of thing."[14]

On the way to the Academy's graduation parade, Eisenhower described the Columbia offer. "Why," he exclaimed to Taylor, a close and admired World War II associate, "I barely got through this place." Taylor had been Superintendent at West Point for nearly two years, and he surmised that his friend was "largely unaware of the nature of the primary duties of a university president with the emphasis on money raising and administration." When Eisenhower told Douglas Black what Watson and Parkinson had said, the publisher thought to himself, "You were naive enough to believe" them. The Trustee recalled, "I think it was amazing that he was told that, and I think it's somewhat amazing that he believed it." Black bluntly criticized the actions of his colleagues on the Board of Trustees: "Parkinson should have known better because he had been on the faculty," but Watson probably did not "even know what the University Council did."[15]

The persistent endeavors of Watson and Parkinson led Eisenhower to agree to discuss the proposition with President Truman, who "heartily" concurred with the Columbia salesmen that the General could "render a worthwhile public service." It might also, Truman could reason, remove Eisenhower from presidential politics in 1948. The Chief of Staff accompanied Truman to Kansas City on June 6-8 for the homecoming of the 35th Division, the President's former outfit. On the third anniversary of D-Day, Eisenhower delivered the keynote address and attended a memorial service. The next day, he and his brothers Arthur and Milton, flew on the Presidential plane to Abilene and visited the family home; the following day he and Truman returned to Washington. The trip had given him the chance to talk with Milton, as well as with the President. On Monday, June 9, he and Mamie left for Fort Monroe, Virginia, where Captain John Eisenhower married Barbara J. Thompson.[16]

Finally, on June 14 the General wrote Watson about their West Point meeting, and he expressed a few doubts, which he had already mentioned, "other than those involving my own qualifications and dislike of New York as a residence." The volume of social activities worried him; his wife, "although extremely capable, . . . is not very strong." Secondly, he needed "an aide, office manager and personal secretary" outside the university hierarchy, and it was important to have an army comrade, since national security questions might be involved. Eisenhower wanted to "select a man whose wife, by reason of friendship and ability, could be of great assistance to Mrs. Eisenhower," and he had in mind for this new position, Assistant to the President, Lieutenant Colonel Kevin McCann, his speech writer and public relations adviser in the Chief of Staff's office. He agreed with Parkinson and Watson's suggestion at West Point that he and Mamie should come to New York "to learn more specifically the nature of our duties." Regarding this visit "as very important," he wrote, "Under no circumstance could I go into such a venture unless I felt assured that there was practically unanimous conviction among those responsible that we would fit properly into the picture."[17]

The same day he wrote Milton and enclosed a copy of his letter to Watson. His brother, after their visit in Kansas City and Abilene, had briefly noted, "The more I think about it, the more I'm inclined to be friendly to the New York idea." The General stated that he just had had a long telephone conversation with the IBM President, who had assured him about the social responsibilities. "He says that in New York particularly all of the entertaining is done either by one of the Trustees—each of whom I presume is a rich man—or by one of the Deans. The President of the College is expected to entertain only when some very distinguished personage comes through the city or where it appears to the advantage of the college for prestige or other reasons to entertain the individual." Watson, continuing his persuasive pitch, had emphasized that the Trustees had had a "lively discussion," and "the faint hope I gave them at West Point last week has gratified them all immeasurably."

These assurances made Eisenhower "a little bit more confident about going further with negotiations." For some reason he listened seriously, and uncritically, to Watson's blandishments and promises; neither he nor his brother, the president of a large state university, was questioning them. Milton, probably assuming that Watson spoke for the full Board, in his reply on the seventeenth expressed his happiness "about the general direction things are taking." Grayson Kirk, Eisenhower's successor at Columbia, later found it "difficult to understand how Eisenhower, with Milton as an academically experienced adviser, could have been so naive as to believe the Trustees' assurances." Did Eisenhower's reference to "President of the College" signify his unawareness, in spite of his administrative experience, that Columbia College was only a part of the University's large, complex structure? By mid-June his determination not "to tie myself—at this time—to any promise" was rapidly weakening. Soon, he and Mamie agreed to meet the Trustee Search Committee in New York on Saturday, June 21, and then to meet the Deans and Directors of the University.[18]

Two days before the Eisenhowers went to New York, columnist Walter Winchell made the startling announcement in the *New York Daily Mirror*: Columbia wanted Eisenhower and there was little doubt about the General's decision to leave the Pentagon and accept the Presidency. Winchell, who had visited Eisenhower during his stay at Pratt General Hospital in Florida, declared that he had been "informed by an indisputable source that the resignation already is in the hands of the President." The War Department released "a cryptic announcement" for General Eisenhower, saying that he "has no intention of leaving his present assignment as Chief of Staff during the current year, and never without the full approval of the Secretary of War and the President." The Columbia Trustees, indeed, had suggested "he consider the presidency," but "he is not in the position to discuss the matter at this time." The following morning the *New York Times* reported on the front page that Eisenhower would accept the position and that President Truman did not object. Chairman Coykendall, though, refused to comment on the report, noting only that the War Department statement spoke for itself; he had indicated, nonetheless, that the Trustees might take some action the next week.[19]

Eisenhower had several opportunities that week, in addition to talking with his brother, to discuss the Columbia proposal and inquire about leading a major university. On Tuesday, June 17, President Truman and General Eisenhower, accompanied by Mrs. Truman and Mrs. Eisenhower, took the presidential train to Princeton, New

Jersey, where they received honorary degrees from Princeton University and had luncheon at the President's house; the next day the General flew to Philadelphia for an honorary degree from the University of Pennsylvania. Then on Friday he met at noon with Vannevar Bush, and they discussed the Columbia presidency; it is not clear whether Eisenhower knew or learned that Bush recently had declined to be considered for the position. Bush had had extensive academic administrative experience, and years later he recalled that he had talked with Eisenhower prior to the General's decision; Bush, indeed, may have suggested a telephone call to his colleague, President Conant, for advice. During the 1930s Conant and Milton Eisenhower had established a good friendship, and the former had played an influential role in the development of Milton's thinking. But that afternoon Conant was "absent," Eisenhower noted, "and so I missed the opportunity that I sought."[20]

Late Friday afternoon, June 20, and into the early evening, Acting President Fackenthal telephoned the University's Deans, Directors, and top administrative officers and asked them to be in the Trustees Room in Low Memorial at 1:45 Saturday afternoon. The request was most unusual; it came several weeks after Commencement, and a number of those called either had left for the summer or had weekend plans. The meeting, consequently, was not largely attended. Professor Harry Morgan Ayres, an outstanding English literature scholar and Director of the Summer Session, considered two possibilities after Fackenthal's telephone call. Either the Walter Winchell article was correct and Eisenhower had accepted the presidency, or Fackenthal had decided that he had had enough—that, after the Baxter and Sproul stories, the newspaper articles about Eisenhower were too much for him to continue in his difficult situation.[21]

Fackenthal opened the Saturday meeting and stated that General Dwight D. Eisenhower would be the next President of Columbia University. The official announcement, he added, would come after a Special Meeting of the Board of Trustees on Tuesday, June 24. Then Coykendall, Parkinson, and Watson led the General through the double doors into the Trustees Room in Low Memorial. Parkinson announced that the Trustees had wanted him all along, though they had lost hope and had approached two other candidates. An informal conversation between Eisenhower and the Deans and Directors followed and, when the General began smoking, contrary to custom in the room, one Dean found a metal wastepaper basket for an ashtray. Toward the end of the meeting Mrs. Watson and Mrs. Eisenhower joined the group.[22]

Earlier, General and Mrs. Eisenhower had met with the Trustee Committee and had "thrashed the whole thing out," and he had said "Yes." At the same time the Trustees had decided that Professor Jacobs should become Provost of the University, the position Fackenthal had held from 1937 to 1945 while administering Columbia. Jacobs "never knew" he had been elected Provost until the Trustees announced both appointments; later, he learned that these Trustees had explored this "very carefully with General Eisenhower" before the General had accepted. Jacobs would, he was told, "be in complete charge of the whole academic program at Columbia." It was a "complete arrangement" or, as Arthur Hays Sulzberger, publisher of the *New York Times* and an influential Trustee subsequently stated, the Trustees considered Eisenhower and Jacobs a "team."[23]

The reasons for Eisenhower's sudden willingness to accept the presidency are complex and, in light of his career, perplexing. He knew he would retire from the Army when his term as Chief of Staff ended in 1948. According to Doug Black, who would become one of Eisenhower's closest and most trusted friends, the salesmanship of Watson had led him to Columbia. The IBM President "wanted to be close to Ike . . . the biggest figure of the day, . . . to be in on the whatever." An ardent Democrat, Watson harbored presidential ambitions for Eisenhower and understood that the prestige of an academic position offered innumerable advantages for a general.

In any case, Watson had discovered the perfect way. At West Point he and Parkinson, also a Democrat, had emphasized cleverly both the opportunity to meet students and the freedom Eisenhower would have to express his convictions—"an opportunity for real service," the General believed—and Watson, by specifically minimizing Eisenhower's involvement with fund raising and the presidential responsibilities of leading a large university, had deceived him. The Trustees, Grayson Kirk emphasized, had not appointed the "wrong" Eisenhower: "I think that's complete canard. The Trustees knew exactly what they were doing." He added that Watson "misled DDE so badly about the actual state of Columbia" that he remained "grumpy about it" for several years. Henry Wriston, President of Brown University and President of the Council on Foreign Relations, came to know Eisenhower well, and he recalled, "He was elected President of Columbia under some misapprehensions, both on his part and on theirs. I know this story because Mr. Eisenhower told it to me, also Thomas J. Watson, Sr., and the two dovetailed exactly." They wanted the General; later, he rather plaintively told Wriston, "I have never been pushed around so much since I was a shavetail." In his *Diary*, Eisenhower acknowledged that "in a way it was a 'stampeding' process, except that it had been first mentioned to me more than a year ago."[24]

"My preference," Eisenhower reflected years later, "inclined me toward a small school in a rural setting." There he could develop "friendly ties with students and faculty," and his "lack of scholarly achievement would be offset by an ability to talk freely and fully about the world." While "I would have loved" such a role, Columbia was "a formidable challenge." Indeed, at Columbia's Special Convocation in early 1947 he had been surprised when Douglas Black told him Columbia College was rather small, and that it would remain so, and that the graduate part of the University was significant. In the fall of 1946 Eisenhower had written "my sole desire and ambition, once I have ended my duties as Chief of Staff, is to retire to private life and to the freedom and the rest that I honestly believe I have earned."[25]

"You can well imagine," he wrote Walter Bedell Smith, his World War II Chief of Staff, that the decision on Columbia was a difficult one. "I had to struggle against every instinct I had. Moreover, I encountered the conviction of many friends that acceptance was a duty." My "real dream," he continued, "was to get a small college of an undergraduate character somewhere in the Virginia or Pennsylvania area or possibly even in the Northwest and to live quietly with Mamie in that kind of atmosphere." He would have an opportunity to "write or not, just as I choose," under those conditions. "I have given up all such dreams for the moment." He was astonished that so many people had insisted that "it was my duty to undertake the job. . . . The matter was first mentioned to me more than a year and a half ago and I had constantly brushed it aside until finally it descended on me in such intensity and backed by so much pressure that I had to give a Yes or No."[26]

Rationalizing the entreaties of Watson and Parkinson, Eisenhower wrote "Swede" Hazlett that many considerations led to his decision. "From my viewpoint, going to Columbia is merely to change the location of my headquarters; perhaps it would be more accurate to say that I am changing the method by which I will continue to strive for the same goals." Promising to take to Columbia his fanatic belief "in the American form of democracy" and in "the practice of true cooperation among sovereign nations . . . until an effective world order is achieved," he hoped "by living them and preaching them I can do some good." Consistently he had refused to consider any proposal "commercial in character," regardless of how "fantastic" it might be. Two and a half years later he recorded in his *Diary* that he had accepted the position because he believed that he could do more at Columbia "than anywhere else to further the cause to which I am devoted, the reawakening of intense interest in the basis of the American system." Nonetheless, earlier, he had written that "the Trustees understand thoroughly two conditions I've laid down. I must convince myself, within a year, that I can be of real service. I must have more leisure and recreation time. . . . If either of these conditions is not met, I'll quit."[27]

He had, in fact, specifically addressed his reservations in a long letter to Parkinson, two days after he had met in New York with the Committee and accepted the offer—and after his appointment had been widely reported in the press—and the day before the Trustees were to meet, formally elect him, and issue the public announcement. The Chief of Staff began, bluntly, "You realize that Mrs. Eisenhower and I have both had very definite inner battles." They still disliked the prospect of living in New York City, and they wanted to "begin leading a somewhat more leisurely life." The hours since Saturday, consequently, have been "filled with anxious and prayerful thought." He expressed no enthusiasm when he added, "I must tell you that while we have come to the conclusion that the finger of duty seems to point in the direction of Columbia, small but definite factors in this conclusion have been two points that are not specifically mentioned in your letter." Watson had told him that he would have help in finding a small home in the country "where we could live as great a portion of the year as might prove feasible." Secondly, Watson had promised that the University would create a position, with reasonable salary, for a personal aide. "These two items may seem selfishly personal but . . . it is only fair that we should state frankly that they have for us a greater importance than normally would be the case."

Chairman Coykendall, he continued in his letter to Parkinson, had given him a book on the duties of Columbia's President. It stated that he was expected to "preside at numerous faculty meetings," and he reminded Parkinson, "I have been assured by all of you that in undertaking this task I would have a minimum of concern with details and that I would be largely master of my own time and activity." Mincing no words, the General asserted, "I am anxious that before the Board meets tomorrow, all of its members understand very clearly the general picture that you, Mr. Watson, and the others have painted to me of the basic purpose lying behind my selection." Eisenhower's task was "to devote my energies in providing internal leadership on broad and liberal lines for the University itself and to promote basic concepts of education in a democracy." He wanted "no misunderstandings of any kind." If this letter, he concluded, did not represent Parkinson's "own idea of the purport of our conversations," the Board Meeting should be postponed "pending further conversations." He hoped that the letter would be taken "in the spirit in which it is written" and that "you will not be disappointed in your choice."[28]

An amazing letter. Had General of the Army Dwight Eisenhower suddenly realized what a vulnerable position he had put himself in? Had he been so overly impressed with his courtship by prominent businessmen that he had lost his proven ability to judge situations? Had he, perhaps during the meeting with the Deans and Directors, begun to sense the dimension of the task he had agreed to assume at Columbia University? Had he unrealistically expected to be merely a presiding officer and was he beginning to understand that the demands were far greater and more complex than he had been led to believe? That he could not be both President and master of his time?

Had he recalled over the weekend a three-hour luncheon and afternoon session he had had in late January with Columbia's Eli Ginzberg? The Professor had visited the Chief of Staff at the Pentagon to discuss a proposed military manpower study, and the General was just beginning to think about the Columbia position. Before the war Ginzberg had pioneered research in manpower and human resources and had launched a brilliant career at Columbia. During his wartime assignment in the Surgeon General's Office he had become closely associated with General Synder, who had arranged the meeting. Two subjects dominated the long conversation. Initially, Eisenhower commented that the Trustees are "talking with me about Columbia. . . . Well, I don't know whether I ought to be a college president." When he added how attractive it would be not to raise funds, Ginzberg bluntly replied, "I don't know how stupid those trustees are but I think they are not so stupid, they are just lying in their teeth. . . . We're in very bad shape." The conversation continued about Columbia for awhile, with Synder remaining silent throughout the meeting, and then the General inquired about Ginzberg's research. If he went to Columbia, he indicated that he wanted to stimulate studies in the military manpower history of World War II. Ginzberg, however, in describing "a not altogether pretty picture about Columbia for him," had given the General a warning.[29]

Over the weekend the General had decided he had to establish clearly his terms, before it was too late. He was, in effect, in his letter to Parkinson issuing an ultimatum to the Board of Trustees. He knew its commitment to an announcement on Tuesday, June 24, only hours after his letter was to arrive in New York. Separately, the General sent Parkinson the same day a second letter in which he formally accepted Parkinson's offer on June 21 of the Presidency; it would not become effective, however, until he had been released from active duty.[30]

Yet, as hard a bargain as he might drive—and he literally gave Parkinson the choice of agreeing or of subjecting the University to a humiliating embarrassment, one far worse than anything Professor Ayres could have imagined on the eve of the Low Memorial meeting—General Eisenhower, after all, missed the point as much as Watson and Parkinson had missed it in their representations. Perhaps, as Douglas Black reflected, and without offering any excuses for his colleagues' actions, many Trustees did not understand the University and its problems, or remember that a university was "involved with much more than simply getting a famous, important, able man to come in."[31] The type of presidency Watson and Parkinson had promised him at West Point in no way could meet the challenges Columbia University confronted. And, no matter how much Eisenhower worried about details, whether they related, for example, to a personal aide, or to housing in the country, or to entertaining, Columbia was an incredibly complicated urban institution in the world's foremost city; it was not a small, rural college. The Chief of Staff of the United States Army and former Supreme Commander, who had skillfully forged a wartime coalition, should have known, in spite of what he was told by Watson and Parkinson, that one cannot run such an organization and be master of his "own time and activity."

Parkinson deliberately misled the Board of Trustees on June 24, as he and Watson had misled Eisenhower about his responsibilities as President; specifically, he read only "some parts" of Eisenhower's letter in his "oral report" at the Meeting. He may have shared Eisenhower's letter with Watson; it would become clear during the fall that Chairman Coykendall had not seen it. Probably only he and Watson knew the extent of the assurances they had given the General at West Point; nonetheless, stretching the truth, he told the Trustees that the Committee was in full agreement with Eisenhower. He added that it would help Eisenhower "to find a country place and would provide for the position" he wanted. The Board's decision, thus, was a formality. When Parkinson later conveyed to the General the Trustees' concurrence, he emphasized that Nicholas Murray Butler, who had left for the summer, was "emphatic and emotional in his enthusiastic approval" of Eisenhower's selection.[32]

The Board of Trustees officially elected General Eisenhower the thirteenth President of Columbia University on June 24. He would join the University as soon as his superiors in Washington released him from active duty, presumably sometime during the first six months of 1948. The official announcement stated,

> The Trustees have sought a man who, as head on one of the great institutions of the city and nation, would not only command confidence and respect but would also carry on and promote those ideals fostered by Nicholas Murray Butler which, in his own phrase, have made Columbia University an important influence in developing New York as the intellectual center of the world.
>
> The Trustees believe that General Eisenhower, in the field of education, as in his former activities, will be a great leader and a worthy successor to the man who for so long has been recognized as one of the foremost of America's educators.

Chairman Coykendall, answering questions from reporters, acknowledged that the Trustees had not discussed an official residence for Eisenhower, as it was assumed Butler would continue to live at the President's House at 60 Morningside Drive. University officials, moreover, declined to state the new President's salary, though newspapers noted that he would continue to receive for life, as a General of the Army, his military pay and allowances.

Chief of Staff Eisenhower, at his first press conference following the Columbia announcement, stated in Washington, "Wherever I am, the interest of the Army and of national security will always be No. 1 with me." The Trustees, he emphasized a few days later, understood that he would "come to Washington any day . . . any time, for any kind of consultation. . . . I am to be here when needed."[33]

The Trustees had voted by secret ballot, and the *Minutes* do not indicate that the Board elected him unanimously; the *Minutes* do indicate, however, that the Board suspended "unanimously" the By-Laws for the election of new Trustees and that the Clerk of the Board was "instructed to cast one ballot" for Eisenhower's election as Trustee and, also, one ballot for Fackenthal's. Eight Trustees, including Butler and Sulzberger, were absent, but the five Trustees who had opposed his selection on June 2 attended the meeting. Black admitted that he did not "toss his hat in the air." He remained annoyed, "miffed," about the way the appointment was "rushed in on about two weeks notice" and without "any briefing" on what it was all about; indeed, only a few of the Trustees had even met Eisenhower. Black knew, furthermore, that "there would be resentment in the faculty because they hadn't been consulted. They weren't carried away as all the Trustees were." Dodge shared Black's sentiments and, evidently, telephoned the editor of the *New York Herald-Tribune* and congratulated the newspaper for an editorial which asserted, "There will inevitably be regrets that the Trustees were unable to find a scholar of the first rank qualified for the post. Plainly. . . they elected to subordinate the question of learning, of the skills in education to the more practical issues of administration."[34]

Interestingly, when Parkinson wrote to the General about the Trustees Meeting, he emphasized that the Deans and Directors at the Low Memorial session on Saturday had been "delighted" and "enthusiastic" about the decision. His letter, however, contained no reference to or even suggestion of Trustee excitement.[35] Did the General become aware of this Trustee opposition and lack of enthusiasm and that it came from some of the most prominent members of the Board? In any event, the decision by the Trustees was as amazing as Eisenhower's letter on the eve of the Board Meeting.

While Eisenhower harbored doubts about what he had decided, the news of his selection received extensive publicity, if not always enthusiastic endorsement. The appointment "greatly pleased" President Emeritus Butler. Although it went against his principles to name a non-academic person, it appealed immensely to his pride to have such a distinguished successor. "It recognizes the now well demonstrated fact that Columbia is much more than an institution of higher learning in the old-fashioned sense of these words." Butler added,

"General Eisenhower's great ability and remarkable character in dealing with world problems are precisely what the world needs today in the administration of a great university. The day-to-day work of Columbia will be guided and administered, as it has long been, by heads of departments and the deans of the several faculties." This last sentence, of course, particularly appealed to the new President; the next day he wrote Fackenthal, "My conception of what will be expected of me in the future was well expressed by Doctor Butler in his public statement, which seems to me clearly to define appropriate functions for a non-professional in such an important position."[36]

When Fackenthal reflected years later on the appointment, he commented, "There was a little unhappiness when the General was invited. Everyone respected him highly. . . . The faculties were quite prepared to receive him with open arms when he came." But only a few weeks after Eisenhower's meeting with the Deans and Directors, the Acting President had told Dean Carl Ackerman, who had returned from Caracas, that there had been no enthusiasm on Morningside Heights for the selection, and he specifically mentioned Deans Pegram and Smith. Dean Carman, not disagreeing with this assessment, put it differently. In the faculty, if its response had been sought, "there would have been lifting of eyebrows and wonderment on the part of some," if they had known that the Trustees were considering General Eisenhower. There would have been "some objections on the grounds that after all, fine man that he was, that he was not a scholar." Carman, a close associate of Pegram and Smith and on the Faculty Committee with them, undoubtedly knew their reactions and that Smith had believed that Fackenthal should have been named President. According to Floyd Taylor, who had done much of the research for the Faculty Committee, no member favored Eisenhower.[37]

Watson and Parkinson, in awe of Eisenhower's immense prestige, had persuaded the General that he had a duty to accept their offer. They thought "this great national leader would be an eminent leader in money-raising," according to Provost Jacobs, who reflected that "I have always firmly believed that the principal reason behind the Trustees' invitation to General Eisenhower, though they would not admit it, was his fund-raising potential, that he would play a tremendous part in this area, then the University's direct need." Because Butler had "genuinely resented anyone else taking part," and had been unable to do anything himself for years, "a whole generation and more had grown up at Columbia completely devoid of any experience with fund-raising activities." The administration and staff were "indoctrinated" against helping, yet after World War II the University faced a "tremendous" need for capital. Probably Watson and Parkinson believed their West Point promises about not having to raise funds: Ike Eisenhower's name, itself, could do the job, and thus his own efforts could be minimal. The key people, Trustee Black asserted, "wanted him in there for fund-raising," and they believed that he could "do anything."[38] The Columbia community, however, did not know the extraordinary arrangements and expected active leadership from Eisenhower to meet this crucial need.

While Eisenhower recoiled from many of the responsibilities of a university president—responsibilities which Watson and Parkinson had had no authority to minimize and the Board was unaware of the terms—the General would bring to the University badly needed publicity, proven administrative and leadership skills, and deeply held convictions. The appointment, itself, gave prominent attention throughout the country and world to Columbia; his executive ability could rejuvenate the University and bring its organization up-to-date to meet the postwar challenges; and his energy, his willingness to undertake a demanding schedule and to make decisions, and his commitment to the youth of America could bring a vitality missing on Morningside Heights for at least two decades.

Eisenhower never pretended to be a scholar—and he would be intimidated by them at Columbia—but his appointment to West Point had given him an opportunity for a college education, and he finished in the top two-fifths of his class. He had, literally, continued his education, with readings and discussions of military history and the classics and with the daily writing of reports, under General Fox Connor in Panama. General Connor later arranged for his assignment to the Army's Command and General Staff School at Fort Leavenworth. This happened, Eisenhower recalled in At Ease, "before I had any chance to get the usual preparatory infantry instruction at Fort Benning or elsewhere. This was like being sent to college without a secondary school education," and one's graduation rank at Leavenworth was crucial "for future advancement." He graduated first in his class, and he also graduated from the War College and the Army Industrial College. In the early 1930s General MacArthur, the Chief of Staff, wanted him in his office, and Eisenhower's ability preparing reports, drafting speeches, and editing material so impressed the General that he insisted that Eisenhower accompany him to the Philippines. Eisenhower returned to the United States soon after the start of the European War in 1939, and after Pearl Harbor his work in the War Department's Planning Division prompted Chief of Staff Marshall to make him the Supreme Allied Commander in Europe.[39]

Eisenhower's appointment by Columbia immediately brought to mind other generals who had become college presidents, from Robert E. Lee at Washington College, now Washington and Lee, and Alexander Stewart Webb's thirty-five-year tenure at City College in New York to Charles Summerall's Presidency of The Citadel. Yet, as the *New York Herald-Tribune* emphasized, Eisenhower "will be the first American general to head a civilian institution of comparable size and will bring to the task a formal academic training received largely at United States Army Schools." The appointment was "without precedent." One day, soon after the announcement, Professor Harry Morgan Ayres listened to the doubts colleagues were expressing about their future President. After a few minutes Ayres said thoughtfully, "You have forgotten one thing, gentlemen—the Guildhall speech General Eisenhower delivered in London." The highly respected literature expert continued, "I believe that to be one of the three greatest speeches ever made in the English language. Only a fine scholar could have written that."[40]

Provost Jacobs extended to Eisenhower "a most cordial welcome to Morningside Heights" in a World-Wide Broadcast. "All Americans are pleased" that Eisenhower "will continue his life of eminent public service." The Provost emphasized in the radio address: "The great leader of American youth in the days when our very existence depended on the decisions he made will have to decide at Columbia matters of far-reaching importance. We welcome him because of his vibrant personality; because he is a true patriot . . . because he is not an educator in the narrow sense of the term. He is much more."[41]

Columbia opened its 194th academic year in the fall of 1947 with a sense of relief. The long interregnum would end soon with the arrival of the popular, energetic, and highly disciplined Eisenhower. The *Columbia Spectator*, calling his appointment "the happiest event in many years" at the University, asserted, "Columbia was fortunate, indeed, in obtaining the services of Dwight D. Eisenhower."[42] Few expressed concern that a definite date for his arrival had not been announced.

In mid-September the General and Mrs. Eisenhower briefly visited the campus to see for the first time the President's House at 60 Morningside Drive, which the Butlers had agreed to relinquish, to find out what the office arrangements would be for him and his staff, to consult with university officials, and to search for a country home nearby. They arrived in a private railroad car from Washington, and Tom Watson and his daughter Jane met them; after breakfast, they drove to the President's House. Butler had been given life occupancy to the house upon his retirement; once Eisenhower had accepted the Presidency, the Trustees faced the problem of asking the Butlers to move. Indeed, on June 30, when Butler offered the General his "forty-four years of experience" and pledged "to try and secure one hundred million dollars" for the University, he had added that he looked forward "to a quiet visit together sometime in the autumn or early winter" with the General after his and Mrs. Butler's "return to 60 Morningside Drive." Upon reading the letter, Eisenhower underlined "60 Morningside Drive" and initialed it.

Both Watson and Parkinson knew Butler well enough to call him "Murray," but they appointed Marcy Dodge, who already had started searching for a "President's" home for the Eisenhowers, to drive out to Butler's home in Southampton and specifically mention the problem. The President Emeritus, delighted with the prominence of his successor—he said it means "capital"—told Dodge they would move as soon as possible. Thus, on July 19 Watson could write to "Ike" that "the matter of the President's house has been settled in a manner entirely satisfactory to everyone." The Butlers were still on Long Island when the Eisenhowers and the Watsons inspected the thirty room, thirty-six-year old Italian Renaissance-style residence.[43]

The Eisenhowers and Watsons then drove onto the campus, a block from 60 Morningside, and were greeted by Dodge and Jacobs in front of Low Memorial Library. As they walked up the steps, past Alma Mater, to the press conference in the Rotunda, Watson reminded Jacobs that, as Provost, he would provide what the General lacked. "I would be able to handle the internal part of the University while Eisenhower did the external," Jacobs recalled. Phil Jessup, his colleague at the School of Law for years, already had called the position "Chief of Staff."[44]

Inside the Rotunda the General, after being officially welcomed to Columbia by the Provost, said he hoped "to talk with various officials of the University while I am here, and possibly get some advance inkling of what a college president is up against, because I know nothing about it." The reporters, though, expressed much more interest in asking questions "about his attitude toward the frequent mention of his name as a possible Republican nominee for the Presidency." Eisenhower replied "that there is no such thing possible in American politics as a draft without artificial stimulus," and he emphasized, "I am not going to be a party to any such draft or anything artificial." The next day the *New York Times* proclaimed, "Eisenhower Here, Avoids A 1948 'No,'" and the lead paragraph referred only to presidential politics, not to his forthcoming presidency of Columbia University. The reporter wrote that the General "would not be a party to a draft," and added, "He refrained from saying he would not accept a nomination if it came to him without any effort on his own part." After the press conference Eisenhower walked through Low Memorial Library to decide where his offices would be, posed for pictures in front of Alma Mater, and then left for the weekend with the Watsons at their summer home in New Canaan, Connecticut.[45] If there were talks for more than a few moments with University officers, there is no record of them, and Eisenhower still had met only a few of the Trustees. Except for his attendance at Dr. Butler's funeral in December, he did not return to Morningside Heights until May, 1948.

The Provost had explained in his welcome that Acting President Fackenthal had been unable to attend the press conference, and Eisenhower did not see him during his brief visit to the campus. For years Fackenthal had served and led the University in the shadow of Butler; now, he had the task of directing the institution when nearly everyone was talking about Eisenhower and waiting for "Ike's" arrival. In all probability, according to Jacques Barzun, Fackenthal could not have seen the way to meet the terrific problems Columbia faced in the late 1940s. He was, the perceptive historian noted, a great judge of people but, because of his deep loyalty to Butler, he was ultimately unable to do things differently.[46]

Yet, in spite of the great overriding problems in the post-war years, like the budget deficit and the need to address a new era, the Administration had handled a number of complex issues, and done so quite successfully. These ranged from the influx of thousands of veterans—many of whom were married and needed housing—to expanding the academic program. These years witnessed, Barzun said, the "heavy onset of the credentials society," and "the pouring in of government money" began. Columbia reorganized the University Extension program for adult higher education and re-named it the School of General Studies; it also established the School of International Affairs with its separate institutions, which included the Program on East Central Europe and the European, East Asian, and Russian Institutes.[47] Still, there could be no plans to modernize the Administration until Eisenhower's arrival—but the date had not been set, and the growing budget deficit continued to overshadow nearly everything else.

That fall Eisenhower, in spite of the pressing demands at the Pentagon as the Cold War intensified, worried about his new job. His concern, though, focused not on the problems challenging the University but on ensuring the arrangements he had discussed with Watson and Parkinson at West Point. Thus, when Chairman Coykendall suggested a few days after Eisenhower's visit to Morningside Heights that he would "be glad to sit down with you and try to give you a clear idea of the situation," the General immediately welcomed the opportunity to discuss "a number of important details . . . with someone in an authoritative position." Until then, however, he needed "advice and information" and, since he could not travel to New York, he was "forced to resort to the use of an emissary," such as Major Robert L. Schulz. Later, when Fackenthal offered to mail "all material sent to the Trustees" for Eisenhower's comment, the Chief of Staff objected: "While I will greatly appreciate receiving anything you think may be of real value in my education for the new job, I must beg you that under no circumstance must you send me anything except those things you think I should see." In mid-October he asked Coykendall if he ever traveled to Washington, as "it would be a godsend to me to have a long and uninterrupted talk with you."[48]

Eisenhower's request undoubtedly resulted from his reading, "Poison in the Academic Ivy," an article he received shortly after Chicago's Robert Hutchins had joined him for lunch in the Chief of Staff's office. The article "succeeded in frightening me very definitely," he wrote Hutchins, especially the "implication that the president and his wife, in a university, are more involved in social activity than anything else!" The publicity surrounding Eisenhower's appointment possibly prompted the critique, "What Makes a Good College President," by the President of the Carnegie Foundation for the Advancement of Teaching.[49]

Eisenhower conveyed his preoccupation with Columbia even when Bill Robinson of the *New York Herald-Tribune* talked with him in mid-October at the Pentagon about writing his wartime memoirs. Robinson had met the General when he had gone to Paris in December, 1944, to arrange the resumption of the European Edition of the *Herald-Tribune*, and now he proposed putting his newspaper's syndicate at the General's disposal, if Eisenhower "planned to do any writing in the future." Their conversation lasted one and a half hours. The General admitted that "life in the Army was really a nomad's life" and he wanted "to establish a permanent home"; in spite of his Columbia decision, according to Robinson, he still "preferred a small home, in a small town, where he could be free to catch up on many books he wanted to read, where he could go fishing and loaf."

Robinson, who along with Douglas Black would be instrumental during the next two months in persuading the General to write his memoirs and would become a regular golfing and bridge partner, was "a little surprised to find him not too enthusiastic about his Columbia University job." The Vice President and business manager of the *Herald-Tribune*, and future President of Coca-Cola, gained the impression that Eisenhower had accepted the position "out of pressure and advice from all sides . . . as a means of settling the issue of his future." He did this, Robinson inferred, "without complete investigation of the function and the responsibilities of the job." Robinson astutely summed up the situation: "This seems, in a way, to be a contradiction of Eisenhower's thoroughness and foresight—and it is!" He added, parenthetically, "But, of course, I may have the wrong impression."

The "terrible demands" of the General's new position—as he saw them as much as seven months before arriving on campus—"appalled" him. Columbia was a much bigger operation than he had assumed and, Robinson noted, "He was not too enthusiastic about the decision he had made." The newspaper executive "came away with the conviction that no public man whom I had ever known or had ever known about, had such intellectual honesty as Eisenhower." Robinson saw Eisenhower as "realistic, practical and disciplined," and he concluded his confidential notes, "His high spirit and his great emotional potentiality might conceivably develop a highly unbalanced entity in a person of lesser intellectual capacity."[50]

A week later, near the end of October, Chairman Coykendall and his wife visited the Eisenhowers at Fort Myer, and they discussed the General's concerns about Columbia. Eisenhower quickly gained "the impression that certain points involved in my early conferences

with Mr. Parkinson's Committee may never have come specifically"
to the Chairman's attention, even though Coykendall had been a
member of that Committee; moreover, it became clear that Parkinson
had not shown Coykendall the blunt letter he had received from
Eisenhower just before the Trustees Meeting on June 24. Perhaps
somewhat startled—and certainly extremely concerned—by what
he had learned during his meeting with Coykendall, the Chief of
Staff left the next morning for homecoming weekend at Kansas State
University. He stayed with his brother and, thus, had an opportune
occasion to reflect on his talks with Coykendall and to discuss his
thoughts about the Columbia situation.[51]

Shortly thereafter, Eisenhower began a long, detailed letter to
Coykendall. Since the Chairman of the Board evidently had not been
given certain specific information, he enclosed copies of his letters
to Watson on June 14 and to Parkinson on June 23. He was, in a
sense, reissuing his ultimatum to Parkinson, and it placed Coykendall
on the defensive. Columbia's President-elect emphasized that he had
had "great difficulty in believing that I possess any particular qualification for the distinguished position," and having expressed the
feeling "that Columbia should select an experienced educator. . . . I
had the temerity to undertake the assignment only because I was
informed that the Trustees were unanimous in their conviction that I
could render useful service." Echoing his earlier comments to
Parkinson, he frankly stated, "If I am in the slightest degree mistaken in my assumption on this point, I should know it at once—it
would be unfair both to Columbia and myself to allow me to come
up there in the face of doubts or mental reservations on the part of
any important person in the institution."

Life for the Eisenhowers at Columbia, he reminded Coykendall,
would be "radically different from what we had so long planned for
our future." He noted that "our official and social life" would be
"more intensive" than if he had accepted "one or more of the attractive offers made to me by prominent publishers." Since the "Committee convinced me that duty pointed to Columbia . . . we mean to
do the best we can, enthusiastically." He agreed with Coykendall's
suggestion to arrive around May 1, 1948, and spend the month "getting acquainted"; furthermore, by April the house at 60 Morningside
will "surely be completely renovated and furnished."[52]

Eisenhower had not concealed his unhappiness from Robinson,
and now Coykendall, who had not initially supported the offer, must

have been stunned to read the letter and enclosures. Yet, the General refused to acknowledge, even slightly, that he himself had not done his homework and had gone into battle unprepared. When Eisenhower finally realized his predicament, it may have been only the continuous efforts of Parkinson and Watson which kept him from changing his mind about Columbia. The two Trustees, of course, were willing to do anything.

Right after Coykendall received the letter from Eisenhower, Tom and Jeannette Watson traveled to Washington and had luncheon with the Eisenhowers at Fort Myer. They discussed the General's "plans for Columbia "with which," Watson soon wrote, "I am in full accord." The IBM President waxed enthusiastic and emphasized the Board's commitment to "the agreement made by Mr. Parkinson and myself." He added, "The Trustees and Faculty of Columbia University are ready and waiting to extend to you a very warm welcome and hope that the date will be soon." Of course, he continued, there was "no question" about the extra secretary, and "if you and Mamie want to steal away and have a little quiet rest," the Eisenhowers and their friends could use the Watson country home.[53]

Coykendall promptly concurred with Parkinson's and Watson's assurances; only a few Trustees know about Eisenhower's qualms, and for them even the possibility of his changing his mind must have been frightening. The blow to the University would be devastating. And, during this period a widely circulated article, highly critical of Columbia and the selection of Eisenhower, could only have increased their anxieties, as well as the General's. "The issue involved in the Columbia appointment," a prominent educator and administrator asserted, "is not that of one man or one institution; it endangers the future of American higher education."[54]

In a detailed three-page letter to Eisenhower on November 17, Coykendall stressed that "the Trustees are unanimous in the belief" that he could perform a notable public service" at Columbia. "We do not expect that you will immediately concern yourself with educational details," and, as for his letter to Parkinson in June, "I think we are in perfect accord." The General's military aide, who "will concern himself solely with matters connected with your activities as an adviser to Washington and other non-University matters," presented no problem. But, the Chairman wondered, was a second military aide, a special assistant, necessary? The Provost can "give you all the immediate assistance you need in academic matters," and he suggested that Eisenhower defer consideration until after he knew the University organization: "As I see it, your first tasks should be to get acquainted with your people and to know and understand the financial resources and limitations by which all activities are controlled." Finally, the General should have "received the plans for office space and for alterations" in the President's House. "The house will be fully furnished, except as to your two bedrooms." Eisenhower's aide, Coykendall added, should talk to the Comptroller "if there are any questions regarding these plans."[55]

Eisenhower had not intended for his letter to carry "an unfortunate implication," the General replied, but he did not retreat. The special assistant remained important, and "it was agreed that he would have nothing whatsoever to do with University matters." Since "a great volume of correspondence and incidental work" fell on Eisenhower, it required a full-time person, and "that individual has necessarily to be acquainted with my attitudes, ideas and purposes." For this reason he had asked the University to create "a position at a reasonable salary." (Eisenhower's pledge that his assistants would handle only non-University matters, however, would be broken with unfortunate consequences for his leadership of Columbia.) The General considered it his personal obligation to supplement, if necessary, the salary of his military aide. He added that he was delighted with his meetings with the Provost, who had made several trips to Washington. Finally, he informed Coykendall that Columbia could announce an arrival date around May 1, 1948, since President Truman had stated that General Bradley would succeed him as Chief of Staff. "I repeat," he concluded, "I am looking forward with great anticipation to participating with you and your associates in the work of Columbia."[56]

Eisenhower, once again personally reassured by Watson and Parkinson, tried to remove Coykendall's doubts by giving him some definite plans; the General now had, however, other pressing matters on his mind. Bill Robinson returned to the Pentagon on December 5, as publishers persisted in their efforts to persuade the retiring Chief of Staff to write his war memoirs. Furthermore, the subject of presidential politics and Eisenhower's availability kept resurfacing. "If it were not," he confided to Milton in December, "for my definite plan of taking a two-month leave between quitting this job and going to Columbia I would take ten days off this instant just to go somewhere and sleep."[57]

In early December President Emeritus Nicholas Murray Butler died, and a few hours after the funeral in Columbia's St. Paul's Chapel on December 9, 1947, Coykendall announced that Eisenhower would arrive in early May and assume his official duties as President on June 7, one week after Commencement. The General had flown to New York for the funeral at the last moment, after initially telling Coykendall that he could not attend. Eisenhower and Butler never had met; over the summer Parkinson had invited Eisenhower to attend the annual dinner of the Pennsylvania Society on December 13, and Butler and Eisenhower had planned to meet prior to the dinner.[58]

Although Eisenhower had not had an opportunity to talk "personally" with Parkinson after the dinner on the thirteenth, his appearance at Butler's funeral and the announcement of his arrival date offered a reassurance to those worried about his plans. Suddenly, however, presidential politics added dark clouds to the question of his future association with the University. Coykendall and Eisenhower, in fact, had discussed the political situation during their meeting in October. The General might complain about "gossip around the country that I am an aspirant for the Republican nomination," but during a recent trip to New Hampshire he had visited Leonard Finder, publisher of the *Manchester Union-Leader* and an ardent Eisenhower supporter. Such activity on the General's part did not dispel rumors and worried Coykendall; he undoubtedly informed Dodge of his conversations with Eisenhower, because Dodge later mentioned to Dean Ackerman his belief that the General's "conscience is troubling him." Evidently, Eisenhower had indicated that he was not interested in being a compromise candidate between Governor Thomas E. Dewey of New York and Senator Robert A. Taft of Ohio at the Republican Convention in June, 1948. That, Ackerman noted in a memorandum of his conversation with Dodge, did not mean he would not accept the nomination." If Eisenhower saw a "ground swell in favor of his nomination, of course he will accept."[59]

The possibility of Eisenhower's political availability, speculated upon almost daily by the media, distracted the Columbia community. Would he resign, even before arriving, and force a new presidential search? After Butler's funeral Dodge had a conversation with Coykendall and Fackenthal, and then wrote to the Acting President, "No one can say how long you will have to continue the pressure you are under." Earlier, when Jacobs had become Provost, he had asked Fackenthal if his family could reside in the former Carlton J. H. Hayes townhouse, which had been reserved for possible use by the Acting President. Fackenthal agreed and had the five-story house on 117th Street renovated by September for the Provost's family. Now, in mid-December, as concern about Eisenhower's future at Columbia grew, Fackenthal wrote Jacobs, "It is highly desirable, I think, certainly for this year and no doubt for several years thereafter that you live near the campus." With the situation at Columbia uncertain, the Acting President wanted to make sure that the Provost would continue to reside on Morningside Heights, less than a block from Low Memorial.[60]

During the fall Eisenhower had reflected at length on "politics" in letters to Beedle Smith, his World War II Chief of Staff, and Milton Eisenhower. He would "not use the language" of William Tecumseh Sherman, the Union General who had stated in 1884, "I will not accept if nominated and will not serve if elected." Eisenhower argued that "the two cases are not parallel." As the stories of his "receptive mood" persisted, he was coming "very close to violating the one underlying principle that I have always believed to be binding on every American. That principle is that every citizen is required to do his duty for the country no matter what it may be." While he believed that no one since "Washington has had any occasion to feel that it was his *duty* to stand" for political office, the validity of the principle kept him from saying "exactly what I'd like to say." A deadlocked political convention, turning to a popular name in a desperate attempt to salvage the party, would never create "any sense of duty." That kind of thing "Sherman answered so emphatically; under the same circumstances I would do the same."

It was most unlikely, he continued, that any group of delegates would feel "such a terrific popular pressure behind them that they would instantly cease any effort to handle their work on a political basis and would respond to such a commitment." Only those circumstances, he believed, "could impart a sense of duty." Thus, by refusing "to use words similar to Sherman's," he punished himself "for adhering to a principle that has become certainly academic." While he had mentioned all this before, "this morning I am a bit more irked than usual by the constant hammering."[61]

An opportunity came in January, he recalled in *At Ease*, "to make it definite that I was not going to get involved in politics." Leonard

Finder, the *Manchester Union-Leader* publisher, had written that a slate of Eisenhower delegates would be entered in the New Hampshire presidential primary in March, 1948. Interestingly, the same day that Eisenhower had written Milton about "politics," October 16, he had flown to Manchester for a dinner and speech to the Community Forum, and he had spent the night at Finder's home. Not surprisingly, Finder vigorously appealed to the General's concept of duty when in January he wrote about the presidential primary. "All that we are attempting is to have the will of the people made so clear that it cannot be obviated by the usual politicians assembled in convention." The publisher also enclosed a copy of his newspaper's front-page editorial endorsement of the General's candidacy.[62]

"I don't know what to say!" Eisenhower jotted down on Finder's letter. Later his assistant Kevin McCann recalled that he and Lieutenant Colonel Paul Carroll, who handled the General's correspondence in the Pentagon, "grabbed the Leonard Finder letter . . . as one where Dwight Eisenhower . . . could make his decision completely clear." They "worked hard drafting" and "we knew his thinking and phrasing." The General took the draft home to Fort Myer over the weekend and made "very minor changes." On Monday he showed the draft to Secretary of Defense James Forrestal, who added a sentence about politics being a noble profession.[63]

"My failure to convince thoughtful and earnest men," Eisenhower's reply began, "proves that I must make some amplification. . . . I am not available for and could not accept nomination to high political office." Then, for several paragraphs, he expressed publicly the inner turmoil with which he had wrestled in his letters to Bedell Smith and Milton Eisenhower: "The bald statement that I would not accept nomination . . . would smack of effrontery." A "flat refusal," more importantly, would appear "to violate that concept of duty to country which calls upon every good citizen." He emphasized, "It is my conviction that, unless an individual feels some inner compulsion and special qualification to enter the political arena—which I do not—a refusal to do so involves no violation of the highest standards of devotion to duty." He remained convinced that a military man should, "in the absence of some obvious and overriding reasons, abstain from seeking high political office."

"In any event," the Chief of Staff concluded in his lengthy reply, "my decision to remove myself completely from the political is definite and positive. . . . I could not accept nomination even under the remote circumstances that it were tendered to me." The letter, published along with Finder's in the *Union-Leader*, was carefully read and reread throughout the country. That evening Eric Sevareid commented on CBS Radio, "The 'dark horse' won't make the race!" He added, "The whole political situation is radically different." Since recent opinion polls showed that the General had "more popular backing than any other Republican and actually more than Truman," Sevareid noted the "unconcealed pleasure" in other political camps. In all likelihood, as biographer Peter Lyon suggested, for Eisenhower "to declare himself unavailable in 1948 meant to foreclose all possibility of ever being President."[64]

Few read the reply more carefully than the Trustees and members of the Columbia University community. Certainly those who had known during the fall of 1947 about Eisenhower's second thoughts and lack of enthusiasm for the Columbia Presidency and, consequently, had realized the implications for Columbia, must have been relieved. The Dean of the Graduate Faculties, George Pegram, immediately wrote in longhand to Eisenhower, "This is just to say 'Bravo!' to your statement published today—not only because it answers any question about your coming to Columbia but even more because it will take a lasting place as one of the finest utterances in our political history."[65]

The Eisenhower boom for President, which peaked in January with the Finder editorial and would reappear during the summer, subsided dramatically during the following months when he started his memoirs and avoided public appearances. On February 7 he retired as Chief of Staff, and the *New York Times* took occasion to connect the "Warrior and Man of Peace." Columbia's President-elect, it wrote, believed that more attention should be paid "to the causes and prevention" of war so that "we should in time attain the same control over its eruption and spread as we have over the physical plagues." Thus, he wanted to introduce into academic curriculum the study of the causes of war and of war itself. America's foremost soldier, the editorial concluded, had made clear in his valedictory that the nation's emphasis was on "peace."[66]

Eisenhower now had time to work on his memoirs, with the date set for him to leave active service in early February and a scheduled arrival at Columbia in early May. Bill Robinson, following his meeting with the General in October, had written that "it is an imperative necessity for the American people as well as the historians of the

world, now and in the future, to have your story." In early December
the Chief of Staff made a commitment that the *Herald-Tribune* executive would have something to do with his book. Doubleday's
Doug Black recalled that "I got this phone call in Garden City from
Bill Robinson, whom I had never met, and he asked me if I'd be
interested in an Eisenhower. I said I was and I didn't want to talk
about it on the telephone, and we made an appointment for the next
day." Eisenhower had received information from the Treasury Department that if "the entire bundle of rights" were sold, he could
receive a capital gains treatment. "We had to put the whole amount
on the line and," Black noted, "we are talking $500,000-600,000,
and in our office at the time we had an editorial committee with
some business people sitting on it. . . . I soon realized that they
didn't have any conception of the scope and size of this thing." They
would go "only up to the normal $150,000, and I said a no go."
Black and his editor-in-chief, Ken McCormick, discussed the proposed project at the Century Association before McCormick left for
a meeting with Eisenhower and Robinson at the Pentagon on December 22. "I said up to $500,000," Black continued. "There was
nobody I could talk to. . . . Mr. Doubleday was ill and in South
Carolina. There was no one I had much confidence in our own organization, and I was pretty much a newcomer." The session in Washington went well, but on the way to the next meeting on December
30 Black started thinking that the offer "would have to be more than
that, not that Ike had made any demands, but they just sensed. We
had an understanding with the *Herald-Tribune*, 50-50; they had first
serial rights and we had everything beyond that, and they put up
another $100,000. . . . So, we had in mind we would make it
$600,000." (Later, when Eisenhower asked Black why he had not
come the first time, the publisher replied that the meeting was an
editorial issue, that he had had a cold, and that he wanted a "second
guess. 'I thought,' Ike commented, 'that was it.'")

As they walked into the General's office, Eisenhower said to Black,
"I think I ought to know you, you are a Columbia man, and all these
prices are way beyond me. We've been talking about the defense
budget for next year, and these figures are way over my head. I was
just a Kansas farm boy." "General," Black responded, "I can understand how you feel, I'm just a Long Island clam boy." They agreed
on $600,000 and, over a light luncheon, Eisenhower said he had not
called Donald Richberg, a prominent Washington lawyer from the

New Deal period who had been advising Eisenhower on taxes. Richberg arrived, noted that everything had been settled, and asked Black, "Can you put that in writing?" As the Doubleday executive said, "Of course," the General interjected, "I don't know why we do that, I have nothing to sue in life." "Well, Mr. Richberg," Black said, "can you imagine anyone suing General Eisenhower?" "No, Mr. Black, I can't." "Ike," Black remembered, "leaned over, took my hand, and that was our deal." Eisenhower called it a "gentlemen's agreement." The handshake, actually, was more than that. It established a lifelong friendship between the General and Douglas Black, who would become his confidant on the Columbia Board, and it confirmed his very close association with Bill Robinson. (One day in Robinson's office with Mamie and Black, Eisenhower said to her, "If anything happens work with these people . . . they'll treat you right.")[67]

Eisenhower had not wanted anything said until he had resigned as Chief of Staff and on February 8 came the front-page announcement, "Memoirs of Gen. Eisenhower To Appear in *Herald-Tribune*." General Eisenhower "wants to write a completely frank account of the military actions he commanded," Black stated, "as well as of his part in the high policy decisions which governed America's role in the war." The book, tentatively titled "Crusade in Europe," Black added, "promises to reveal much new information that until now has only been guessed at." That same day, Eisenhower recalled in *At Ease*, "I started on a writing program, at a speed that a soldier would call a blitz." Working sixteen hours a day, he completed the draft of his five hundred-page memoir on March 26. Joseph Barnes, the foreign news editor at the *Herald-Tribune,* told Eli Ginzberg that on one occasion Eisenhower dictated, without stopping, five thousand words that required almost no editing, and Barnes had "never seen such a performance." Eisenhower would have to wait six months before he could sell the manuscript as a package to the *Herald-Tribune* and Doubleday and qualify for the capital gains treatment.[68]

On March 29 at the Pentagon Eisenhower showed Black and Robinson the manuscript for their consideration. As the General had noted before starting the project, they were providing "the checkers and researchers to determine the complete historical accuracy of every statement made before they actually accomplish its purchase." He already had the assistance of his aide, Kevin McCann, and at his suggestion Doubleday had hired General Arthur Nevins, who had been on his wartime staff. During the next month McCann, Nevins,

Ken McCormick, and Joseph Barnes played prominent roles with Eisenhower on the project, and they completed most of the work before he moved to Columbia University.[69]

During the meeting in the General's office the conversation turned from the manuscript to politics and "especially the efforts of some Democrats to draft him as a candidate in place of Truman." Eisenhower said he knew "they were desperately searching around for someone to save their skins," and he revealed "for the first time," according to Robinson, "his political beliefs when he said that his good friends back in Iowa would be shocked and chagrined at the very idea of his running on a Democratic ticket for anything." He added, facetiously, that "he must have been a grown man before he ever saw a Democrat." When McCann inquired about General MacArthur's political strength, Eisenhower said, "My God, anything would be better" than a MacCarthur candidacy."

Robinson concluded that there was "not the slightest chance of any situation or circumstance within the Democratic Party that would induce him to run on that ticket." The newspaper executive added, "I am still persuaded, however, that if he were honestly drafted at the Republican Convention, he would accept the nomination." Indeed, if a Dewey-Taft stalemate were to provide an opportunity for MacArthur, the favorite of right-wing Republicans, Robinson believed that "Eisenhower would be more than eager to accept the bid." A week earlier he had written Helen Reid, the *Herald-Tribune's* publisher, that "Eisenhower was the only American in public life with the ability, experience, integrity, and devotion to country qualified to be President at this important juncture of our history." He urged that she consider, "without further delay," the possibility that the "*Herald-Tribune* declare itself for General Eisenhower for President."[70]

With the manuscript finished, the Eisenhowers accepted Robinson's invitation to Augusta National Golf Club. During April he played golf and bridge, watched the Masters Tournament, met a group of wealthy men who became known as the "gang," and discussed politics. Mamie enjoyed meeting the members and their wives; she came to like Augusta "immensely" and would be "very happy there." Besides Robinson, the "gang" included investment banker Clifford Roberts, who made Augusta "golf's most prestigious tournament" and would soon handle the General's investments; Coca-Cola's chairman Robert Woodruff; City Service's W. Alton (Pete) Jones; corporation lawyer George Allen, the only Democrat and President Truman's close friend; and Ellis (Slats) Slater, the president of Frankfort Distilleries. All would be bridge regulars with the General at 60 Morningside Heights and golfing partners at Blind Brook Country Club in Westchester County and Deepdale Golf Club on Long Island. They would support Eisenhower's favorite projects at Columbia and form the Citizens for Eisenhower for President in 1951; they would, of course, regularly join Eisenhower whenever he returned to Augusta National and, thanks to the *Herald-Tribune's* Helen Reid, Robinson had the newspaper's private plane available.[71]

Eisenhower resumed his public appearances as soon as he reached Columbia. Every new president of a major university faces innumerable commitments during his first few months, and Eisenhower was not just any new president—a year earlier Fackenthal had written that he hoped the General would not be embarrassed "by our desire as a community to become acquainted with you and Mrs. Eisenhower." Just before leaving Fort Myer, he complained, "My schedule of appointments for the first month there has already grown to appalling proportions. If current indications provide any index of what my future life there is to be, I shall quit them cold." [72]

Yet, he had accepted more than a few non-university invitations. Columbia offered him a forum from which to express his convictions, and he looked forward to using that forum. Kevin McCann, whose presence in Low Memorial as the General's assistant would be so controversial, later wrote, "In return for the vitality that Eisenhower brought to Columbia, he received among other things an invaluable opportunity to express himself on matters which his military status had forbidden him to discuss openly." [73]

He had wondered if his strong beliefs "would fit into the academic world" and, for that reason, had told the Trustees before accepting the position, "All I can bring you is the convictions I have always held. I am not going to change my spots." He asserted that "Freedom of the individual, presupposing faith of a religious character in the integrity of the individual man, is the first leg on which democracy stands." Freedom of thought provided that basis for his philosophy of education. That spring Allan Nevins reviewed a book of Eisenhower's speeches. "It is not strange that with this interest in youth and its training," the well-known Professor of American History concluded, "General Eisenhower should have chosen education for the second part of his career. . . . To the guidance of young people he will bring a genuinely philosophical mind."[74]

Later, the General recalled: "My difficulty in reaching a decision was a natural fear that I could hardly hope to discharge the responsibilities in an enterprise so different from all my experience." But, he added in *At Ease*, "I saw in Columbia, because of its standing among American educational institutions and its influence on the educational process, opportunities as large and rewarding as the environment might be strange and difficult." He had accepted the position with "no illusions that I could contribute anything academically," believing instead that he "could probably learn to run the place efficiently." Crucial, though, for him was that "I saw an opportunity to advance education in citizenship, to promote faith in the American way of life among its youth who will be the leaders of America in the near future."[75]

By 1948 Eisenhower, his brother Milton argued, had a well developed philosophy of what education should be doing. He opposed, strongly, the extreme degree of specialization, which had existed even at the undergraduate level during the prewar years. As problems become more and more complex, he saw that the specialist was inadequate and that education should help each person to find evidence and to reason objectively, critically, and creatively. He hoped that this would be done within a moral framework during college years. Eisenhower firmly believed, according to the Kansas State University president, that the student should receive certain fundamental values to prepare him for life or for graduate studies.[76]

His postwar interest in education has been explained in a slightly different light by Dean Philip Young of the Graduate School of Business and a close associate and friend of the President at Columbia and later in Washington. The General's experience with G.I.'s during the war had emphasized and given focus to his concern for citizenship education. On the eve of the North African invasion in 1942 Eisenhower had written a classmate and friend from the Fort Leavenworth Command School, "The Allied cause is completely bound up with the rights and welfare of the common man. You must make certain that every GI realizes that the privileged life he has led is under direct threat. His right to speak his own mind, to engage in any profession of his own choosing, to belong to any religious denomination, to live in any locality where he can support himself and his family, and to be sure of fair treatment when he might be accused of any crime—all of these would disappear if the Nazis win this war." Dean Young reflected, "Eisenhower told me that in his informal get-togethers or pep talks with groups of G.I.'s, such as in the blacked-out mess halls of Normandy, he was asked again and again, 'General, what are we fighting for, anyway?'" The Supreme Commander had wrestled with the issue, and Young added, "I am sure that nagging question, consciously or unconsciously, was in the back of his mind when he accepted the Columbia offer, for here was a tremendous opportunity to get across to the youth of America what it all meant."

On the other hand, Young thought that the General's new friends in the business world—and he was the son of General Electric's Owen D. Young—saw things differently. They had a political goal for Eisenhower—certainly Tom Watson did—and they could work toward this goal while Eisenhower was doing his job. "As far apart as these views were," Young added, "they were welded together, but only after his political friends had done their best to persuade him to accept the Columbia offer."[77]

On Sunday morning, May 2, 1948, General of the Army Dwight D. Eisenhower, who had been on leave from the Army since early February, received a farewell salute from the ceremonial Third Army Regiment at Fort Myer. "It was an emotional day" for the General and Mrs. Eisenhower, General Snyder remembered. "The garrison was lined shoulder to shoulder on each side of the road from Quarters One in Fort Myer down the main road of the garrison to the turn at the Chapel, and from there on down to the exit gate at the foot of the hill beyond Arlington Cemetery. Tears appeared frequently in the eyes of each of them," as Sergeant Leonard Dry began driving them to their new home at 60 Morningside Drive and Columbia University.

When the Eisenhowers arrived late that Sunday afternoon, some two hundred persons welcomed them, including nine-year-old David Syrett, son of an Assistant Professor of History. The boy wanted Ike's autograph. (Fifteen years later, when Eisenhower returned to the campus for the first time since becoming President of the United States, his picture was again taken with young Syrett, by then a graduate student in history, and newspapers printed both photographs.)[78]

*   *   *

It would be improper to conclude, as Peter Lyon did in *Eisenhower: Portrait of the Hero,* that "It was wrong all around: wrong for the trustees to have selected him, wrong for him to have accepted. . . . It was worse than wrong, it was cruel." Columbia needed a dynamic President who had administrative skills and could bring publicity, and General Eisenhower had those abilities. The difficulty lay in the misplaced expectations. Few knew that Parkinson and Watson had misled him about his responsibilities and that he had allowed himself to be deceived. Thus, while the University community looked to Eisenhower to be a President who would bring recognition, strong leadership, and fame in the tradition of Nicholas Murray Butler, the General had anticipated that he could be master of "his own time and activity." The failure of the Trustees to define clearly—and publicly—the duties and the responsibilities of the University's top two executives contributed to these misplaced expectations; then, when Eisenhower's doubts surfaced and resurfaced, his concerns had little to do with the complexities of a great urban university in the postwar age. And, correspondingly, the few Trustees during 1947-1948 who knew about his reservations worried more about whether he might change his mind than about the various expectations on campus, which they did nothing to dispel.

Indeed, only a few Trustees had even met the President-elect, and the full Board did not know what he had been promised and that he had been reassured. As President of Columbia University he would not have to take the lead with the faculty, the curriculum, and fundraising. Nor was it known, consequently, that Watson had told the new Provost that he would be responsible for all internal matters at the University. These difficulties were compounded by the necessity to wait nearly a year for the General's arrival and by the persistent accounts of his involvement in presidential politics. The University would have been "better off," according to Provost Jacobs, "if Fackenthal had been President," not Acting President, for that year.[79]

Eisenhower had "questioned his desire to accept the responsibilities of a great 'inanimate' organization such as Columbia University," Snyder wrote. "Nevertheless, as time wore on, it became apparent that he was going to react favorably to the demands of the Trustees of this institution." The Columbia decision and the completion of *Crusade in Europe*, his personal physician emphasized, had lifted "a heavy load" from his shoulders. "He acted like a mushroom popping forth from the ground in the spring."[80]

Notes

1. Robert H. Ferrell, ed., *The Eisenhower Diaries* (New York, 1981), July 24, 1947, p. 142; Dwight D. Eisenhower, *At Ease: Stories I Tell to Friends* (New York, 1967), p. 336.
2. Marcellus H. Dodge to Tom Parkinson, March 14, 1947, Trustee Special Committee folder (TSC), Central Archives, Columbia University (CACU).
3. John G. Jackson to Parkinson, April 4, 1947; Dodge to Parkinson, April 2, 1947, and two letters on April 5, 1947; Dodge to Watson, April 13, 1947, TSC folder, CACU.
4. Watson to Dodge, April 22 and 25, 1947; Dodge to Watson, April 13, 1947; Dodge to Parkinson, March 14 and May 3, 1947, ibid.; *New York Times,* April 17, 1947.
5. The Trustees of Columbia University in the City of New York, *Minutes,* May 7, 1947, CACU; Frederick Coykendall to Parkinson, May 15, 1947; Dodge to Parkinson, May 12, 1947, TSC folder, CACU; Philip Jessup, personal interview, June 16, 1977, Norfolk, Ct.
6. Dodge to Parkinson, May 12, 1947, TSC folder, CACU.
7. Jessup, interview, June 16, 1977; *New York Times,* February 1, 1986; Dodge to Parkinson, May 11 and 19, 1947; Dodge to George L. Harrison, May 25, 1947, TSC folder, CACU.
8. Eisenhower to Louis Marx, May 14, 1947, and Eisenhower to Milton Eisenhower, May 29, 1947, *The Papers of Dwight David Eisenhower: The Chief of Staff,* vol. VII (Baltimore, Md., 1978), ed. Louis Galambos, 1716, 1737-38; Douglas Black, personal interview, June 6, 1973, New York, N. Y. For a discussion of Watson and Eisenhower, David L. Stebenne's forthcoming article, "Thomas J. Watson and the Business-Government Relationship, 1933-1956."
9. Campbell wrote: "I have no exact recollection as to the young Trustee who spoke to me after the meeting. I wish I had noted his name in my diary. I didn't because I probably thought it was not important." Campbell to author, November 8, 1981, and February 21, 1982, and personal interview, February 25, 1964, Washington, D.C.; Dodge to Parkinson, May 19, 1947, TSC folder, CACU.
10. Eisenhower to Milton Eisenhower, May 29, 1947, *PDDE,* VIII, 1737-38.
11. For Watson's message, see *PDDE,* VIII, 1738; Black, interview, June 6, 1973; Trustees, *Minutes,* June 2, 1947, CACU. The *Minutes* do not mention the vote. Was Rector Fleming on the Search Committee and did he oppose Eisenhower's selection because the original grant from Trinity Church provided that the President "shall be a member of and in communion with the Church of England," even though Columbia considered that provision no longer legally binding? There appears to be no mention of the provision in the files of the Trustee Search Committee, and Fleming's papers at Trinity Church remain closed. See Trustees, *Minutes,* April 3, 1950, CACU, and chapter VII.
12. Eisenhower to Milton Eisenhower, May 29, 1947, *PDDE,* VIII, 1737-38; Milton Eisenhower, personal interview, July 26, 1972, Baltimore, Md.
13. Kevin McCann, *Man from Abilene* (New York, 1952), pp. 161-64; Kevin McCann, personal interview, July 25, 1972, Gettysburg, Pa; Milton Eisenhower, interview, July 26, 1972; Eisenhower to Milton Eisenhower, April 20, 1943, *PDDE,* II, 1097-98; Steve Neal, *The Eisenhowers* (Lawrence, Kans., 1984), pp. 161-62.
14. Harry J. Carman, personal interview, December 1, 1961, New York, N. Y.
15. Alden Hatch, "The Prexy Plan of General Ike," *Collier's,* September 13, 1947, p. 11; Maxwell D. Taylor, *Swords and Plowshares* (New York, 1972), p. 116; Douglas Black, interview, 1967, Oral History Project (COHP); Black, interview, June 6, 1973.
16. *PDDE,* VIII, 1744, fn. #3 and IX, 2373-74.

17. Eisenhower to Watson, June 14, 1947, *PDDE*, VIII, 1757-58.
18. Milton Eisenhower to Eisenhower, June 10, 1947, and Eisenhower to Milton Eisenhower, June 14, 1947, *PDDE*, VIII, 1759; Milton Eisenhower to Eisenhower, June 17, 1947, Eisenhower MSS., Dwight D. Eisenhower Library, Abilene, Kans. (DDEL); Grayson Kirk to author, March 13, 1992.
19. *Daily Mirror*, June 19, 1947; Howard M. Snyder, "Summary of Year 1947," Snyder MSS., DDEL; *New York Times*, June 20, 1947.
20. Vannevar Bush, *Pieces of Action* (New York, 1970), p. 210; Eisenhower to James Bryant Conant, June 26,, 1947, *PDDE*, VIII, 1786, and IX, 2375. Conant visited the Chief of Staff in Washington on July 1, 1947; later, he would become Eisenhower's High Commissioner to West Germany. Stephen E. Ambrose and Richard H. Immerman, *Milton S. Eisenhower: Educational Statesman* (Baltimore, Md., 1983), p. 75.
21. Harry Morgan Ayres, "Recollections of June 21, 1947," Eisenhower Files, Columbiana, Low Memorial, Columbia University.
22. Ibid.; Hatch, "Prexy Plan," *Collier's*, September 13, 1947, p. 11; Carman, interview, December 1, 1961; Albert C. Jacobs, personal interview, February 5, 1965, Hartford, Ct; Black, interview, June 6, 1973.
23. Albert C. Jacobs, "Memorandum" to author, March 10, 1958; Arthur Hays Sulzberger, personal interview, March 27, 1958, New York, N. Y.; R. Gordon Hoxie, personal interview, January 18, 1980, New York, N. Y.
24. Black, interview, June 6, 1973; Kirk to author, March 13, 1992 and January 16, 1997, and Oral History Interview, January 14, 1987, COHP; Harry Wriston, Oral History Interview, 1968, COHP; Ferrell, ed., *Eisenhower Diaries*, July 24, 1947, p. 143.
25. Eisenhower, *At Ease*, pp. 336-37; Black, interview, June 6, 1973; Eisenhower to Bert Andrews, November 26, 1946, *PDDE*, VIII, 1399-1400.
26. Eisenhower to Walter Bedell Smith, July 3, 1947, ibid, 1799-1800.
27. Eisenhower to Edward Everett Hazlett, Jr., July 19, 1947, ibid., 1836-38; Ferrell, ed., *Eisenhower Diaries*, December 31, 1947, p. 145, and c. January 1, 1950, p. 169; McCann, *Man from Abilene*, pp. 165-66.
28. Eisenhower to Parkinson, June 23, 1947, *PDDE*, VIII, 1775-76.
29. Eli Ginzberg, Oral History Interview, May 14, 1975, OHDDEL; Eli Ginzberg, personal interview, December 11, 1990, New York, N. Y.
30. Eisenhower to Parkinson, June 23, 1947, Eisenhower MSS., DDEL.
31. Black, interview, 1967, COHP.
32. Parkinson informed Eisenhower that "both letters have been filed with the Clerk of the Board," so Dodge may have learned about the assurances. Parkinson to Eisenhower, June 26, 1947, Eisenhower MSS., DDEL.
33. *New York Times*, June 25 and 28, 1947; *New York Herald-Tribune*, June 25, 1947; Eisenhower to Congressman Francis Case, July 1, 1947, *PDDE*, VIII, 1793.
34. Trustees, Minutes, June 24, 1947, CACU; Black, interview, June 6, 1973; Carl W. Ackerman, memo, August 5, 1947, Ackerman MSS., Library of Congress (LC); Editorial, "Columbia's New President," *New York Herald-Tribune*, June 25, 1947.
35. Parkinson to Eisenhower, June 26, 1947, Eisenhower MSS., DDEL.
36. *New York Times*, June 25, 1947; Eisenhower to Fackenthal, June 26, 1947, *PDDE*, VIII, 1786-87.
37. Frank D. Fackenthal, Oral History Interview, 1956, COHP; Carman, interview, December 1, 1961; Ackerman, memo, August 5, 1947, Ackerman MSS., LC. An interesting question is whether Taylor, who had worked with the *Herald-Tribune's* editorial board, inspired the critical editorial on the appointment.
38. Jacobs, interview, February 5, 1965; Jacobs, "Memoirs," 1974; McCann, interview, July 25, 1972; Black, interview, June 6, 1973.

39. Eisenhower, *At Ease,* chapters XIV-XV; Stephen E. Ambrose, *Eisenhower: Soldier,*
     General of the Army, President-Elect, 1890-1952 (New York, 1983), chapters 6-7.
40. "Topics of the Times," *New York Times,* June 25, 1947; *New York Herald-Tribune,*
     June 25, 1947; Question Reynolds, "Mr. President Eisenhower," *Life,* April 17,
     1950, p. 144.
41. Jacobs, World-Wide Broadcast, July 29, 1947, Eisenhower MSS., DDEL.
42. Editorial, "President `Ike,'" *Columbia Spectator,* September 25, 1947.
43. *New York Times,* September 12, 1947; Joseph Campbell, personal interview, Febru-
     ary 5, 1964, Washington, D.C.; Nicholas Murray Butler to Eisenhower, June 23 and
     30, 1947, and Watson to Eisenhower, July 19, 1947, Eisenhower MSS., DDEL;
     Eisenhower to Watson, August 21, 1947, *PDDE,* IX, 1889-91; Kirk to author,
     March 13, 1992.
44. *New York Times,* September 12, 1947; Jacobs, "Memorandum" to author, March 10,
     1958, and "Memoirs"; Philip Jessup to Jacobs, July 3, 1947, Jacobs MSS., Bentley
     Historical Library, Michigan Historical Collections (MHC).
45. *New York Times,* September 12, 1948.
46. Jacques Barzun, personal interview, April 5, 1979, New York, N. Y. In a letter on
     July 17 Eisenhower had invited Fackenthal to Washington and hoped that they
     could have "a good long period" together sometime the next two weeks, but no
     meeting occurred. Eisenhower to Fackenthal, July 17, 1947, Eisenhower MSS.,
     DDEL.
47. Barzun, interview, April 5, 1979.
48. Coykendall to Eisenhower, September 15, 1947, Eisenhower MSS., DDEL;
     Eisenhower to Coykendall, September 17, 1947, and to Fackenthal, September 18,
     1947, *PDDE,* IX, 1925-26, 1928-30; Fackenthal to Eisenhower, September 19,
     1947, CACU; Eisenhower to Fackenthal, September 22, 1947, and to Coykendall,
     October 13, 1947, Eisenhower MSS., DDEL.
49. Joseph August Brandt, "Poison in the Ivy," *Saturday Review of Literature,* Janu-
     ary13, 1945, pp. 5-7; Eisenhower to Robert Maynard Hutchins, October 13, 1947,
     PDDE, IX,1972-74; O. C. Carmichael, "What Makes a Good College President,"
     New York Times Magazine, September 7, 1947.
50. William E. Robinson, "Confidential notes," October 17, 1947, Robinson MSS.,
     DDEL; Richard Kluger, *The Paper: The Life and Death of the New York Herald-
     Tribune* (New York, 1989), pp. 359-60, 423.
51. Eisenhower to Coykendall, November 12, 1947, *PDDE,* IX, 2055-57.
52. Ibid.
53. Watson to Eisenhower, November 18, 1947, DDEL. Parkinson would remind
     Eisenhower about Butler's "enthusiastic approval." See Parkinson to Eisenhower,
     June 26, 1947 and October 27, 1948, DDEL.
54. Monroe Emanuel Deutsch, "Choosing College Presidents," *School and Society,"*
     October 25, 1947, reprinted in *American Association of University Professors Bul-
     letin* , XXX (Autumn, 1947), 520-24.
55. Coykendall to Eisenhower, November 17, 1947, CACU.
56. Eisenhower to Coykendall, November 22, 1947, *PDDE,* IX, 2078-80.
57. Eisenhower to Milton Eisenhower, December 9, 1947, ibid., 2127-28.
58. *New York Times,* December 7, 10, 1947; *Columbia Spectator,* December 8, 10,
     1947; Eisenhower to Coykendall, December 7, 1947, CACU; Eisenhower to Watson,
     December 8, 1947, *PDDE,* IX, 2121-22; Eisenhower to Parkinson, June 13, 1947,
     ibid., VIII, 1756-57; Eisenhower to Parkinson, December 15, 1947, ibid., IX, 2138-
     39.
59. Eisenhower to Milton Eisenhower, October 16, 1947, ibid., 1986-88; Ackerman,
     memorandum, January 1, 1948, Ackerman MSS., LC.

60. Dodge to Fackenthal, December 121, 1947, CACU; Fackenthal to Jacobs, December 16, 1947, Jacobs MSS., MHC; Jacobs, "Memoirs."

61. Eisenhower to Walter Bedell Smith, September 18, 1947, and to Milton Eisenhower, October 16, 1947, *PDDE*, IX, 1933-34, 1986-88.

62. Eisenhower, *At Ease*, p. 354; *PDDE*, IX, fn. #1, 2193.

63. McCann, interview, July 25, 1972. In *At Ease*, pp. 334-35, Eisenhower, however, wrote, "I worked over the draft of the letter carefully. . . . After four or five or six revisions of the letter, I decided to let it cool over the weekend. I did not take a copy home with me to Fort Myer."

64. Eric Sevareid, CBS News, Eisenhower MSS., DDEL; Peter Lyon, *Eisenhower: Portrait of the Hero* (Boston, 1974), p. 379. The assumption was that Governor Dewey would defeat President Truman in 1948 and run for reelection in 1952; in 1956 Eisenhower would be sixty-six.

65. Pegram to Eisenhower, January 24, 1948, Eisenhower MSS., DDEL.

66. Editorial, "Warrior and Man of Peace," *New York Times*, February 16, 1948.

67. Black, interview, June 6, 1973; Eisenhower to Robinson, December 17 and 20, 1947, and Eisenhower to Joseph E. Davies, December 23 and 31, 1947, *PDDE*, IX, 2148, 2153, 2159-60, 2174-75.

68. *New York Herald-Tribune*, February 9, 1948; Black, interview, June 6, 1973; Eisenhower, *At Ease*, pp. 324-29; Ginzberg, interview, December 11, 1990.

69. Eisenhower to Davies, December 23, 1947, *PDDE*, IX, 2159-60; Black, interview, June 6, 1973; McCann, interview, July 25, 1972; Arthur Nevins, Oral History, 1970, COHP; When Nevins and Eisenhower planned "a final lengthy session" in early June, Eisenhower invited him to stay at 60 Morningside. Eisenhower to Nevins, May 17, 1948, Eisenhower MSS., DDEL; Robinson, memorandum, April 1, 1948, Robinson MSS., DDEL.

70. Robinson, memo, April 1, 1948, and Robinson to Helen Reid, March 24, 1948, Robinson MSS., DDEL.

71. Clifford Roberts, interview, 1968, COHP; Ambrose, *Eisenhower*, 476-78; Lyon, *Eisenhower*, 383-84; David Owen, *The Making of the Masters: Clifford Roberts, Augusta National, and Golf's Most Prestigious Tournament* (New York, 1999), chapter 7; Kluger, *The Paper*, 423.

72. Fackenthal to Eisenhower, July 7, 1947, Eisenhower MSS., DDEL; Eisenhower to Edward "Swede" Hazlett, Jr., April 28, 1948, *PDDE : Columbia University* (Baltimore, 1984), X, 47-49.

73. McCann, *Man from Abilene*, p. 172.

74. Hatch, "Prexy Plan," *Collier's*, September 13, 1947, p. 11; Allan Nevins, review of *Eisenhower Speaks*, in *New York Times Book Review*, May 16, 1948.

75. Eisenhower, *At Ease*, p. 337; Ira Henry Freeman, "Eisenhower of Columbia," *New York Times Magazine*, November 7, 1948, pp. 13ff.

76. Milton Eisenhower, interview, July 26, 1972.

77. Philip Young, personal interview, June 15, 1977, Van Hornesville, N. Y.; Eisenhower to Leonard Gerow, October 10, 1942, cited by Stephen E. Ambrose, "Eisenhower's Legacy," in Gunter Bischof and Stephen E. Ambrose, ed., *Eisenhower: A Centenary Assessment* (Baton Rouge, La., 1995), p. 255; Young to author, March 2, 1982.

78. Howard M. Snyder, "Summary of Year 1948," Snyder MSS., DDEL; *New York Herald-Tribune*, May 3, 1948; *New York Times*, May 3, 1948, and November 22, 1963; Lyon, *Eisenhower*, p. 381.

79. Lyon, *Eisenhower*, pp. 382-83; Carman, interview, December 1, 1961; Jacobs, personal interview, February 5, 1965, Hartford, Ct; Jacobs, "Memoirs."

80. Snyder, "Summary of Year 1948, Snyder MSS., DDEL.

3

President Ike Arrives

In a moment of weakness I listened to the blandishments of a couple of your Trustees and here I find myself with this gigantic organization of my hands, and I don't know a goddamn thing about it.
—Dwight D. Eisenhower,
Spring, 1948

It would take a book to give even a glimpse of the task that now belongs to General Eisenhower.
—*Washington Post,*
August 1, 1948

He could have had any gift in the power of the people to bestow. He chose to remain Ike, his integrity intact, loved and trusted by a nation. This man led the force that saved the world from chaos and slavery. Yet he seeks no reward except in further service.
— *New York Times,*
February 9, 1948

Dwight Eisenhower walked into the President's Office in Low Memorial Library for the first time on Monday, May 3, 1948, and faced a busy schedule. The morning's appointments started with Director of Public Relations Harron, Dean Carman, Provost Jacobs, and Trustees Dodge and Coykendall, then luncheon with Acting President Fackenthal and the Trustees at the Men's Faculty Club, followed by a press conference, a Trustees Meeting, and an informal meeting with Trustees in his office. "Seriously and frankly," he told a host of reporters and photographers, "I am going to try to learn the requirements of a new and very important position. I have no idea of carrying over anything except for the experience that I have had that may prove valuable." The assistants from Washington, he emphasized, had accompanied him to Columbia "merely to carry on the work that cannot be cut off." The University community "frightened" him, he admitted, and the task would be difficult. "I have nothing to say about education. I don't know enough about it, . . . I am coming to learn." The President-elect added, "I'm just a Freshman around the place." Most of the questions, however, concerned presidential politics and foreign affairs, ranging from the Cold War to the critical situation in Palestine; Eisenhower, "cordial and patient," became "unmistakably serious," according to the *New York Sun* reporter, "when the inevitable political questions popped up."[1]

The following noon at the Union Club Eisenhower, delivering his first public speech in civilian clothes, enthusiastically supported the decision to turn the School of Business into a graduate school with an expanded program. "Eisenhower Ready To Aid U.S. System," the *New York Times* proclaimed; Columbia's incoming President would "help the educational world to improve and perpetuate the American economic system." He argued that in the United States business and education had "created more public benefits" than those created by any other economic system in the world. "Our country has done the best of any" in producing happiness, prosperity, individual rights, conveniences, and security.

It was "more than coincidence," he declared, that the Trustees at his first meeting the previous day had approved Dean Young's plan for a Graduate School of Business. Young, who had served as Deputy Administrator of Lend-Lease during World War II, had spent a year on Wall Street before accepting the challenge of pulling the Business School together and giving it a focus. As the Dean initiated changes, he received cooperation from the faculty, gave a reception at his apartment for the faculty to meet Eisenhower, and welcomed collaboration with business in New York to solve "live problems," as part of the course of instruction. "Participation by the faculty and staff in a wide variety of businesses, coupled with the exposure of the students to actual live business operations," Young told the audience, "creates a basis for sound business education."[2]

Tom Watson had invited some 160 prominent guests from industry, education, the arts, politics, and government to the luncheon, and they warmly received the words of Eisenhower and Young. The IBM President in his remarks stressed that the new Graduate School would help provide the well-trained minds needed by business in future years. In late June Eisenhower delivered two addresses for Watson at the dedication of a new IBM facility in Poughkeepsie and in mid-July two more at the IBM facilities in Endicott, New York.[3]

On May 5, his third day at Columbia, Eisenhower spoke at the University Club to a hundred professional and business leaders attending a luncheon of the International Committee for Mental Hygiene. His deep concern about the wastage of human resources had been "one of the numerous reasons" taking him to the University, and it led him to what would be one of his most important projects at Columbia. He had discussed the problem and his proposed speech with Professor Eli Ginzberg, with whom he had talked in 1947 at the Pentagon and who during the war had conducted a series of studies and recently had been Director of the War Department's Resources Analysis Division. The General, drawing on his wartime experiences, emphasized in his speech that mental and emotional instability had had "far-reaching consequences" in the armed forces. The Army, he recalled, had rejected "hundreds of thousands" as mentally unfit, and the entire armed services had rejected some two million men. Arguing that if people understood one another there would be "no danger of war," he called the nation's manpower "one of our most treasured resources." Delighted that the International Conference on Mental Health in London that summer would investigate causes of strife, unrest, and discontent, he hoped it might achieve "a small answer. . . . If in the measurable future we don't find some way of eliminating the cause of war, our grandchildren will find it most unhappy to live."[4]

In early June Eisenhower, as honorary chairman of the American Overseas Aid Organization for the United Nations Appeal for Children, again stressed his concern. He asked one thousand persons at the Waldorf-Astoria, "How can we expect children struggling to keep alive to hold to ideas that will maintain them, as disciples of peace?" With half of the world's children hungry and "searching for the garbage heaps," he urged support for the AOA-UNAC and for Americans "to save food and produce more of it." There would be no peace for Americans "until we are all bound together in common concept of the fundamentals of the problem."[5]

These early speeches demonstrate that, as President-designate of Columbia, Eisenhower had wasted no time in presenting themes he considered vital and, as intended, his comments received prominent attention in the media. The day after discussing the problem of mental health, he addressed the issue of American and European Security at a meeting of the Chamber of Commerce of New York; earlier that day he had become a trustee of the Carnegie Endowment for

International Peace, carrying on, in the words of the Endowment's chairman, John Foster Dulles, "the tradition so splendidly established by Dr. Butler."[6]

During this busy first week at Columbia a Republican Congressman from Nebraska criticized the General's retirement benefits, specifically his military assistants, on the floor of the House of Representatives, and this received considerable publicity. The Chairman of the House Armed Services Committee, asked by reporters for his opinion, quickly informed Eisenhower, who had testified often before his Committee, that he had been "entirely misquoted" in the press on the subject. To quiet the controversy, the General asked Secretary of Defense James Forrestal: Did the United States Government want him to stop answering "calls that may be made upon me?" Forrestal discussed this question with President Truman, who "feels very strongly that you . . . must have help . . . if you are to continue to perform the many public and semi-public activities" and "he also feels very strongly . . . that it is of importance to the Government that you continue with these activities." At Forrestal's urging, on May 21 Eisenhower addressed the Commercial Club of Chicago, and a few weeks later he delivered a lecture at the National War College on the problems of the Allied Command.[7]

The General's military assistants included a chauffeur, Sergeant Leonard Dry, who had been with him since the North African campaign and would be Mamie's favorite chauffeur at Columbia; Sergeant John Moaney, who had joined Eisenhower's household staff in 1942 and would remain with the family for well over three decades; Major Robert L. Schulz, a former industrial traffic manager who had been commissioned in the Army in 1942 and had served with the General in the Pentagon since the war; and a private secretary. Schulz had the responsibility to make sure "things will always work out," or as he recalled, "I was concerned about how much can be done in so many hours without conflicts." He made all the General's travel arrangements, and he supervised the preparations for Eisenhower's arrival at Columbia. Consequently, under Schulz's direction, the President's office and house were set up and organized around his military staff.[8]

Eisenhower had requested that the President's offices in Low Memorial Library be relocated. Butler's office, one floor above the Rotunda level, could be reached only by a private elevator from the Office of the Secretary of the University. During the General's brief visit to the University in September, 1947, he had looked around Low Memorial and, as the group reached the west side—the location of the distinguished Plimpton Library—he said, "I think this will be a good area," and the Plimpton Library was moved.

He later recalled that he had insisted his office be on the main floor, just off the Rotunda. "There, I hoped, both students and faculty might have direct and easy access to their President and I would not feel immured in a remote citadel." The extensive alterations were undertaken, and his office in the presidential suite occupied the southwest corner of Low Memorial Library. Next to it, and between the President and the Provost, was the office of Major Schulz, his Administrative Aide, and Kevin McCann, the Special Assistant to the President—the aide that the General had requested that the Trustees appoint—and two secretaries. This office had large plate-glass windows on the hall to Eisenhower's office, which provided an additional check on anyone who had entered the suite at its main entrance off the Rotunda, where two receptionists sat. The President's Office also had a separate, private entrance.[9]

The University also spared no expense on renovations of the President's House at 60 Morningside Drive. Only the Butlers had lived in the large four-story building, and there had been no alterations since its construction in 1912. Mrs. Butler, in fact, had told Trustee Black, Chairman of the Buildings and Grounds Committee, "I hope you are going to fix it up for the new President." (When Watson's secretary told Black to get things progressing on the house, the Trustee replied, "B & G will take care of these matters in due course, and I wish you would tell this to Mr. Watson.") The University acquired the services of Dorothy Draper, a well-known interior decorator. She restored the library and dining room on the first floor, the marble staircase to the second floor with a large reception hall, and two smaller rooms. The major changes were a new kitchen in the basement, a new elevator, and extensive remodeling for living quarters for the Eisenhowers on the third floor and guest rooms and maids rooms on the top floor. On the roof an old "water room" was converted into a penthouse retreat, where they spent considerable time. Here, members of the "gang" regularly played bridge, and Eisenhower had a studio for painting. "Mrs. Eisenhower and I," the General wrote, "have not ceased wondering how you were able to accomplish such a complete transformation," and he expressed to Draper "our delight and satisfaction." The Columbia community assumed that 60 Morningside, with its expensive renovations and refurbishing, would be used for University functions. The limited entertaining that spring and early summer—only five occasions, ranging from a working luncheon with Provost Jacobs, Trustee Black, and Paul Davis of the Development Office to a small dinner for the University Fund committee and a stag dinner for fifteen Trustees— would set a disappointing pattern.[10]

Acting President Fackenthal, for his part, had anticipated problems with the General's staff in Low Memorial. "It is desirable," he wrote to the Provost and to the Secretary of the University, that you continue to be "familiar with what goes over the President's desk. . .

We must be quite sure that matters are not permitted to fail of attention because of someone's absence or because of burial on someone's desk." In spite of Fackenthal's admonition, the front office under Schulz's preparation and with the subsequent arrival of McCann took on more than a few Pentagon characteristics.

Schulz and McCann had very different responsibilities under President Eisenhower; nonetheless, in the eyes of the University community both quickly came to be seen as "traffic cops," or "barriers," or "a safeguard" for the President. McCann, a gifted writer, had responsibility for the General's correspondence and would establish a very close association that lasted until the General's death. He quickly assumed more and more influence and control over the President's office, even though Eisenhower had stated specifically to the Trustees that his Special Assistant "would have nothing to do with University matters." After working with Schulz on the renovation at 60 Morningside and knowing McCann through his association with Eisenhower on *Crusade in Europe*, Black saw the two aides as keeping "the big fellow" to themselves. Schulz and McCann, he added, "didn't know anything about the University." They were, Fackenthal emphasized, "still protecting a world figure, instead of putting him into a new community." They had, he added, the great "ability to make the wrong appointments, either for speaking or consultation." Fackenthal saw the developing situation as a "tactical mistake," and Jacobs later called it the "greatest weakness" of the Eisenhower administration. Grayson Kirk, Jacobs' successor in the Provost's Office, recalled that Schulz saw it his duty "to interpose himself between the outside world and the General," and he kept the faculty away, "sometimes with disastrous consequences."[11] Schulz and McCann, however, were used to running the Chief of Staff's office;

they applied their experience to the President's office in Low Memorial and the demands the General faced in his new position.

During General Eisenhower's first weeks, when he made prominent appearances in New York City, he had a full schedule of appointments in Low Memorial; moreover, he spent a full day at Teachers College with Dean William Russell, and he held a stag dinner for the Trustees at the Links Club; he and Mamie gave a dinner for the University's Deans and Directors and their spouses at the Men's Faculty Club; and they attended several dinners at the Watsons'. The day-long Commencement festivities, even though he was still President-designate, also included a black-tie dinner the previous evening for the honorary degree recipients. A few days later on June 7 in the Trustees' Room, with the Deans and Directors present, Eisenhower officially assumed the Presidency when he received the keys to the University; meanwhile, he had set aside a day for work on *Crusade in Europe*. In mid-June he informed Provost Jacobs that he needed more office space, writing "in the very near future give this matter your very careful attention."[12]

One Saturday morning, soon after arriving on the Morningside Heights campus, he asked Dean Carman to come over to his office. It was only the third time the two had met, the first being when the historian, who never forgot that he was an upstate "farm boy," had escorted the General at the University's Special Convocation for World War II leaders in February, 1947. A magnificent teacher with an unmatched sense of civic responsibility, Carman passionately believed in the importance of a liberal education, broadly conceived. "He communicated to everyone associated with him," Eisenhower recalled, "his zest for Columbia College and for living a full life," and the General wanted to talk with the Dean. He told Carman he had thought of becoming president of a small rural college where he "could be very useful." But, he complained, "in a moment of weakness I listened to the blandishments of a couple of your Trustees and here I find myself with this gigantic organization on my hands, and I don't know a goddamn thing about it." Thumping his fists on his desk, he pleaded, "You have got to help me!" Doug Black, Eisenhower's closest non-golfing friend, reflected years later, "I don't think that he had any idea what a complicated thing Columbia University was or is. No idea of it whatever."[13]

With his busy schedule and somewhat overwhelmed by his campus demands, he declined a number of invitations. He did not attend the dinner of the Alumni Association of the University's Journalism School, even though Doug Black delivered the principal address. He refused several honorary degrees; Fackenthal and Congressman Clifford Case of New Jersey persuaded him, however, to reconsider an invitation from Rutgers University. Paraphrasing Fackenthal's argument, Eisenhower accepted the offer, emphasizing that "the historic association between Rutgers and Columbia fully justifies an exception in this instance." He also received honorary degrees from James Phinney Baxter at Williams College and from Charles Seymour at Yale University. These and other appearances that spring kept his name prominently in the spotlight on the eve of the Republican and Democratic presidential nominating conventions.[14]

During the press conference at the Men's Faculty Club on May 3 the reporters had concentrated on partisan politics and not his new position at Columbia. When asked, "if either political party" nominated him would he accept, he seriously replied, "I wrote a letter in January which I presume you all have read. Nothing in the situation has changed the convictions which I then uttered. It was honest. I slaved a long time writing it and I meant exactly what I said. There is not a word in it that misrepresents what I mean. I stand by that." The reporters, nonetheless, had persisted. What would he do if President Truman did not run for election? "You people," he said, "can think up the most impossible assumptions. I cannot see how any one single person's opinion or act could change me." What, then, about a "mass petition" on his behalf? "I have tried to make myself very clear," he added. "I assure you I am honest." According to the *Columbia Spectator*, he considered the possibilities of such a draft "in the realm of fantasy." One journalist, however, observed in his article that the General had not answered the last question directly.[15]

The Eisenhower "boom" had lost momentum after the Finder letter in January and during his writing of *Crusade in Europe*, but it rapidly regained strength with the publicity generated by his arrival at Columbia and the forthcoming conventions. The boom, indeed, overshadowed everything he did during his first two months and disrupted the University. Very soon a "procession of politicians, most of them Democrats, lined up outside his door" in Low Memorial. A number of prominent Democrats either disliked President Truman or were convinced that he could not win the election that fall, and they wanted to dump him or persuade him to step aside for another candidate. Journalist Marquis Childs, who interviewed Eisenhower in May in his Columbia office and wrote him in July that "Naturally I shall be careful of the confidences which you have been kind enough to give me," reported that "at least eight senators and a half-dozen governors made the pilgrimage" to Columbia. These politicians presented the argument that the times "demanded a man of Eisenhower's great stature and prestige who could rise above ordinary political considerations." Trustees and businessmen Parkinson and Watson, meanwhile, did not need to line up to see Eisenhower. They saw Columbia as "a stepping stone" for him, as a Democrat, to the White House and, according to Provost Jacobs, "Watson wanted him to get the Democratic nomination for 1948."[16]

Eisenhower had been at Columbia for only a couple of weeks when Bob Harron suggested that the General hold a press conference on the fourth anniversary of D-Day; since June 6 was a Sunday, Harron proposed scheduling the conference for Monday the seventh, the day Eisenhower officially assumed his Columbia duties. The General agreed, realizing that it would be an excellent opportunity to talk about the importance of D-Day. When he asked Harron on June 3 if the press had been notified, the Public Information Director replied that the notice was going out that afternoon. "I don't think you had better," Eisenhower stated. "I have received word that I think is reliable." He had been told that the *Herald-Tribune* would publish on Sunday, June 6, the recent Roper Poll which showed that Eisenhower could win the Presidency as either a Democrat or a Republican and that the voters in both political parties preferred him over any other candidate. "If that happens," Eisenhower commented, "and then we have a press conference on Monday, the questions are going to be about that and not about D-Day." He added, "They're going to think I'm running for President and I don't want it." Harron, consequently, did not schedule the press conference, and the *Herald-Tribune* published on the sixth the Roper Poll which demonstrated Ike's enormous popularity. It also printed photographs of Eisenhower under the caption "Four Years Ago and Today: Eisenhower Gets a New Command."[17]

Ike Eisenhower, the D-Day anniversary, and Columbia University all received widespread publicity, in addition to the Roper Poll, on Sunday, June 6. William Zinsser, feature writer for the *Herald-Tribune*, noted that four years and a day after the Allied landing in Normandy General Eisenhower would assume the Presidency of Columbia University. "Although this may seem to be a less difficult beachhead, the two tasks have much in common. Like the force General Eisenhower commanded in 1944, Columbia is huge and complex, with divisions doing practically every kind of work and operating as almost independent units." Some 31,000 attended the University's various branches; the faculty and staff exceeded 3,000 persons; and in the summer some "18,000 relative strangers descend on the University from practically every part of the world." This "many-sidedness . . . strikes the visitor." The task for the new President would be "to develop Columbia to its fullest possible effectiveness as one of the leading American institutions." To do this Eisenhower would have to "expand the campus beyond its present constricting limits and bind the University's many divisions into a closer unit." Zinsser, a prolific writer, asserted, "Those who watched the smooth operation of Eisenhower's war-time headquarters, which was an organization of polyglot groups and strong-willed commanders, feel that his experience and personality make him peculiarly fitted to bring Columbia's divisions into line." Zinsser saw "exciting possibilities" for the General's new command, and he concluded, "It could be said that the job he undertakes tomorrow, which is again to lead young people to important objectives, is but the peace-time extension of the job he began in Europe four years ago today."[18]

Historian Allan Nevins, also writing on D-Day, asserted in the *New York Times*, "No one can visit Morningside without feeling great energies vibrating there" and he stressed Columbia's metropolitan, national, and international characteristics. Yet, because it lacks funds, "it is estopped from rendering still further services to business, industry, and government and social activities, as well as to education." He predicted that with her new President Columbia's "greatest years lie before her, and she knows that she will share them with a nation which has become the first power on the globe, and a city which has become a world capital."[19] Columbia had good reason to be pleased that weekend.

And Eisenhower was right about the proposed press conference. The newspaper correspondents, in spite of the D-Day anniversary and his officially assuming Columbia's Presidency, would have concentrated on politics. Bill Robinson had told him about the Roper Poll and when his paper would publish it. They had spent the afternoon of June 2 together, and he and Doug Black met with the General the next afternoon to discuss *Crusade in Europe*. Robinson, a perceptive political observer and partisan Republican, during the winter and spring had seen Eisenhower frequently at meetings and while playing golf and bridge. He confidentially told the *Herald-Tribune's* Helen Reid that Eisenhower saw the Democratic party in a "terrible state. . . . He points out that it is a mixture of extremes on the right, extremes on the left, with political chicanery and expediency shot through the whole business." The General described himself "as a Liberal Republican, . . . the sound, responsible, middle-of-the-road party." Robinson was worried, however. "Despite all of this," he added, "it is barely conceivable that in certain circumstances he would not resist an overwhelming draft as a Democratic candidate for the Presidency." He continued. "If the Republicans were to nominate a narrow and limited man who might be or become a political opportunist in the White House, great pressures from all sides might lead General Eisenhower to listen to the voice of the people."[20]

While Robinson might know Eisenhower's political thinking, the General's partisan beliefs did not matter that spring: voters of both major political parties wanted him to be the next President of the United States. Some twenty thousand letters, postcards, and telegrams urged his candidacy. The correspondence overwhelmed his staff, which replied to over eight thousand writers, the General himself signing one thousand letters. Under sociologist Robert K. Merton's direction, Columbia's Bureau of Applied Social Research analyzed the mail and, in Merton's words, this marked "the first time that a person in public life has acquired a full picture of masses of correspondence reaching his office." The Bureau reported that "The Collective Portrait of DDE . . . is focused on his *personal qualities,* rather than his career, chief among these qualities being *sincerity* and *competence.*" The writers saw him *primarily as a statesman and administrator, . . .* as *a non-militaristic military man, . . . a charismatic leader.*" His entire career, according to the letters, had served the nation, and the public did not identify him with special groups or political parties. *"The General has thus become, through his public activities, a living symbol of unity . . . he had, so to speak, earned through action the right to speak in the name of unity."* This material, Merton concluded, suggested "the important hypothesis, supported also by social research, that *slogans do not move people if the slogans do not correspond to the easily visible realities of the case."*[21] This "full picture" documented the enormous following Eisenhower had among the American people when he became President of Columbia.

"No one knew whether he was a Democrat or a Republic," the *New Yorker's* political commentator Richard H. Rovere observed. "For all anyone knew, he might have been a Greenbacker or a Social Credit Crank. No one knew whether he knew what he was." People knew or believed, though, that "he could win an election." Indeed, Rovere emphasized, "the mystery of his beliefs" had created "the vast popular front movement" for him, "a movement embracing Chester Bowles and Alf M. Landon, the Americans for Democratic Action and the remnants of the Liberty League."[22]

By late June, 1948, after Governor Dewey had captured the Republican Party nomination, many Democrats and New Dealers desperately wanted to draft Eisenhower. Few believed that the badly divided Democrats with anyone else could defeat Dewey. While these people "seemed to have no idea of what views on domestic policy, if any, the General held," journalist Marquis Childs wrote, "doubts on this score were brushed aside as irrelevant." Florida's Senator Claude Pepper, an ardent New Dealer, urged the delegates to the forthcoming Democratic Convention "to pick the ablest and strongest man available," obviously meaning Ike.[23]

As the Fourth of July weekend approached—and the Democratic National Convention would begin a week later—the Eisenhowers celebrated their thirty-second wedding anniversary with the "gang" at 60 Morningside. Ellis "Slats" Slater recalled that one evening an enthusiastic crowd of some two-to-three hundred persons gathered outside and chanted "We Like Ike," and the General went out on the balcony and waved to the cheering fans. With the political pressure on Eisenhower mounting, McCann and Harron began to prepare a statement reiterating his position. "The way things are coming along now," Eisenhower commented, "we may have to use this thing, but we'll hold it." Then, he added, "If we have to let this go over the weekend, I hope we don't have to, but if we do and it happens to be Sunday, I don't want it to go before six o'clock Sunday, because I don't want that so and so [Drew Pearson] who broadcasts at six o'clock to have it. If it has to go, wait until after six o'clock."

The need did not occur, and on Monday, the holiday, Eisenhower played golf at Blind Brook, and Harron waited in his office for any developments. A few minutes after Harron returned home for dinner, Major Schulz called and asked him to come to the President's House. When he reached 60 Morningside, the General, McCann, and Harron discussed the situation, and Bill Robinson tinkered with the statement. Finally, at nine o'clock, Eisenhower said "All right, there it is." Harron returned to his office, called the news services, and at ten-thirty met with fifty to sixty reporters who had quickly gathered on Morningside Heights. Eisenhower's statement read, "I will not, at this time, identify myself with any political party, and could not accept nomination for any public office or participate in partisan political contest."[24]

"I want to tell you how magnificently," Marquis Childs wrote the General the day after the statement, "you have handled this extraordinary phenomenon of the 'Eisenhower boom.'" Childs knew of no parallel in American history when a man, "so definitely the choice of a great majority of the American people," had said "'no' again and again and again." Eisenhower replied immediately, acknowledging that for thirty-six hours he believed he had been "completely out of the woods" but then on the morning on the eighth he had heard that he was "still vulnerable--the thing seems incomprehensible, but I have become convinced it is still serious." The news, undoubtedly, had come from public opinion analyst Elmo Roper, Jr., who had visited Eisenhower in Low Memorial on the mornings of July 7 and 8 and had also talked with Robinson on the seventh.[25]

Roper's news that the General was "still vulnerable" prompted Eisenhower to write James Roosevelt, the California State Democratic Chairman and late President's son, who ardently supported Eisenhower instead of Truman for the Democratic presidential nomination. Meanwhile, Truman had his friend George Allen, a "gang" guest that weekend at 60 Morningside, ask Eisenhower specifically to remove his name from consideration. When Allen failed, the President asked the Secretary of the Army, Kenneth Royall, to call the General; he did and the two of them over the telephone drafted Eisenhower's message for Roosevelt and, also, for Senator Pepper. The General asserted: "No matter under what terms, conditions, or premises a proposal might be couched, I would refuse to accept the nomination."[26]

The excitement for Eisenhower prompted Childs to write an article, and he noted that the General's letter on the eighth "naturally pleased me very much." Replying from Philadelphia on July 13, the day after the Democrats had convened and before they reluctantly nominated Truman, the journalist said that he had completed the article for *Collier's*, entitled "Why Ike Said No." Childs observed, "As you say, it is incomprehensible and I have often thought of your description of the whole business as an effort to seek a miraculous or a magical way out of problems that can never be solved in that fashion."[27]

"As the polls show," Alden Hatch wrote to "General Ike," "you are most certainly the real choice of the American people; and there is no doubt, that had you not spoken again, you would have been nominated and elected." While the General's aide McCann later sought to dismiss these activities as a "minor eruption by the Democrats and relatively few Democrats, well-heeled Democrats I must say," and asserted that Eisenhower's statement "left no further room for doubt," the activities were not minor. Bob Harron, moreover, was left with a very different impression about the General's statement; Eisenhower, he reflected, "didn't slam the door. There was a phrase in each of those like 'at this time' or something like that." Harron quickly added, however, that if Eisenhower had had any political ambitions in 1948 he would not have supported so strongly several controversial decisions after he arrived at Columbia that spring.[28]

During this period Eisenhower had been pulling the blinds on his office windows, and the incessant political activities had distracted and disrupted for the University. His attention had been diverted from Columbia's pressing demands by politics and checking the final stages of his war memoirs, which were scheduled for publication in the fall. He had, consequently, emphasized in his press release "the important duties I have undertaken as President of Columbia." A few days earlier the Italian Ambassador had bestowed on the General his country's Grand Cross of the Military of Italy. Before the ceremony Eisenhower had said to the newspaper reporters, "I thought all you people would be in Philadelphia," at the Republican Convention—one photographer replied that he was "better off here." The next day Columbia's President welcomed twenty-eight European students visiting the United States on a tour sponsored by the American Field Service. Then on July 6, in the midst of pressures from many Democrats on him, he opened the University's forty-ninth summer session; two days later he introduced Eleanor Roosevelt at the opening of the Summer Session Institute[29]

At a convocation the next day he awarded his first honorary degree to Venezuelan novelist and educator Romulo Gallegos, that country's first President elected by popular vote. The *New York Daily Mirror's* photo caption read, "'Ike' Honors a Good Neighbor After His Third and Final 'No.'" The public address system, however, had ruined the General's speech. "Oh, was he mad," Harron recalled, "and he stomped back into his office and that vein was sticking out on his forehead." Newsreel men quickly told Harron, "Bob, he has got to stay. He said something in that speech he had not told us before and the newspapers have it. We are in trouble if we don't." "Holy gees," Harron replied, "have I got to go in" and ask the General to come out? "So, I went in," and Eisenhower, perhaps showing the strains of the previous week, replied, "Do you mean to say I've got to go out and talk with those so and so's again?" "Well, General, it might mean the jobs of some of them if they don't get what the newspapers have gotten, and the newspapers have your speech as you said it." Quickly, Eisenhower agreed. "All right, come on." They went out to the newsreel men, and he stuck out his hand. "Boys, how are you? Now what is it I can do for you." (The President also said "Fix it," referring to the public address system. It was replaced before the Installation and, according to Barzun, "everybody has been grateful ever since.")[30]

His first weeks had, indeed, been hectic, and when he had walked initially into the President's Office on Monday, May 3, he had to have sensed that the academic year 1947-1948—the year the University had waited for his arrival—had been a difficult one. In addition to the mounting budget deficit and the general affairs of the University, the issue of freedom of speech on the Columbia campus had stirred up critical publicity in the Cold War atmosphere of 1948. The former Chief of Staff suddenly became associated with an academic freedom controversy at a time when members of both the Republican and Democratic parties were intensifying their pressure on him to become a presidential candidate.

The previous December Provost Jacobs had refused to allow Howard Fast, author of *Freedom Road* and *Citizen Thomas Paine* to speak on campus. The *Columbia Spectator* saw a denial of free speech, and in an editorial argued that the House Un-American Activities Committee, with "a definite hostility toward leftist individuals," has succeeded in applying "pressure" on Columbia's campus. Fast, one of the sixteen leaders of the Joint Anti-Fascist Refugee Committee, was appealing his conviction on a contempt citation for refusing to produce material for the House Committee. Jacobs asserted that "no convicted person should be accorded the privilege of the University forum to argue his case." He added: "When Mr. Fast is cleared under the law, the request of a student organization to have him speak will be honored." The University, consequently, raised no question about permitting Arnold Johnson, the legislative director of the Communist Party, to speak to Columbia's Marxist Study Group in Pupin Hall a few days later on December 17. Liberal critics, nonetheless, accused the University of retreating "before the incipient threat of attack" by the House Un-American Activities Committee. However, the city-supported colleges—Brooklyn, City College of New York, and Hunter—followed the Columbia lead.[31]

Then, soon after General Eisenhower's arrival at Columbia, the Hearst press, the *New York World Telegram*, and *Counterattack* accused the University of supporting communists when the Polish Government offered $30,000, over a three-year period, for establishing the Adam Mickiewicz Chair of Polish Philology, Language, and Philosophy. On May 5 Acting President Fackenthal accepted the gift and informed the Polish ambassador that "the first incumbent of so distinguished a chair" would be Professor Manfred Kridl, an eminent scholar on the Smith College faculty. The University regarded the new Chair, in honor of Poland's great nineteenth-century poet and ardent nationalist, "as a means of expanding its offering in Polish studies and of making Columbia a national leader . . . in building closer educational and cultural ties between our two nations."[32]

Over Memorial Day weekend a delegation from the Polish-American Congress requested that Columbia University rescind the grant, but the Provost refused. Suddenly, on the eve of the presidential nominating conventions, "all hell popped." Arthur Pruden Coleman, for twenty years an Assistant Professor of Slavic Languages, charged that the Communist Government of Poland was controlled by "Moscow and the Comintern" and that it engaged in a campaign of "academic infiltration" at Columbia under the guise of ostensibly honoring Poland's great poet. Then on July 1 Coleman, who had been planning a biography of the Mickiewicz and objected to the use of the poet's name by the Communist government, dramatically resigned. He vigorously asserted that if he had not done so "I would be conniving at the sort of intellectual 'collaboration' for which the conscience of the entire guild of professors the world over now blames the professors who stayed at their posts and drew fat salaries during Hitler's regime."[33]

The outburst and ensuing publicity provoked a sharp debate within Low Memorial, which was already sensitive to charges of communist influence on Morningside Heights. On May 25 Eisenhower, not yet President, had had to respond to criticism from the family of one of the University's major benefactors, Michael Idvorsky Pupin. His daughter bitterly had protested the December speech by the communist Arnold Johnson to the Marxist Study Group in Pupin Hall, and she threatened to have her father's name removed from the building. Unsatisfied by the Provost's reply that Columbia sought to allow "free and open discussion on all subjects of public interest," and his assurance that Columbia intended "no degradation or slur upon your father's monumental service," her husband wrote Eisenhower and the Trustees and enclosed his wife's correspondence. "Will Columbia," he asked, "agree to keep traitors out of Pupin Hall?" Denouncing other recent speakers, he warned about "Kremlin agents . . . among our school and college teachers and administrators." Eisenhower immediately replied, expressing his "personal conviction," since he had not been at Columbia long enough to know the specifics. He had accepted the Presidency "only because of a passionate belief in the American political plan," and he asserted that "the virtues of our system will never be fully appreciated by us and our children unless we also understand the essentials of opposing ideologies." He had "complete faith in the integrity and democratic purposes" of Columbia's administrators. The University seized the opportunity to send Eisenhower's reply to alumni.[34]

The letter had been written, however, before the eruption over the Adam Mickiewicz Chair, and pressure grew to change the decision and to return to the Polish Government the first payment of $5,000. Robert Harron argued that accepting the money was not "a smart thing" for Columbia, and he believed that it would cost the University in bad publicity far more than the $10,000 a year it received from the Communist Government. Fackenthal, partly responsible for the initial decision, then proposed a compromise: Columbia should tell Warsaw to keep the money and Columbia would establish the Mickiewicz Chair and pay for it herself.[35]

Events in the Cold War—and in late June the Soviets had started their blockade of the Western Sectors of Berlin—that spring had linked the Polish Chair with the Chair of Czechoslovak Studies at Columbia. In 1946 the University had honored at a dinner Jan Masaryk, the American-educated Czechoslovakian Minister of Foreign Affairs and son of the founder and first President of the Czechoslovak Republic, Thomas G. Masaryk. That evening Fackenthal announced the Chair in honor of the elder Masaryk and the Prague Government's gift of $7,500 with an additional $15,000 in 1947. In early 1948, however, the communist coup d'état in Czechoslovakia pulled the country behind the "Iron Curtain," and the death a few weeks later of Jan Masaryk under mysterious circumstances produced an outrage of anticommunist sentiments throughout the United States. Public opinion added to the pressure on Eisenhower and the University to reverse the Polish Chair decision.[36]

In this anti-communist atmosphere new charges circulated that Columbia was sponsoring communist infiltration and that certain faculty members were communist sympathizers. The *San Francisco Examiner*, in an editorial entitled "Coddling Communism at Columbia," criticized the Masaryk and Mickiewicz Chairs and, particularly, Eisenhower's role in the Polish affair. The Hearst paper proclaimed that Eisenhower's decision "SHOULD MAKE THE COUNTRY REJOICE THAT IT WILL NOT BE SUBJECT TO HIS DECISIONS AS PRESIDENT OF THE UNITED STATES." Columbia's Henry Steele Commager, teaching during the summer at the University of California at Berkeley, sent to Eisenhower the editorial, which added that, because of the General's World War II decision, Allied troops had not occupied Czechoslovakia, "THEREBY ESTABLISHING THE RED FLAG IN CENTRAL EUROPE." The newspaper specifically criticized, in addition to Kridl, Masaryk Professor Roman Jakobson and Professor Ernest Simmons, the Executive Officer of the Department of Slavic Languages. These attacks were spearheaded by Sigmund J. Sluszka, a former student of Coleman's at Columbia and the chairman of the Polish-American Congress. Sluszka described Kridl as "a noted Marxist," and he sought the removal of Simmons. He boasted that he could "reach every newspaper, radio, syndicate and press association in the U.S.A. for publicity." He remained silent, however, when reminded by the fact that during 1947-1948 he had "eagerly attempted to establish the contact with the Polish Government."[37]

Eisenhower decided to support the Provost fully on the Polish Chair. He accepted Coleman's resignation, and he asserted in his letter that he had done so only after the Provost personally had outlined to Coleman the University's policy. "You may be certain that if I ever find that the incumbent of the Chair or of any similar Chair steps aside from his academic assignment to infiltrate our University with philosophies inimical to our American system of government, the Chair will be at once discontinued." Professor Kridl had been appointed, he stated, "solely by Columbia without advice or suggestion from non-University sources" and Columbia students would be able "to learn more about . . . a country that has suffered so much. A great deal of the trouble in the world today is traceable to a lack of understanding of the cultures of various countries." Having emphasized this theme, he concluded, "I intend to do all in my power to remedy this situation." Coleman promptly and vehemently expressed his disagreement with Eisenhower, and the University received numerous letters supporting Coleman's position. He denied that Kridl, "paid as he will be by funds made available by the present Polish regime, will be able to carry on his teaching at Columbia under conditions of true scholarship." The Assistant Professor added: "I am thoroughly convinced that lack of understanding between the American people and the Polish people, the latter suffering under communism, will grow rather than be diminished by this regrettable decision by General Eisenhower."[38]

Columbia's President believed that the University should "maintain a dignified silence" in regard to these charges, and he would explain his position in a long letter to the Trustees on September 20. Before leaving for his summer vacation, Eisenhower had received a confidential file on Coleman from Arthur Hays Sulzberger of the *New York Times*, and he gave the file to Provost Jacobs with instructions to "develop such further facts and statements" for a letter.

An extensive investigation by Jacobs provided the material for the President's letter to the Board. Eisenhower explained that the Provost had talked with R. Gordon Wasson, Vice President in Charge of Public Relations at J. P. Morgan and Company and a Columbia alumnus who knew very well the three professors accused of being communist sympathizers. Wesson had spoken with assurance about two of them, Kridl and Jakobson, and was "not really concerned about any difficulty for the third professor," Simmons. He commended the University for furthering studies of various areas in Europe and hoped that "the University would not give in to the various pressures."

The problem of public relations for the University, though, concerned Wesson. He recommended that Jacobs "talk separately with a number of newspaper persons," and in a letter to Sulzberger he referred to the "hullabaloo in the press" and commented, "The University is doing a superb job, quite unique, in the evolution of Slavic studies. . . . The recent criticisms have been monstrously unfair, in my judgment, and uninformed." During the meeting with Wasson, Jacobs had suggested the possibility that Eisenhower might speak out "on academic freedom and his aversion to various subversive activities," and the public relations expert considered it "an excellent idea." Eisenhower liked the suggestion—he would speak on academic freedom during his Installation Address—and concluded his report to the Trustees, "I am convinced, on the basis of investigations that nothing could be more fantastic to assert that any of them is tinged with communism." Jacobs later recalled: "I think we came out a plus on the thing."[39]

The academic freedom controversy illustrated the opportunity Eisenhower had at Columbia—one he had not had in the Army—to speak on matters he considered important, and numerous occasions during his first months in office enabled him to develop and express his thoughts on important issues, ranging from the growing anti-communist movement to federal aid to education. In January, when Columbia College had awarded Fackenthal the Alexander Hamilton Medal—the first Medal had gone to Nicholas Murray Butler in 1947—Eisenhower had traveled from Washington and spoke as Chief of Staff, not as president-designate, at the Waldorf-Astoria dinner. The Army, he noted, "exists to protect a way of life," and he saw "a direct relationship" between the Army and the University under Fackenthal. The program at Columbia contemplated a student who would do more than absorb a college education; he, because of character, personality, social-mindedness, would make of his abilities and training an instrument of public service as a citizen of the world. Eisenhower's presence at the Hamilton Dinner, however, was viewed by some critics as attracting more attention than the medal recipient "though, if he had not made the special trip from Washington for the dinner, the criticism would have been worse."[40]

In retrospect, it was probably inevitable that Eisenhower would not communicate with Fackenthal after his arrival at Columbia. The Acting President, at the time of Eisenhower's appointment, had been named a Life Trustee and the Chairman of the Board's important Committee on Education, as the Trustees, aware of the burdens they had placed on him over the years, sought to make amends. "The General never sent for me," Fackenthal reflected, although the Trustees had asked him to be available to assist the new President, and he had offered to do so. Perhaps, as Professor Raymond Saulnier suggested, Eisenhower sensed that Fackenthal had a very different concept of a university. For Fackenthal Columbia's purpose was "teaching and research period," not building citizenship. In any event, the former Acting President felt alienated and resented the arrangement set up by Eisenhower's staff in Low Memorial; yet, perhaps Fackenthal, by occupying Butler's old office, did not help the situation. Indeed, Eisenhower, as Jacobs sadly observed, in turn seemed to resent Fackenthal's presence in that office. "They really never got together," he added, and this put him "in a difficult spot."[41]

Fackenthal had inherited from Butler a growing budget deficit and the lack of a successful fund-raising program; Butler, in fact, had not even had a development office. Fackenthal had established one under the direction of Paul H. Davis. It would, however, take time to launch a program, and Fackenthal might have had some helpful advice for the new President; he had, though, only one official appointment with Eisenhower during those first months. The University may have had a large endowment, but the operating losses had forced the Provost in early 1948 to increase tuition from $450 to $600 a year, beginning in September. Even with the increase, Jacobs projected a deficit for 1948-1949 of over one million dollars. Students, especially veterans—the new tuition figure exceeded the G.I. Bill allowance—argued vigorously that endowment funds should be used to cover the rising expenses and took their protest to Trustees. The Administration, however, remained steadfast.[42]

In early June, 1948, the Development Office submitted a memorandum to President Eisenhower and the Trustees. When Butler retired in 1945 he had requested to devote his time to securing large gifts and had aimed for $100,000,000, a figure he had set for the University in 1939. The Development Office in 1948 projected the need of $170,000,000, and "the securing of such funds is the responsibility of the entire Columbia organization, including deans, directors, faculty, alumni, students, and friends of the University." The President was to be "head of this activity." Translated, the Development Office proposed a decentralized program, with each school and division raising funds for itself; thus, the professional schools—especially business, law, and medicine—with wealthy alumni would be in a better position than the other schools, except for Columbia College. A few days later, before the memorandum had gone to the Trustees, Eisenhower emphasized to a group of some six hundred Columbia College alumni and their wives that the University "needs lots of money. I've sent men to their death. I've seen men engaged in a mighty struggle for life and death. Why should $170,000,000 scare us?" He said that he had made three speeches that day and, as the *Times* reported, "he intimated that he would have to reduce his outside activities to perform his duties on Morningside Heights."[43]

On July 15 Eisenhower gave an informal stag dinner for fourteen Trustees at 60 Morningside. Initially, he discussed with them the development plan. The University's deficit for the academic year, ending June 30, was $1,457,701.35, and the Provost projected for the following year a deficit of $1,444,900.70, without payment of over $430,000 to amortize the loan taken in 1948. Jacobs had informed the President that the Development Plan Committee on the thirteenth had adopted a report "under which it is believed Columbia University is destined to develop most successfully." The period of talk had come to an end, Eisenhower asserted, and it was something on which "They emphatically agreed."

For the dinner meeting the Provost also had prepared background material on other matters which "you may desire to discuss with the Trustees this evening." One memorandum provided information on the grants from foreign governments to endow chairs at the University, in the event the Trustees might have questions about the Adam Mickiewicz Chair, the protests, and the resignation of Professor Coleman only a few days earlier. Jacobs also included for discussion a proposal "to establish a maximum statutory" retirement age for academic and administrative staff, since the present situation "has not been satisfactory." The President, on his notes of the meeting, wrote, "Retirement plan—compulsory."

Finally, the Provost wondered whether the President wished to discuss the recommendations for reorganizing the Administration. For the Provost this subject was nearly as crucial as a successful development program. Fackenthal had had the firm of Booz, Allen and Hamilton thoroughly study the Administration, and a University Committee, under Doug Black, had been considering its recommendations. In his memorandum to the President, Jacobs stated that two of the four vice presidents positions suggested in the Booz, Allen report, one for business relations and one for development, were "entirely justified," but he was not sure about the title of Vice President.

As for a Vice President for student relations, the Provost preferred that no action be taken "for the time being," since it "raises some very difficult points" that need "to be worked out with extreme care." For the final position, educational affairs, Jacobs wanted the advice of Dean Pegram of the Graduate Faculties. The Provost's memorandum concluded: "I think it is going to be very important for you to have someone, give him what title you will, who will be in effect your Chief of Staff, in military parlance. It seems to me very important that there be such a person upon whom you may rely when you are called away from the University to act in your behalf."[44]

The President informed Jacobs a few days later that he had told the Trustees that Paul Davis would have a development program ready for their approval in the fall, and that he expected to have ready "a specific plan" for retirement of University officers. "Will you," he asked, "please have such a plan drawn up?" As for administrative reorganization, the President wanted to "be prepared to submit a definite plan." Eisenhower, who had left New York for a week in Vermont with General Nevins, concluded, "I hope that during the summer you will have these matters looked into most intensively so that during September you and I, with other interested parties, may go over them in detail and be completely prepared for the October meeting."[45]

In late July the Eisenhowers left Morningside Heights for an extended vacation in Colorado. "The General seemed to be taking a new lease on life," his personal physician wrote. "He adjusted easily to the duties of that great institution." Making "good use of his spare hours," General Snyder added that Eisenhower played golf and bridge two evenings a week. On Saturdays bridge often would start at four o'clock in the penthouse and, after a buffet supper, it would continue until "they cared to disperse along toward midnight." Snyder resided at 60 Morningside that summer since the General, concerned about Mamie, had wanted him to accompany the Eisenhowers to New York and had asked Professor Ginzberg if he could find a place for General Snyder on his staff. "I just can't," Eisenhower had said, "put any more military on the payroll" and Ginzberg, directing a study of New York State hospitals for Governor Dewey, hired Synder as a consultant. General Synder recalled that during one of his brief absences for the hospital report Mrs. Eisenhower became ill and another doctor gave her a shot of penicillin. She had "an anaphylactic reaction and was covered over the neck, shoulders, and other parts of her body with hives." Consequently, Snyder added, "This so frightened her that she would never permit any doctor to give her penicillin." As for the University's new president, General Synder knew that Eisenhower needed "activity to keep well," and he was very pleased with the General's condition.[46]

Columbia had welcomed Eisenhower's arrival. "We all knew that the General was a great organizer, and it was a time when Columbia needed a good deal of reorganization," Professor Jacques Barzun recalled. "So, we were very eager to have the new President." West Point's Commandant Maxwell Taylor reflected, "I always thought that he took over that position with sincere enthusiasm, expecting to have the opportunity to exercise his remarkable qualities of leadership on the student body of Columbia." Yet in August, during the Eisenhowers' vacation, the Trustee Committee on Finance asked the Provost to attend in the President's absence because "of the urgency of some of the requests" before it. Provost Jacobs, for his part, found himself turning to Fackenthal, who had retired and was on vacation, for advice on various "matters pertaining to the University." "That summer, I admit," Jacobs later commented, Eisenhower "should have been around and he wasn't."[47]

Notes

1.   At the end of the press conference Eisenhower prepared for a brief newsreel talk. *New York Sun*, May 4, 1948; *Columbia Spectator*, May 4, 1948; Press Conference transcript, May 3, 1948, Eisenhower MSS, Dwight D. Eisenhower Library, Abilene, Kans. (DDEL).

2.   *New York Times*, May 5, 1948; Philip Young, personal interview, June 15, 1977, Van Hornesville, N. Y.

3.   *New York Times*, May 5, 1948; Louis Galambos, ed., *The Papers of Dwight David Eisenhower: Columbia University* (Baltimore, Md., 1948), XI, 1563, 1565 (*PDDE*).

4.   *New York Times*, May 6, 1948. Eli Ginzberg, personal interview, December 11, 1990, New York, N. Y.; Eisenhower to Frank Whittemore Abrams, December 18, 1948, *PDDE*, X, 374-77; ibid., p. 195. When *Cosmopolitan* asked to publish his remarks, Eisenhower replied that he did not want "any remuneration" and suggested a scholarship at Teachers College, and a Cosmopolitan scholarship was established in June. Ibid., X, 81-82.

5.   General George Marshall, the Secretary of State, had urged Eisenhower to accept the honorary position. Eisenhower to Marshall, May 28, 1948, *ibid.*, X, 90-91; *New York Times*, July 9, 1948.

6.   Ibid., May 7, 1948. On May 7 Eisenhower asked Secretary of Defense James Forrestal for his reaction to the Chamber of Commerce speech, *PDDE*, X, 61-62; Eisenhower to Alger Hiss, May 19, 1948, ibid., 76-77.

7.   Eisenhower to Walter Andrews, May 7, 1948, and to James Forrestal, May 11, 1948, ibid., X, 58-60, 62-63, and 70, 112.

8.   Dwight D. Eisenhower, *At Ease: Stories I Tell to Friends* (New York, 1967), p. 323; Colonel Robert L. Schulz, personal interview, March 11, 1958, White House, Washington, D.C.; Bruce Wonnacott, personal interview, November 11, 1977, Middlebury, Vt.

9.   Robert C. Harron, personal interview, February 5, 1965, Hartford, Ct; Eisenhower, *At Ease*, p. 342; Helen King, Oral History Interview, May 12, 1975, Eisenhower

Library (OHDDEL); Jacobs, memorandum to author, March 10, 1958; Frank D. Fackenthal, memo, August 28, 1947, Central Archives, Columbia University (CACU).

10. Douglas Black, personal interview, June 6, 1973, N. Y., New York; Eisenhower, *At Ease*, pp. 341-42; *New York Herald-Tribune*, February 8, 1948; *Columbia Spectator*, April 30, 1948; Eisenhower to Dorothy Draper, June 5, 1948, Eisenhower MSS., DDEL; Albert C. Jacobs, personal interview, December 31, 1973, Ann Arbor, Mi.; "Disbursement," Mamie Doud Eisenhower MSS., DDEL.

11. Jacobs, interview, December 31, 1973; King, oral history, 1975, OHDDEL; Young, interview, June 15, 1977; Eisenhower to Coykendall, November 22, 1947, *PDDE,* IX, 2078-80; Black, interview, June 6, 1973; Fackenthal, Oral History Interview, 1956, COHP; Jacobs, "Memoirs"; Grayson Kirk, January, 1987, COHP.

12. "Chronology," *PDDE*, XI, 1557-60; Eisenhower to Jacobs, June 15, 1948, CACU.

13. Harry J. Carman, personal interview, December 1, 1961, New York, N. Y.; Eisenhower, *At Ease,* p. 345; Black, interview, June 6, 1973.

14. "Chronology," *PDDE*, XI, 1556-62. Seymour had asked Marcy Dodge to urge Eisenhower to accept the Yale degree.

15. *New York Times*, May 4, 1948; *Columbia Spectator*, May 4, 1948; Clippings, Carl W. Ackerman MSS., Library of Congress (LC).

16. Marquis Childs to Eisenhower, July 6, 1948, Eisenhower MSS., DDEL; Childs, *Eisenhower: Captive Hero* (New York, 1958), p. 112; Jacobs, personal interview, February 5, 1965, Hartford, Ct, and interview, December 31, 1973.

17. Robert C. Harron, personal interview, February 5, 1965, Hartford, Ct; *New York Herald-Tribune*, June 6, 1948.

18. William Zinsser, "Columbia Confronts Eisenhower With a Complex, Difficult Job," *New York Herald-Tribune*, June 6, 1948.

19. Allan Nevins, "University City Within the City," *New York Times*, June 6, 1948.

20. "Chronology," *PDDE*, XI, 1559-60; Robinson memo to Helen Rogers Reid (personal), June 21, 1948, Robinson MSS., DDEL.

21. "Political Mail," August 9, 1948, and Robert K. Merton to Eisenhower, Jacobs, and George Pegram, memorandum, September, 1949, Eisenhower MSS., DDEL. Merton had planned to publish his findings, and Joan D. Goldhamer (a Bureau staff member) concluded that "the decision to abort the study . . . clearly reflected the military habits of Eisenhower and his staff. Goldhamer, "General Eisenhower in Academe: A Clash of Perspectives and a Study Suppressed," *Journal of the History of the Behavioral Sciences*, 33 (Summer, 1997), 241-59. McCann undoubtedly made the decision to suppress publication in August, 1949, when he was drafting Eisenhower's important St. Louis speech to the American Bar Association.

22. Richard H. Rovere, "The Second Eisenhower Boom," *Harper's*, May, 1950, p. 33; Rovere, Oral History Interview, 1968, COHP.

23. Childs, *Eisenhower*, p. 113; Lyon, *Eisenhower*, p. 386.

24. Eisenhower to Harron, memorandum, July 5, 1948, *PDDE,* X, 124-26; Ellis D. Slater, personal interview, September 1, 1972, Edgartown, Ma.; Harron, interview, February 5, 1965; Kevin McCann, personal interview, July 25, 1972, Gettysburg, Pa.; *New York Times*, July 6, 1948. Harron wrote Eisenhower on July 10 that the original of the statement "has already joined the prized and carefully preserved heirlooms of the Harron family." Eisenhower MSS., DDEL.

25. Childs to Eisenhower, July 6, 1948, Eisenhower MSS., DDEL; Eisenhower to Childs, July 8, 1948, *PDDE*, X, 128-29; "Chronology," ibid., XI, 1564.

25. Eisenhower to Roosevelt, July 8, 1948, *PDDE*, X, 129-31 and 125; Arthur Krock, *Memoirs: Sixty Years On the Firing Line* (New York, 1968), pp. 242-44.

27. Childs to Eisenhower, July 13, 1948, Eisenhower MSS., DDEL; Childs, "Why Ike Said No," *Collier's*, August 28, 1948, pp. 14-15, 76-77.

28. Alden Hatch to Eisenhower, July 6, 1948, Eisenhower MSS., DDEL; McCann, Oral History Interview, 1966, COHP; McCann, interview, July 25, 1972; Kevin McCann, *Man from Abilene* (New York, 1952), p. 170; Harron, interview, February 5, 1965.

29. *New York Times*, June 25 and July 7, 9, and 10, 1948; *New York Herald-Tribune*, June 26 and July 7 and 10, 1948; "Chronology," *PDDE*, XI, 1564.

30. *New York Daily Mirror*, July 10, 1948; Harron, interview, February 5, 1965; Jacques Barzun, personal interview, April 5, 1979, New York, N. Y..

31. *New York Times*, December 16 and 18, 1948; *Columbia Spectator*, December 5, 1948; Jacobs, "Memoirs."

32. Fackenthal to Poland's Ambassador, Josep Winiewicz, May 5, 1948, CACU.

33. *New York Times*, June 1, July 12, 13, and 16, 1948, and July 17, 1974; *Newsweek*, July 19, 1948, p. 78; Jacobs, interview, February 5, 1965; Jacobs, "Memoirs."

34. Eisenhower to Louis Graham Smith, May 25, 1948, *PDDE*, X, 84-87.

35. Jacobs to Eisenhower, memorandum, July 15, 1948, CACU; Harron and Jacobs, interview, February 5, 1965.

36. Harron and Jacobs, interview, February 5, 1965; Press Release, "Masaryk Chair,' November 21, 1946, Jacobs MSS., Bentley Historical Library, Michigan Historical Collections (MHC); Jacobs, "Memoirs."

37. Commager had sent the editorial for Eisenhower's "entertainment," not his "edification." Eisenhower to Commager, July 29, 1948, *PDDE*, X, 170-71; *New York Times*, July 17 and August 2, 1948.

38. Eisenhower to Coleman, July 12, 1948, to Arthur Hays Sulzberger, July 27, 1948, and to Jacobs, July 27, 1948, *PDDE*, X, 139-41, 162-68; *New York Times,* July 13, 1948.

39. Eisenhower to Trustees, confidential, September 20, 1948, and Jacobs, confidential memo, July 31, 1948, CACU; Jacobs, interview, February 5, 1965.

40. *New York Times*, January 16, 1948. For some criticism of the dinner, see Ackerman to Carman, January 17, 1949, "Do *not* mail CWA," Ackerman MSS., LC.

41. Black, interview, June 6, 1973; Fackenthal, Oral History Interview, 1956, COHP; Raymond J. Saulnier, personal interview, June 13, 1991, New York, N. Y.; Jacobs, interview, February 5, 1965. For example, Fackenthal would ask Jacobs to "explain" the Associated Colleges of Upper New York to Eisenhower or to "give the General a little briefing on the Morningside Heights, Inc., since David Rockefeller wants to see him." Fackenthal to Jacobs, May 26 and June 14, 1948, CACU.

42. Jacobs, "Memoirs"; *New York Times*, February 11, 1948; *Columbia Spectator*, February 11, 12, 18 and March 5, 1948. Initially, six Trustees, including Fackenthal, urged a reconsideration of the increase.

43. *New York Times*, June 12, 1948. President William McGill of Columbia saw the Development Office memo in 1970 and exclaimed: "Migod, we have learned nothing! We are still on the same projects." Development Office memorandum, June 8, 1948, CACU.

44. Jacobs to Eisenhower, memoranda, July 14 and 15, 1948, CACU; Jacobs, interview, December 31, 1973,

45. Eisenhower to Jacobs, July 19, 1948, *PDDE*, X, 152-56.

46. Snyder, "Summary of Year 1948," Snyder MSS., DDEL; Ginzberg, tel. message for Eisenhower, July 29, 1948, and Jacobs to Ginzberg, July 31, 1948, Eisenhower MSS., DDEL; Ginzberg, interview, December 11, 1990.

47. Jacques Barzun, interview, April 5, 1979; Maxwell Taylor, *Swords and Plowshares* (New York, 1972), p. 116; Jacobs to Fackenthal, August 6, 1948, CACU; Jacobs, interview, February 5, 1965.

4

Launching His Columbia Crusade

To assign the university the mission of ever strengthening the foundations of our culture is to ennoble the institution and confirm the virtual importance of its service.

—Dwight D. Eisenhower,
Installation Address,
October 12, 1948

Columbia is aware that it must grow and improve to meet the needs of the nation and the world. This is the challenge facing President Eisenhower. No man is better suited to meet the challenge.

—*Columbia Spectator,*
October 12, 1948

Last spring when he stepped out of his role as America's First Soldier to accept appointment as head of one of the world's first universities, there may have been some who questioned whether such a transition could be made. President Eisenhower's future conduct of Columbia must provide the final answer. But his inaugural address shows that he has a clear grasp of his responsibilities. . . . In her new President Columbia has a valiant champion of the academic freedom that determines, in the final analysis, the stature of an institution of learning.

—*New York Times,*
Editorial,
October 13, 1948

The Eisenhowers left Denver by train after Labor Day weekend, and the train trip gave him time to think about the beginning of his first academic year at Columbia. He knew that his schedule would be extremely hectic and demanding, yet he had to have had a great sense of anticipation. As his private railroad car crossed the Great Plains to Chicago and on to New York, he looked forward to his Installation as the thirteenth President of Columbia, an occasion which offered an unparalleled opportunity to articulate his beliefs in a ceremony receiving worldwide publicity. He planned to present to the

University's Trustees, at his first meeting as President, an ambitious development plan and his proposals to reorganize the administration, so that under his leadership Columbia would "contribute markedly toward the perpetuation and strengthening of the American democracy."[1] He had initiated, moreover, during his first days at Columbia, a project on human resources with Professor Eli Ginzberg and, upon receiving Ginzberg's report in October, he anticipated taking the next steps toward a major study of the problem. Finally, his World War II memoirs, *Crusade in Europe*, eagerly awaited by the media and millions of Americans, would be published in November. Even though a presidential campaign was underway in 1948 and the popular general had remained aloof, the spotlight would continue to shine brilliantly on him that fall.

He had had, furthermore, his first extended vacation since before World War II. He had traveled to Vermont, Wisconsin, and Colorado; he had gone fishing in the San Luis Valley and the Colorado Rockies and played golf in Denver; and he had limited his public appearances to a minimum. He had held a press conference on his arrival in Denver, delivered a nationwide radio address for the United Nations Crusade for Children in mid-August, and made several appearances, all on August 31, for the Columbia Alumni Club of Colorado, a hospital dedication in honor of a World War II colleague, and a military review. He was well rested; he had been away from Low Memorial Library from July 17 to September 9, with the exception for three days in late July, and his vacation had not been interrupted by the University.[2]

The Columbia community also shared the sense of excitement as Eisenhower returned to the campus and opened the 195th academic year. He welcomed a capacity audience of students, faculty, and guests in McMillin Theater to the opportunity that the University offered with its "great faculty . . . to prepare yourselves for effective citizenship in the greatest of all free democracies. . . . That, to my mind, is the greatest ambition any American can hope for." As the *Columbia Spectator* noted, the famed "Eisenhower grin" was evident, and afterwards he talked informally with the student body of Columbia College. The next day he addressed the students at Barnard, the first formal opening exercises at the women's college since its founding. In introducing President Eisenhower, Dean Millicent McIntosh saw the University as "entering upon a new period" and being "fortunate" with its new leader.[3]

A week later, at Columbia's first all-College assembly since the outbreak of the war, Eisenhower delivered his first speech to the undergraduates. Dean Carman conducted the ceremony and introduced the President, who acknowledged that Columbia was far from his vision of "some nice, secluded, undergraduate college—maybe out in the hills of Pennsylvania or Virginia." He was glad, he added, to learn from the Dean that "the very heart of this University was composed of Columbia College" and that he could "at least revise my old ambitions sufficiently to impose upon you . . . one brief meeting where we could get together." He emphasized to the students that "you have not been given the facilities here that you deserve." Specifically, he mentioned the condition of the gymnasium, Baker Field's inadequacy, and the lack of a student center for the College. The *Spectator*, in a front-page editorial, found "most encouraging" the words of Eisenhower and Carman. "What both speakers repeatedly emphasized was that Columbia has not forgotten that its undergraduate students must grow and mature in more than an intellectual sense. The spiritual, social, non-academic functions of Columbia must rank with the scholastic standards it so proudly claims."[4]

Earlier, on Saturday the 20th, he had gone to Washington to participate in a conference at the Pentagon and meet with Secretary of Defense James Forrestal, and at the strong urging of Dean Carman and Provost Jacobs he had returned to New York in time to attend that evening the traditional dinner for freshmen in John Jay Hall. Six hundred students heard Dean Carman, New York District Attorney Frank S. Hogan, the president of the Alumni Association, and the well-known football Coach Lou Little extend their "heartiest welcome." The *Spectator* called the dinner "the most outstanding of its kind since World War II" and reported that the General arrived as "the 'inanimate' guest-football which bore the inscription, Columbia 21-Army 20" was being introduced. The previous fall at Baker Field Columbia, with a spectacular fourth quarter and sensational catches, had ended Army's record of thirty-two games without a defeat. Eisenhower, whose collegiate football career at West Point had been cut short by a serious knee injury, referred to the big upset and stated, "If Army had to lose its winning streak I'm glad it was to Columbia. Future battles, however, are not won by calling attention to bygone victories. Let us all look ahead."[5]

In the opening weeks of the academic year the University saw that it had an energetic, charismatic President. His enthusiasm and his pleasure in talking with students were obvious, and his presence infused a vitality and a spirit of optimism unknown on Morningside Heights since the heyday of Nicholas Murray Butler. Commenting that Columbia's new leader "is different than" Frank Fackenthal or Butler "and one cannot go into Low Memorial Library without realizing the somewhat changed atmosphere," Carman observed, "His marvelous smile, humor, humility, downright honesty, and great wisdom combine to make him an almost perfect fit for mid-twentieth century Columbia."[6] Dramatically, the University had regained momentum, and neither Columbia nor its new President, moreover, had to worry about the distractions of presidential politics.

It was an auspicious beginning that September for the eminent institution approaching its bicentennial in 1954, and Eisenhower's actions those first few weeks sharply illustrated the different atmosphere and the prominent attention he brought to his new position. On September 17 he went up to Baker Field at 218th Street and Broadway to watch the Columbia football team practice, and he was photographed with Lou Little, who had been offered a few months earlier the coaching position at Yale. Little had been at Columbia since 1930, and in 1934 his team had scored a stunning upset over Stanford in the Rose Bowl. Eisenhower and Little, in fact, had met on the football field in 1924 as rivals, when Eisenhower was coaching the III Army Corps team and Little's Georgetown University team won by a point.

In February, 1948, before the General had left Washington, Columbia alumni had given him "the mission of saving Lou for the University." Two prominent alumni, General William Donovan, the Director of the Office of Strategic Services during World War II, and District Attorney Frank Hogan, took Little down to Fort Myer to see Ike. Columbia's President-designate personally appealed to the coach, asserting, "Lou, you cannot do this to me. You're one of the reasons I am going to Columbia." Little, somewhat flustered, asked for some time and then the two reminisced for awhile. The coach returned to his hotel room and, as Eisenhower soon learned, called his wife in New York and said, "Stop packing. We're not going." The story quickly circulated and became famous on Morningside Heights; that fall a Columbia law school alumnus wrote, "You never will, in your entire time as president of the university, do anything which will elicit more universal approval."[7] On September 25 Eisenhower saw Columbia defeat Rutgers 27-6 in the opening game at Baker Field.

The *New York Times* reported that "a famed new rooter" joined 28,000 fans in "the largest gathering" to watch the launching of a new season. At half-time the Rutgers marching band had spelled "IKE" in front of the Columbia stands.[8]

More publicity came, some from entirely different, and surprising, fronts. At Mamie Eisenhower's urging, the General was one of a hundred notables who contributed a painting for an auction to benefit the Urban League Service Fund. It occupied a place of honor, as did Winston Churchill's "View of the City Gate of Marrakech," painted after World War II's Casablanca Conference and presented to President Franklin D. Roosevelt. While still at Fort Myer, Eisenhower had been fascinated as he watched Thomas E. Stephens begin a portrait of Mamie. The General, Schulz recalled, was encouraged by Stephens "to try his hand . . . at painting Mrs. Eisenhower. He had a lot of fun doing it." That evening Mamie asked Schulz to get "some canvases . . . framed, and an easel, not a beginner's set but a starter's set of oil paints," and it was her Valentine's Day gift. As Eisenhower wrote in *At Ease*, he found "the attempt to paint absorbing." His painting for the show was a copy of a painting and, a newspaper noted, "The general's head of an Indian in a broad-rimmed hat against a pale sky holds the colors of the sun-bleached rocks and the purple shadows of the West." A photograph of it appeared in newspapers and "brought a lot of attention" to the New York exhibit. His artistic effort sold for $2,600.[9] Meanwhile, he had flown to Corning, New York, for the opening ceremonies of a new memorial stadium, and he had addressed 10,000 persons; he had gone to Grand Central Station for dedication of the new Twentieth Century Limited, a New York-Chicago train; he had received from Ethiopia's Minister to the United States an award from the Emperor of Ethiopia, Haile Selassie I, for his wartime leadership; and Governor Dewey had sent him a "DDE" car license plate, "the only three-letter private license plate in the State."[10]

Then near the end of September he made one of his remarkable speaking appearances at the Jewish Theological Seminary of America, a neighboring institution on Morningside Heights. He had had a busy day in Low Memorial, with discussions ranging from the Russian Institute to the publication of *Crusade in Europe* and meetings with Dean of Faculty Pegram and Trustee Chairman Coykendall. He also had written a long letter to Secretary Forrestal about "the prospects" for Soviet-American relations looking "darker . . . than they have yet."[11] He had, consequently, had no time to read the notes Kevin McCann had prepared for his talk at the convocation opening the Seminary's sixty-second year. He had asked Provost Jacobs to accompany him and, just before they were to leave, he called McCann into his office and asked, "What did you say about the 'seed of Abraham'?" McCann told him in a couple of sentences, and the President and Provost, as they walked the few blocks to the Seminary, talked casually and arrived a few minutes before the ceremonies began.

David Sarnoff, the president of RCA, welcomed Eisenhower, "an eminent American—our neighbor on Morningside Heights." Then former New York Governor Herbert H. Lehman, Chairman of the Seminary's Board, honored Eisenhower as a "beloved counsellor of our people in peace as in war," and the Seminary's President, Doctor Louis Finkelstein, conferred the honorary degree. "Dictators" would have us believe "that men are merely animals," Eisenhower told the audience of 400 persons, "but we believe that because men have each been born with a soul they have inalienable rights and none can take them away. These rights can never be destroyed." He continued. "That belief came from the ancient Jewish leaders. They taught and gave their lives in this belief." Specifically, "they taught us that although man is made of the dust of the earth, having had the breath of life breathed into him, he is a living soul. On this belief," the General asserted, "is based the doctrine that the American army fought to defend. In this sense all the free world is the seed of Abraham, Moses and the ancient kings." Then, "admitting the need for theological seminaries . . . and the necessity for giving this education to teachers," he said "we must grant their right to designate themselves, as in this instance, 'Jewish.'" But, "except for some such limited use as this," he concluded, "my hope is that in the future development of this country . . . the day will come when in speaking of an American there will be no reason for applying a qualitative adjective of any kind." With these words Columbia's President expressed sentiments in striking contrast to those of his predecessor, Nicholas Murray Butler. Years later Provost Jacobs would still recall with admiration that Eisenhower had delivered "a brilliant address without a note."[12]

During this period, as he began planning for his first official Trustees meeting and preparing his Installation speech, the General increasingly worried about the deterioration in Soviet-American relations. Negotiations to lift the Soviet blockade of Berlin, and thereby end the Allied airlift to the city, had collapsed, and he found the news "completely depressing." In his letter to Forrestal he had hoped that "the very existence of this critical problem" should make "your task of coordinating the several fighting services" easier. The interservice rivalry between the Army, Navy, and Air Force, unfortunately, had not been solved by the National Security Act of 1947, and discussions during 1948 over the forthcoming defense budget had intensified the disagreements. "I believe that the time has come," he wrote to Forrestal, "when everyone must begin to think in terms of his possible future duty and be as fully prepared for its performance as is possible."[13] The Secretary, who during the summer had called two top-ranking officers out of retirement and had considered ordering Eisenhower back to active duty, immediately thanked the General for his "thoughts." A few days later, when the Russians denounced the American proposal for the control of atomic weapons, Eisenhower added that he had been "desperately hanging onto a period of three or four days" in late October to go to Washington. He emphasized the "great gravity" of the situation, because "I believe that our diplomatic opponents have finally demonstrated their intention of avoiding any path that might lead to even partial settlement of our differences." He concluded this letter, shortly before his first Trustees Meeting on October 4, by telling the Secretary, "I shall always answer to any quick call, and there are very few days indeed that I could not cancel out all engagements and rush down for a talk."[14]

That afternoon the Board of Trustees meeting was one of those days. In July he had invited the Trustees to a stag dinner at 60 Morningside. Fourteen attended, and many of them had their first opportunity to view and hear the General describe some of his cherished World War II mementos. During the evening they discussed informally "a number of affairs of interest to the University," including development and organization plans and a compulsory retirement proposal. After the meeting he reported to the Provost in detail what he had said, and he instructed Jacobs to examine the matters "intensively" so that the two of them could discuss the proposals in September and he would be prepared for the October 4th meeting.[15]

Administrative reorganization and a vast development program were, undoubtedly, among the least exciting matters he considered during the busy September weeks, but they were, also, most pressing if he were to launch successfully his crusade for youth and citizenship. During World War II he had created a unified command system for the Allies, overcoming extremely complex problems.[16] On the eve of his Installation he probably assumed the Board's support for his plans, since he already had discussed his proposals with the Trustees in general terms. The General would ruefully discover, however, that the system at a university was entirely different, if equally complex, and that many Trustees might not realize how vital a matter was or know enough about how the University worked to see the necessity for prompt action. The adoption of a proposal which Eisenhower considered important often took much longer than he had anticipated.

The issue of a compulsory retirement plan demonstrated some of the difficulties. The University did not have an automatic plan, and he had suggested that "administrative personnel should be retired at something like 65 or 66 and teaching personnel at something like 68." Over the summer a special committee, appointed by Jacobs, essentially recommended the age of sixty-eight for everyone appointed by the Trustees. President Eisenhower sent this report to the Board, adding, "I intend at the proper time to urge certain changes in these recommendations." When the Provost prepared material for Eisenhower for the October meeting, he reminded him of the committee's recommendation and stated, "You desire 65 or 66 for members of administrative staff." It was not until the spring of 1949, however, that the Trustees agreed, effective in 1950, that academics retire at sixty-eight and administrators at sixty-five; by that time Eisenhower had voluntarily bound himself to retirement at sixty-five and wanted to enact a compulsory retirement plan for Trustees.[17]

Nor did the Board, which had met earlier for luncheon at the Faculty Club, act on reorganization. Doug Black's Special Committee had recommended the establishment of two Vice Presidents, one in charge of business affairs and the other in charge of development, but had not made an overall proposal. The University's operations had been divided "into three relatively distinct factions—business, development, and education" and the Committee emphasized "the dominance of education." It foresaw, consequently, a senior Vice President of the University whose "principal task would be educational" and who would "act for the President in the event of the latter's disability or absence." Jacobs had made a similar proposal in July, which Eisenhower had supported. Since the two proposed positions required an amendment to the University's Statutes and "the more complex problem" in the educational area required "much study" before a formal proposal, the Trustees "laid over" reorganization for another meeting.[18]

By this time it already had been a long meeting for the Trustees, who had not met since May. They had had to endorse the many actions of several committees, including the establishment of the Bancroft Prizes (one of the awards went to Allan Nevins for *The Ordeal of the Union*, the first two volumes of what would become his monumental eight-volume history of the Civil War), and the approval of an extra appropriation for the overrun on the renovations and redecorating of 60 Morningside and the new Low Memorial offices for the President and his staff. They had discussed a variety of issues—the *Minutes* would contain well over two hundred typewritten pages—from Eisenhower's report on the amount of gifts received by the University to Professor John Krout's detailed report on the preparations for Eisenhower's Installation.[19]

A development plan and fund-raising had been a top priority at his dinner with the Trustees in July, and he had stated "that it was quite necessary for the period of talk begin to come to an end and the period of action take over." The University's "serious financial condition"—Eisenhower emphasized that Albert W. Putnam, Chairman of the Trustees Finance Committee, "unqualifiedly describes the situation as dangerous"—would dominate much of Low Memorial's thinking during 1948-1949. The operating deficit for the previous year had been over one million dollars with "a probable deficit of $1,444,900.70 as of June 30, 1949." As Putnam noted, until necessary funds could be raised, "it is equally important that everyone should practice the strictest economy consistent with carrying out our present work effectively." Eisenhower, in fact, earlier had emphasized "the present effort for the maximum reduction in current expenditure" in a memorandum "To Deans, Departmental Officers, and Administrative Officers."[20]

The Board endorsed on October 4, not surprisingly, the proposals for a development program with the goal of raising over $200,000,000 by 1954, the Bicentennial. Black had presented for the Development Committee a masterful eighteen-page statement, discussing all facets of the University from its "Cultural Foundation" to its contributions and role in the community, its professional staff and students, and its facilities and educational program. The

Committee's "primary recommendation" was "the maintenance and improvement of the excellence of the University staff and parallel with this careful selection of the best students." So that "Columbia University will continue to press forward," the Committee recommended major improvements to the physical plant from laboratory equipment to Butler Library, the construction of a gymnasium and student center, the reconstruction of Baker Field, for faculty "the assurance of adequate housing with good neighborhood schools," and the expansion of several major academic programs and schools.[21]

The report emphasized that "Columbia stands at the gateway to the United States." While it saw no need to recall that for decades foreign dignitaries had first visited Columbia and Nicholas Murray Butler when they came to America, it noted that "Since the United Nations began deliberations at Lake Success, more than ever before Columbia University had become aware of its key geographic position." It envisioned "the gradually developing contacts between the various secretariats" of the U.N. and the University staff; it was unnecessary to add that General Eisenhower's presence on Morningside Heights would serve as a magnet for foreign leaders and publicity. Indeed, the report closely linked together Columbia's "gateway position," the development program, and Ike Eisenhower.[22]

"Columbia, With Inauguration of Eisenhower," a headline in the next Sunday's *New York Times* read, "Will Launch A Vast Development Plan." With the General's Installation, Benjamin Fine, the paper's education editor, wrote that Columbia would "enter a new era of educational development . . . the most ambitious expansion program ever undertaken by any college or university." Eisenhower explained that he had participated in preparing the program, which included a long-range building plan. The project, though, called for much more: a major scholarship program, a dynamic arts center, an expanded role for Teachers College "in its service to the nation in the field of education," expansion for the medical and law schools, and the beginning of the Graduate School of Business. "Columbia," Eisenhower asserted, "must develop men and women who will be effective, responsible and unselfish citizens of this democracy." Fine observed, "It is almost staggering" to watch the launching of what might well be a quarter-billion-dollar educational project. The *Times'* editor concluded, "The effect on all colleges and universities throughout the country should be salutary. Columbia University has implicit faith in the future of the democratic way of life."[23]

That weekend Eisenhower and Columbia completed preparations for his Installation on Tuesday. He welcomed family members to 60 Morningside and fought to recover from a bad cold, which had forced him to cancel all engagements from Wednesday through Saturday, including a speech at the Federation of Jewish Philanthropies Dinner. The previous weekend Milton Eisenhower had cleared three days to come to New York and give "such help as you think I can" on the Installation speech. That same weekend Ike had been invited to play bridge by Ely Culbertson, the international bridge authority. Eisenhower, an excellent player who would make opportunities to find a good game and frequently discussed bridge hands in his correspondence, explained facetiously to Culbertson, "I am working on a world-shaking address for my forthcoming inauguration." He added that he had "help on those two evenings with a man whose judgment and ability I value highly."[24]

Columbia had offered him a public forum in the cultural and business center of the world and, while he was not an academic and made no pretense to be one, a strong speech could show his ability and determination to lead the great University. It could, moreover, convey his passionate concerns about the challenge America faced in the growing Cold War. Columbia, furthermore, had given him in his first few months on Morningside Heights some important issues to discuss, such as academic freedom.

The two brothers, working closely with McCann that weekend, were determined to take the opportunity to launch his crusade for democratic citizenship, and undoubtedly they discussed his communications with Forrestal. As Eisenhower soon reflected, "I attempted nothing more than to outline what I believe to be a few of the important guideposts that we must observe if we are to steer a straight course."[25] He would have an audience of nearly twenty thousand persons, unless rain forced the ceremonies to move into the Cathedral of St. John the Divine, a few blocks from the campus, and they would include representatives from universities throughout the nation and the world and prominent dignitaries from many governments.

Officials arranged carefully for this great occasion. Professor Kirk, who had been asked by Fackenthal to chair the planning committee, recommended either a small, in-house ceremony, a modest one with some guests, or a large one with representatives from all major universities and prominent dignitaries. Kirk met regularly with

Sulzberger's corresponding Trustee Committee—because of Colonel Schulz and McCann, he recalled, he was "never allowed to go over any of the plans with DDE personally"—and the Trustees "opted for the big show." To accommodate the extensive media coverage, a special stand was built on the Kent Hall side of the rostrum for television cameras, movie cameras, and photographers.[26]

The official ceremonies began Monday evening, following an afternoon rehearsal. The Eisenhowers and Coykendalls gave a formal, three-hour buffet reception in the Rotunda of Low Memorial for two thousand invited guests, and special exhibits of Columbiana had been arranged in the Rotunda's display cases. During a break in greeting the University's guests Mamie Eisenhower was heard to say "I'm not going to put up with this, I'm getting tired," but she returned to the receiving line. On Tuesday Eisenhower spent several hours in the office before a buffet luncheon for 125 family and friends at 60 Morningside. Because of the huge crowd arriving for the Installation, he was escorted to Butler Library at one-thirty and his family left for their front-row seats. The University had allocated some 6,500 tickets to students, 4,500 to alumni, 1,300 to faculty, 1,000 to non-academic staff, and 5,700 to guests. Finally, after the ceremonies Dean Philip Young would give a reception at the Faculty Club for the academic representatives, the Trustees, and University officers, and the Eisenhowers would give a cocktail party for 150 guests at their house. "President Eisenhower comes to us at a critical moment," the *Columbia Spectator* asserted on the morning of the Installation. "Columbia is aware that it must grow and improve to meet the needs of the nation and the world. This is the challenge facing President Eisenhower. No man is better suited to meet that challenge."[27]

An extra intensity must have infused the General on October 12 as he reviewed his speech. President Truman, in the midst of a "whistle-stop" campaign tour in his up-hill battle against Governor Dewey, had declared in a telegram, "The sense of moral and spiritual values which made you invincible in war will inspire and guide you as you assume the leadership in one of our great American institutions of learning." Earlier, Eisenhower had heard from Forrestal, who had talked with Truman, and the Secretary wanted to know when the General would be in Washington, so "we can talk fundamentals: Policy, budget, and our whole military-diplomatic position." The President concluded his message, "I know you will rise to the opportunity for continued public service which becomes yours today."[28]

The tolling of bells in St. Paul's Chapel began shortly before two o'clock on Tuesday, October 12, and the gray, overcast skies could not mute the richly colored robes and gowns of distinguished scholars and educators from throughout the country and world.[29] Between the great columns of Low Memorial hung pendant blue banners, and other University buildings were decked with blue-and-white banners and the Stars and Stripes. The main academic procession, paced by processional music, marched solemnly in double file through the middle of the audience from Butler Library north across South Field and South Court and climbed the stone steps to the platform in front of Alma Mater and Low Memorial. Dignitaries from the world's oldest universities—Bologna, Oxford, Paris, Cambridge, and Florence—led the procession, and representatives from over three hundred American universities and colleges followed, including Harvard's James Conant, Yale's Charles Seymour, Pennsylvania's Harold Stassen, and Princeton's Harold Dodds, and some two hundred other presidents. The President and Provost, followed only by the mace-bearer and Chairman Coykendall, walked last. Before reaching the platform they passed Mamie, John, and Barbara Eisenhower; Eisenhower's four brothers, with President Milton Eisenhower representing Kansas State and Edgar Eisenhower the College of Puget Sound, attended, as did many of the General's prominent World War II colleagues.[30]

Soon the Installation began, and Coykendall rose for the traditional presentation of the University's Charter and Keys to the new President. As he said, "I also hand you these keys symbolic of the open doors of all our academic buildings for the care and use of which you are now responsible," the sun burst through the clouds and blue skies appeared. A reporter wrote that "the cloud rack dispersed. Skylike blue water showed through the openings. The sun hit on edges of cloud. It burnished the crown and eagle perched on the flagpoles." As Eisenhower grasped "the giant-size ring with the giant-size keys, the sun pounced on them and set them afire."[31]

"My heart is torn with doubt," President Eisenhower began, that my words can "convey anything of the intensity of my sincerity. . . . This gathering" of Columbia's friends convincingly demonstrates "universal respect for this university as a fruitful agent in the promotion of human knowledge and human welfare." He asserted, "I am privileged to participate in this ceremony. If this were a land where the military profession is a weapon of tyranny or aggression—its members an elite caste dedicated to its own perpetuation—a life-long soldier could hardly assume my present role." In America "the army is the servant of the people. . . . Duty in its ranks is an exercise of citizenship." Thus, "the soldier who becomes an educator . . . finds himself . . . engaged in a new phase of his fundamental life purpose—the protection and the perpetuation of basic human freedoms."

"Today's challenge to freedom and to every free institution," he declared, "is such that none of us dares stand alone. . . . All must be joined in a common profession—that of democratic citizenship; every institution within our national structure must contribute to the advancement of this profession. . . . Democratic citizenship is concerned with the sum total of human relations. . . . The educational system, therefore, can scarcely impose any logical limit upon its functions and responsibilities." There is "one immutable, incontestable fact . . . those who know our way of life place upon one thing greater value than upon any other—and that priceless thing is individual liberty." This "freedom has been won" but it is essential to "be ever alert to all threats to that freedom. . . . Thus, one danger arises from too great a concentration of power in the hands of any individual or group: The power of concentrated finance, the power of selfish pressure groups, the power of any class organized in opposition to the whole—any one of these, if allowed to dominate is fully capable of destroying individual freedom as is excessive power concentrated in the political head of state. . . . A paternalistic government can gradually destroy, by suffocation in the immediate advantage of subsidy, the will of a people to maintain a high degree of individual responsibility."

"It follows," he continued, "that every institution built by free men, including great universities, must be first of all concerned with the preservation and further development of human freedom—despite any contrary philosophy, or force that may be pitted against it. At all levels of education, we must be constantly watchful that our schools do not become so engrossed in techniques, great varieties of fractionalized courses, highly specialized knowledge, and the size of the physical plant as to forget the principal purpose of education itself—to prepare the student for effective personal and social life in a free society. From the school at the crossroads to a university as great as Columbia, general education for citizenship must be the common and first purpose of them all. I do not suggest less emphasis on pure research or on vocational or professional training; nor by any means am I suggesting that curricula should be reduced to the classical education of the nineteenth century. But I deeply believe that all of us must demand of our schools more emphasis on those fundamentals that make our free society what it is and that assure it boundless increase in the future if we comprehend and live by them. . . . There is a growing doubt among our people that democracy is able to cope with the social and economic trials that lie ahead. Among some is a stark fear that our way of life may succumb to the combined effects of creeping paralysis from within and aggressive assault from without. . . . Only by education in the apparently obvious can doubt and fear be resolved. . . . To assign the university the mission of ever strengthening the foundations of our culture is to ennoble the institution and confirm the vital importance of its service. . . . Dependence by the country upon the schools for this vital service implies no infringement of academic freedom."

As he neared the end of his twenty-minutes address, he declared, "There will be no administrative suppression or distortion of any subject that merits a place in this University's curricula. The facts of communism, for example, shall be taught here—its ideological development, its political methods, its economic effects, its probable course in the future. The truth about communism is today an indispensable requirement if the true values of our democratic system are to be properly assessed. Ignorance of communism, fascism, or any other police-state philosophy is far more dangerous than ignorance of the most virulent disease. Who among us can doubt the choice of future Americans, as between statism and freedom, if the truth concerning each be constantly held before their eyes? But if we, as adults, attempt to hide from the young the facts in this world struggle, not only will we be making a futile attempt to establish an intellectual 'iron curtain,' but we will arouse the lively suspicion that statism possesses virtues whose persuasive effect we desperately fear."

"The American university," he argued, has a responsibility to the community. It "does not operate in an unreal world of its own, concerned solely with the abstract," and the "preservation of the American way . . . demands a working partnership between universities and all other free institutions. . . . Partnership is the proof and product of unity."

"Columbia University," he concluded, "will forever be bound by its loyalty to truth and the basic concepts of democratic freedom." From Columbia will come scholars, statesmen, skilled professionals, and great leaders in every area, "but Columbia shall count it failure, whatever their success, if they are not all their lives a leaven of better citizenship. . . . My personal dedication is in the manner of my illustrious predecessors . . . to devote my energies to the support of Columbia's able and distinguished faculty, in the service of America, in the service of all humanity."[32]

The huge crowd gave Ike an enthusiastic ovation, and the impressive Installation ceremonies came to an end as the audience stood for the University's choir singing of "Stand, Columbia!" and the benediction. Then President Eisenhower, following the mace-bearer, led the main procession back across the campus to Butler Library with the sun still shining on Morningside Heights.[33]

That evening Edward R. Murrow reported on CBS News that Eisenhower, among "the colorful robes and hoods of the Universities of Rome, Oxford, Paris, San Marcos, Iran and all the rest," at first "seemed rather out of place in that colorful academic setting." And, when he began speaking, "you realized that this was something considerably out of the ordinary for a speech by a College President. Here was no display of synthetic erudition, no labored effort to be complicated." Eisenhower, the prominent broadcaster declared, was "laying it on the line, so that all could understand." Murrow played recorded excerpts of the General talking about the danger "from too great a concentration of power," his explaining the University's principal task to emphasize "those fundamentals that make our society free," and his making his position clear that "the facts of communism . . . shall be taught here." It was, according to Murrow, "quite a speech. . . . Those words, spoken in the Cold War atmosphere by a lesser man would have produced the cry of 'subversive' or 'un-American' in some well-advertised quarters. That charge is not likely to be leveled against Eisenhower." Murrow did not "pretend to know" whether Eisenhower would be successful at Columbia, "but his record shouts that he is a man who means what he says; and it is possible to conclude that those who believe in academic freedom have this day secured a very powerful ally."[34]

Others shared Murrow's assessment. The *New York Daily Mirror* described the speech as "a long and brilliant inaugural address before one of the greatest assemblages of world educators in this city since the turn of the century." For *Newsweek*, "There had never been anything quite like it in the 194-year history of Columbia University," and certainly there never had been anything like it on television. Eisenhower had made the occasion "unique," and the magazine emphasized that he had "pledged to defend what Alma Mater stood for as vigorously in peace as he had in a victorious war." "The traditions of that great university are in safe hands," the *New York Times* asserted. Columbia has "a valiant champion of the academic freedom that determines, in the final analysis, the stature of an institution of learning." Eisenhower's address, the *Times* added, "shows that he has a clear grasp of his responsibilities," and the "inauguration was an auspicious beginning. It suggests that, in rising to it, he will not only win for himself distinction in a new field, but will insure for Columbia continued primacy among the world's most famous and ancient universities." From Washington, Supreme Court Justice Felix Frankfurter wrote, "How can I avoid applauding when the head of a great university proposes to save this democracy through candid and truthful education!" Even the late Nicholas Murray Butler, *Newsweek* suggested, "seemed to feel that the irresistible Eisenhower could replace the irreplaceable Butler."[35] As the elaborate ceremonies came to an end, few were questioning Columbia's greatness or her bright future under Eisenhower.

His whirlwind schedule continued. The next day he visited the Brookhaven National Laboratory; on October 14—his fifty-eighth birthday—he attended the New York Board of Trade anniversary dinner at the Waldorf; and the following day he traveled to Albany for an honorary degree from the University of the State of New York. Back in the city, on Saturday morning he participated in the dedication of the Riverdale Country School's new site overlooking the Hudson River in the Bronx, and twelve hundred persons heard him stress that "Education for peace is more than ever necessary" and "An American school which welcomes students from other lands takes a vital step in this direction."[36]

From Riverdale he went directly to Columbia's Homecoming ceremonies at Baker Field where he welcomed 2,000 alumni. Declaring that it was important for future graduates "to be tied with affection" to Columbia, he asserted, "If we want a field house badly on this site, we can get it. We can get more material for Lou Little and then we wouldn't be wondering whether we were going to beat those fellows." The opposition that afternoon—"those fellows"—was the University of Pennsylvania, and on the way from his talk to the stands and during the game he was besieged for autographs. As much as he loved football, henceforth he often would arrive late and leave early to avoid being disruptive. Some 35,000 fans, many undoubtedly prompted to attend by the opportunity to see Ike, watched the game, which Pennsylvania won with only thirty-two seconds remaining.

Homecoming "climaxed with a big social affair in John Jay in honor of General and Mrs. Eisenhower," Dean Carman wrote. "The whole first floor of John Jay was converted into Central Park even to the zoo and the animals! . . . At 12:30 midnight the Eisenhowers departed in a hansom cab which the boys had arranged for. It really was a great evening for all."[37] Not surprisingly, a *New York Times* staff member in early November wrote that "General Eisenhower has taken Columbia the way he took the Normandy beach. . . the entire university population of 35,000—students, professors, officers, trustees and janitors—has happily surrendered and adores its conqueror." The article glowed with praise, emphasizing Ike's charm, energy, and leadership abilities and stressing that "the five-star president devotes a fourteen-hour day to the complex needs of his job." The *Spectator's* Max Frankel wrote that "articles on Columbia activities in the nation's publications are becoming the rule rather than the exception."[38]

"My schedule has been terribly overcrowded for the past two weeks," Eisenhower told Doug Black in mid-October, "and the week ahead shows little promise of improvement." Columbia commitments constituted many of the demands on his schedule; in addition to his regular office appointments on the day he wrote to Black, he attended the opening of the Institute of Arts and Sciences in McMillin Theater. The next day he presided over his first University Council meeting, where all the faculties were represented. "Ladies and Gentlemen, I understand that the tradition is that there is no smoking in this room. We will have very short meetings." He "rifled" through the agenda with no discussion, Dean Carman recalled. "He applied an Army technique and the sad thing about it from my point of view is that, while he was doing this, he was nevertheless conscious that something was wrong, and I've often wished I'd had a camera to have had the expressions on the faces of the members of that Council. . . . They were just dumb founded." The Dean added, "It always had been so smoothly handled, you know." Jacobs recorded that the

President "did not do well," and henceforth the Provost "took over his duties in this regard." ("I remember him complaining," McCann stated, "about some of the stuffed shirts on the faculty who seemed to be, well, trying to show him up.")[39]

The following day he toured with Jacobs and McCann a former Army camp, Shanks Village, which had been renovated for housing for some 1,500 Columbia veterans and their families. He had written a short article, based on McCann's draft, for the October *Reader's Digest*, and a second article would appear in February; the $25,000 he received for each went for a scholarship fund. Yet, many appearances in October and early November were not Columbia related, from a Boy Scouts of America meeting at the Biltmore Hotel to luncheon and dinner engagements at the Waldorf. "He is a great worker," Carman observed, "and has permitted himself to become overloaded with commitments for speeches and addresses . . . no human can long endure that kind of schedule."[40]

While Eisenhower's office was flooded with requests for personal appearances—and many were declined—it is not clear why McCann and Schulz permitted so many off-campus speaking engagements and appearances. His Installation Address had conveyed a commitment to Columbia University, and that October—with Governor Dewey still heavily favored to defeat Truman for the Presidency— the likelihood of a political future for the General was minimal; moreover, pressing University issues, particularly finances and an overdue reorganization of the administration, demanded attention. McCann and Schulz before coming to Columbia had long tried to keep the pressure from him, but they now allowed his calendar to be full, and often it seemed at the expense of the Columbia community. Grayson Kirk, for example, had been denied appointments with Eisenhower to go over the Installation ceremonies. More damaging, they had refused to allow Robert Livingston Schuyler, who had delivered the faculty's welcome at the Installation, to see the President. The professor wondered if the General might address the graduate students in the large historiography class and discuss the historians and books he liked. Twice Schulz, saying that "the President didn't have time for anything like that," turned away the professor. As the Provost wrote, McCann and Schulz, whose office was between his and the President's, set themselves up "as a screen to keep the President from persons. This they did most effectively, with the result that the faculty felt they could not get to the President." Helen King put it bluntly. A long-time secretary at the University, she had been asked to work in the President's office, and "nine times out of ten," when she set up an appointment, "Schulz would—as he said—'Kill it.'"[41]

Professor Schuyler, frustrated in his attempts to see Eisenhower, finally mentioned the difficulty to R. Gordon Hoxie, a Ph.D. candidate he knew in the Faculty of Political Science and the Provost's assistant. Hoxie noted that the President, "everyday at high noon, and he is so punctual just like it's D-Day Invasion," left his office "and marches down the steps and over to 60 Morningside Drive." Hoxie suggested that Schulyer should be walking one noon from Fayerweather Hall toward the steps in front of Low Memorial and cross paths with the President. The next day Schulyer did exactly that and Eisenhower, as he left the office, saw "the fair figure of Professor Schuyler . . . and he waved and you could almost hear it echo off Butler Library." "Oh, Professor Schuyler," he said, "I've been wanting to meet you and tell you what a wonderful oration you gave at my Inauguration and to ask you whether there is anything I could ever do for you." "Well," Schuyler replied, "as a matter of fact there is. Would you come and address the historiography class?" Eisenhower agreed and, McCann recalled, "jumped in with both feet and made out a list of books he wanted to go through and asked me to get them from Butler Library. . . . He was working with the books spread all over his desk." Hoxie, who attended the lecture, reflected that Eisenhower "spoke with passion and deep knowledge about two of the college's most illustrious former students, Alexander Hamilton and John Jay," and Eisenhower "made such a big hit with those students." This particular appearance may have been a popular success; nonetheless, stories about the President's inaccessibility gained currency on Morningside Heights.[42]

McCann and Schulz kept Eisenhower's calendar free for late October, and he and Mamie left for Washington on the 27th. For three days he attended conferences with Forrestal, the three Chiefs of Staff, and other top defense leaders. While he had stressed "the importance of a united front on the security establishment," the impending presidential election occupied everyone in the capital. Public opinion polls continued to give Dewey a comfortable lead over the President and predicted a change in the nation's leadership, which would mean not only the White House but also Cabinet and sub-Cabinet positions would change. In this situation, few officials contemplated long-term planning. The Eisenhowers stayed over for the weekend to see old friends, and Ike played several rounds of golf at Burning Tree with George Allen, Bill Robinson, and Clifford Roberts, and in the evenings they played bridge.[43]

He flew back to New York Monday in time for a morning tour of the Medical Center with Dean Rappleye and the November Board of Trustees Meeting, followed by a meeting of the Trustees' Development Committee. Afterwards, Eisenhower began drafting a long personal letter to each Trustee "in the hope of keeping the Trustees abreast of facts and plans affecting the University." It specifically addressed finances, development, reorganization, and the "urgent need for expanded facilities" to maintain Columbia's standards. The letter would undergo many versions, and Eisenhower carefully edited the final draft before sending it on November 17.[44]

Tuesday, November 2, was election day; during the previous week political activity had increased on the campus, and two presidential candidates had spoken. Irwin Edman, the popular and witty Professor of Philosophy, had introduced Norman Thomas, the Socialist Party leader, to students in McMillin. The *Spectator*, though, gave far more publicity to Henry A. Wallace's visit. Wallace, Franklin D. Roosevelt's Vice President during the war, had broken with the Truman Administration and the Democratic Party over its anti-Soviet Cold War policies and had formed the Progressive Party. Mark Van Doren, a Professor of English and a Pulitzer Prize winner, introduced Norman Mailer, author of the best-selling *The Naked and the Dead*, to the over-flowing crowd of 1,600 in McMillin. Then, declaring his support for Wallace, Van Doren asserted, "The Third Party, although not perfect, is some kind of an answer for the American people to promote better and more serious politics." The Progressive candidate warned his audience about the plans of Congressman J. Parnell Thomas and his House Committee on Un-American Activities to attack Columbia's curriculum and curb academic freedom. He believed, though, that "the purity of academic research is guaranteed here at Columbia" and that Eisenhower "will not fold up as some other university presidents have folded up before the extraordinary Thomas Committee."[45]

Later, Eisenhower, interested in the reaction to Wallace's appearance on campus, asked Bruce Wonnacott, his student driver who lived at the President's House for two years, "Have you talked to many of the kids about the Wallace visit?" "Well, quite a few,"

Wonnacott replied. "Some think he is a real 'Class A nut,' and there are other people who like his political notions, and then there are those who like his agricultural accomplishments." Eisenhower commented, as he would several other times to Wonnacott on his trips around the city, "Well, you know, it has been fascinating to talk with some of these kids. . . . They are wild raving radicals when they are here in school and they get a lot done and have fresh ideas. They graduate from college and in a couple of years they're conservative Republicans, and I've never figured this out. I think it is a great shame," he continued. "It has always disappointed me that there is this great fire you get in a school like this among so many of the kids and there is a process that starts upon graduation and getting a job and work and a lot of fire goes out of what they have."[46]

Eisenhower, himself, had avoided all political activity during the campaign, just as he had rejected political opportunities during the Eisenhower "boom" in 1948. Indeed, as Stephen Ambrose has concluded, "It stretches the truth, perhaps, but only slightly, to say that Eisenhower, in 1948, turned down the Presidency of the United States." Election night the golfing trio over the weekend in Washington joined him at 60 Morningside for dinner and bridge. During the summer he had discussed foreign affairs with the Republican candidate, and he assumed that Dewey would win and run for re-election in 1952. Eisenhower had, therefore, according to Roberts, "felt no sense of obligation to his country to respond" to the "overtures from politicians."[47]

During the evening it became apparent that the election might be close and that Truman had a chance of winning. George Allen, a Democrat, had pulled away from his party during the campaign and had not helped raise money for the President. As they played bridge, Roberts recalled, Allen "began to get not only excited but nervous as well because he had assumed there was no doubt . . . and he knew the General was not too happy about the Democrats that were in charge in Washington." Allen soon left the room to use the telephone and try to mend fences, while Roberts saw that Eisenhower was "just as disappointed as Robinson and I were." The General, indeed, had "a worried look . . . an unhappy man." Roberts began to wonder whether Eisenhower had made the right political decision for 1948; years later he was unable to remember Eisenhower's exact words that evening, but he thought that the General had "indicated quite clearly to me that he also was having second thoughts about his decision to stay clear of political involvement."[48]

Truman's amazing victory changed everything for Eisenhower; November 2 was the darkest night of Eisenhower's life, according to his son John. Suddenly, he was thrust back into the political spotlight, regardless of what he did or would do. The Republicans needed a strong candidate for 1952. Without referring to the election, Eisenhower wrote Forrestal on the 4th that he shared the Secretary's "concern over the state of world affairs" and concluded, "I can scarcely think of any chore that I would refuse to do wherever people in responsible positions feel that I might be able to help." Forrestal replied, "That was quite a day Tuesday," and a couple of days later he suggested to Truman that Ike be brought to Washington for three-to-four weeks to deal with the Joint Chiefs of Staff and the unification problem. When Eisenhower congratulated Truman on his "great victory," he reaffirmed his "loyalty to you as President" and repeated that he was always "ready to attempt the performance of any professional duty for which my constitutional superiors believe I might be specially suited." The President, replying that "I always know exactly where you stand," asked the General to see him on his next trip to Washington.[49]

Eisenhower had informed the Trustees at the November meeting that the demands on his time emphasized the importance of reorganization. He, nonetheless, continued to maintain a back-breaking schedule. On a Sunday evening he and Mrs. Eisenhower participated in a traditional hearth fire lighting ceremony on campus, and during this period he had dinner with Harvard's President Conant, attended an Academy of Political Science dinner downtown, and went to a number of events at the Faculty Club, from a luncheon for deans to a development program dinner and a junior faculty reception. He joined 35,000 fans at Baker Field and watched Columbia defeat Navy, 13-0. The capacity crowds—and General Eisenhower's presence—caused a problem for the police and prompted them regularly to go to him around seven minutes before the end of the game. He recalled: "The police come and say, 'General, we've got to get out of here ahead of the crowd, or we'll have a big jam at the gate and we'll be in trouble.'" "So," Eisenhower added, with a bit of a grumble, "I have to get up and follow them out, whether we're winning or whether we're losing; and, if we're losing, people probably say: 'Look at the General, leaving before the end of the game, guess he doesn't have much faith in his Columbia team.'"[50] Non-Columbia events, aside from office appointments, included the Chamber of Commerce of New York dinner at the Waldorf; an American Heritage Foundation trustee dinner; an address at a stag dinner of the New England Society, and an address when he became an honorary member of the Lawyers Club. He also attended the Army-Stanford football game at Yankee Stadium with Secretary of the Army Kenneth Royall and several generals. When Eisenhower declined an invitation, Trustee Sulzberger was delighted, "Frankly," the publisher of the *New York Times* wrote just before Thanksgiving, "I have been worried about the number of things you are taking on and all the speeches you have been called upon to make."[51]

A few days earlier Sulzberger and the other Trustees had received the long letter Eisenhower had been preparing and sent on November 17. Initially, the President bluntly stated: "The experience of the past year and the current one points to the inescapable truth that unless our income soon approximates the outgo, our situation will become precarious, if not desperate." Yet, there was, he emphasized, a limit to budget cutting before sacrificing "the quality and character of our educational system." This meant that the Development Program "requires the enthusiastic support of all of us."

Then, elaborating on the importance of reorganization, he wrote, "I have found it impossible to respond to legitimate public service, education and other important calls upon my time and simultaneously to give to University matters the attention they deserve." At 60 Morningside he had placed most of his books in the den on the third floor. He had worked there on the final stages of *Crusade,* and for his correspondence and memos he would write out his thoughts on a yellow pad and then use his Dictaphone—and the Dictabelts would be taken to his office for transcription—where he had a machine in his office desk. He regularly arrived at Low Memorial shortly after 8:00 A.M., and he stayed late, rarely going downtown at noon for luncheons. Helen King, who "took a lot of his dictation, and he really had a tremendous vocabulary," recalled that "one of his tricks would be to dictate to me for about an hour and then he would say, 'Let me call Al Jacobs in now.'" The Provost, she added, "was actually running things on the academic side," and the President "would then say to me, 'Now read that to Mr. Jacobs and see what he thinks and maybe get some suggestions.'" He had made Provost Jacobs his chief of staff, and he proposed in his letter to the Trustees an office "whose incumbent will be properly designated and remunerated as my chief assistant." This was important, because he could not "assure the Trustees" that he "might not, at any time, be called back to governmental service on either an indefinite or temporary basis."[52]

The General and Mrs. Eisenhower went to Washington on Saturday, November 20, for a colleague's funeral at Walter Reed Chapel; while there he had an opportunity to discuss with Forrestal "the possibilities you suggested to me about personal service." Back in New York he wrote to the Secretary on the 24th: "Naturally, if anything more than a very temporary assignment were contemplated I think you and I would have to get together in advance." The General concluded that he probably would be in Washington "again, for a few hours, possibly next week." Meanwhile, Columbia's President had informed Doug Black, after returning from the funeral in Washington and talking with Forrestal, that he "should like to see someone (my own choice is Mr. Jacobs) set up very quickly as the number two man with suitable title and remuneration. Personally, I should like to call him 'Chancellor'. . . in the event of my enforced absence for some weeks, [it] would give him a title completely indicative of his authority to act decisively."[53]

Perhaps the General, with his vast managerial experience during World War II and in the Pentagon, was beginning to realize the complexity of Columbia: the University required an administrative officer with the proper title and authority, and that he could not, in his words, be "master of my own time and activity." Certainly he could not be such a master when demands from Washington and non-Columbia speaking engagements were added to his Columbia calendar. He had suggested the term "Chancellor" for the new position, though "President" would be the more appropriate term, with Eisenhower assuming the position of "Chancellor of Columbia University." Then, released from the demanding administrative responsibilities and everyday detail, he could be Columbia's spokesman and ambassador without disrupting the University, and, also, fulfill his national security commitments as a five-star general. This arrangement, essentially, would have corresponded to that which Watson and Parkinson had offered him in 1947, without Trustee authorization; it is, moreover, the arrangement Watson specifically had mentioned to Jacobs. Unfortunately, Trustees Watson and Parkinson had not made their proposals from any understanding of Columbia's administrative needs and postwar problems. If the Trustees had recognized the situation and made these arrangements formal, it is unlikely that Eisenhower during his Presidency would have spent so much time on reorganization plans and personnel; it is, moreover, unlikely that his frequent absences from Morningside Heights would have provoked such criticism.

During this period a major Columbia event appeared on his calendar, and the President's response to demands placed on him proved unsettling. The Tenth Annual Convocation for the Maria Moors Cabot Prizes had been scheduled for November 18-19, and Jacobs had informed Schulz over the summer that "these are very important occasions . . . put them down definitely on the President's calendar." Eisenhower, though, did not attend the dinner on the 18th. Prior to the luncheon and awards ceremony the next day, Dean Ackerman of the Journalism School, who had organized the event, met with Eisenhower to outline the Convocation's proceedings, which would honor four journalists for advancing "International Friendship in the Western Hemisphere." In a scathing memorandum, located in Ackerman's personal papers, the Dean privately described Eisenhower's explosion when the President heard that each recipient would give a speech. Then, the President learned that he, also, should deliver "a few remarks at the end" and "with an angry expression . . . stopped abruptly . . . and exclaimed 'If anyone asks me to make a speech again I'm going to desert. I've made five speeches in three days and I'm not going to speak today.'" Years later Ackerman, increasingly bitter about Eisenhower's Presidency of Columbia, emphasized that "throughout the luncheon and ceremony and in the news photographs it was evident that President Eisenhower was uneasy and unhappy. At no time was the familiar Eisenhower smile visible."[54]

Perhaps the pressures were taking their toll on the General. Only two days earlier he had informed the Trustees that he required a chief assistant and he might "be called back to governmental service," and that evening, after the Cabot ceremony, he took the train to Washington for a funeral. And, while he was away, Professor Harry Morgan Ayers died. A prominent scholar and outstanding leader in the field of adult education, Ayres was the Director of the Summer Session, which recently had had some 18,000 students, and of the School of General Studies; earlier he had highly praised to colleagues the General's Guildhall Address in London. His death forced President and Mrs. Eisenhower to cancel an elaborate tea and cocktail party at 60 Morningside for prominent faculty and spouses on Sunday.[55]

That weekend also saw the eagerly awaited publication of *Crusade in Europe*. Throughout the fall, the stunning election results and the intensifying Cold War notwithstanding, it would have been difficult, if not impossible, to miss publicity for the General's wartime memoirs. Doug Black's Doubleday and Bill Robinson's *New York Herald-Tribune* had conducted a massive pre-publication campaign since late September, and newspaper syndication started on November 7, the Sunday after the election. On November 18 Black gave "the first book made" to Mamie, and on the 22nd the Blacks celebrated the publication with a dinner party at their Park Avenue apartment. The next day some 1,800 persons heard the General address a book-and-author luncheon. *Crusade in Europe* was also a Book-of-the-Month Club selection, and the following night he had dinner with the Club's president. During the next two years Doubleday would sell some 275,000 copies.[56]

Crusade in Europe delighted the General's fans, and they greeted it with enthusiasm and critical acclaim. *New York Times* correspondent Drew Middleton asserted that the memoir had a "deep honesty, a simplicity and a sense of importance of what was done in those years" and it belonged "to the first rank of war memoirs." In the *Herald-Tribune's* "Weekly Book Review" Robert E. Sherwood called it "A Great Soldier's Story of a Great War: Eisenhower Simply and Courageously Sets Down the Record." Sherwood, who had won two Pulitzer Prizes as a playwright, had served as a Franklin Roosevelt speech-writer and had just written *Roosevelt and Hopkins: An Intimate History* covering the war period; he emphasized that Eisenhower's book offered "a heartening demonstration of what we are pleased to call Americanism at its best." Others concurred. Liberal political writer Richard Rovere considered *Crusade* "a document that sometimes comes close to splendor." Merle Miller described it as "probably the best book ever written about any war by an active general, with the possible exception of Julius Caesar." Allan Nevins wrote: "Nothing in a long time has given me such pleasure as your far too generous inscription in the volume of your *Crusade in Europe*." According to McCann, Nevins said that he had started reading *Crusade* as his train was leaving Washington and that "he became so absorbed in it that the first thing he knew he was in New York" and had missed his stop at Princeton for a lecture and had to take another train back. When Fox Connor, Eisenhower's "history" mentor, thanked him for a copy, the General replied, "I doubt very much that I should ever have been in a position to prepare such a memoir, had it not been for the guidance and counsel I got from you."[57]

Eisenhower had sold every right, including subsidiary rights, to *Crusade in Europe*, qualifying him for a capital gains tax instead of a personal income tax. While Eisenhower received nearly $500,000, after taxes, the book's fantastic sales primarily benefited the publishers. In 1966 Eisenhower, as he was finishing *At Ease*, asked Doubleday for the figures, and he wrote, "At least 1,170,000 copies of *Crusade in Europe* were sold in the United States and there were contracts for twenty-two foreign language editions." *Crusade* would withstand the test of time; it was, Stephen Ambrose has asserted, "a book worthy of the man and his services to the nation."[58] The new President of Columbia University had published a major historical account of World War II after arriving in the academic community on Morningside Heights.

The Eisenhowers spent Thanksgiving, 1948, at 60 Morningside, and he had much for which he could be thankful. It had been a tremendously hectic and strenuous fall, especially the previous week; it had, also, been an extremely exciting and rewarding time. As hard as it was to believe, his Installation at Columbia and the publication of his wartime memoirs had made him even more popular and had brought widespread recognition to the University. He had established a close relationship with the Provost for administering the University, and he had presented for Trustee consideration a series of proposals to address pressing problems. Plans for a major human resources study, an important program for him, were progressing rapidly, and he had worked with Professor Ginzberg and Provost Jacobs on a letter which would go to fifty-five business and public affairs leaders in mid-December. He had, furthermore, been invited by the prestigious Council on Foreign Relations to lead a study group on the long-term implications of the European Recovery Program. "That was," McCann emphasized, "a good thing for Dwight Eisenhower as President of Columbia University."[59]

He also faced that Thanksgiving, however, matters of grave concern, and probably he failed to notice several warning signs on the horizon at Morningside Heights. Stories circulated that he did not have time or want to see the faculty and that his public commitments downtown came at the expense of University functions; moreover, it was becoming known that he had appeared very uncomfortable at the University Council meeting and he had lost his temper prior to the Cabot Awards. On the national level, the problems of military reunification and the difficult situation in Washington deeply worried him, especially as Cold War tensions grew and increasingly demanded his attention and time. He would be meeting with President Truman and Secretary Forrestal within a few days, and he knew that he would be called to duty in Washington, but he had no idea whether it might be "a temporary assignment" or "short term, possibly to be followed by one of some month's duration." He could only wonder how disruptive this might be for Columbia and whether the Trustees would respond to his proposals. After all, they had learned only a few days earlier that the University's new President might be leaving for a few weeks, at the minimum, and this had to be terribly disconcerting for them. Their memories of the long interregnum between Nicholas Murray Butler and Dwight Eisenhower and of Columbia's problems during those years remained vivid and unpleasant. Yet Eisenhower, nonetheless, could take pleasure that Thanksgiving in the successful launching of his Columbia crusade for youth and citizenship.

Notes

1. Dwight D. Eisenhower to Thomas J. Watson, October 26, 1948, *The Papers of Dwight David Eisenhower: Columbia University*, vol. X (Baltimore, Md., 1984), ed. Louis Galambos, pp. 271-72 (*PDDE*).

2. Ibid., p. 161; *New York Times*, August 18 and September 1, 1948.

3. *Columbia Spectator*, September 23, 24, 1948; *New York Times*, September 23, 1949; *Newsweek*, October 18, 1948; Ira Henry Freeman, *New York Times Magazine*, November 7, 1948, pp. 90-91.

4. *Columbia Spectator*, September 29, 1948; Editorial, "At Last," ibid.

5. Jacobs to Eisenhower, September 13, 1948, Central Archives, Columbia University (CACU); *Columbia Spectator*, September 23, 1948, and October 27, 1947; *PDDE*, XI, 1569-70.

6. Harry J. Carman to Father Ford, November 2, 1948, Carman MSS., Butler Library, Columbia University.

7. Dwight D. Eisenhower, *At Ease: Stories I Tell to Friends* (New York, 1967), pp. 346-47; *PDDE*, X, 15; Joseph Lang to Eisenhower, October 11, 1948, ibid., 252; Robert C. Harron, personal interview, February 5, 1965, Hartford, Ct. For a "Profile" on Little, see R. O. Boyer, "Drive, Drive, Drive," *New Yorker*, October 9, 1948.

8. *New York Times*, September 26, 1948; Eisenhower to Robert Clarkson Clothier, September 28, 1948, *PDDE*, X, 235.

9. Robert L. Schulz, Oral History Interview, Columbia Oral History Project (COHP), 1968. Schulz added that in *At Ease* Eisenhower "contends that this took place at Columbia University, which is not right." Eisenhower, *At Ease*, p. 340; *New York*

Times, September 26 and October 14, 1948; Eisenhower to Mildred Anderson Considine, September 22, 1948, *PDDE*, X, 217-18.

10. Ibid., X, fn. #6, 189; fn. #4, 198; fn. #6, 187; and fn. #1, 185.

11. Ibid., X, 1570; Eisenhower to Forrestal, September 27, 1948, ibid., 230-34.

12. "Notes of the Remarks," box 34, Lewis L. Strauss Papers, Herbert C. Hoover Library, West Branch, Ia; "Convocation," The Jewish Theological Seminary of America, September 27, 1948; *New York Times*, September 28, 1948; Albert C. Jacobs, Oral History Interview, 1968, COHP; Jacobs, memorandum to author, March 10, 1958; Jacobs, personal interview, February 5, 1965, Hartford, Ct.

13. Eisenhower to Forrestal, September 27, 1948, *PDDE*, X, 231-34.

14. Eisenhower to Forrestal, September 27 and October 4, 1948, ibid., 231-34, 239-40. On October 8 Forrestal asked Eisenhower to "let me know" his schedule. Ibid., fn. #4, p. 239.

15. Jacobs to Eisenhower, July 15, 1948, CACU; Eisenhower notes, July 15, 1948, and Eisenhower to Jacobs, July 19, 1948, CACU. On September 20, 1948, Eisenhower sent to the Trustees a confidential nine-page letter with four appendices discussing the Polish chair. Ibid.

16. *The Papers of Dwight David Eisenhower*, vol. I (Baltimore, Md., 1970), *The War Years*, ed. Alfred D. Chandler, Jr., "Introduction"; Stephen E. Ambrose, *Eisenhower: Soldier, General of the Army, President-Elect, 1890-1952* (New York, 1983), chapters 9-20.

17. Jacobs to Eisenhower, July 10, 1948, CACU; Eisenhower to Jacobs, July 19, 1948 *PDDE*, X, 152-56; Eisenhower to Trustees, September 22, 1948, CACU.

18. In adopting a faculty report prepared under Fackenthal's direction and stemming from the Booz, Allen, and Hamilton study of Columbia's administration, the Committee recognized that the "larger problem" had to be "considered as a necessary preliminary to any partial solution." Trustees of Columbia University in the City of New York, *Minutes*, October 4, 1948, CACU; *PDDE*, X, 153-56.

19. Trustees, *Minutes*, October 4, 1948, CACU.

20. Eisenhower to Jacobs, July 19, 1948, *PDDE*, X, 152-56; Trustees, *Minutes*, October 4, 1948, CACU; Putnam to Eisenhower, November 19, 1948, CACU; Eisenhower to Deans, Departmental Officers and Administrative Officers, October 22, 1948, *PDDE*, X, 265-67.

21. Trustees, *Minutes*, October 4, 1948, CACU; *PDDE*, X, fn. #4-10, 154-55.

22. Trustees, *Minutes*, October 4, 1948, CACU.

23. Benjamin Fine, "Education in Review," *New York Times*, October 10, 1948.

24. Milton Eisenhower to Eisenhower, September 16, 1948, Dwight D. Eisenhower Library (DDEL); Eisenhower to Ely Culbertson, September 24, 1948, and to General Alfred Gruenther, June 16 and July 28, 1948, *PDDE*, X, 225-26, 111-12, 168-69.

25. Kevin McCann, personal interview, July 25, 1972, Gettysburg, Pa.; Eisenhower to Felix Frankfurter, October 18, 1948, *PDDE*, X, 250.

26. Grayson Kirk to author, March 13, 1992; Kirk, Oral History Interview, January 14, 1987, COHP.

27. Much of the careful planning had been done by Jacobs and Krout, since Kirk had been away for much of the summer. John A. Krout, personal interview, July 22, 1963, New York, N. Y.; Kirk, Interview, January 17, 1987, COHP; Trustees, *Minutes*, October 4, 1948, CACU; *New York Times*, October 12, 1948; Albert C. Jacobs, "Memoirs," 1974; "Disbursements," Mamie D. Eisenhower MSS., DDEL; Editorial, "A Great Man . . . Meets A Great Challenge," *Columbia Spectator*, October 12, 1948.

28. President Truman to Eisenhower, tel., October 12, 1948, DDEL; Forrestal to Eisenhower, October 8, 1948, ibid.; *The Forrestal Diaries*, ed. by Walter Millis (New York, 1951), pp. 498-500.

29. Did Eisenhower worry about the weather and moving the ceremony indoors? At the Pennsylvania State University commencement in 1955, President Milton Eisenhower worried about the storm clouds and asked Eisenhower, the commencement speaker, for advice. The former President of Columbia replied: "I haven't worried about the weather since June 6, 1944." Fred Greenstein, "Eisenhower's Leadership Style," *Eisenhower: A Centenary Assessment*, ed. by Gunter Bischof and Stephen E. Ambrose (Baton Rouge, La., 1995), p. 63.

30. Columbia University, Installation of Dwight David Eisenhower as Thirteenth President, October 12, 1948. At least eight of the official representatives had been considered for Columbia's Presidency. See, also, *The 1949 Columbian* (Baltimore, Md., 1949), pp. 22-25.

31. Meyer Berger, "Rich Color and Solemn Pageantry of Middle Ages Greet Eisenhower," and Russell Porter, "Eisenhower Takes Office At Columbia: Stresses Freedom," *New York Times*, October 13, 1948.

32. "Text of Eisenhower's Speech," *New York Times*, October 13, 1948.

33. Porter, "Eisenhower Takes Office," ibid.

34. Edward R. Murrow, "With the News," October 12, 1948, DDEL.

35. *New York Daily Mirror*, October 13, 1948; *Newsweek*, October 18, 1948, p. 90; Editorial, "A Soldier-Educator Speaks," *New York Times*, October 13, 1948; Felix Frankfurter to Eisenhower, October 15, 1948, *PDDE*, X, 250.

36. *PDDE*, XI, 1572; ibid., X, fn. #4, 251; *New York Times*, October 17, 1948.

37. *New York Times*, October 17, 1948; *Columbia Spectator*, October 18, 1948; Carman to Father Ford, November 2, 1948, Carman MSS., Butler Library.

38. Freeman, "Eisenhower of Columbia," *New York Times Magazine*, November 7, 1948; Max Frankel, "Morningside Becoming Country's 'Newsmaker,'" *Columbia Spectator*, October 18, 1948.

39. Eisenhower to Black, October 18, 1948, *PDDE*, X, 250-51; Ibid., XI, 1572-75; *New York Times*, October 21, 1948; Jacobs, memorandum, March 10, 1958; Harry J. Carman, personal interview, December 1, 1961, New York, N. Y.; McCann, interview, July 25, 1972.

40. McCann, interview, July 25, 1972; Carman to Father Ford, November 2, 1948, Carman MSS.

41. Grayson Kirk to author, March 13, 1992; R. Gordon Hoxie, personal interview, June 9, 1995, New York, N. Y.; Jacobs, memorandum to author, March 10, 1958; Helen King, Oral History Interview, May 12, 1975, Eisenhower Library (OHDDEL).

42. Hoxie, interview, June 9, 1995; McCann, interview, July 25, 1972; R. Gordon Hoxie, "The Federalist Student," *American Heritage* 50 (December, 1999), pp. 26-27.

43. Eisenhower to Forrestal, November 4, 1948, *PDDE*, X, 283-84, and XI, 1574.

44. Eisenhower to Fackenthal, November 17, 1949, ibid., X, 303-306.

45. *Columbia Spectator*, October 25, 28, and 29, and November 1, 1948.

46. Bruce Wonnacott, personal interview, November 9, 1977, Middlebury, Vt.

47. Ambrose, *Eisenhower*, p. 464, 478; Roberts, Oral History Interview, September 12 and 29, 1968, COHP.

48. Ibid.

49. Ambrose, *Eisenhower*, pp. 464, 478; Eisenhower to Forrestal, November 4, 1948, and to Truman, November 18, 1948, *PDDE*, X, 283-84, 310-11; Forrestal to Eisenhower, November 5, 1948, DDEL. For Eisenhower's July 23 meeting with Dewey, see *New York Times*, July 24, 1948.

50. Albert C. Jacobs, "The Eisenhower I have Known," March 10, 1964, Twilight Club, Hartford, Ct.

51. For Eisenhower's November schedule, see *PDDE*, XI, 1574-78; *New York Times*, November 7 and 14, 1948; Sulzberger to Eisenhower, *PDDE*, X, fn. #1, 328.

52. Eisenhower to Black, November 17, 1948, DDEL; the same letter (to Fackenthal), with extensive annotations is in *PDDE*, X, 303-306; Bruce Wonnacott, who described the General's dictating in the den, would often run errands to the office. Wonnacott, interview, November 7, 1977; Jacques Barzun, personal interview, April 5, 1979, New York, N.Y.; King, interview, May 12, 1975, OHDDEL. Eisenhower had had a Dictaphone recorder installed in his Low Memorial desk but, according to a Dictaphone technician, it never worked properly. See William Doyle, *Inside the Oval Office: The White House Tapes from FDR to Clinton* (New York, 1999), p. 73; also Kirk, interview, September 3, 1987, COHP.

53. Eisenhower to Forrestal, November 24, 1948, ibid., 322-23; Eisenhower concluded, referring to the December Board meeting, "I am quite sure that prompt action is indicated as wise and desirable." Eisenhower to Black. November 22, 1948, ibid., 316.

54. Jacobs to Schulz, July 20, 1948, CACU; Ackerman, "A Secret Report on the Tenth Annual Maria Moors Cabot Convocation," November 26, 1948, Carl A. Ackerman MSS., Library of Congress; Ackerman, "The Story of General Eisenhower," unpublished manuscript, 1957, ibid.; *Columbia Spectator*, November 22, 1948.

55. Ibid., November 23, 1948; Jacobs, memorandum to author, March 10, 1958; "List of Guests," Mamie D. Eisenhower MSS., DDEL.

56. Douglas Black, personal interview, June 6, 1973, New York, N.Y.; *PDDE*, X, 299, 268.

57. Drew Middleton, *New York Times Book Review*, November 21, 1948; Robert E. Sherwood, *New York Herald-Tribune*, November 21, 1948; Steve Neal, *The Eisenhowers* (Lawrence, Kans., 1984), p. 243; Allan Nevins to Eisenhower, January 16, 1949, CACU; McCann, interview, July 25, 1972; Eisenhower to Fox Connor, January 3, 1949, Eisenhower MSS., DDEL.

58. Eisenhower, *At Ease*, pp. 326-29; Ambrose, *Eisenhower*, pp. 474-75.

59. Jacobs to Eisenhower, November 10, 1948, CACU; Ginzberg to Jacobs, November 24, 1948, ibid., *PDDE*, X, 374-77; Michael Wala, "An 'Education in Foreign Affairs for the Future President': The Council on Foreign Relations and Dwight D. Eisenhower," in *Examining the Eisenhower Presidency*, ed. Shirley Anne Warshaw (Westport, Ct., 1993), pp. 1-16; McCann, interview, July 25, 1972.

MR. PRESIDENT
EISENHOWER
A CLOSE-UP

APRIL 17, 1950 20 CENTS
YEARLY SUBSCRIPTION $6.00

LIFE/TIMEPIX, photo by Arnold Newman

This was Eisenhower's fourth appearance on the cover of *Life* and his first as a civilian. Author Quentin Reynolds presented a flattering description of Eisenhower at Columbia, and the cover story–and its title–provoked widespread controversy at the University.

Eisenhower, IBM's Thomas J. Watson, right, and Provost Albert C. Jacobs, left, climbing the steps to Low Memorial during the General's brief visit in September, 1948. Trustee Watson, who played a major role in the General's Columbia decision, told Jacobs, to "handle the internal part of the university while Eisenhower did the external." *Photograph: Family possession*

Eisenhower's Installation as President on October 12, 1948. The view from Butler Library looks across South Field and South Court to the platform in front of Low Memorial. *Columbia University*

Eisenhower and Provost Jacobs in the procession at his Installation. Seated to the General's right are Mamie Eisenhower and John S. D. Eisenhower.
Photograph: Dwight D. Eisenhower Library

Eisenhower receiving the University's Charter and symbolic keys at his Installation from Frederick Coykendall, Chairman of the Board of Trustees.
Photograph: Columbia University

Eisenhower talking with the Columbia football team and Coach Lou Little at Baker Field. Earlier, the General had persuaded Little to stay at Columbia.
Photograph: Dwight D. Eisenhower Library

Columbia's Homecoming on October 16, 1948, "climaxed with a big social affair" honoring Mamie and General Eisenhower, and "12:30 midnight the Eisenhowers departed in a hansom cab."
Photograph: Dwight D. Eisenhower Library

President Eisenhower talks with Eleanor Roosevelt prior to her speech at the 1949 Forum on Democracy. *Photograph: Dwight D. Eisenhower Library*

Eisenhower, President-Elect of the United States, saying farewell to Columbia in front of Alma Mater on January 16, 1953. Dean Harry J. Carman, Eisenhower's closest friend among the faculty, is on the left with an open coat and glasses. *Photograph: Dwight D. Eisenhower Library/New York Herald-Tribune*

President Eisehhower, Major General Howard Snyder, the General's personal physi-cian and long-term consultant to the Conservation of Human Resources Project, and the Project's Director, Eli Ginzberg. *Photograph: Society, Vol.16, No. 6, September 1979*

5

Return to Duty: Ike's First Leave

Sec. Nat. Defense has called me to Washington for quick survey of
difficulties in way of achieving efficiency in coordination of defense
services. Idea is that I am to come here about Jan. 21, '49 to work as his
military consultant for 2-3 months to iron out many of these difficulties.

—Dwight D. Eisenhower,
Diary, December 13, 1948

From the date of my assumption of my present post it was, of course,
understood between the Columbia Trustees and me that urgent public
business would always have first claim on my time. It has now developed that the consultative and advisory functions . . . will, during the
near future, require for their accomplishment almost a full allocation of
my time.

—Dwight D. Eisenhower
to Frederick Coykendall,
February 7, 1949

On Monday, November 29, the Eisenhowers, who had spent a
quiet Thanksgiving in New York, left on the night train for Washington. The General knew that Secretary Forrestal and President
Truman wanted him to return temporarily to the Pentagon, but he
did not know how long the assignment might last and what impact
his absence would have on Columbia. He already had been in the
nation's capital twice that month, and he would make two more
trips in December before enjoying a two-week Christmas Holiday
in Denver. As his chauffeur drove the Eisenhowers that evening
from 60 Morningside Drive to Pennsylvania Station, the General
could not know that his return to duty in January would last longer
than he had anticipated and that, after a few weeks, he would discover that he would no longer be able to split his time between
Columbia and the Pentagon; nor could he know that, in spite of his
enormous energy and discipline, he would suffer a serious illness
and be unable to return to Columbia until mid-May.

Then, during the summer Eisenhower, more conscious of his health and the dangers of a hectic schedule, would take a two-month vacation in Wisconsin and Colorado. All this meant an extended absence from his Presidency of Columbia University: when he left in January, he was removed from involvement in the University's day-to-day activities and this occurred while he was still largely unfamiliar with the complex academic world of Columbia; moreover, the University—and he—lost the dramatic momentum his leadership had provided during the fall. By the time Eisenhower returned full time to Morningside Heights in mid-September, 1949, his chief of staff had decided to leave the University and the sense of excitement and enthusiasm following his arrival had disappeared. His first leave from Columbia would be pivotal for his presidency.

Secretary Forrestal had briefed Eisenhower during the fall about the problems with the 1949-1950 defense budget and the constant bickering among the Joint Chiefs of Staff. The 1947 National Security Act had not provided for a single chief of staff and had not achieved the desired unification. The Secretary sought the General's assistance at a time when the Berlin blockade crisis remained tense and the position of Chiang Kai-Shek's Nationalists in China, in Forrestal's words, was "going through a rapid process of deterioration" and "a vast amount of American-bought equipment" had been surrendered to the Chinese Communists. Yet, in spite of the Cold War situation, the JCS had not even worked out, according to Eisenhower, a "basic and firm strategic concept" in case of a Russian attack. The armed services could not agree on major responsibilities, and arguments erupted over the Navy's determination to build a super aircraft carrier, as a movable base for intercontinental atomic strikes, and the Air Force's insistence that the new B-36 bomber should play the primary role. By late November the Secretary had persuaded the Joint Chiefs to agree on an "intermediate" budget program of $16.9 billion, whereas President Truman still insisted on a $14.4 billion defense "ceiling."[1]

Eisenhower arrived in Washington in the midst of these discussions. First, though, he talked on with the Secretary of the Treasury and, then, the Commissioner of Internal Revenue about the capital gains treatment for his proceeds from *Crusade in Europe*. After a luncheon with Secretary Forrestal, he attended a meeting of Army commanders with Chief of Staff General Bradley, and he met with

W. Averell Harriman, the President's Special Representative to the Economic Cooperation Administration in Europe and former Ambassador to the Soviet Union. The day ended with Eisenhower playing bridge at the Alfred Gruenthers'; General Gruenther, the Director of the Joint Staff, JCS, was a close friend, colleague, and bridge partner—in July the *New York Times* bridge columnist had analyzed a bridge hand Eisenhower and Gruenther had played as partners the previous week.[2]

The General had been called to Washington because of the difficulties in coordinating the armed services, and the following afternoon, December 1, he met with Truman and Forrestal at Blair House—the White House was undergoing a major restoration. Forrestal earlier had expressed to the President his serious problems with the JCS and their inability to agree on strategic planning. He had suggested, consequently, inviting Eisenhower "to come down, only with your approval, of course, to sit with us for a period of three or four weeks." Truman supported the request, and Eisenhower agreed to serve as the Secretary's military consultant. That same day, probably at the meeting, Forrestal presented the President with his proposal for a $16.9 billion defense budget, and Eisenhower agreed to return to the capital briefly the next week for specific discussions about his assignment and for a series of appointments with top military officials. Years later, he recalled in *At Ease*, "I was assured that even if my new task called for long hours occasionally, the work would still be compatible with my University role and even profitable to Columbia."[3]

Meanwhile, he had pressing commitments at Columbia. During the fall Ginzberg had been finishing his report, "Adjustment to Work," and as soon as Eisenhower returned to the campus he discussed with Ginzberg and Provost Jacobs the report and the covering letter, which would be sent to prominent leaders in business, labor and public affairs. Eisenhower hoped, Ginzberg has recalled, that work on the military records of World War II would lead to "a better understanding of what had happened with manpower utilization and mal-utilization as a part of the war experience." Or, as Eisenhower wrote in *At Ease*, he had realized during the war that "we had seriously neglected the full education and preparation of our young people to be vigorous and productive members of society. This neglect was tragically tabulated, among young men, in those armed forces rejection records of the years 1940-1945."[4]

Eisenhower had emphasized this subject in one of his first speeches at Columbia, and Ginzberg has emphasized that "very few people believed . . . what a lively role he played and how far he went to conceptualize these issues and that he was in a very real sense of the term, the innovator of these studies." Jacobs had sent the professor's proposals and covering letter to the University's deans for comments and approval. Eisenhower discussed the replies and suggested that Ginzberg should add a labor leader to the list of potential contributors. Ginzberg also added, at the suggestion of Dean Young, a greater emphasis on civilian manpower.[5]

Eisenhower's letter, which went through some "eighteen drafts," went to fifty-five leaders on December 18. He discussed "the wastage of manpower through mental and emotional failures" and how his attention had been "drawn forcibly to the matter during the war." In late 1944 the "lack of manpower" had "badly strained" battle units on the European front, yet "rejections and discharges of men for mental defects reached a total of more than two million." The military records for "a down-to-earth study" were available, and he enclosed Ginzberg's report, entitled "Adjustment to Work," to demonstrate Columbia's "capacity and qualifications" for such an undertaking. Eisenhower concluded that he wanted "a volume of considered opinion" before proceeding and seeking financial support. "If this project is worth doing, the sooner we get it under way, the better." The proposal intrigued Walter Reuther—the labor leader—but he considered the title "manipulative." Ginzberg, who had been reading about Teddy Roosevelt, "discovered that TR was interested in the Conservation of Human and Natural Resources," and retitled the project, the Conservation of Human Resources. Eisenhower and Ginzberg had taken a major step in launching one of his most significant achievements at Columbia.[6]

After talking with Ginzberg upon his return from Washington, Eisenhower immediately addressed another central concern: decentralization. From the start the General had recognized the importance of strengthening the administrative organization of the University and over the summer he had considered a proposal for establishing four vice presidencies. This decentralization would give greater responsibility to the various schools and departments and relieve the President's Office of decisions which he believed should be made at a lower level. During the fall he had discussed reorganization proposals with the Provost, and at the October Board Meeting

Trustee Black's Special Committee on Reorganization had recommended, as part of a larger plan, the establishment of two vice presidents, one in Charge of Business Affairs and the other in Charge of Development. Each would be "answerable to the President."

The Trustees, however, had "laid over" the two proposals and had "deferred" action at the November meeting. On December 2 Eisenhower and the Committee decided to present to the Board on December 6 these amendments to the University's Statutes with the recommendation that under the "Officers of Administration" the new vice presidents follow the Provost. Details for the other two vice presidents, however, still had not been worked out. They did not formally consider, moreover, for Trustee action Eisenhower's request for a "properly designated . . . chief assistant," the proposal he had mentioned to the Trustees in mid-November with the specific recommendation of Provost Jacobs for the position.[7]

As the University prepared to reorganize the office of business affairs, a publicity blunder badly embarrassed the community. Frederick A. Goetz, Treasurer since 1916, had retired on November 1, and Joseph Campbell, the Assistant Treasurer since 1941 and the supervisor of accounting for the Manhattan Project at Columbia during the war, had resigned on October 1. In neither case, however, had there been a public announcement, and when the University realized this, it issued "an immediate press release." Unfortunately, the *New York Herald-Tribune* reported that Campbell would succeed the retiring Goetz; further complicating the situation, Campbell's marriage to Goetz's daughter was dissolving.[8]

Other matters may have been of less pressing concern for Eisenhower, but his schedule remained full during the day and evening. The first night back in New York he attended the Varsity "C" Club annual awards dinner and the following evening a black-tie dinner at the apartment of Trustee Arthur Hays Sulzberger and his wife, Iphigene Ochs Sulzberger, a prominent civic leader and a Barnard College Trustee. Earlier, Eisenhower had indicated that a prior commitment would prevent him from going to a Saturday morning meeting of the Association of American Universities at the University Club; however, he did go for awhile, probably because President Conant had urged him to attend "at least part" of the meeting. Afterwards, he had lunch at 60 Morningside with Dean Ackerman and a World War II colleague.[9]

That Saturday night the History Department held its annual black-tie dinner at the Men's Faculty Club, "complete with the young men and the old men together," and Jacques Barzun has recalled that Dean Carman had the "bright idea of asking whether the President might be free and might want to join us." It was a distinguished department; Professor Schuyler was the Acting Chair, and its members included past presidents and future presidents of the American Historical Association and Pulitzer Prize winners. Eisenhower, who had just published *Crusade in Europe*, accepted the invitation, and "we had guaranteed that he would not be asked for a speech or any formal offering." During the after dinner conversation, as they sat around a large horseshoe shaped table, one of the historians quoted Winston Churchill's remark about the "soft-underbelly" of Europe. Eisenhower, according to Barzun, "got quite huffy at that and said 'That is one of the most ignorant remarks made by anybody,' and he proceeded to give us, without any prompting, a history of the campaigns, beginning with Thucydides and the Peloponnesian War that had taken place in the south of Europe which, as we all know, is a mass of mountains, and he went right on to the Austrian War of 1866, the German-Austrian War." The General's talk, the brilliant, articulate European intellectual historian emphasized, was "a masterly performance and with hardly a hesitation in words." Henry F. Graff, a very junior member and just beginning a life-long career in the department, has recently written, "In a dazzling talk delivered without notes and with uncommon insight and learning, he spoke of the great captains of history who had preceded him on the battlefields of Europe. Let no one ever tell you he was not an historian, that he was not one of us."A senior professor, however, clearly was not impressed when Eisenhower made a gaffe and referred to his "magnus opus." Audibly commenting—and embarrassing his department colleagues—Barnard's medievalist kept asking Lynn Thorndike, the Graduate Faculties' medievalist, "Lynn, shall we tell him now?" Nothing could detract, though, from a delightful evening and, as Eisenhower walked around the corner to the President's House next door, he looked forward to a quiet Sunday and possibly wondered how long his assignment in Washington would take him away from Morningside Heights.[10]

Whether or not he had specifically discussed with a few Trustees his conversations with Truman and Forrestal, on December 6, the morning of the Board Meeting, syndicated columnists Joseph and

Stewart Alsop reported that Eisenhower was "the obvious choice" to serve as temporary "chairman" of the Joint Chiefs of Staff. Those familiar with the scheme, the Alsops asserted, realized "it would be unfair to ask General Eisenhower to leave Columbia University for more than a brief period. But a mere three or four months would be quite sufficient to do the essential job."[11]

The Trustees met at the Men's Faculty Club for a luncheon before their meeting, and they faced a dilemma. Significantly, Black, Dodge, and Watson did not attend, and the *Minutes* contain no reference to the General's pending departure for Washington. The Trustees adopted the recommendations for the two vice presidents, but why did they not receive any recommendation to "set up very quickly" the "number two man"? Had Eisenhower convinced himself, and a few Trustees, that he could do both jobs, including the speaking commitments he had already accepted for the winter, by splitting his time between Columbia and the Pentagon? Or, more likely, did the Trustees worry that any action would seem hasty, in response to the newspaper article, and send the wrong message? That it would convey the impression that Eisenhower would be away for a long time? That he might not return? Yet, if they did not act, would they be subjecting the Administration to weeks or months of severe strains, especially at a time of serious budget questions? While the Trustees undoubtedly recognized that they faced a major challenge to the leadership of Columbia, once again, they did not seem to know how to respond to the problem.[12]

Early Thursday morning, December 9, the General flew to Washington for the day, and he, Secretary Forrestal, and the President worked out the terms of his assignment. On the 13th, when he returned to the capital for three days, he outlined the plan in his *Diary*. "Sec Nat. Defense has called me to Washington for quick survey of difficulties in way of achieving efficiency in coordination of defense services. Idea is that I am to come here about Jan. 21, '49 to work as his military consultant for 2-3 months to iron out many of these difficulties." He continued. "Basic & firm strategic concept is 1st requirement. Once this is achieved much else will fall in line," and "Final approval of plan must be given by President and then complete & loyal adherence to decision must be *demanded & obtained*." During this mid-December trip the press reported, "Eisenhower To Be Forrestal Adviser"; the *New York World-Telegram*, after stating that the General will be "on leave" from Columbia, emphasized that "his first assignment . . . will be to fight the battle of the budget. He is expected to appear frequently before Congressional committees. . . . He may put on his uniform again." Columbia quickly announced that Eisenhower's military duties would not require a leave of absence, but Forrestal, acknowledging that he badly needed Eisenhower's help, wrote in his diary, "With Ike here for sixty days I think we can get the pattern set and prove its workability by pragmatic experience."[13]

With the date of his appointment established, Eisenhower recorded, "Returned from Washington on fifteenth, in time to go to Yule-log lighting in John Jay Hall, then to dinner at Links Club." A snowstorm had forced him to take the train, instead of flying, to attend the Yule-log ceremony, an important College event for over thirty years. Mrs. Eisenhower, Provost Jacobs, and Dean Carman accompanied the President, who apologized for his late arrival. He appealed for "a vacation from the perplexing problems confronting all of us. . . . Let's have a Merry Christmas. . . above all else let's have some good will and a sense of humor." Carman reminisced that Eisenhower "loved young people" and it was "beautifully done." After the ceremony, Eisenhower told a *Spectator* reporter that the *World-Telegram* story was "not to be taken too seriously."[14]

During the next week he sought to clear his desk before leaving for Christmas and New Year's in Denver. His health had been good that summer and fall, which was "very comforting" to Dr. Snyder, who had moved to Butler Hall, only three blocks from 60 Morningside. His wife came up from Washington for the holidays, and several times that week the Snyders and General and Ann Nevins joined the Eisenhowers for cocktails and dinner. "General and Mrs. Eisenhower appeared very happy and very contented" and, Snyder added, "We always seemed to have so much to laugh about and enjoy. There may have been some after-dinner indulgence. . . ."[15]

At his Low Memorial office Eisenhower, before leaving for his vacation, regularly saw Paul Davis, responsible for long-range development, in addition to his usual appointments. He also attended cocktails and a buffet with alumni from the School of Business alumni, a Rockefeller Foundation luncheon, an Association of University Teas meeting with Mrs. Eisenhower, and a luncheon at Tom Watson's—Watson visited him two days later in Low Memorial. On December 21, just before departing on the train for Colorado, he appeared at the quarterly University Council meeting. He asked Provost Jacobs, however, to request the Dean of the Graduate Faculties to Chair the meeting for him, and for the Provost to represent the President's Office. Perhaps he realized how bad the October meeting had been; in any event, never again would he attend a University Council meeting.[16]

The juxtaposition of events that afternoon foreshadowed much for Columbia. He had decided not to preside over the major academic body at the University, at a session for which he, the President, was the designated chair; moreover, his departure for a two-week Christmas vacation, on the eve of a two or three month leave, worried the Administration. The combination could be seen by the community as demonstrating a lack of leadership by the President and that he minimized his Columbia responsibilities. The Provost realized that Eisenhower's absence during the winter months and the ensuing distractions would have a major impact on his schedule. He would have to know what commitments—University and non-University—Eisenhower would not fulfill, which the Provost would have to do in his stead. During the holidays, for example, Jacobs delivered on behalf of the President a talk to the University's Alumni Federation. Then, in response to an inquiry about communists on the faculty, he issued a statement for the President on the importance of academic freedom and that a faculty member "who is pledged to follow 'the party line' is" not "free to seek and to speak the truth. To allow the infiltration of such persons into the faculties of universities would tend to defeat the very ends which academic freedom is designed to attain."[17]

The Eisenhowers' train arrived back in New York City on Monday, January 3, in time for him to attend the Trustees luncheon at the Men's Faculty Club and a meeting of the Committee on Reorganization with Trustees Black and John G. Jackson, a New York lawyer, before the Board Meeting. During the fall Eisenhower, who wanted to expand the Board with trustees from other parts of the country, had discussed the possibility with Jackson. The lawyer determined that this would require the New York State legislature to amend the University's Charter; his Committee on Legal Affairs, consequently, proposed a Charter amendment, which was discussed and referred back to the Committee. (In late January Jackson informed Eisenhower that the University's legal counsel worried that the state legislature, given the opportunity, might try to "pack the Trustees with appointees of its selection.") Next, the Reorganization Committee reported informally on proposals for the last two of four vice presidents, a Vice President of the University, a crucial position given the President's absence, and a Vice President in charge of medical affairs, and gave notice that it would move to amend the Statutes at a future meeting.[18]

President Eisenhower had wanted a mandatory retirement program ever since his arrival on Morningside Heights, and the Committee on Education presented its report on "automatic and optional retirement" for discussion. The proposals, which also required amending the Statutes, specified the retirement of officers of the administration at "the age of 65 years" and officers of instruction at "the age of 68 years." The Committee gave formal notice that at the next Trustees Meeting it would "move the adoption" of the amendments. (Eisenhower, thwarted in his plan to expand the Board itself, later in 1949 proposed that Trustees, themselves, retire at the age of 70; this was presented to the Board at its November 7, 1949, meeting, and it was "tabled" by a Trustee on December 5.)[19]

Two days later General and Mrs. Eisenhower left on an afternoon train for Washington. Earlier, at breakfast, he showed his involvement with the Boy Scouts when he pinned the Boy Scout emblem on the city's 500,000th member, a 12-year old, and the Greater New York Council of the Boy Scouts of America opened a fund drive for $2,000,000 in a ceremony at the Waldorf-Astoria. That evening at the Gruenthers' Ike played bridge and Mamie mah-jong. The next night they dined informally with Secretary Forrestal and President Truman, and the imminent resignations of Secretary of State George C. Marshall and Under Secretary Robert Lovett, one of Forrestal's closest friends, must have been disconcerting for both Eisenhower and Forrestal. In December an optimistic Eisenhower had written, "I insisted that I *not* get into the *current* budget struggle when I go down to *consult & advise* with Forrestal." His two *Diary* entries that first week of January, however, reflected his budget concern, his determination that "decisions once reached *all* are to carry out faithfully, loyally & enthusiastically," and his preoccupation with a lack of leadership. "The President has to show the iron underneath the pretty glove," and he noted that Forrestal, whose mental health was deteriorating, "is looking badly." Eisenhower sensed a growing complexity and dimension—and perhaps a greater time commitment—to his task in Washington. Referring to Forrestal, he wrote, "Except for my liking, admiration and respect for his great qualities I'd not

go near Washington—even if I had to resign my Commission completely. To a certain extent these same feelings apply to H.S.T.—but
he does not see the problems so clearly as does Jim—and he does
not suffer so much due to the failure to solve the problems. I like
them both." As he returned to Morningside Heights Saturday afternoon, he acknowledged "the mess we are in."[20]

Eisenhower, meanwhile, had not forgotten the human resources
project, and he arranged for Ginzberg to talk with Forrestal. The
professor, "very unnerved" by the Secretary's anxious appearance,
described what the General and he had in mind. It excited Forrestal,
and he offered to help pay for it and supply personnel; moreover, he
assured Ginzberg that the Department of Defense would cooperate
fully. "Look, it is very tempting this business about money," Ginzberg
reported to Eisenhower, "because Phil Young and I are not finding it
all that easy, but I don't think it is right for you, and I'm not sure it is
right for the research project." He explained: "I could conceive that
we're going to come out finally with sets of findings which are going to be embarrassing the Department of Defense, and they are
going to start to raise troubles about publication and release. . . . So,
from purely scholarly results getting into the public domain, I just
don't like it, it's not comfortable. I don't know who will be the Secretary of Defense when this happens." Secondly, Ginzberg added,
"I don't want to be even the indirect source of any embarrassment to
you. . . you are the president of a non-profit institution. I don't think
it is appropriate to ride on your old connections, and somebody in
the press is going to take potshots at you using military connections
to get this funded. . . . We'll get the money." Eisenhower agreed.[21]

Eisenhower had only a week and a half in New York before reporting to duty at the Pentagon, although he planned to return regularly to Columbia for a few days at a time. He had important commitments on his calendar, in addition to the usual meetings, and he
wanted to send the first of several long letters to the University's
alumni and friends. Eisenhower, who seldom went downtown at
noon, during this period attended a series of midtown luncheons.
They included Tom Watson's for General Maxwell Taylor at the Union
Club, one at the Columbia University Club, a General Motors Corporation luncheon at the Waldorf-Astoria, and the Texaco Roundtable
and luncheon at the Chrysler Building, which Mrs. Eisenhower also
attended. At the Century Association he participated in the Carnegie
Corporation of New York's discussion on higher education. Over the

weekend he went shooting on Long Island, and one of his companions was Alden Hatch, who had written "The Prexy Plan for General Ike" for *Collier's* in 1947. Several nights later he had dinner with another well-known author and journalist, Henry Junior Taylor.[22]

An engagement at the prestigious Council on Foreign Relations took him back downtown that first Monday evening. During the fall the Council, which supported an internationalist foreign policy, had asked him to lead a study group on "the problems of aid to Europe," and he had invited a number of distinguished leaders to an organizing meeting and dinner on January 10. The idea, originally, had been to study the economic implications of the Marshall Plan, but by early 1949, with Washington moving towards the formation of the North Atlantic Treaty Organization and with Eisenhower as chairman, the group's emphasis shifted to military concerns. The members, "well informed about the latest developments," discussed at the session "the very strong interdependence between the Marshall Plan and the Alliance." General Eisenhower, according to one writer, "reported that the Truman administration was willing to do everything possible to support and strengthen a western European defense community." During the next two years the Council's meetings would broaden Eisenhower's understanding of the interplay between economics and politics in foreign policy.[23]

While Eisenhower benefited from his association with the European study group, the Administration's China policy and the collapse of the Nationalist forces created a political uproar in Washington and caused some consternation on the General's staff. At a time when the China bloc was bitterly criticizing the failure of the United States to help Chiang Kai-Shek's government against the communists, the Columbia College Alumni Association had decided to award the Alexander Hamilton Medal at its annual dinner on January 11 to an esteemed alumnus, V. K. Wellington Koo, Nationalist China's Ambassador to the United States. During Koo's remarkable diplomatic career he had played a key role in his country's admission to the League of Nations, and he had been one of China's delegates to the San Francisco United Nations Conference in 1945.

Kevin McCann saw a politically sensitive situation for the General, and on the afternoon of the ceremony he went to Bob Harron, the University's Director of Public Relations, and stated, "We better not have any photographs of Koo and Eisenhower." Harron assumed that this represented the General Eisenhower's wishes. "So," he recalled, "we got down to the reception" at the Biltmore Hotel. "The General and Mrs. Eisenhower were up in the suite with Provost and Mrs. Jacobs, and the reception was underway. The photographers came to me and said: 'Now, let's get a picture of the guest of honor, General Eisenhower, and Frank Hogan and get out of here.'" Harron, following McCann's instructions, told them, "I'm afraid you are not going to be able to get the picture of the General because he is going to be late. Why don't you take Mr. Koo and Frank Hogan and let it go at that." "No," they said, "we'd like to get the General."

The photographers then saw the General and Mrs. Eisenhower walking into the room and exclaimed, "There he is, right now, we can get him and get out." Harron went over and told Eisenhower, "General, the photographers are very insistent. They would like a picture of you, with Mr. Koo and with Mr. Hogan, but I can still dodge it if you think it is best." "Why," he replied, "why not take the picture. He is our guest of honor. Sure, we'll take the picture. Where do you want it?" Harron realized that the Chinese political situation was "not on his mind at all but Kevin was protecting him. . . . So, we got the picture and I went to Kevin and said, 'Why did you tell me that?'" Eisenhower's assistant merely commented, "Oh, he'll cross you up every once in a while" and laughed it off. Years later Jacobs, listening to Harron recall the episode, commented, "McCann was hired solely to write speeches for Eisenhower. He went way beyond the call of duty." While Harron never doubted "the sincerity of Kevin's loyalty to the General," it easily could have been an awkward public relations situation.[24]

During his brief time in New York Eisenhower had maintained a highly active and visible schedule, and his long letter to Columbia's alumni and friends would serve a public relations purpose and, as Davis noted, "prepare the way for the Columbia Fund solicitation." The University sent the letter after he had returned to Washington for Truman's Inauguration and reported to duty; moreover, the letter did not mention his departure, thereby conveying the impression that he was on duty in Low Memorial. The second and third letters, furthermore, would be mailed in February, while he was still in Washington, and neither contained any reference to his absence.[25]

During the fall Davis had assumed an increasingly influential role, and his office had prepared the initial draft, after consultations with Eisenhower and Jacobs. More than once Eisenhower told Dean

Carman, "You know, I think that the Trustees got me here with the idea that I would be a money raiser. I hate to raise money. I made it perfectly clear to them that I wouldn't be a money raiser. I will do my part. I will give dinners and luncheons, I'll make speeches, I'll shake hands, I'll explain the needs of the University." When Carman quipped in, "Well, Mr. President somebody has to put the bee on them," the General asserted, "It won't be me, never." He saw Davis working hard and willing "to put the bee on them." Jacobs recalled that "Ike leaned toward Davis and thought he was quite a guy." Carman added, "I think he was enthusiastic about Paul Davis because Paul Davis was tackling and was brought here to tackle this difficult problem of securing funds for the institution. It boils down to that."[26]

Davis took more and more of Eisenhower's time and established an elaborate organization. His methods, according to Major Schulz, were not "pleasing" to the General but Eisenhower realized that Davis had a professional reputation. Jacques Barzun, who became Provost years later, noted that Eisenhower was sent to a big foundation for a large grant, being told that with his prestige it would be just a matter of form; on the contrary, Barzun recalled, the foundation officers put Eisenhower through a grilling. After a few minutes he told the group, "Gentlemen, I know absolutely nothing about the subject which you want to discuss with me. I was not briefed and I am not prepared. I'm merely carrying to you something which the Trustees of the University and you are supposed to have worked out between you." Such a confrontation, Barzun added, would have badly embarrassed the General and, thereafter "you couldn't get him to go anywhere." Davis, McCann observed, "would use Dwight Eisenhower, of course, and in some ways Eisenhower would resent it. You don't like to be merely a tool to a vice-president." According to Harron, Davis "used to be in there at 8:30 in the morning and sit on Eisenhower's lap."

Still, Columbia only had had Butler as a fund-raiser, and Davis had "an almost insuperable obstacle" to overcome at Columbia. In the fall he had formed the Columbia Associates, with an annual membership fee of $1,000 and a membership goal of five hundred graduates and friends, to help launch the development program. Although by January it had only fourteen members (eight of them, including Eisenhower, were Trustees) and several had joined only after persuasive letters from Eisenhower, Davis saw the program as a start.[27]

Yet, in spite of Columbia's financial needs, Eisenhower worried more and more about federal aid to education and "the trend toward governmental centralization." He observed that "the American Museum of Natural History is nearing bankruptcy" and that "undoubtedly, the final answer will be 'federal aid.'" Writing in his *Diary* on January 14, he commented,. "Columbia University is feeling the effects, disastrously. Taxes leave prospective donors to university income so little in the way of spare income that only the most strenuous efforts keep us going at all. So," he added, "since this is typical of nearly all the privately endowed universities, we hear more and more, from educators themselves, of 'federal aid for education.' It is a dangerous slogan." While he acknowledged that the government could properly act "in certain limited fields," he argued that "federal money to support institutions, free grants of money to use as university authorities may desire," was an "immoral" proposition, "and its adoption, in this general sense, will lead to statism and, therefore, slavery."

"To help stop" this trend, Columbia's leader stated, "is one of the reasons I've taken on this strange, difficult, and often frustrating task." Specifically addressing some of the problems in his job, he declared, "The older trustees, officials, and friends of the university fear a businesslike organization (or so it seems). They move, think, and act slowly and fearfully. They won't see that we are living in a modern age, where leadership must manifest itself in terms of teams and that such teams must be interlocked in purposes and in operation." Concluding his *Diary* entry, he assessed the situation, "Financial support for Columbia must come from thousands (the days of the $100 million gift are gone or going fast). And money is the central university problem as of now."[28]

The President's letter "To Alumni and Friends" on January 20 stated the thoughts he had been stressing at Columbia:

> My job at Columbia is one of facilitating the educational and research work now going on in the University, of helping the faculty, students, and Alumni in working together. The job of "running" Columbia, in a detailed sense, is much too great for one man. It is a team effort of a high order.

He discussed physical plant needs and mentioned, specifically, "an adequate gymnasium on Morningside, a student center, and a field house for varsity and intramural sports at Baker Field." He noted his surprise at the "paperwork"—"I thought I was leaving those mountainous white piles forever" in Washington—and that he had insisted "that most projects be stated in one-typewritten page." He continued,

Our program is not one of expansion in terms of students and faculty. It is one of re-equipping ourselves and enlarging our assets in the light of present cost conditions in order to do our job with traditional Columbia excellence. . . . Columbia must obviously do more than prescribe courses and grant degrees no matter how advanced. It must furnish its share of leadership to education, not just for independent education, or for higher education, but for all education.

Columbia is a gift-supported university. . . . Columbia will remain congenial to new ideas, and to the testing and evaluation of all ideas. Its functions, I think, are national and human, not local and partisan.

Echoing a theme from his Installation Address, he concluded, "A major Columbia objective, I believe, is the training of youth for effective citizenship."

That morning he flew to Washington, and after President Truman's Inauguration he rode in the parade in Secretary of the Army Kenneth Royall's car; that evening, after attending the Inaugural Ball with Mrs. Eisenhower, he had a "chat" with the President at 11:15 P.M. The next morning he reported to the Pentagon and began his meetings with top military officials.[29]

On January 27, after the General attended a briefing for the House Subcommittee on Military Appropriations, the Eisenhowers left on an afternoon train to New York and attended a dinner given in honor of General Courtney Hodges and Admiral Thomas C. Kincaid. One sentence in a long *Diary* entry that day summarized his thoughts for the previous week: "The bitterness of the fight between Air and Navy is so noticeable that it is never absent from any discussion."[30]

He had only two working days in New York, since he and Mrs. Eisenhower tried to keep Sundays for themselves, and he had to pack much into his schedule. He discussed with Dean Smith of the School of Law his address to the New York State Bar Association the next night. McCann had shown Smith a draft; the subject was "bureaucracy" and Smith told the General that lawyers knew enough about bureaucracy. It was "a mistaken topic" and Smith suggested that he should talk about something he knew more than lawyers did. Eisenhower then went to an American Press Institute seminar and luncheon on campus, an alumni meeting at Columbia Presbyterian Medical Center at 168th Street, and finally downtown for a Friday dinner and evening session of his study group at the Council on Foreign Relations. That meeting undoubtedly had been scheduled for when he would be in the city.[31]

On Saturday, after Eisenhower met with Provost Jacobs, Dean Carman told him about the First Columbia College Forum on Democracy and asked him to give the "lead-off" talk to over a hundred high school student leaders on February 12. They discussed the program and soon Eisenhower was saying "This is wonderful. I'm delighted" but, he added, "I have to be in Washington that morning. I can't do it." The Dean could not refrain from replying that that was "a great disappointment to us. Is there any other time you could fit into the program?" Eisenhower sat silently for a few moments and then asked, "What time did you say this was?" "I said 11:30." "All right, Harry, I'll do it. I'll tell you, I've got a committee in the Pentagon that morning, meeting at nine o'clock. I'll get that committee started and then ask someone else to take over and say I'll be out for a short time. Then I'll hop a plane and I'll be here and you meet me at the office."[32]

Before the day was through, he had delivered two major addresses. At the Waldorf-Astoria he spoke at the Women's Colleges Conference to 2,000 New York alumnae of seven women's colleges. His theme reflected his worry about whether "we can make certain of survival of this wonderful American system, whose intricacies and complexities seem to demand more and more dependence on centralized government. . . . Unless women," he concluded, "are equally able along with men to detect that we are drifting toward something we hate with all our hearts, then we are doomed." For the Bar Association talk that evening, also at the Waldorf, he accepted Smith's suggestion. He spoke about Russia and Berlin to an audience of 1,200 persons and it was, according to Smith, "a hit." Both speeches received favorable press coverage.[33]

Once again, the General had demonstrated his energy, stamina, and resiliency; in many respects the visit to New York was a big success, but he had had little time in Low Memorial for Columbia. Had he, perhaps, returned primarily because he had agreed to the two prominent speaking commitments downtown and, consequently, had scheduled the Council on Foreign Relations meeting for a Friday evening? When he left Penn Station on the train in a heavy snow storm Monday morning, January 31, he planned to return to New York the following two weekends. Even he, though, had to question how long he could maintain such a strenuous schedule.

He had authorized sending on February 3 his second letter "To Alumni and Friends." "One of the happiest aspects of my new job," he began, "is getting away from my desk and visiting our Schools and Colleges to see how things are going." Describing Teachers College as "one of the foundation stones of the American educational system," and refuting the notion "about 'pinkos' at TC," the General expressed his "conviction that the leaders and faculty of Teachers College are supporting the assertion that the first mission of our schools is to prepare our youth for effective citizenship in a free democracy." Columbia, "engaged in a crusade,. . . intends to listen to all ideas, including those hostile to our own, but we also intend to devote ourselves to the task of making sure that our students understand America. We cannot win this crusade without your help," and he stated the "ways in which you, as an Alumnus, can help." The Columbia Fund would be writing alumni and friends and, Eisenhower concluded, "I hope that every one of us will put his shoulder to the wheel."[34]

The General during the week in Washington certainly would have preferred to think about the teacher being "the most important person in American society" rather than what he was recording in his *Diary*. He had had a series of briefings in the Navy Department, and the Navy had blocked his "idea of majority rule" in the Chiefs of Staff. What is now known as the "Revolt of the Admirals" was underway, and Forrestal, previously Secretary of the Navy and now "highly discouraged," sadly acknowledged that he trusted only a few in the Navy. "It must have cost him a lot," Eisenhower wrote, "to come to such a conclusion." Two days later Eisenbhower added that Truman and Forrestal "are going to have to get tough! and I mean tough!" It had been a bad week.[35]

When he returned to New York for the weekend and a Trustees luncheon and meeting on Monday, February 7—and to receive an honorary Phi Beta Kappa membership from Columbia's chapter and attend a Carnegie Corporation dinner—he had concluded that his Columbia obligations would have to take second place. No longer could he do both. His aide, Bob Schulz, recalled that during this period they would "go up to New York, be met by a car, go to Columbia, get a little work done, go down to a dinner at the Waldorf, usually, over to Penn Station, into a train, and do it all over again. And frankly," Schulz said, "there were days that I didn't know whether I was waking up in New York or Washington. And he must have been the same way. It was a rat race, pure and simple."[36]

Before a Saturday luncheon at the Union Club, Eisenhower had appointments with Doug Black, Philip Jessup, and General Marshall. The generals undoubtedly talked about the Washington situation, and four days later Eisenhower visited Marshall, who had been admitted to Walter Reed General Hospital, and then had a "long conversation" with the President. Jessup, on leave as Hamilton Fish Professor of International Law and Diplomacy, had been the Deputy Chief of the United States Mission to the United Nations and was directly involved in delicate negotiations with the Soviets over ending the Berlin Blockade. President Truman had just appointed him Ambassador at Large, and Eisenhower granted him another leave.[37] Black had become Eisenhower's closest friend on the Board of Trustees, and the General needed to talk with him not only about the proposed reorganization amendments but also his situation. Since he could not maintain his University commitments during the coming months, they discussed letters that he had had prepared for the Trustees and for the Deans and professors.

The President informed Chairman Coykendall of his decision, and the Trustees received the letter at the Monday Board Meeting. It was brief and to the point:

> From the date of my assumption of my present post it was, of course, understood between the Columbia Trustees and me that urgent public business would always have first claim on my time. It has now developed that the consultative and advisory functions which I have been performing in Washington will, during the near future, require for their accomplishment almost a full allocation of my time.
>
> While I am hopeful that this condition will not persist longer than some seven or eight weeks, I felt it my duty to call the present condition to the attention of the Trustees, with the assurance that I will continue to give to the University every possible attention that these overriding governmental preoccupations will permit.

After the Meeting Coykendall informed the press that the Trustees, "cognizant of the tradition of public service which has characterized Columbia's long history," gave "full approval" to the General's "important work in Washington." The *Spectator* reported, "Duties As Adviser Claim Eisenhower," and the *New York Times* stated, "EISENHOWER GETS TIME TO AID ARMY" and the subheads added "School Heads Carry On" and "No Acting President Named."[38]

The Trustees had had for their consideration important amendments to the Statutes creating a Vice President of the University and a Vice President in charge of medical affairs. They adopted the proposals, but Eisenhower's announcement gave them pause and they expressed reservations. The *Minutes*, of course, did not reflect their concern and hesitation. (The *Minutes* of the next meeting, March 7, interestingly stated "tentatively adopted" for those February proposals, and the Committee's further amendments at that March meeting differed considerably.) It had been agreed that Eisenhower, Marcy Dodge, and Doug Black would meet when the General returned to New York on Saturday, February 12. As Eisenhower subsequently acknowledged, the new proposals "would more nearly conform to the general ideas of the majority of Trustees" than the ones previously adopted. The Board had had no difficulty in passing the mandatory retirement provisions, effective in June, 1950, for administrative officers and academic personnel.[39]

Afterwards, President Eisenhower notified the Columbia community that he would be absent until mid-April. He stated that he had hoped "to divide my time between Washington and the Columbia campus, spending three days a week here in the fulfillment of local and University commitments . . . a just and practical compromise between compelling loyalties to the country and to Columbia." During the past week, however, "it became evident . . . I could not keep many significant University appointments on my calendar." He had a commitment to "spend nearly all of the next sixty days in Washington. From this commitment I can except only a University engagement for February 12, the Trustees Meeting in March, an engagement in Chicago late in February when I open the American Red Cross campaign for 1949," and he added "any emergency here at the University which may demand my presence."[40]

The General flew to Washington on the 8th, and during the week he had two "off-the-record" meetings with Truman. He agreed "to act as Chairman of JC/S for a brief (I hope) period," and he worried that "Pres. & Mr. F. apparently assume that I have some miraculous power to make some of these warring elements lie down in peace together.!!!!" (Secretary Forrestal's health continued to deteriorate during February, and on March 1 the President asked for his resignation.) Eisenhower returned to New York for the Student Forum, as he had promised Dean Carman, on Saturday, the 12th.[41]

First that morning, though, came the question of reorganization and the University's Statutes, and before his meeting with Trustees Black and Dodge the General discussed with Provost Jacobs what he wanted and considered "urgently necessary." He then met with them and, after reaching a "verbal agreement," he prepared a letter for Black: "This letter is to assure you that the changes you now propose in the planned scheme of University reorganization have my full approval." He emphasized that for months he had favored "establishing an individual in the organization who would serve as my principal assistant . . . and who would be recognized in the statutes as my 'alter ego' and successor during my necessary absences from the University or in the event of an emergency." Separately, he wanted the three vice presidents of Education, Business Affairs, and Development. "You now assure me," he added, "that in your opinion these changes will not only be welcomed by the Trustees but you believe also that they will be promptly accomplished, so that the whole matter can be cleared up, including the approval of new appointments, not later than the March meeting of the Trustees."

"With these assumptions and understandings," Eisenhower expanded the duties of Provost Jacobs. Next in line of "Officers of Administration" after the Provost came the Vice President of the University (Education), and he proposed Dean George Pegram, whose "great accomplishments, prestige, and character will instantly give to the post that distinction which it must always have." For the Vice President of Development, he nominated Paul Davis, who was "discharging the duties of this office as General Secretary." For the Vice President of Business Affairs position, he wrote that he was waiting for recommendations. He specifically reminded Black that the Trustee had assured him this new arrangement "would more nearly conform to the general ideas of the majority of Trustees than the one contained in the amendments recently made in the statutes." He planned to attend the March 7 meeting but, if a special meeting should be held, as Dodge had suggested, Eisenhower made clear that he doubted his ability to attend.[42]

By this time Dean Carman had arrived to take him over to Earl Hall for the College's First Forum on Democracy, attended by 130 secondary school student leaders. "As we walked out of his office," Carman recalled, Eisenhower said "Now, tell me again what this is? . . . What do you want me to say?" The Dean replied "It is entirely up to you. This is Lincoln's birthday, incidentally, and you come from the western part of the world. These are young men. Why don't you talk about some ideals which are down so deep." They already were "inside and walking upstairs," Carman continued. "It was packed, jammed, the photographers and all those there, and we walked right up on the rostrum." Ushering the President to his seat, Carman immediately went to the lectern and introduced him.

"There is a kind of dictatorship," Eisenhower began, "that can come about through a creeping paralysis of thought," and once again he emphasized the dangers of "federal intervention . . . this constant drift toward centralized bureaucratic government. . . a swarming of bureaucrats over the land." Continuing, he declared, "I believe it is things such as that we must watch today if we are going to be true to the standards that Lincoln gave to all of us." Carman timed him, remembering "He talked for seventeen minutes and when that was finished you could have taken it and sent it right off to the printer without a change, even the commas. It was a magnificent talk." Henry Graff recalled, "I was sure I was listening to the best extemporaneous speaker I had ever heard. He spoke with deep sincerity" and, referring also to the General's Guildhall Speech in 1945, the historian added, "He was a master of words."[43] On Sunday Eisenhower took the late night train back to Washington.

Before returning to New York for the March Trustees Meeting, he had flown to Chicago for the dinner and his speech launching the 1949 American Red Cross campaign. He spoke to five thousand persons, and the talk was broadcast nationally. McCann, Paul Davis, and Dean William Russell of Teachers College had joined him in Chicago, and McCann and Davis accompanied Eisenhower to a luncheon the next day at the Blackstone Hotel which Edward Bermingham and a few others attended. Bermingham had graduated from Columbia in 1909 and had been a highly successful partner at Lehman Brothers and at Dillon, Read until he retired early in 1940; he was a charter member of the Columbia Associates and the University's Fund Committee. That afternoon Eisenhower spoke to Columbia alumni at a reception and cocktail party and, then, demostrating his commitment to general education for citizenship and his interest in Teachers College he appeared briefly at a dinner with Dean Russell—two weeks later Eisenhower nominated Russell to became the first President of Teachers College in over fifty years.

That evening Bermingham gave a small dinner in the General's honor at the Chicago Club. The financier initially had suggested the dinner the day after Dewey's defeat, and he invited some of the city's most prominent businessmen and leaders to meet Eisenhower and listen to the General discuss the Columbia Associates and development program. "The dinner was a grand affair," Eisenhower wrote, "I am very fond of quail. . . . The entire party was relaxing and a memorable occasion." Davis also attended the dinner, and during this Chicago trip his aggressive fund raising tactics evidently alienated Bermingham. The former investment banker, already a close friend and adviser to the General, soon wrote that he was "out of sympathy with some growing tendencies of the development plan" and would not renew his membership on the University Fund Committee; he also informed Davis of his resignation from the Columbia Associates. When Eisenhower asked why, Bermingham stated that Columbia's fund-raising lacked "the traditional fineness and subtlety in keeping with its great dignity," and he urged Eisenhower not to be closely involved in the development program.[44]

The Trustees on March 7, after a tour of Columbia College and a luncheon, adopted the re-organization proposal, expanding the Provost's authority and adding, according to the President's request, a Vice President in Charge of Medical Affairs with the appointment Dean Willard C. Rappleye to the position. Afterwards, Coykendall announced that the new organization plan established "a principal assistant to the president . . .who will be recognized as the president's 'alter ego' and successor during his necessary absences or in the event of emergency." In effect, the Chairman emphasized, "Professor Jacobs has been performing the duties outlined by the new position for some time."[45]

The Trustees and Eisenhower gave the Provost two specific assignments. In order for the University "to proceed promptly with detailed reorganization," they appointed Jacobs chairman of a board, whose members included the three Vice Presidents, the Controller, and Joseph Campbell, the newly elected Treasurer. Second, Eisenhower directed "the sternest kind of re-examination" to bring the budget "as close to a balance as seems feasible" and had issued orders that "the 1950-1951 budget must be brought into balance."[46] Following the meeting Eisenhower led another session of his study group at the Council on Foreign Relations before resuming his duties in Washington; the previous week he had flown to New York one afternoon for a Deans' meeting and an address before 500 members of the New York City Bar Association.[47]

Shortly after the Trustees Meeting the Provost elaborated on the press release announcing the recent appointments. Addressed "to professors and administrative officers," he gave the background for the reorganization and presented the statutes for the new vice presidencies, emphasizing that the Vice President of the University was "head of the educational system." This meant, as critics quickly charged, that Deans, Directors, and Department Officers no longer had direct access to the Provost or President. Jacobs then gave the statute amendment for the Provost's Office and those designating the "Acting President," with the first four in the order of succession being the Provost, the Vice President of the University, the Dean of the Faculties, and the Dean of Columbia College. The Board on Reorganization, Jacobs noted, had instructions to prepare a plan establishing "definite lines of responsibility and authority applicable to all phases of the University's activities, functions and personnel, and to make recommendations . . . at the earliest practicable date" for the Trustees. "It is proposed," the Provost concluded, "to seek, determine, and put into effect improvements in the University administration and it is expected that this will be done by an orderly evolution."[48]

These significant administrative changes quickly gained a new importance. The situation in Washington was bothering the General more and more. "I am so weary of this inter-service struggle for position, prestige and power," he wrote on March 14, "that this morning I practically 'blew my top.' I would hate to have my doctor take my blood pressure at the moment." Five days later, after a series of JCS conferences, he bluntly began a *Diary* entry, "The situation grows intolerable." On March 21, after a staff meeting and Congressional testimony, Eisenhower attended "a rather lengthy" luncheon at the Association of Motion Pictures in Washington, and Major Schulz picked him up to take him to the Statler Hotel, where they were staying. He had not felt well when he had left for the Pentagon in the morning and, when the General got in the car, Schulz recalled lighting "a cigarette for him, and he threw it away. He said, 'My stomach is bothering me.'" He asked where General Snyder was and told Schulz, "You might ask him to drop in to see me." At the hotel they took Eisenhower to his room—by this time his stomach was bloated and "getting larger. It seemed like a balloon"—and Schulz immediately had a plane sent to fly Dr. Snyder down from New York. The doctor's diagnosis was "acute gastroenteritis," and he recommended complete rest.[49]

Eisenhower acknowledged in *At Ease* that he had been "struck with an attack of a most distressing kind (one that foreshadowed the ileitis attack of 1956)" and that "I was so ill that I lost touch with events." Snyder, he added, "treated me as though I were at the end of the precipice and teetering a bit. For days, my head was not off the pillow." A week after the attack Eisenhower, Snyder, and Schulz flew on President Truman's plane, *The Sacred Cow,* to Boca Chica, Florida, and upon leaving Washington he told reporters, "I'm not as puny as I look."[50]

The General convalesced and underwent detailed laboratory tests at the President's retreat at the Key West naval base. On March 30 General Snyder reported for the press that "the General is picking up very rapidly," and soon he was getting some exercise by practicing golf for thirty minutes. Eisenhower had not smoked since falling ill and, feeling better one morning, asked Snyder to "get him a package of cigarettes." Snyder pleaded with him to stop and the General, who smoked a "customary four packs," replied "I'll just have to quit." He did.[51]

On April 7 the Joint Chiefs arrived at Key West to resume discussions with Eisenhower about the 1950-1951 defense budget, and Secretary of Defense Louis Johnson, who had succeeded Forrestal, arrived on the 10th. General Snyder insisted, in spite of the important deliberations, that Eisenhower have time between sessions to rest and in the evenings they watched movies, including *The Secret Life of Walter Mitty* and *The Egg and I.* On April 12 the meetings ended and the General flew on *The Sacred Cow* to Augusta, Georgia. "Finally he decided," Cliff Roberts remembered, "the only way he was going to get better was to move out of there and come up to Augusta," and when he arrived he was "a very weak and a very sick man." Mamie Eisenhower joined him while he continued his recuperation, and in a few days he was playing golf and painting.[52] Meanwhile, rumors circulated that Eisenhower might not return to Columbia, and this added to the administration's difficulties as it addressed the budget crisis.

In recent years Eisenhower's illness in 1949 has provoked a controversy. A prominent cardiologist, Dr. Thomas Mattingly, who had been a consultant following Eisenhower's heart attack in 1955, argued that "gastroenteritis" was a cover-up by Dr. Snyder, a "deceptive diagnosis" for a mild heart attack. The General, Mattingly asserted, had "sanctioned and collaborated in" the deception, as he wanted "to keep his records free of any disease or physical abnormalities which might interfere with subsequent promotions and assignments." The implication: presidential ambitions and politics required deception. Clarence Lasby, however, has found the evidence "overwhelming" that "the problem really was with the stomach and not with the heart." General Eisenhower, he persuasively has concluded, "did not have a heart attack in 1949 and did not participate in a cover-up."[53]

Columbia's President, of course, could not attend the Trustees Meeting on April 4. He had sent a telegram to Coykendall, regretting "the circumstances" which prevented his presence and thanking those who had expressed concern. The Provost, present by invitation, discussed the President's business and was authorized to tell the academic departments that the budget for 1949-1950 was being restudied and that final adoption would be postponed until the May meeting. When Black reported to Eisenhower about the meeting, he emphasized that the Provost was "doing a terrific job" on the budget, and he assured the General that "everyone was in favor of your taking every bit of the time that your doctor suggests."[54] The President's first year at Columbia, nonetheless, was ending on a down note.

Jacobs' long, detailed letter about the deficit went to the major administrative officers immediately after the Board Meeting. The Trustees, he emphasized, had postponed adopting the 1949-1950 budget because of the necessity to restudy "with great care the budget provisions . . . to reduce materially the estimated deficit." The 1947-1948 deficit had been nearly $1,500,000 and for 1948-1949 "a deficit of at least $1,500,000 is clearly indicated." The Trustees, he added, had resolved that the 1950-1951 budget "must be balanced," and to do so, the 1949-1950 budget "will have to be reduced substantially below that of 1948-1949," since next year's income "may well be below" the current year. He proceeded to outline eleven steps, consequently, that had been taken. While "no decreases in academic salaries" would occur and departments could proceed with "recent nominations in regard to junior appointments," unfilled positions have been "eliminated," medical school tuition increased, and budgets for Building and Grounds and the Libraries reduced; he asked administrative officers "to economize . . . without lowering our academic standards" and stated "it is intended" that the recent administrative organization "will result in budgetary savings." Thus "consolidating our position" shall enable Columbia "to go forward confidently on a sound and firm basis." He concluded by urging support for the Development Program; gifts, though, had not noticeably reduced the current deficit and clearly did not play a significant role in the proposed budget. Several days later he wrote to the University's students. He explained the budget crisis and a one-sixth reduction in student aid and fellowships; he emphasized that the students should know what the University was doing to balance the budget, since the tuition increase the previous year had "decreased by half the deficit,"[55]

Throughout Eisenhower's illness Jacobs regularly informed him about major matters and kept other Columbia material from reaching the General's desk. The University's confidential letters for persons nominated for honorary degrees, however, caused a problem because they required the President's signature. Helen King had prepared the letters and "they went off to Georgia or wherever he was and they didn't come back"; finally, they came back with "a straight line drawn down" and "a little note from Schulz" to have them done for someone else's signature. Jacobs did discuss the budget in general terms in his letters to the General and by late April he reported considerable progress on the 1949-1950 budget and "significant steps toward the balanced budget we must have in the year 1950-1951." Carman, who was close to the budget decisions, described the situation in a letter to Columbia's Louis Hacker, Harmsworth Professor of American History at Oxford, 1949-1949. The Dean emphasized that Jacobs has "had the full brunt of the budget as far as the Trustees are concerned. The Trustees have been very hard-boiled."[56]

Eisenhower's absence removed him from the budget battle and ensuing criticism; it also, however, encouraged rumors which distracted the University and worried the Provost. *Newsweek*, just before the General's illness, had viewed his Washington assignment as "only the first step toward a return to full-time public life—possibly culminating in 1952." In Oklahoma a *Tulsa Tribune* editorial declared that "The begging job irked the General. So now speculation is current as to whether or not Eisenhower's leave of absence . . . may or may not mean his permanent departure from Columbia." The *Spectator* printed a long letter, which referred to the *Newsweek* article, under the heading "Suggest Eisenhower Resign." For its April 1st issue, the College's student paper reported that the "Academy of Motion Pictures Arts and Sciences awarded the coveted 'Oscar' for Best Supporting Role to Provost Albert C. Jacobs of Columbia University." Perhaps it was during this period that the *Spectator* editor went to Dean Carman and showed him the draft for a devastating editorial, asking "why is this man our president?" The College's Dean knew that this "would have simply added fuel to what was already developing." He asked the editor not to publish "Have We a President or Haven't We One?" and saved Eisenhower "from an editorial which would have been a scathing thing." And the more Jacobs substituted for Eisenhower, whether it be for a speech downtown, at an important Teachers College Alumni Dinner, or awarding the Pulitzer Prizes, the more it reminded people of the General's absence from Columbia.[57]

The Provost decided, consequently, to address directly "Rumor in the University." He selected an event which would receive widespread publicity, the dinner of the American Press Institute Seminar of City Editors on April 11. Twenty-three city-editors had been invited by Dean Ackerman, and Jacobs informed the experienced journalists that those attending the Institute's seminar a few years earlier had been told, "We are here because we recognize the tremendous social responsibilities which are ours, responsibilities of a scope and complexity scarcely dreamed of by newspapermen a short generation ago." He added, commenting on the saying that "two principal ingredients in a newspaperman's professional diet are fact and rumor," that "Here, at Columbia, we are fast becoming intimately acquainted with rumor—rumor with a Capital 'R.'"

First, he recalled that during 1948, in the months before and immediately after Eisenhower's arrival at Columbia, "we were inundated with predictions, constantly repeated and enlarged, that our new President would never arrive, or, having arrived, would shortly make his exit at the call of a political convention." He continued. "Against all those rumors we had no defense and no-counter weapon except the statement, 'General Eisenhower is not interested in political office.' We had to wait until fact gave the lie to rumor."

"This year," the Provost emphasized, "the barrage has been even more varied and unceasing. Last week opened with a statement that Mr. Truman is cozying up to General Eisenhower with an eye to '52; it closed with a flat statement"—Jacobs did not mention the newspaper, the *New York World-Telegram*—"that General Eisenhower was fed up with Columbia and Columbia with him," and if the Secretary of Defense "would have him, he would like to be Chairman of the Joint Chiefs-of-Staff or Commander of the defense forces to be established under the North Atlantic Pact." And, Jacobs continued, "a myriad of rumors, as wild or even wilder," existed, "possessing only one trait in common—lack of a truth element that might make an eventual scoop."

Jacobs acknowledged that Eisenhower had had "some apprehension" as a professional soldier upon arriving at Columbia and that "he had some difficulty adjusting himself to what he called 'the vertical living conditions of New York City.'" However, every one of Eisenhower's plans, the Provost asserted, "including this afternoon when he talked to Columbia long-distance from Key West, every last one of them is based on his firm belief that he will be President of Columbia for years to come." Eisenhower's Washington "service has, of course, kept the General away from the University a good deal and has prevented him from seeing as much as he would like of students and staff . . . . But, while here, he has, I assure you, put in full days during which he has devoted himself enthusiastically and energetically to the duties of the University." Provost Jacobs continued, "Again I say—that against these rumors we have no defense and no counter-weapon except the statement: 'President Eisenhower is returning to Columbia.' Again, we will have to wait until fact gives lie to rumor." In conclusion, the Provost also denied "emphatically" to the newspaper editors that "Columbia is predominantly 'red'" and asserted that "academic freedom must be preserved."[58]

The rumors, nonetheless, persisted while Eisenhower continued his recovery and played golf and bridge at Augusta National. Dean Ackerman told Jacobs that his speech had been "widely read," but that "speculation" would persist until Eisenhower returned to Morningside Heights. During their conversation, according to the Journalism Dean, McCann came into the Provost's office and said "he did not know where Defense Secretary Johnson got the information that General Eisenhower was going to spend two or three weeks more in Washington. . . . It was not the General's intention to return to Washington." McCann added that "he thought the struggle of conscience was over but he did not know whether the General was going to resign his commission in the Army." Jacobs replied that he had told Eisenhower that "he did not think it was necessary or desirable" to resign, but Ackerman inferred from the conversation between Jacobs and McCann that the General "has been struggling with the issue . . . in order to be completely free to give his time to the University."[59]

Eisenhower was still at Augusta when the Trustees met on May 2 and adopted the budget for the 1949-1950 academic year. The Provost had cut expenses by nearly $800,000 and estimated an income increase of approximately $168,000. The estimated deficit would be "just over $300,000," and "the Trustees," Jacobs reported to Eisenhower after the meeting, "seemed very pleased with what we had done in bringing income and expense closer together." Progress had been made on the road to a balanced budget for 1950-1951. The Trustees did request, however, that Eisenhower appoint a committee to study thoroughly "the educational and financial system" and make recommendations no later than the December, 1949, meeting for possible Trustee action in balancing the budget.

Furthermore, the Committee on Development proposed, and it was adopted, that in the reorganization of the executive offices "attention be given to an effective grouping of the functions and responsibilities related to procurement of gifts, grants, and bequests." A Special Meeting to consider a Development Committee Report was scheduled for June 7. Marcy Dodge, later emphasizing to Jacobs that the appointment of Treasurer Campbell as Acting Vice President in charge of business affairs "is now entirely up to you and the President," assured him that the Board would act on the nomination. The Provost, who also discussed the appointment with Trustees Putnam and Jackson at the Downtown Association, soon recommended Campbell on Eisenhower's behalf to the appropriate Trustee Committee. "It has been impossible," Jacobs argued, "to proceed further with this reorganization" until the Business Affairs position has been filled.[60]

Eisenhower, who found the budget report "encouraging" and "a tonic not found elsewhere," expressed his hope that Jacobs could find "an equally effective solution . . . that will minimize my personal attendance at semi-business dinners and cocktail gatherings . . . upon my return to Morningside Heights." A few days later Dodge wrote the Provost, "Evidently you are the man of the hour so far as saving the strength of General Eisenhower is concerned. . . . All I can say is I hope you are successful." Eisenhower, meanwhile, had written the Secretary of Defense that he would be in Washington for several days, and he arrived from Augusta on May 11. He attended three JCS meetings, a War Council meeting, an Economic Development luncheon with the President and Cabinet, a luncheon with Johnson, and an off-the-record meeting with Truman before flying to New York on Friday evening, May 13. New York newspapers reported his return to work in Low Memorial on Saturday, with the

Herald-Tribune adding it was understood that the General would meet with the JCS "in Washington about once a week."[61]

Since the Provost's Office had been handling University affairs for the President, Eisenhower had few Columbia matters on his desk. The Trustees had requested a committee to examine the University's finances and to make recommendations to the Board for balancing the budget, and Eisenhower noted in pencil "Provost see me re this DE." Jacobs, in turn, would pencil in his name and Vice Presidents Pegram, Davis, and Rappleye, and Treasurer Campbell. The President also reminded the Provost of "the most pressing importance" of the Organizational Committee's duties. Until "a comprehensive and detailed plan" is developed, "there is bound to be confusion and delay in all our work, particularly in the all-important business of promoting the University's standing in the fund-raising field." As soon as Commencement was over, Eisenhower noted to Jacobs: "I desire that you give first priority to the completion" of this work.[62]

Though back on campus, he continued to delegate responsibilities to the Provost; meanwhile, he reduced his own schedule. He wrote to his brother Milton that he and Mamie would "leave New York about the 20th of July" for summer vacation and that he planned "to take not less than a total of 10 weeks' leave during the year." He added, "If I am not able to keep up to this leave schedule. I will simply quit all my jobs except that of helping out in Washington."[63]

During his first weeks back at Columbia he arranged to play golf three or four times a week and kept those evenings free from engagements. His Augusta friends had made him an honorary member at Blind Brook, in Port Chester, near the Connecticut border, and he also played at Deepdale, Roberts' club on Long Island. The evenings were for bridge at 60 Morningside, and they occurred so often while they were at Columbia "because Mamie didn't like his going out without her to other places. And she didn't care how much he played bridge, she was perfectly happy to have him play bridge all evening or all day long during a holiday, just as long as he played at home." May 25, less than two weeks after his return, he flew to Washington for the day to attend Forrestal's funeral—the former Secretary had committed suicide during the night of May 21-22— and, then, a meeting with Johnson and the JCS.[64]

The President's emphasis on fund-raising stemmed not only from the budget deficits but also from Paul Davis' report in mid-April on the Development Program. In 1946 Columbia had had a $40,000,000 goal over a ten-year period, but this "objective was entirely inadequate" and by the time of Eisenhower's Installation the figure had jumped to $210,000,000—"into the stratosphere." Success, Davis wrote, would "require major adjustments, the greatest adjustments being in terms of thinking, talking, and work habits of our entire University group in relation to gift procurement activities." The Trustees Development Committee would have for membership those "most experienced in sales and promotion" and they would have no other assignments. The administrative officers, he emphasized, in this new system would "assign at least one-fourth of their time to development activities and at least three-fourths of that one-fourth specifically to gift procurement and gift procurement organization." Writing with a rhetorical fervor which would appeal to Eisenhower, Davis asserted, "The struggle, the fierce competition, the battle for survival that is inherent in the American pattern of life should be accepted as a part of the life of an independent university, and in that part everyone should participate." Emphasizing that "development is hard work," he concluded, "No one should look back and long for the old days when the president of the University supplied us with money, but should welcome the opportunity to enter into the spirit of the team as full participants in the competitive struggle."[65]

That Davis' message and plan would strike a responsive cord in Eisenhower was not surprising. "The General disliked raising money," Dean Carman stated, "and I can see perfectly how he would be pleased to have that responsibility lifted from his shoulders by someone else, and the someone else around here he thought could do it was Paul." The proposal did not entrust the President with a primary responsibility; moreover, Davis was energetically taking the leadership and assigning everyone, as part of the team, a significant role. The General saw this as an effective arrangement and believed that the sooner the University's organization was completed along the lines of the Trustees' fund-raising emphasis, the sooner the Development Program could proceed.[66]

Prominent academics, though, viewed Davis and his proposals differently. Ackerman had stated at a conference of Deans that it would be difficult for Deans to raise money, when it was known that under the re-organization they did not have direct access to the President or the Provost and, he added, "Heretofore Deans have not been responsible for deficits which they had nothing whatsoever to do with, either as cause or effect." Furthermore, Ackerman argued that Davis' system "cannot be applied to newspaper, magazine, radio and other industries because they cannot be pressured into action by the customary methods of fund raising campaigns."[67]

Dean Carman, emphasizing how Davis could be "almost brutal in accomplishing his own particular ends," asserted "that fully one-third of my time is spent on development and money raising." Yet, he recalled, "I shall never forget coming up from downtown in a taxi and, boy, I never got such a going over from a fellow as I got from Paul, because Paul felt I was not playing the role that I ought to play as Dean of Columbia College. I wasn't getting out and hitting hard enough to get money for the institution." Jacques Barzun, after noting that Davis "infuriated some of the older and most distinguished members of the faculty," considered the Vice President "a vulgarian and a fool and an incompetent." The Provost, meanwhile, must have wondered how he could devote one-fourth of his time when, for months, he had been doing most of the President's duties in addition to his own. Even Kevin McCann in the President's Office saw that "the academic people resented Paul very much . . . and that there was deep resentment against Paul Davis."[68] Davis' proposals, nonetheless, proceeded with Eisenhower's support, and the Trustee Committee on Development would submit its long report at the Special Meeting on June 7.

On June 1 President Eisenhower conducted his first Columbia University Commencement. Eighteen thousand persons attended the ceremony in front of Low Memorial and heard him stress, "We are belabored by the demagogues of the right and left, both of whom would turn back the clock of history to the days of regimented humanity." Warning about "the modern preachers of the paternalistic state," he declared, "Blinding themselves to the inevitable growth of despotism, they—craven-like—seek, through government, assurance that they can forever count upon a full stomach and warm cloak or—perhaps—the sinister-minded among them think, by playing upon our fears, to become the masters of our lives. In the years ahead," he declared, "the fundamental struggle of our time may be decided between those who would further apply to our daily lives the concept of individual freedom and equality; and those who would subordinate the individual to the dictates of the state." Provost Jacobs read the citations for the honorary degree recipients who included the actress Helen Hayes MacArthur; the *New York Herald-Tribune's* president, Helen Rogers Reid; Nobel Prize-winner Hermann Joseph Muller; Charles Wilson of General Motors; the historian Arnold Toynbee; the former president of the Rockefeller Foundation, Raymond B. Fosdick; the British Ambassador; and Generals Lucius Clay and Omar Bradley. Among recipients of the University Medal of Excellence were librettist Oscar Hammerstein II and composer Richard Rodgers, who had received a Special Pulitzer Citation for *Oklahoma* and whose *South Pacific* was playing on Broadway with enormous fanfare. It was a memorable 195th Commencement for Columbia.[69]

President Eisenhower, who "wouldn't even read the citations for the honorary degrees," according to Jacobs, decided not to hold the traditional reception after the ceremony for the University's distinguished guests, and Provost and Mrs. Jacobs honored them at the Men's Faculty Club. Mamie Eisenhower regretted the invitation from Loretta Jacobs, writing that they would have "house guests." The guests, also guests of the University, were honorary degree recipient Clay and his wife, and they went to 60 Morningside Drive; the Bradleys attended the official reception. When Doug Black arrived at the Eisenhowers' after the reception, the General introduced him to Clay, who had just retired from the Army as Commander in Chief, U.S. Forces in Europe, and Military Governor for the U.S. zone in Germany. Black and Clay, and possibly the *Herald-Tribune's* Bill Robinson, discussed a proposal for Clay's memoirs, which would be published by Doubleday in 1950.[70]

Suddenly, during the week after Commencement, the administration—and the reorganization plan—were shaken by Provost Jacobs' decision to leave the University. One Saturday in April two representatives from the University of Denver had appeared in Low Memorial without an appointment and asked him for recommendations for a new Chancellor of the University. They then invited Jacobs to luncheon on Monday and asked if he would consider the position. Jacobs, who previously had declined an offer to become Director of the Commonwealth Foundation, knew that his wife never had enjoyed living and raising their children in New York City and that she was upset about the strenuous schedule he had had for months. Loretta Jacobs, whose father had been a Regent of the University of Michigan for over three decades, immediately expressed her strong interest, and they officially visited Denver the first weekend in May. Thereafter, she waged "a virtual campaign," according to the Provost's Assistant, R. Gordon Hoxie, to persuade her husband to accept the Denver offer. When she invited a few of their close Columbia friends for his forty-ninth birthday on May 21, her theme was "We'll be the '49ers going west" and the party's decorations included pioneers, covered wagons, and '49ers. Adrienne Swift, his long-time secretary, was at the Jacobs residence in the townhouse on 117th Street that evening with her husband, the Manager of the Faculty Club, and she realized that Mrs. Jacobs "wanted out, though he loved Columbia and would have stayed." A few days later Jacobs, faced with the responsibilities of Commencement and torn by conflicting pressures, received an extension from the University of Denver for his decision.[71]

Harry Carman knew that "the General was very much taken back about this" and went to Professor John Krout. Jacobs had recommended Krout, the Chairman of the History Department, to succeed the late Harry Morgan Ayres as Director of the School of General Studies and of the University Summer Session, and he had recently appointed him Dean of the Graduate Faculties to succeed George Pegram. Carman and Krout, long-time colleagues and friends of the Provost, knew the family pressure on him but "went to Jacobs and almost on bended knee," according to Carman, and "said 'my God, Al, are you crazy?'" Jacobs, who acknowledged that Davis was "one of the very unhappy associations at Columbia during the Eisenhower regime" and felt that he had "the inside track," replied that the Vice President was "making him increasingly useless to this place." Carman and Krout quickly stated, "Listen, keep your shirt on. We are willing to wager money with you that in two or three months Paul Davis will be out of here."

The Provost confided in only a few persons about the offer, and his closest associates at Columbia—from Carman and Krout to Pegram, Dean Smith, Campbell, and Trustees Dodge and Warren— realized how overworked he was fulfilling the President's and Provost's responsibilities. As Dean James Kip Finch, Dean of the School of Engineering, would write, "You have been burning the candle at both ends and in the middle. Enthusiasm for and devotion to work is essential but we only live once. At the clip you were going it could only end in a short tour of duty." They had, thus, a hard time asking him to continue doing what he had been, especially when Carman recently had written to Professor Hacker that "Jacobs has worked like a dog" and the Dean wondered if Eisenhower "is in good enough shape to undertake many duties which are certain to come his way.[72]

Eisenhower did everything he could to keep his chief of staff.[73] "It upset the President, to be very frank," Hoxie recalled, "several Trustees said that to me." Watson and Parkinson, after all, had assured the General, when he had accepted the Presidency, that Jacobs would stay on for a while, and he had come to rely heavily on the Provost as they developed a close friendship and mutual admiration. "Eisenhower," Jacobs recalled, "tried to get me to stay." As early as November the General had suggested calling Jacobs' position "Chancellor," meaning President; now, Jacobs added, "Ike said: 'I'll make myself Chancellor and make you President.'" Marcy Dodge, knowing Loretta Jacobs' sentiments about living in the City, offered to purchase for the University a home for the Jacobses within commuting distance.[74]

Jacobs had agreed to call the University of Denver late on the afternoon of June 7, and he turned down the offer. Dodge wired Jacobs that George "Warren and I delighted to hear of action taken last evening." Mrs. Jacobs, convinced that he would accept, before the decision had flown to her family's home Ann Arbor with a daughter; she called from the airport in Michigan and, though he could be seen walking home, she decided to go on to Ann Arbor and then call back. When she did, she was stunned. A lengthy conversation ensued, and Jacobs returned to Low Memorial and called Denver. When he finally reached the Board Chairman, he asked to reconsider his decision, and a meeting was arranged for June 10 in Chicago. As Adrienne Swift noted, Jacobs "went with the family. . . he never was back and forth with things like that, he was quite decisive."

Loretta Jacobs quickly returned to New York, and Eisenhower canceled his appointments for a meeting with her in his office on the 9th. It must have been an unusual occasion for the former Supreme Commander. Not only was his chief of staff leaving, he was unaccustomed to discussing his professional matters with women; and, now, he was trying to persuade Loretta Jacobs to change her mind so that the Provost would remain at Columbia. Eisenhower's efforts, Jacobs wrote, "did not impress Loretta one iota." She remained convinced that "I must get out of New York." Years later, when she recalled her meeting with the President and his offer of the Chancellor-President proposal, with a tone of regret she said, "It might have made a difference if it had been clearer sooner." On June 16th Jacobs reluctantly wrote to President Eisenhower, "I talked with Denver yesterday and am going ahead with the offer they have given me. I see no other solution. I appreciate very greatly your sympathetic understanding." Lou Little, with a marvelous sense of irony, wrote to Al Jacobs that it was an "odd turn of fate," considering when he had wanted to leave Columbia.[75]

The Provost emphasized that he had told Denver he would remain in New York as long as Eisenhower wished and "until after I complete in addition to my regular work the several important missions I mentioned yesterday." The next day he prepared a detailed memorandum for the President, specifically listing the undertakings they had discussed for the Provost:

> These include, among others, recommendation of a Vice President of the University to succeed Dr. Pegram; recommendation of a Dean for Columbia College to succeed Dean Carman; recommendation of a Dean for the School of Engineering to succeed Dean Finch; recommendation of a Provost of the University to succeed myself; recommendation of a Registrar . . . ; final resolution of the Director of University Admissions . . .; the further implementation of the reorganization of the University; the work in regard to budget and finance which you have asked me to assume; and, lastly, the final resolution of the Vice Presidency in Charge of Business Affairs.

Eisenhower relied on the Provost for this work; these were, Jacobs wrote, "very important matters affecting the future of the University." While the Provost did not "know how long it will take me to make the necessary recommendations to you," he emphasized that he intended "to forego most if not all of any vacation this summer."[76]

Eisenhower would be away from Columbia for two months that summer; while he was gone, Jacobs worked on the various recommendations. Many had considered Eisenhower and Jacobs "a team," but that arrangement and the General's reorganization plans had unraveled. When he returned to Morningside Heights in September, his chief of staff would be leaving for Denver in mid-October and significant personnel changes in the Administration were pending. For the President, the scene and atmosphere differed considerably from when he had started his tour of duty in Washington the previous fall.

Notes

1. *The Forrestal Diaries* (New York, 1951), ed. Walter Millis, pp. 532, 535-36; Eisenhower, *Diary*, December 13, 1948, *The Papers of Dwight David Eisenhower*, vol. X (Baltimore, Md., 1984), *Columbia University*, ed. Louis Galambos, pp. 365-68 (*PDDE*).

2.   Ibid., XI, 1578; Eisenhower to Gruenther, July 28, 1948, ibid., X, 168-69; *New York Times*, July 25, 1948.
3.   Forrestal to Truman, November 9, 1948, cited by *PDDE*, X, 282, fn. #3; ibid., 365-68; Dwight D. Eisenhower, *At Ease: Stories I Tell to Friends* (New York, 1967), p. 352.
4.   Eli Ginzberg, Oral History Interview, May 14, 1975, Dwight David Eisenhower Library (OHDDEL), 1975; Eli Ginzberg, personal interview, December 11, 1990, New York, N. Y.; Eisenhower, *At Ease*, pp. 350-51.
5.   Ginzberg, interview, 1975, OHDDEL; Albert C. Jacobs to Eisenhower, November 10, 1948, with Eisenhower's handwritten note, Central Archives, Columbia University; (CACU); Ginzberg to Jacobs, November 24, 1948, and Ginzberg's report, "Adjustment to Work," ibid.
6.   Eisenhower to David Dubinsky, December 18, 1948, CACU; see, also, Eisenhower to Frank Abrams, December 18, 1948, *PDDE*, X, 375-77; Ginzberg to author, May 4, 1999.
7.   The Trustee Committee had asked Fackenthal to work on reorganization with a faculty committee. Trustees of Columbia University in the City of New York, *Minutes*, December 6, 1948, CACU; Eisenhower to Frank Fackenthal, November 17, 1948, and Eisenhower to Douglas Black, November 22, 1948, *PDDE*, X, 303-306, 316.
8.   *New York Herald-Tribune*, November 29, 1948; Jacobs to Eisenhower, December 3, 1948, CACU; see also *Columbia Spectator*, November 29, 1948.
9.   *PDDE*, XI, 1578-79; Eisenhower to Deane Waldo Malott, November 22, 1948, James Bryant Conant to Eisenhower, December 1, 1948, and Henry Merritt Wriston to Eisenhower, December 6, 1948, ibid., X, 318-19, 333-34, 352-53.
10. Harry J. Carman, personal interview, December 1, 1961, New York, N. Y.; Jacques Barzun, personal interview, April 5, 1979, New York, N. Y.; Henry F. Graff, personal interview, June 13, 1991, New York, N. Y.; Graff, letter to the editor, *Presidential Studies Quarterly*, XXV (Fall 1995), 862-63.
11. Joseph and Stewart Alsop, "Matter of Fact," *New York Herald-Tribune*, December 6, 1948.
12. Trustees, *Minutes*, December 6, 1948, CACU.
13. Eisenhower, *Diary*, December 13, 1948, *PDDE*, X, 365-68; *New York World-Telegram*, December 15, 1948; Robert Harron, memorandum, December 15, 1948, Eisenhower MSS., DDEL; *Columbia Spectator*, December 16, 1948; Millis, ed., *Forrestal Diaries*, p. 540.
14. Eisenhower *Diary*, December 17, 1948, *PDDE*, X, 369-71; *Columbia Spectator*, December 16, 1948; Carman, interview, December 1, 1961.
15. Howard M. Snyder, "Summary of 1948," Snyder MSS., DDEL.
16. *PDDE*, XI, 1580-81; University Council, *Minutes*, December 21, 1948; Jacobs to George Pegram, December 14, 1948, CACU.
17. Albert C. Jacobs, "Memoirs," 1974; *New York Times*, January 1, 1949.
18. *PDDE*, XI, 1581-82; Trustees, *Minutes*, January 3, 1949, CACU; Jackson to Eisenhower, December 28, 1948, and January 26, 1949, ibid.; see also *PDDE*, X, 286, and fn. #2, 329-30.
19. Ibid.; Trustees, *Minutes*, November 7 and December 5, 1949, ibid.; see also *PDDE*, X, 153, 673-74.
20. *New York Times*, January 6, 1949; Eisenhower, Diary, December 17, 1948, January 7 and 8, 1949, *PDDE*, X, 369-71, 398-400, 401-403. The slightly different wording for the January 7 entry is in *The Eisenhower Diaries*, ed. by Robert H. Ferrell (New York, 1981), p. 152.
21. Ginzberg, interview, December 11, 1990.

22. *PDDE*, XI, 1582-83.
23. Michael Wala, "An 'Education in Foreign Affairs for the Future President': The Council on Foreign Relations and Dwight D. Eisenhower," in *Examining the Eisenhower Presidency*, ed. Shirley Anne Warshaw (Westport, Ct.,1993), pp. 1-16.
24. Robert C. Harron, personal interview, December 1, 1961, New York, N. Y.; Harron and Albert C. Jacobs, personal interview, February 5, 1965, Hartford, Ct; *New York Times*, January 12, 1949. Koo warned that a "militant Communism" enslaving China would endanger free peoples everywhere. *Columbia Spectator*, January 13, 1949.
25. Davis sent Jacobs on December 31, 1948, a two-page memorandum outlining the proposed letters. Jacobs gave the memorandum to Eisenhower when the latter returned from Colorado on January 3, and the General proposed to discuss it informally with the Trustees that afternoon. CACU.
26. Carman, interview, December 1, 1961; Jacobs, interview, February 5, 1965.
27. R.Gordon Hoxie, personal interview, November 10, 1978, N. Y., New York; Robert L. Schulz, personal interview, March 11, 1958, Washington, D.C.; Jacques Barzun, personal interview, April 5, 1979, New York, N. Y.; Kevin McCann, personal interview, July 25, 1972, Gettysburg, Pa.; Robert C. Harron, interview, February 5, 1965; Paul H. Davis to Eisenhower, January 7, 1949, CACU. See also "Proposed Plan of Columbia Associates," October 27, 1948, CACU, and Eisenhower's letters to Watson on October 15, to Sulzberger on October 21, and to John D. Rockefeller, Jr., on November 18, 1948, *PDDE*, X, 247, 260, 312-13.
28. Eisenhower, *Diary*, January 14, 1949, *PDDE*, X, 430-32.
29. Eisenhower "To Alumni and Friends," January 20, 1949, ibid., X, 441-44; Fn. #2, ibid., 446.
30. Eisenhower, *Diary*, January 27, 1949, *PDDE*, X, 448-51.
31. Young B. Smith, personal interview, April 26, 1959, New York, New York; *PDDE*, X, 1585.
32. Carman, interview, December 1, 1961.
33. *New York Times*, January 30, 1949; Carl W. Ackerman, unpublished manuscript, Ackerman MSS, Library of Congress (LC); Smith, interview, April 26, 1959.
34. Eisenhower "To Alumni and Friends," February 3, 1949; *New York Times*, February 4, 1949; His third letter would be sent on February 24, 1949, and the *Washington Times-Herald* headline read, "Ike Tells Alumni Vigilance Is Cost of Free America," February 27, 1949; *PDDE*, X, 462-65, 505-508.
35. Eisenhower, *Diary*, February 2 and 4, 1949, ibid., 461-63, 465-66.
36. Robert L. Schulz, 1968, COHP.
37. *PDDE*, XI, 1586; *Columbia Spectator*, February 18, 1949.
38. Eisenhower to Frederick Coykendall, February 7, 1949, *PDDE*, X, 479; *Columbia Spectator*, February 8, 1949; *New York Times*, February 8, 1949.
39. Trustees, *Minutes*, February 7 and March 7, 1949, CACU; Eisenhower to Black, February 12, 1949, *PDDE*, X, 486-89.
40. See Eisenhower to Harry Carman, February 7, 1949, ibid., 477-79.
41. Eisenhower, *Diary*, February 9, 1949, *PDDE*, X, 483-85; *New York Times*, February 12, 1949.
42. Eisenhower to Black, February 12, 1949, *PDDE*, X, 486-89.
43. Carman, interview, December 1, 1961; *New York Times*, February 13, 1949; *Columbia Spectator*, February 14, 1949; *PDDE*, X, fns. #3, 439, and #5, 479; Henry F. Graff, "Two Who Liked Ike," *Columbia* (February, 1985), p. 18; Graff, interview, June 13, 1991.
44. *New York Times* March 1, 1949; Eisenhower to Bermingham (with guest list), March 4, 1949, Eisenhower MSS.; *PDDE*, X, fn. #4, 520; ibid., XI, 1589; Bermingham to Eisenhower, July 13 and July 23, 1949, Eisenhower MSS., Dwight David

Eisenhower Library (DDEL); *PDDE*, X, fn. #2, 707; Peter Lyon, *Eisenhower: Portrait of the Hero* (Boston, 1974), pp. 390-91.

45. *New York Times*, March 8, 1949. *Time's* article on the appointments included a photograph of the Provost with the caption "an alter ego." March 21, 1949, pp. 47-48.

46. Trustees, *Minutes*, March 7, 1949, CACU; Eisenhower to Jacobs, March 8, 1949, and Eisenhower to Coykendall, March 9, 1949, *PDE*, X, 535-38.

47. *Columbia Spectator*, March 4, 1949; *PDDE*, XI, p. 1590.

48. Jacobs to Professors and Chief Administrative Officers, March 15, 1949, CACU; Eisenhower to Jacobs, March 8, 1949, *PDDE*, X, 535-36.

49. Schulz, interview, 1968, COHP; Snyder, "Summary of Year 1949," Snyder MSS., DDEL; Eisenhower to Henry H. Arnold, March 14, 1949, and *Diary*, March 19, 1949, *PDDE*, X, 544-46 and fn. #7, p. 547. Snyder earlier had written that Eisenhower's "anger explosion caused me great concern." "Summary of Year 1947," Snyder MSS., DDEL.

50. Eisenhower, *At Ease*, pp. 332-33, 354-55; *New York Times*, March 29, 1949.

51. Snyder, "Summary of Year 1949;" Snyder MSS., DDEL; *New York Times*, March 29, March 31, April 1, 1949; Eisenhower, *At Ease*, pp. 354-55. Just before the illness, the General's office had informed Provost Jacobs that Eisenhower would attend the Dean's Day luncheon on Saturday, April 2, and the Trustees Meeting on April 4. Jacobs to Dodge, March 22, 1949, CACU.

52. "Chronology," April 7-12, 1949, *PDDE*, X, 1592-93; *New York Times*, April 13, 1949; Roberts, personal interview, September 12, 1968, COHP. According to Snyder, this was the first painting he had "done from real life." Snyder MSS., DDEL.

53. Clarence G. Lasby, *Eisenhower's Heart Attack: How Ike Beat Heart Disease and Held on to the Presidency* (Lawrence, Kans.,1997), pp. 39-50.

54. Trustees, *Minutes*, April 4, 1949, CACU; Eisenhower telegram to Coykendall, April 3, 1949, and Black to Eisenhower, April 5, 1949, *PDDE*, X, 553.

55. Jacobs to Major Administrative Officers and Executive Officers of Departments, April 4, 1949; Jacobs to students, April 7, 1949, CACU.

56. Jacobs to Eisenhower, April 8, April 10, April 15, and April 24, 1949, Eisenhower MSS.; see also *PDDE*, X, 567; Helen King, Oral History Interview, May 12, 1975, OHDDEL; Carman to Louis Hacker, May 23, 1949, Carman MSS., Butler Library, Columbia University;

57. *Newsweek*, March 21, 1949; Editorial, *Tulsa Tribune*, "Challenge to College Presidents," March 26, 1949, PF 1916-52, #1, DDEL; *Columbia Spectator*, March 24 and April 1, 1949; Carman, interview, December 1, 1961. During that winter and spring Jacobs would often ask his assistant, R. Gordon Hoxie, "on very short notice, as was often the case when I had to pinch-hit for President Eisenhower, to give me several key lines which I could easily and quickly develop." Jacobs, "Memoirs."

58. Press Release, American Press Institute Address by Jacobs, April 11, 1949, ibid.; *New York Times*, April 12, 1949; The *World-Telegram* article was on April 9, and Jacobs hoped that Robert Harron could find its origin: "I am much worried about it." Jacobs to Harron, April 11, 1949, CACU.

59. Ackerman memo, April 19, 1949, Ackerman MSS., LC.

60. Trustees, *Minutes*, May 2, 1949; Jacobs to Eisenhower, May 3, 1949; Dodge to Eisenhower, May 16, 1949; Dodge to Jacobs, May 3, 1949; Jacobs to Dodge, May 5, 1949; Jacobs to Frank D. Fackenthal, May 17, 1949, CACU. Earlier, Dodge had hoped that Jacobs would get an assurance that Eisenhower would be at Commencement. Dodge to Jacobs, April 27, 1949, ibid.

61. Eisenhower to Jacobs, May 3, 1949, *PDDE*, X, 567; Dodge to Jacobs, May 9, 1949, CACU; Eisenhower to Johnson, May 3, 1949, *PDDE*, X, 568-70, and *PDDE*, XI,

1593; *New York Times* and *New York Herald-Tribune*, May 15, 1949.

62. Dodge to Eisenhower, May 16, 1949, with pencil notations by Eisenhower and Jacobs, CACU; Eisenhower to Jacobs, May 31, 1949, *PDDE*, X, 597.

63. Eisenhower to Milton Eisenhower, May 13, 1949, ibid., 580-81.

64. Ibid., and XI, 1594-95.

65. Davis to Jacobs, "Development Program," April 12, 1949, CACU. The memorandum Eisenhower received, "Major Changes Indicated for Development Activities," was dated April 18, 1949, see fn. #3, *PDDE*, X, 597-98.

66. Carman, interview, December 1, 1961.

67. Ackerman, undated memorandum (March 1949?), Ackerman MSS., LC.

68. Carman to Hacker, May 23, 1949, Carman MSS., Butler Library; Carman, interview, December 1, 1961; Barzun, interview, April 5, 1979; McCann, interview, July 25, 1972.

69. *New York Times* and *New York Herald-Tribune*, June 2, 1949. The night before Commencement the Eisenhowers gave a dinner at 60 Morningside for the honorary degree recipients. John H. H. Lyon to Mamie Eisenhower, May 26, 1949, and "Disbursement," May 1949, Mamie D. Eisenhower MSS., DDEL.

70. Jacobs, interview, February 5, 1965; Jacobs, memorandum to author, March 10, 1958; Mamie Eisenhower to Mrs. Albert C. Jacobs, May 24, 1949, CACU; Black, interview, June 6, 1973; Eisenhower to Lucius Clay, July 6, 1949, *PDDE*, X, 676-77.

71. Jacobs, interview, February 5, 1965; Jacobs, "Memoirs"; Jacobs MSS., Letters "Leaving Columbia," Bentley Library, University of Michigan; R. Gordon Hoxie, personal interview, November 10, 1978, and June 9, 1995, New York, N.Y.; Adrienne Swift, telephone interview, December 5, 1993, Sarasota, Fl.

72. Carman, interview, December 1, 1961; Smith, interview, April 26, 1959; James Kip Finch to Jacobs, October 25, 1949, Jacobs MSS., Bentley Library; Carman to Hacker, May 23, 1949, Carman MSS., Butler Library.

73. Eisenhower, through some friends in Denver, had known about the vacancy and some of the university's problems. Eisenhower to Milton Eisenhower, January 29, 1949, and Eisenhower to Palmer Hoyt, June 2, 1949, *PDDE*, X, 455-56, 602-603.

74. Hoxie, interviews, November 10, 1978, and June 9, 1995; Carman, interview, December 1, 1961; Jacobs, interviews, February 5, 1965, and December 31, 1973; Swift, interview, December 5, 1993; Smith, interview, April 26, 1959; Jacobs, "Memoirs," p. 190.

75. I remember vividly that afternoon and evening. I did not want to leave New York, and I knew my father wanted to stay at Columbia. I went downtown and got two tickets for the Giants-Cardinals night game at the Polo Grounds; I answered the first call from my mother and, later, went to the office with Dad. After waiting awhile, he sent me up to the game—I arrived after Stan Musial had hit a two-run homer; Dad arrived in time for Musial's second home run, and the Giants lost. Letters, "Leaving Columbia," Jacobs MSS., Bentley Library; Jacobs, "Memoirs," 1974; Swift, interview, December 5, 1993; Loretta Jacobs, conversation after she had listened to tape recorded interviews with Black, Carman, Hoxie, and McCann, October 2, 1979; Jacobs to Eisenhower, June 16, 1949, Eisenhower MSS., DDEL.

76. Jacobs to Eisenhower, ibid.; Jacobs to Eisenhower, June 17, 1949, CACU.

6

Toward His Columbia Mission

I am not, now or in the future, going willingly into politics.
—Dwight D. Eisenhower,
Diary, November 3, 1949

Actually, I believe that if a man were able to give his full or nearly full attention to such a job as this, he would find it completely absorbing. . . . As long as I am here, you can believe that I am not only interested in the task, but I still believe it to offer a way in which I may render some service to the public at large.
—Eisenhower to
Swede Hazlett,
February 24, 1950

President Eisenhower had not forgotten about his vision for Columbia during his extended absence and illness; indeed, during the weeks after Commencement he looked forward to his two-month vacation and planning for the coming year. He had agreed to deliver several major speeches which would give him the opportunity to explain to large audiences his views and hopes, as well as his philosophy of government; these speeches would also raise the issue of presidential politics. Determined to maintain a reduced schedule before leaving for Wisconsin and Colorado, he limited his non-Columbia appearances and played golf at least twice a week at either Deepdale or Blind Brook. He did, however, make a half-dozen trips to Washington and reconvene his Council on Foreign Relations Aid to Europe group for two meetings, the first since his illness.

Yet, for Eisenhower to have the freedom to pursue his proposals for Columbia, he had first to think through his concerns about the cuts in the Department of Defense budget; moreover, he had to make important appointments to his administration of the University, only months after his major reorganization plan. The Washington ques-

181

tion was easier to answer. His frustrations had grown during his JCS meetings and his conversations with President Truman, Secretary Johnson, and Secretary of State Dean Acheson, and he decided to end his tour at the Pentagon. Commenting on the Administration's proposed defense budget, in early June he complained, "We work like the devil on an agreement on a certain sized budget—and then are told to reduce it." After a JCS session on the 17th, he prepared a detailed memorandum on June 21; at a meeting on June 28, it became clear that Johnson wanted further cuts; the General recalculated his figures, which Johnson cut, again; finally, Eisenhower sent the Secretary a long memorandum on July 14. Three days later he recorded in his *Diary* that Johnson wanted him to come back "to Washington as Chairman of JC/S. . . . Of course, I'll not do it." Years later he recalled that "as military budgets were reduced and reduced, I finally had to say, 'You don't want me. I can't agree with this.' . . . Secretary Johnson kept making it less and less and I asked to be relieved. Now, I cleaned up the loose ends of the assignment, and returned to Columbia."[1]

Loose ends, however, also faced him on Morningside Heights, as he resumed his duties at Columbia. He had viewed the University's reorganization plan during the previous spring as an essential step toward better management and, now, as he confronted replacing his Provost, he told the students at the opening of the Summer Session "I do not know why the teacher as a professional man or woman does not get the recompense, the remuneration to which he is so justly entitled. . . . It is a good cause for which to fight." He attended meetings with the Committee on Instruction from several Departments, wanted from Provost Jacobs a "retirement" proposal for Trustees over seventy, and spent considerable time on correspondence. He joined Harvard's Conant and fourteen other prominent educators, as members on the National Education Association's Educational Policies Commission, in recommending that Communists be excluded from teaching. "Such membership," the report asserted, "and the accompanying surrender of intellectual integrity, render an individual unfit to discharge the duties of a teacher in this country." Teachers, however, should not be called Communists "carelessly and unjustly" and, similarly, textbooks should not be called "Red." The national convention adopted the report, 2,995 to 5.[2]

The NEA report came at the time when Democrat John S. Wood, Chairman of the House Committee on Un-American Activities, had requested from some seventy-one colleges and high schools "a list of textbooks and supplementary reading . . . which are being used by your institution" to determine if they presented a Communist slant. Columbia's Henry Steele Commager immediately protested that the request posed "a potential threat to academic freedom." For the historian, "the real danger," he told Eisenhower, was "in the all-embracing proscription of whatever members of committees may suppose to be 'subversive' or 'un-American.'" The Provost advised that the General's reply to Wood "should be neither a flat defiance nor should it agree." On reading the proposed letter he still thought it was "a little too much on the defensive," and he preferred using Vice President Pegram's draft. Eisenhower, agreeing, wrote the Congressman that Columbia did not "keep on file . . . a complete list of books that are used as textbooks"; he did send "several specimen lists of books" placed on "reference" by professors at the library. Meanwhile, Wood's committee members, who had not been consulted, called on him to end his inquiry, and he did.[3]

Eisenhower also ventured into the controversial issue of federal aid to education, when a Congressman sought his views. Hoping that he would not have to testify before a Congressional Committee, he expressed in his reply the "basic principle" that "I definitely oppose every unnecessary intervention." He believed that certain areas of the country, lacking adequate tax revenue, might receive "federal aid, under formulas that would permit no abuse, no direct interference of the federal authority in educational processes." He did not oppose, moreover, "federal contractual arrangements with schools for scientific research" and "certain types of fellowships and scholarships to meet unusual federal requirements." A few days later he confided to Milton Eisenhower, "If I had dreamed that my letter to the committee was going to get the publicity that it did, I should undoubtedly have conferred with you." He emphasized, though, that "95 percent of the people who write to me about this vigorously support my personal stand."[4]

His views received more publicity during Teachers College's eighth annual conference on school administrative problems in early July. After a long discussion, Earl J. McGrath, the U. S. Commissioner of Education, warned that without federal aid soon children "will not be educated to live in this democracy," and participants enthusiastically supported him. Then Columbia's President, who had remained silent, replied critically to the argument for federal aid to "wealthy" states. He defended, however, assistance "in areas where it is needed" and supported the role of the "forty-eight sovereign states" in education, adding that he was "a more violent advocate" for such aid "than most of you here." A heated exchange followed; finally Eisenhower, smiling, ended the discussion on federal aid by stating, "There is no use trying to convince me."[5]

Eisenhower's position on federal aid to education prompted journalists to speculate on his presidential ambitions for 1952; they did not know that on July 6 Governor Dewey had gone to 60 Morningside for a two-hour conversation about politics with the General. The Governor, Eisenhower wrote, "assumes I am a Republican & would like to be President . . . and that only I . . . can save this country from going to Hades in the hand basket of paternalism—socialism—dictatorship." When Dewey urged him to "run for governor of New York State," Eisenhower responded, "I shall *never want* to enter politics. I shall never willingly seek a vote." The Governor, nonetheless, argued that Eisenhower would, "if you want to preserve Democracy," and he "refused to take a final answer of 'no.'"[6]

Politics, however, was not the pressing issue on Morningside Heights that summer. Eisenhower's directive to Provost Jacobs on June 24 focused "on decentralization as the basic principle of Columbia administration." He believed that most decisions should be made at the department level and that that would increase responsibility and loyalty; it would, moreover, enable him to focus on the Univeristy's mission to serve the nation. Yet, the University's top administrators worried about the pending appointments, which would be crucial for managing the institution. For Provost, Carman wrote to Jacobs that much depended "upon the nature of the job." If the General "must have someone at his beck and call, as you have been, . . . he might as well have an assistant." But if the Provost "is to have all the power and responsibility, which have been yours, then . . . your successor ought to be the most talented man we can find." And, the Dean added, referring to the Vice President of the University, "There is only one George Pegram and I know it is futile to think that we can find another like him." Yet the President, without addressing the importance of personnel and pending decisions, was insisting that decentralization "must be applied in delineating the functions and authorities of the several principal administrative officers." Consequently, he instructed Jacobs that the Provost's office should be relieved "of all possible details so that he can be, in effect, the internal administrator of the University."[7]

Eisenhower had delegated to Jacobs responsibility for the search for the Provost's successor, as well as the replacements for Vice President Pegram and Dean Carman—both had to retire in 1950 under the new statutes—and the appointment of a permanent Vice President for Business Affairs. Earlier, Jacobs had made two significant appointments. The *Times'* Sulzberger had accepted responsibility for being Chairman of the Bicentennial Committee. Then, when Oxford University had wanted Louis Hacker to stay in England after his year as Harmsworth Professor of American History, the Provost had asked him over the telephone to return to Columbia and become Director of the School of General Studies, and he agreed.[8] The President, in many respects, remained largely unfamiliar with the internal arrangements of the University and its personnel, except for a few key officers. He almost seemed unaware of the significance of the appointments still to be made, and he would leave for the summer on July 22.

Ambassador at Large Philip Jessup quickly became Jacobs' first choice for Provost. Jacobs wrote his former Law School colleague and, after a telephone call, traveled to Washington for a meeting on July 13. He offered Jessup the Provostship or the office of the Vice President of the University for Education; he specifically told Jessup that "the Trustees might very well carry forward the recommendation that the Provost assume the title of President of the University and the President that of Chancellor." Jessup promised to consider the matter "very seriously," and a week later Eisenhower, while in Washington for the JCS and a meeting with Secretaries Acheson and Johnson, also discussed the positions with Jessup. Yet, as Jacobs confided to Dean Smith about the Ambassador, "it would be very hard for him, after some thirty years, to leave a career which he has devoted to international affairs."[9]

Years later Jessup stated that Eisenhower also had given him the understanding that "I would succeed him" when he retired, but the international scholar added, "I was not interested in college or university administration." He telephoned his reply to Jacobs on August 1 and sent a long letter to Eisenhower's Low Memorial office. "I am in the international business and it is in my bones. . . . I know I would not be happy in another field." Jessup ventured the suggestion that Eisenhower become Chancellor of Columbia University with a President primarily responsible for educational policy. The General acknowledged, "I must admit I had high hopes," though the decision did not surprise Trustee Dodge, who still believed "it was worth the try." Barnard's Raymond "Steve" Saulnier, who would be the Chairman, Council of Economic Advisers, 1956-1960, during the Eisenhower Administration, has emphasized that Jessup was "made to order for the presidency of a large eastern university." Indeed, that summer Dean Acheson, the senior member of the Yale Corporation, gave the Ambassador "the impression that if I were interested" in the Yale presidency "the Corporation would act favorably on the recommendation." Jessup, in effect, that summer declined the presidencies of Columbia University and Yale University. For Columbia at least, Jessup's negative reply meant it was unlikely he would go to Yale.[10]

The Provost, while waiting to hear from Jessup, began concentrating on other appointments, especially Carman's important position as Dean of Columbia College. He interviewed members of the College's faculty for recommendations, and Lawrence Chamberlain, recently promoted to Professor of Public Law and Government, became the leading candidate. Jacobs, in fact, had discussed Chamberlain's name for the Deanship during his conversation with Jessup in Washington; the Ambassador had known the professor "extremely well" and believed he would "in every way make an excellent successor to Dean Carman," and Jacobs prepared a memorandum to that effect. Although Carman would suggest him for the Provostship after Jessup's refusal, he become Dean of the College in 1950.[11]

During Eisenhower's summer vacation the Provost had to address issues raised by three of the four vice president positions established by Eisenhower's reorganization in March. The Vice President in charge of Business Affairs did not worry him. He had recommended Joseph Campbell's appointment as Acting Vice President; in September he would talk with Trustees on the Committee on Finance about making the title permanent, and they "enthusiastically endorsed" the proposal. An unexpected problem for Jacobs, however, arose concerning the Vice President for Development when "every Dean came to me and asked me to tell the President to get rid of Davis."[12] As for the position of Vice President for Education, the senior office under the Provost, little could be done until Jacobs' successor had been named.

When Eisenhower arrived at Mamie Eisenhower's parents in Denver, after fishing in Wisconsin for two weeks, Jessup's letter refusing the Provostship was waiting for him. Initially, he asked Jacobs to circulate the letter "on a confidential basis, to several of our Trustees" to assure them "we are moving to obtain the finest possible individuals for the University" and to give them the Ambassador's comments. "It is still my conviction," he wrote, "that we must move promptly and decisively." He wanted Jacobs to get his "slate prepared instantly, incorporating in it the broad general opinion or approval of selected faculty members" and then call or come to Denver. "Even if we cannot fill the whole slate at this moment . . . select the man to take over your position so that he may actually begin work under your tutelage." The General added, "The only thing I insist upon is that the man that we select as Provost, and the man that we select as Vice President of Education be of the caliber appropriate to the Presidency of the institution."[13]

With Jessup out of the running, Jacobs recalled that, "because of Eisenhower's short experience" at the University, "there had to be someone from the faculty who had had a fair period of service and who ranked well." It was, he emphasized, "imperative that there be someone with academic stature and background at Columbia." Replying to a thoughtful letter from Carman, he had written, "I am entirely convinced, with the situation as it is, that the Office of Provost must continue to be much as it has been in the past year." But, after Jessup's decision, he told Smith, "I do by no means think that my successor must be able to take over if and when the President retires." Jacobs soon focused on Grayson Kirk, Director of the European Institute and Professor of International Relations. Kirk, who had been the Chairman of the Faculty Committee for Eisenhower's Installation, had a number of outside activities, and this posed a major concern. It was questionable, moreover, whether Kirk would consider the position and whether high administrative officers would support him for it. Schuyler Wallace, the Director of the School of International Affairs, talked with the Provost and afterwards wrote to Jessup that the Ambassador had made "the wise decision"; he added that, though Jacobs had not made a "final decision," he suspected that Kirk would make it for the Provost by arriving "at the same conclusion you did."[14]

In mid-August Jacobs suggested Kirk for the Provostship after the Professor had agreed "to forego many of his outside activities."

With that condition understood, Deans Carman and Smith supported the recommendation. The Provost had not offered Kirk the Chancellor-President package he had proposed to Jessup. Yet Kevin McCann, managing Eisenhower's desk in New York, recalled that "representing the President of the University, I had to go over to Grayson Kirk's office and assure him that, in case of any change in the presidency, the Provost would probably succeed as President of the University." If McCann gave that assurance, it would have been without Trustee authorization. On August 22 Jacobs informed the Trustees that Eisenhower had decided to nominate Kirk and had directed that the nomination be sent to the Trustee Committee on Education "for action under summer powers." Marcy Dodge, vacationing on Martha's Vineyard, quickly telegraphed Frank Fackenthal, the Committee Chair, who was on vacation in the Poconos, and asked if Fackenthal could meet him in New York. Only a few days earlier Dodge had wondered in a letter to Fackenthal if Jacobs "is tired . . . or seems sorry of his decision. He has gone so far there is no possibility of turning back now with honor is there?"[15]

"I have your letter about the Provostship and am prepared to go along with the recommendation," Fackenthal immediately informed Jacobs, "though I must say I have some reservations on the candidate's personality for that kind of job; I have no question as to his ability." The former Acting President of Columbia University continued. "There must be no misunderstanding on the Acting Presidency; in my judgment that should now be moved back to the Vice President." And, referring to Jacobs' reference to "action under summer powers," Fackenthal advised "there should be some discussion and not just mail or telephone consent." The Provost promptly forwarded Fackenthal's comments to Eisenhower in Denver. Dodge, returning to New York, called on Kirk and recommended to Fackenthal that Kirk be asked to meet Committee members. "If he does I am not at all sure they will vote for him at once." Jacobs, Dodge added, "has to be told there will be some delay." The Trustee had decided, however, not to talk with Jacobs, though he did with Vice President Pegram, who suggested the name of an outside candidate. Dodge concluded, "I have some uneasiness in my mind. . . . I wonder if the General really knows Kirk and has put his mind on the problem or is taking Al Jacobs' opinion entirely?" Board Chairman Coykendall, though, from Maine informed the Provost, "I am much pleased with your choice of Grayson Kirk." Jacobs sent those comments to Eisenhower, who would not return to Columbia until mid-September, and he informed the President that Fackenthal had scheduled a Committee meeting for September 8.[16]

The Committee met with Eisenhower on September 26 and reported favorably on Kirk's nomination, and the President announced the appointment after the Trustees Meeting on October 3. Fackenthal's Committee, however, at the Board Meeting proposed Amendments to the Statutes which significantly changed the arrangements that Eisenhower had painstakingly obtained at the Trustees Meeting on March 7. The Committee moved to place the Vice President of the University (Education) "immediately following the President and to remove the Provost from the line of succession"; moreover, the Amendments eliminated the provision under which the Provost would become Acting President and placed the Provost, among officers of the University, in line after the four Vice Presidents. The Board adopted these changes on November 7, 1949; meanwhile, the Trustees removed the word "Acting" from Campbell's title.[17]

Eisenhower had returned from his long summer vacation with plans he wanted to implement to fulfill Columbia's mission. Welcoming students to the beginning of Columbia University's 196th year, he declared in late September, 1949, "I know that you will make the best of the advantages spread before you,...so that you may better yourselves, your families, your home communities and your country." At the official opening ceremonies, which included a formal academic procession, he added, "I have now entered my sophomore year."

That day he emphasized themes that he would develop throughout the year. "Life is certainly worthwhile only as it represents struggle for worthy causes," and he expressed scorn for those "seeking perfect security. . . . I should think that the best example of it would be a man serving a lifetime in a federal prison." Encouraging the students to embrace opportunity, which "you will meet here at every turn, everyday—all the time," he hoped that they would "grow to love the fight that opportunity brings." That evening at the opening of the School of General Studies he introduced a new course, "American Values in World Perspective." America's friends abroad, he asserted, "can be determined by whether or not they are struggling for freedom and peace." Meanwhile, a proposal circulated about a course Eisenhower might offer in the College's Contemporary Civilization Program.[18]

At Barnard College's opening convocation he talked about the educational system and American freedoms, and he mentioned his concerns for the future. Stating that schools in Germany before the war had bred a "fanatical devotion to wickedness," he told 850 students that "as long as there are fine privately endowed institutions in this country to establish the standards, and as long as public education is supported by diffused governments—that is by cities and states rather than the federal government—we are in no danger of any such thing." He then went to Baker Field to watch Lou Little's football team practice, and the next day he saw Columbia defeat Amherst. In his Orientation Lecture to the College's freshmen he admitted that as a youngster he had "wanted to be another Hans Wagner," the Hall of Fame Pittsburgh shortstop, and that the new undergraduates might dismiss "the aphorisms of an old fuddy-duddy." He asserted, nonetheless, that education helps "to pierce the hazy clouds of misunderstanding reflected in the daily news." Referring to international problems, he added, "Any country which treats the individual as a dignified human being is our friend."[19]

Eisenhower energetically launched the new academic year, after missing the entire spring semester of 1949, and the University's opening ceremonies gave him the opportunity to express some of the ideas he considered vital. On his return to Morningside Heights he was well rested; he had gone fishing in Wisconsin, and he had played golf almost daily in Colorado and gone fishing in the Rockies; he had had time to think about how he wanted Columbia "to fulfill its purpose," and he could look forward to concentrating on his proposals without major interruptions. He was determined to protect himself from too many commitments, and he had declined an offer from Secretary of Defense Johnson to become Chairman of the Joint Chiefs of Staff, "permanently, or at least, indefinitely." Still, the General maintained an active schedule, including prominent speeches away from Morningside Heights. These speeches raised, once again, the issue of presidential politics, in spite of his insistence that he had no such interest. Moreover, in spite of his dislike for fund raising, his proposals for Columbia required separate efforts by him, at the same time that University-wide opposition to Davis' Development Office was growing and the University's financial needs remained pressing. He would, furthermore, begin working with a new Provost, Grayson Kirk, in late October; while he hardly knew Jacobs' successor, Eisenhower was aware that the Provost's position had been central to the University's reorganization plan during the previous spring. That fall the administrative arrangements and top personnel for the institution would be considerably different, and President Eisenhower concentrated his energies more and more on the pursuit of his mission for Columbia, instead of administrative leadership.

For Eisenhower—and the press—the fall, however, had started on Labor Day in St. Louis, nearly three weeks before the General returned to New York and the beginning of Columbia's academic year. Interrupting his Colorado vacation, he spoke at the opening of the American Bar Association's seventy-second annual convention. Kevin McCann had been working on the speech in New York, and in late August he wrote, "I have taken the liberty of showing this latest revision to John Krout, Louis Hacker, and Douglas Black, representing a very sound critical group." They were "very pleased with it" and "none of them suggested any alterations." Black, though, proposed "omitting the last paragraph." McCann agreed and reminded Eisenhower that he could make "any revisions . . . up to the moment of delivery."

America's future, the General declared in a speech eagerly awaited by the media, "lies down the middle of the road between concentrated wealth on one flank and the unbridled power of statism or partisan interest, on the other." Fundamental principles "still dictate progress down the center, even though there the contest is hottest, the progress is sometimes discouragingly slow." Agreement on those principles, nonetheless, "provides the setting within which can always be composed any acute differences." The middle way, thus, was not a "neutral, wishy-washy one," he told the lawyers and friends. "It is the area in which are rooted the hopes and allegiance of the vast majority of our people." With his audience frequently interrupting him with applause and three times with a standing ovation, he warned against an "ever-expanding federal government. . . . We will not accord to the central government unlimited authority, any more than we will bow our necks to the dictates of the uninhibited seekers after personal power in finance, labor, or any other field." The *New York Herald-Tribune*, agreeing that "the middle of the road is no easy path," asserted that "the ideal has seldom been more thoughtfully stated." The *New York Times* declared that Eisenhower "drew heavy applause when he stated that the country's present high standard of living was 'not the result of political legerdemain or crackpot fantasies of reward without effort, harvests without planting.'"[20]

The speech prompted *U.S. News and World Report* to consider the General "actively engaged in a program aimed at a 1952 presidential nomination," and a few weeks later it stated that he remained "in front among Republican contenders for the 1952 presidential nomination due to his active campaigning." Former U. S. Representative Clare Boothe Luce, the wife of *Time* and *Life's* Henry R. Luce, met with Eisenhower and very earnestly advised him, he wrote, "to keep on speaking out on points of my own beliefs in govt, etc." Senator Arthur H. Vandenberg, the architect of Republican support for the Truman Doctrine, the Marshall Plan, and the recently ratified North Atlantic Treaty, asserted, "The sane philosophy of the 'middle road' is indispensable to the preservation of our threatened national unity. No one," he insisted, "can lead this indispensable 'revival' quite so well as you. This means more than meets the eye." The *Herald-Tribune's* Robinson immediately sent "four or five copies of the paper" and stated, "Everyone here was deeply impressed. . . . Your middle-of-the-road theme is brilliantly timed."

"We might have a discussion some evening," Robinson soon suggested, "with a few of our friends who had manifested extraordinary interest in the subject." The newspaperman probably was referring to more than the speech. George E. Allen, Clifford Roberts, and Robinson had visited Eisenhower in Denver just before the Bar Association speech. Allen, in fact, brought a message from President Truman: an offer of the New York State Democratic nomination for U.S. Senator in the 1949 special election. The General would not consider the offer—Allen immediately telephoned the White House—and in September he recorded in his *Diary,* "What I dread is the faint possibility that circumstances & people could combine in some way to convince me I have a duty in politics. But I do not believe it—and if I should ever, in the future, decide affirmative on this point it will be because I've become *over*-sold by friends!"[21] Despite his disclaimer, he had reopened the subject of presidential politics on the eve of his return to Columbia.

Throughout the fall he did little to close the door. Amid the University's opening activities, he delivered an address before 10,000 persons at the dedication of the Harlem Y. M. C. A. boys building. No people, he argued, "have come so far on the road to understanding, citizenship and culture in eighty-five years as has the Negro race." Once again denouncing "Federal security" and the trend to "let the Government do it," he praised the building as an example of

"Americanism at its best, . . . an investment in the future of America." While he declined Carman's invitation to attend the freshman dinner at John Jay—he worried that "I'll be in danger of repeating myself" when talking at freshmen orientation a few days later—he attended, instead, a meeting and dinner for his study group at the Council on Foreign Relations.

In early October the annual session of the Educational Policies Commission, meeting outside New York City, received widespread publicity when it amplified its June statement that "members of the Communist party of the United States should not be employed as teachers." While adhering "to its previously stated position," the educators—and Eisenhower had attended a number of the sessions—"wished also to emphasize again that citizens should be especially alert . . . to defend the essential need of their schools for freedom of teaching and learning." Admitting that Soviet Russia's recent explosion of an atomic bomb alarmed the American people, the Commission stated, nonetheless, that "State laws requiring special oaths for teachers . . . impair the vigor of local school autonomy and thus do harm to an important safeguard of freedom in education."[22] Warnings against loyalty oaths, however, became increasingly unpopular in the United States and, as the "Red Scare" grew during the year, Columbia and Eisenhower would be called upon to defend academic freedom.

In spite of such meetings out of town and a brief trip to Washington, Eisenhower maintained an active schedule on campus, ranging from his administrative duties to ceremonial occasions. He held a luncheon at 60 Morningside for the University's Deans to discuss development, and a few days later he had a series of meetings with Deans and Trustees at the Faculty Club, followed by a session with the Trustee Committee on Development. He invited the senior staff for a luncheon at 60 Morningside prior to the October Trustees Meeting, and afterwards Trustees joined members of the School of Business for cocktails at the Men's Faculty Club; Eisenhower, though, had a long-standing commitment at the Link's Club and did not remain for the informal dinner. The next day he made visits around Columbia College.[23]

During this period he and the Provost had a meeting at 60 Morningside, and Jacobs conveyed to the President "the urgent message from all the Deans" that Vice President Davis "must go. . . . I told him the story and I didn't mince any matters," Jacobs recalled.

"Davis was a thorn in the side of amicable living at Columbia, and the worst of it was he was not accomplishing anything." Davis, meanwhile, had arranged a luncheon at the house in connection with plans for the University's Bicentennial. That morning, at a meeting with Jacobs, the General said, "You'll be at lunch today, won't you?" "Hell, no," the Provost replied, "I haven't been invited." "The hell you're not invited!" When Jacobs arrived with the President, he remembered "how upset Davis was."

Over the summer, when Trustees Dodge and Warren had raised some questions about Davis, the General stated, "I am convinced that he knows his business and is an asset to the organization." When Eisenhower subsequently told Douglas Black, "I think I have to let that fellow go," the Trustee replied, "I think he has done a good job, Ike. He doesn't seem to have gotten along with people. . . . I think he has great qualities of leadership." The World War II Supreme Commander bluntly asserted, "Doug, he is a hell of a leader if no one is following him." That November, after Bob Harron entered a Philadelphia hospital, Davis informed the Public Information Office that it was now an adjunct to the Development Office and reported to him. Harron's assistants quickly went to Kirk, who proceeded to tell Davis that no changes would occur until Harron returned—and none occurred even then. Davis left Columbia in early 1950, and the Development Office was decentralized, with an Acting Coordinator instead of a Vice President. It was reported with his "resignation" that "Columbia received $10,000,000 in gifts, grants, and bequests" in Davis' three years; Eisenhower, though, in 1948 had announced the need for $170,000,000, and Davis' 1948 and 1949 memoranda for the Trustees had projected a $210,000,000 goal for the Bicentennial. "A lucky break for Columbia," Dean Smith wrote. "We can now make a fresh start in the problem of raising money."[24]

Eisenhower launched the first building phase of the Development Program when he broke ground over Homecoming Weekend, 1949, for a new field house at Baker Field. In his talk he predicted that the University's expansion would continue. At the picnic luncheon on the baseball diamond before the Yale football game, which Columbia lost badly, he told 2,500 alumni and families that "nothing can defeat Columbia." During the picnic, the *Times* noted, "the small fry of alumni . . . surrounded the General, asking for and receiving autographs." On his fifty-ninth birthday a few days later the fifty-piece First Army Band surprised the General. Shortly before noon it appeared on the lawn outside his Low Memorial office and, with several hundred students present, played "Happy Birthday," "Roll Out the Barrel," "Lili Marlene," and "The General's March." The President walked out to thank the band, and then he and Mrs. Eisenhower went over to John Jay, where they had lunch with Lou Little and the football team. The squad sang "Happy Birthday," and he told the players he intended to attend all future games, except for the Army one, since he "wouldn't know which team to root for. . . . I'll probably save myself from high blood pressure by staying home and listening to the game over the radio."[25] They had not played Army during Eisenhower's first year; eight days later at West Point the Cadets slaughtered Columbia, 63-6, thereby gaining a measure of revenge for Army's stunning loss at Baker Field in 1947.

On the first anniversary of his Installation the *Spectator's* editorial gave the President a less pleasant birthday present. Acknowledging that those "in immediate contact with him . . . are full of high praise," the *Spectator* declared, "The rest of us who know him only through the newspapers are not just sure what his job is, much less how well he has done it." It emphasized that he had "made many speeches . . . many trips away from campus" and "met many people. Perhaps in the near future our chief officer will have the time to meet some of us in the ranks on Morningside Heights." The college paper concluded, "It would be too bad, if the important tradition of unity and understanding within the Morningside community were abandoned now."[26]

While the *Spectator's* opinions might easily be dismissed as normal undergraduate complaining, especially since Eisenhower had demonstrated far more interest in the College than in any other part of the University, criticism was mounting. It was generally acknowledged that he had been away more than he had been on campus, and he had delivered speeches frequently downtown and out of town. Moreover, Major Schulz and, to a lesser extent, Kevin McCann guarded his appointments on campus carefully and became even more protective after the General's illness. "They were all the time," according to Dean Carman, "trying to shield him and safeguard him. They didn't have the knowledge of things academic." Mrs. Eisenhower later acknowledged that even she had heard that Schulz, absolutely loyal to her husband, had "hurt a lot of people" and did "a lot of harm."[27]

The Eisenhowers, furthermore, did "very little entertaining of the administration and faculty," even though, as Jacobs and others emphasized, the President's House at 60 Morningside Drive had been extensively renovated at great expense. The academic community had assumed that the house would be used for University functions and not just working luncheons. The Eisenhowers, however, never saw 60 Morningside Drive as an integral part of the Columbia community; it was where he could relax and play bridge with members of his gang twice a week—on Saturdays that often included an informal dinner—and paint in the penthouse, and where they could enjoy John and Barbara's visits and the grandchildren. Mamie Eisenhower, moreover, wanted to keep Sundays free for the two of them. During this period, Dr. Snyder recalled that he "spent practically all Sunday from early morning until late evening at the Eisenhower home." In the penthouse the General "would get out his color box and canvas and go to work. We would chat about old Army days and friends we had mutually known." When Alice Snyder was in the city, Dr. Snyder added that "Mamie would get Alice and Ann Nevins and sit down at Canasta which she so loved, and I would join them for a fourth, and we would play until midnight, or later."[28]

The Eisenhowers limited their entertaining to a few Trustees, dignitaries, and friends; seldom were Columbia personnel invited, Mamie Eisenhower explained, since her husband saw them on campus. (Noting that Eisenhower seemed to want to limit this side of his life to his personal friends, Roberts recalled, "I don't know of a single instance where any of the Columbia people were ever involved.") The Trustees included the Watsons, the Blacks, and occasionally the Sulzbergers; the friends were the Robinsons, the Roberts, the George E. Allens, Ellis D. Slater and his wife Priscilla, who became one of Mamie's closest companions, the Gruenthers, the Clays, the Walter "Beedle" Smiths, the W. A. "Pete" Joneses, General and Ann Nevins, the Snyders, and Columbia's Phil Young and his wife. For the occasional formal dinners—elaborate and "just as grand as they could be," according to the college student living in the house—some three thousand crystal dining room chandelier drops would be cleaned and dried by hand. The smaller dinners, also, were "just beautifully done." Mamie Eisenhower remembered that 60 Morningside "lent itself beautifully for state functions and important occasions, and people came from all over the country and world to see them."

The Butlers, though, had used the President's house for both state occasions and University entertaining. While the evenings had been "exceedingly stiff and formal," until Butler's later years 60 Morningside remained the social center of the University. The difference under the Eisenhowers stunned the community. "Don't overlook the fact," Carman acknowledged, "that under President Butler's years that the house was used certainly more extensively along those lines." Lionel Trilling, the brilliant literary critic, observed that the entertaining "in the big house with its old 19th century massive charm" served a useful University function. The professor considered it "significant" that the Eisenhowers "never revived those dinners." Indirectly, these failures supported the *Spectator's* editorial and conveyed the impression that the Eisenhowers lacked interest in knowing and enjoying the Columbia community.[29]

President Eisenhower reinforced this view with his apparent reluctance to participate during October in the 90th birthday celebration for John Dewey, who had started teaching at Columbia in 1905 and had achieved worldwide recognition as the country's most distinguished philosopher and educator. In July Trustee George Warren reminded Schulz that President Eisenhower was no longer ill and that "very substantial people have accepted" the invitation, but Schulz tersely replied, "The General has already reconsidered the request on several occasions." Vice President Pegram, emphasizing the significance of the occasion, then informed McCann that Dewey was "one of the most renowned scholars among those who have served at Columbia."

Professor Irwin Edman, a student and colleague of the progressive educator for thirty-two years, helped arrange three days of festivities, which included a testimonial dinner at the Commodore Hotel on October 20 for distinguished guests from all over world and sessions at Teachers College on the 22nd. Eisenhower decided, before departing for his summer vacation, that he would not go to the dinner, and this presented a potential problem. Fackenthal expressed his concern to Jacobs that if Harvard's Conant, or other prominent university presidents, attended the dinner, Eisenhower's "absence would not be understood." Trustee Sulzberger, moreover, told the Provost that Eisenhower should be one of the dinner's sponsors. At Jacobs' request, Pegram learned that Conant would "not be present at the dinner"—that removed one possible embarrassment—and in September McCann finally indicated that the General would deliver a tribute to Dewey on the Saturday evening occasion at Teachers College.[30]

Over the years different stories evolved and overlapped about Eisenhower and Dewey's birthday celebration. One version had Eisenhower accepting Edman's invitation for the dinner. Then, as Jacques Barzun recounted, "a couple of days before the dinner Irwin had a direct call from the President saying 'I very much wanted to come to the dinner honoring your professor friend, but I really can't. I have a very old army buddy who is coming on that day, and he is coming over to 60 Morningside Drive. We want to have a chat about old times, so I must ask you to excuse me.' Irwin then said to the President, 'We're terribly sorry, Mr. President. It is for a former colleague and professor but he is very famous, known for the world over and I may tell you that Prime Minister Nehru, who is in the country, is attending the dinner.' The President then said 'Well, Oh, in that case, well, I'll see.' He did come."[31]

Eisenhower went, but he attended the evening celebration at Teachers College, not the Commodore Hotel dinner, where 1,500 persons had heard "leaders and scholars the world over" pay tribute to Dewey's contributions to fields ranging from philosophy and education to art, labor, and the law. The *Times'* front-page caption read, "World Cheers Dewey at Lively 90." India's Pandit Nehru, in a surprise appearance, stated, "There are few Americans who have influenced my thinking and actions. Among them is John Dewey." Fackenthal represented Columbia; Eisenhower had testified that morning before the House Armed Services Committee but had returned to New York in the afternoon. Two nights later he spoke at the Teachers College celebration—interrupting an evening of dinner and bridge in the Penthouse—but it would be recalled on campus over the years that he had appeared only briefly and spent all his time with an Army crony. Whether he spent only a few moments—and he had delivered a tribute—was not the issue. He had not gone to the Commodore Hotel dinner, and it had been difficult to get him to appear on the 22nd.

Irrespective of Eisenhower's opinions about the soundness of Dewey's educational philosophy, prominent faculty thought he should have endeavored more to pay his respects to the distinguished, though controversial, professor. Political Scientist David Truman, who did not arrive at Columbia until the following year, recalled vivid faculty resentment about "the non-sharing of values of a great man" and the belief that "Ike should have made an effort on an occasion of this sort to pay respects to a great man." To the academic community the evening illustrated a lack of rapport by the President on a very special occasion, and it prompted many to conclude that Eisenhower "begrudged the University."[32]

The General, actually, had entertained Nehru earlier in the week, when the Indian Prime Minister had been honored at a special Columbia University Convocation. The Eisenhowers gave a state dinner at 60 Morningside Drive for Nehru and his party, which included his daughter Indira Gandhi. The evening ceremonies in the Rotunda of Low Memorial celebrated "a champion of the underprivileged peoples, his devotion to the noble ideals of universal peace and understanding have won him the respect and acclaim of all mankind." The Provost then awarded Nehru the honorary degree; though he well knew that Eisenhower was not "at home in academic life," he thought that the President, who spoke, should have conferred the degree on "this important occasion."

The Prime Minister, before a capacity audience of 600 invited guests, delivered a major address, broadcast worldwide, on international relations. "The very process," India's leader declared, "of a marshalling of the world into two hostile camps precipitates the conflict which it is sought to avoid." Espousing the doctrine of nonviolence, Mohandas K. Gandhi's political heir attacked western imperialism and called for an end to the world armaments race. The "colossal expenditure of energy and resources on armaments," he stressed, can not solve the problem of world peace. The Prime Minister, finishing his address, took off his glasses and turned to President Eisenhower. Remarking that the citation had made him feel "very humble," he said, "The scene that I see here under your distinguished presidentship will long remain in my mind. . . . I shall prize that honor of being a fellow member with you of this great university above all the other honors that have come my way, and I shall prize it not only in my individual capacity but as I believe that the honor was perhaps meant for something more than the individual—as a symbol and representative of India."[33] Columbia's tribute to India's Nehru had become, also, a recognition of and publicity for the University and her President.

Eisenhower, himself, had an important speech on his mind. He had agreed the year before to deliver the opening address at the eighteenth annual *New York Herald-Tribune* Forum at the Waldorf-

Astoria. Helen Reid, the newspaper's president, in June had reminded him about the talk, when she expressed how much Columbia's honorary degree had meant to her. "For months," Eisenhower had written in August, he had wondered how to address a question asked by Bernard Baruch. The elder statesman, worried about the growing power of the central government, had urged the General to use Columbia to explore where to draw "the dividing line between government and personal responsibility. . . . If an institution such as Columbia with its vast intellectual resources cannot come to grips with this issue, how can we ordinary citizens be expected to?" While Eisenhower was in Colorado, McCann wrestled with the problem, and the General "broached the subject" in September at a luncheon with the University's alumni in Denver. "I saw on the Columbia faculty," Eisenhower wrote in *At Ease*, "an immense pool of talent, scholarly and humane in its comprehension of human needs and aspirations, above the bias of sect and party. At first I thought of it as a sort of intellectual Supreme Court which could search through the entanglements of the problems before us and by dispassionate study, and with imaginative and profound thought, propose solutions that would win acceptance." During the fall, according to McCann, "he clarified his thinking," on his conference proposal as he prepared for the *Herald-Tribune* talk.[34]

The two-evening program at the Waldorf-Astoria addressed the question, "What Kind of Government Ahead?" Following General Eisenhower's opening speech on October 24, Democratic Party leaders, including North Carolina's Senator Frank Graham, Governor Adlai E. Stevenson of Illinois, Senator Hubert H. Humphrey, Jr. of Minnesota, and Representative Franklin D. Roosevelt, Jr. of New York presented their solutions for the national's welfare. Republicans would speak on the second night. Columbia's President titled his remarks, "The Individual's Responsibility for Government," and ABC broadcast his speech. Pointing to the nation's coal and steel strikes, he said, "Two great American industries are today shut down because a few men cannot see eye-to-eye on specific problems of employee and employer responsibility. If they—of undoubted loyalty to America—can dare calamity by their failure to agree on a far more simple decision, how can the plain citizen determine the dividing line between his own and the Government's responsibilities?" He proposed "a convocation of leaders in every field with the faculties of our great universities. . . . The task is to promote social and

economic welfare without jeopardy to individual freedom and right."
The conclusions, Eisenhower argued, "would certainly emphasize the
truth, 'More and more bureaus, more and more taxes, fewer and fewer
producers; the final result is financial collapse and the end of freedom.'"[35]

The *Herald-Tribune's* Forum attracted leading politicians from both
parties, and Eisenhower, who professed no political ambitions and
whose popularity remained undiminished, had spoken first. It was,
perhaps, no coincidence that the Democrats, not the Republicans,
followed him to the podium. He had recently declined a major speaking engagement, he wrote in his *Diary*, "on the basis of partisanship—I stick to my determination not to appear with a definitely
Republican or Democratic party." The *Herald-Tribune's* Bill
Robinson, who gave a dinner for Eisenhower at the Waldorf before
the speech and who had had dinner and played bridge with the General prior to his appearance at the John Dewey celebration, knew his
close friend's sentiments and could have arranged for Eisenhower
and the Republicans to speak on separate nights and to avoid a partisan association for the General. Shortly after the Forum talk,
Eisenhower would confide that "Personal political problems, which
I thought had been solved forever by my several public statements
in 1948 . . . are now plaguing me again." With no acknowledgment
that his speeches were reopening the issue and admitting that "individuals of some prominence . . . have either flatly stated or hinted
broadly that *I* am to be a political figure in 1952," he wrote, "I am
not, now or in the future, going willingly into politics." He concluded, though, "I cannot say to anyone that I would *not* do my best
to perform a *duty*."[36]

Indeed, his focus that fall, Eisenhower insisted, remained on the
conference proposal, and he had his staff "now working on a definite plan for carrying out the idea." During the previous summer the
brothers W. Averell and E. Roland Harriman had offered Arden House,
their large family estate some fifty miles outside New York City, to
Columbia. Because of the University's bad financial situation and
the projected annual costs involved, neither Jacobs, Pegram, nor
Campbell was enthusiastic about the offer—Campbell considered a
$5,000,000 endowment a "requisite"—and Eli Ginzberg, a member
of the original review committee, "couldn't figure out what Columbia could do with a residential structure in poor shape." Eisenhower,
though, saw the property as an opportunity for his "convocation"
ideas. "Since I saw you last," Eisenhower told Averell Harriman on

November 30, "there has been scarcely a day in which I have not had a conference with some individual concerning the possibility of Columbia University's use of Arden House." Yet he realized that "productive utilization of the property" would take time and require "some combination of projects" until Arden House developed "into a great center of conferences." Eisenhower expressed the conviction that he and Harriman still held "the vision of a great cultural center where business, professional, and governmental leaders could meet from time to time to discuss and reach conclusions concerning problems of a social and political nature." The General, meanwhile, planned for early December a well-publicized two-week trip to Texas, where he would talk about the idea.[37]

Soon after the Waldorf speech Eisenhower flew on a Doubleday & Co. plane to Madison, Wisconsin, for a meeting of the Presidents of the American Association of Universities. Perhaps underscoring his lack of comfort with academics, he mentioned—a year after his Installation—that he was a "freshman president" attending the sessions "to learn what I can." Returning to New York, he reported on the sessions to Grayson Kirk, who had assumed the Provostship in late October. Over the weekend he undoubtedly discussed the *Herald-Tribune* Forum and politics while he played bridge with Roberts and Robinson. On Sunday he went to West Point, visiting John and Barbara Eisenhower and his grandchildren, nineteen-month-old David and five-month-old Barbara Anne; John Eisenhower had been an Instructor of English at the Military Academy since September, 1948.

On Monday he discussed with the Trustees Committee on Education the proposed amendments to the University's Statutes concerning the positions of Provost and Vice President of the University, and the Board adopted these at the Meeting on November 7. Other important matters included the search for a successor to Pegram and Eisenhower's desire to establish a retirement age for Trustees. It appeared, though, that such an amendment "might impair the validity" of the University's Charter; thus, instead, "resolutions" would be presented to the Board proposing that after January 1, 1950, each Trustee upon election to the Board file his resignation "to take effect . . . after he attains the age of seventy years" and become a "Trustee Emeritus." These resolutions were "laid on the table" for the next meeting.[38]

In mid-November at the Men's Faculty Club the General handed Governor Dewey a comprehensive report on the New York State hospital system which had been conducted by Professor Ginzberg and the School of Business. "This was a big occasion," Ginzberg recalled. "It was an important report; *The Times* ran six articles on it six days in a row." The reception also provided the opportunity for both the Governor and Eisenhower to criticize government interference and federal aid to education. The President, when asked by newsmen at the luncheon about politics, replied, "I don't think I'll have to get involved in partisanship as long as I live." Yet, after the ceremony, the Governor and he retired to 60 Morningside Drive for "another long talk." Dewey "remains of the opinion that I must soon enter politics or," Eisenhower recorded, "be totally incapable of helping the country when it will need it the most. . . . He wants me to run for Gov. of N.Y. in 1950. I said 'No.'" The General, though, agreed to talk with him again. "Every day," Eisenhower concluded, the question of his own political ambitions "comes before me. . . . I'm worn out trying to explain myself."[39]

While Eisenhower maintained an active schedule in Low Memorial that fall, evidence suggests that he continued to be less involved in day-to-day affairs. In early November he traveled to Indianapolis to address the American Legion's National Executive Committee; the next week he went to Annapolis for several days of meetings with the Service Academy Board, which was considering the creation of an Air Force military academy. While there, he watched Navy defeat Columbia, 34-0, and the dismal football season distressed the Columbia Alumni Football Committee. Later, at Valley Forge he presented the Freedom Foundation's first annual awards to 121 recipients. Special awards went to Columbia Law School's Judge Harold R. Medina for his "administration of American justice under law," while presiding over the recent convictions of eleven Communist Party leaders, and to baseball player Jackie Robinson for his anti-communist testimony before the House Committee on Un-American Activities. From Valley Forge, the General went to alumni meetings and speeches in Cincinnati. Over Thanksgiving he and Mrs. Eisenhower drove to West Point for their granddaughter's christening. In late November, just before leaving for Texas, he launched a $250,000 fund drive for Columbia College, half the funds to support scholarships and half for the completion of the field house at Baker Field; he also urged a greater emphasis on athletics for a balanced program "between scholastics and athletics."[40]

The President's travels and avoidance of major academic functions increasingly raised questions and criticism. He did not attend the annual Maria Moors Cabot Awards ceremony for journalists furthering hemispheric friendship and understanding, the awards occasion which in 1948, evidently, had angered him so much. He continued, moreover, to miss or avoid participation in academic affairs. "We would gather in the Trustees Room at three in the afternoon for a meeting of the Faculty of Political Science," the Faculty's secretary Jacques Barzun recalled. "He would come in and shake hands and chat and be very pleasant, and then he would come over to me and say 'I am expecting an important long distance call from Washington and I'd hate to interrupt the meeting, so you sit in the Chair and you take the meeting, and I'll sit on the sidelines in case my opinion is needed. But, you run the formal meeting. On only one of those three occasions was there a long distance phone call." He went on a duck and pheasant shoot in Connecticut, leaving Provost Jacobs to install James A. Pike as Chaplain of the University and Professor Reinhold Niebuhr to deliver the main address. Grayson Kirk emphasized, "Routinely, after I became Provost, he would call me in before a stated meeting of the University Council and say that he was too busy to preside. He always added that if he finished his work in time he would come in and take a seat on the sidelines, which, of course, he never did."[41]

Columbia's President, however, did not have during 1949-1950 the excuses for his absences from these and other meetings that he had had during his hectic fall of 1948, when he began commuting to Washington, and during the winter and spring, 1949, when he returned to the Pentagon and later became ill. Then, in December, 1949, he was in Texas when the Board of Trustees held its regular meeting—at that session Parkinson and Watson would have nothing to do with the proposal on the retirement of Trustees, and the resolutions were "tabled," not to be "brought up again unless specifically requested by a Trustee."[42]

All this signaled a lack of University leadership by the President, and it led gradually to an estrangement from large segments of the Columbia community. Some explanations are obvious; others less so. Initially, Eisenhower was not comfortable with academic matters, whether it be awarding an honorary degree at a special convocation or presiding over faculty meetings. By not attending University Council meetings, Grayson Kirk argued, Eisenhower "destroyed his leadership with the faculty." This created, according to Lionel Trilling, "an offensive contrast with Butler, who intellectually responded to everything and was not just a presiding officer." Kirk also noted, emphatically, "the harm done to Eisenhower's campus relations by Schulz and McCann."

The General was "simply overawed," Barzun commented. "At a couple of occasions, I remember one Class Day exercise, he would make a point of his non-academic, non-intellectual training." This "non-enjoyment in getting into things academic on his part," Dean Carman related, "was because he didn't know, it was ignorance, he didn't understand." He had, the new Provost added, a "curiously ambivalent feeling about the University, especially the faculty"; he had the non-academic's suspicion of professors while being timid about the faculty. Carman, worried about the direction things were taking on campus, began to work on a plan to have Eisenhower visit College classes and become more involved. But, as Ginzberg commented, Eisenhower "never found the way of responding to anything substantive on the campus" and nothing within at the University gave him "a real kick . . . a central focus." Thus, while the President had had "an auspicious start," Trilling remembered, it "gradually and quickly disintegrated. . . . I began to sense that he was nowhere in relation to the University." These assessments—whether from Carman, Jacobs, and Kirk, or Barzun, Trilling, and Ginzberg—came from members of the academic community who had devoted their professional careers to Columbia and had an extensive knowledge of the University.[43]

*   *   *

"I accepted, after long urging, the presidency of Columbia in the belief," Eisenhower wrote at the first of the year, 1950, "I could do more than anywhere else to further the cause to which I am devoted, the reawakening of intense interest in the basis of the American system." Why, then, did he miss what were considered important academic functions for the President? "The Columbia faculty," he believed, "was capable of taking the lead in studying and analyzing the national viewpoint on the vast social, political, and economic problems thrust upon us after World War II. Eisenhower believed that with such a venture they would amplify the University's role so that its influence would not be restricted to classrooms or scholarly conferences." This led to "the idea of a truly national assembly. . . .

Working toward this idea became an absorbing pursuit for me through most of 1949."

He increasingly realized, however, that the faculties of Columbia had a different research agenda and did not share his vision for the University and his commitment to citizenship education. Kevin McCann emphasized, "The faculty didn't try to learn Dwight Eisenhower," and he recalled that Mark Van Doren, the eminent author and Professor of English, "was just against Dwight Eisenhower and most things he represented." As Eisenhower complained about faculty meetings, "stuffed shirts on the faculty," McCann noted, "he could become stiff." He believed that he could spend his time better elsewhere, especially as he sought "to control his activities" after his illness. Consequently, he turned more and more toward what he saw as the vital goals for Columbia, from Ginzberg's human resources project to developing a program for citizenship education and his conference proposal. Columbia's Presidency, he realized, gave him the forum and opportunity to convey his message and seek his objectives for the University.[44]

Another reason might explain the General's concentration on expanding "the moral and intellectual strength of Columbia, a power for good throughout the country and Western World," instead of addressing the University's internal problems. During his difficult first year with an unfamiliar job he had had a close, confidential relationship with Jacobs, but he never established that rapport with Kirk. General Snyder, who saw Eisenhower daily and worked closely with Ginzberg on the Human Resources Project, early in the fall told the Professor that the General's "judgment about Kirk had been premature and wrong." McCann, who had urged Kirk to accept the Provostship, later admitted that "there was never between those two the relationship there was between Dwight Eisenhower and Al Jacobs." Eisenhower's trusted friend Doug Black knew that the President and new Provost were never close, and he acknowledged that he, also, was not close to Kirk. McCann, in fact, emphasized that "Doug was beating his head trying to figure some way" to bring Jacobs back to Columbia, and Adrienne Swift, who for many years worked closely with Jacobs and then Kirk in the front office, observed that the Doubleday publisher thought that that was important. During the fall of 1949 Eisenhower, attracted to his plans for Columbia, uncomfortable with academics, and without his accustomed chief of staff relationship, devoted himself independently to the reawakening of interest in the American system.[45]

Kirk faced, consequently, an awkward situation and a difficult challenge. The Trustees had reduced considerably the Provost's authority; moreover, since senior Vice President Pegram's successor had not been selected, the Trustees asked him to stay on, in an advisory capacity, for another year. With the University's administration in transition, the *Spectator* reported, with Kirk's confirmation, that Columbia once again had turned to Philip Jessup, offering him Pegram's position; the Ambassador, however, again declined.

Newsweek added to the leadership problem, declaring, "General Eisenhower is thinking seriously of quitting the presidency of Columbia University. He may ask the Trustees to allow him to become Chancellor, leaving him as front man and speechmaker for the university but getting routine administration off his shoulders." The General, the magazine continued, "would like to keep his connection with Columbia, but it's no secret that he is increasingly unhappy in his present job. He now simply doesn't have time to be a college president and fill his schedule of appearances and speeches." While neither Eisenhower nor the Trustees were considering the "Chancellor" idea that fall, the story drew attention to Eisenhower's less active involvement in the University's daily administrative matters, and this proved unsettling. McCann referred to the period as "four rough and rugged days." To address the leadership problem, Kirk found it necessary to ask the University's four Vice Presidents "to set up a regular weekly meeting" with him "to discuss high-level matters affecting University policy. It is anticipated that Kevin McCann will meet frequently with us." McCann, thus, would be the liaison between the President's Office and senior Vice President Pegram, the other Vice Presidents, and the Provost.[46]

Eisenhower, soon after the *Newsweek* article hit the stands, delivered a highly controversial and political speech at the St. Andrew's Society dinner at the Waldorf-Astoria. The *Times* headline read "Eisenhower Urges 'Dogs,' Not Caviar," while the *New York World-Telegram* called the speech an attack on the welfare state and asserted that in political circles it was regarded as a bid by the General for the 1952 Republican presidential nomination. Columbia's President, defining a "liberal" as "a man in Washington who wants to play the Almighty with your money," told the 1,100 cheering persons of Scottish ancestry or birth that he preferred Thomas Jefferson's liberalism preaching the best government being that which governed least. Too many Americans seek "an illusory thing called security" at the expense of individual liberty. "Maybe we like caviar and champagne when we ought to be out working on beer and hot dogs." He had seen, he stated, white crosses on the graves of thousands of men who had died "because they believed there was something more than merely assuring themselves they weren't going to be hungry when they got to be 67." The next morning beer cans and hot dogs appeared in a necklace around the statute of Alexander Hamilton on the Morningside Heights campus.[47]

"Being content with beer and hot dogs," the *Columbia Spectator* caustically asserted, "has never been part of the American tradition we know. The one we know assures any citizen that he may some day eat champagne and caviar, and in the White House at that." The *Spectator's* editorial was picked up by the nation's wire services—according to Max Frankel, the *Times'* campus stringer, it "ran prominently, and the news reverberated through press and radio"—and it declared, "We don't know, of course, but we are willing to bet beer and hot dogs weren't on the menu at the Waldorf-Astoria." The editorial described Eisenhower as the man "who doubles as president of the university," and Frankel has recalled that it "assaulted the general as no one had assaulted him since the Battle of the Bulge"; a University spokesman acknowledged that the President was in Texas and could not be reached for comment.[48]

Following the St. Andrew's speech, Eisenhower left on the trip he had planned for months. He flew to St. Louis, where he met Mamie Eisenhower, who had traveled by train, and they continued to San Antonio by a special train, instead of the usual private railroad car. In June he had expressed his personal beliefs in a long letter to Amon G. Carter, the publisher and editor of the *Fort-Worth Star-Telegram* and a friend, that Columbia University had the opportunity to do "something effective to perpetuate our basic ideals for practice by our grandchildren." The World War II hero, born in Texas, appealed to wealthy Texans for fund-raising; the trip included private luncheons and dinner, several scheduled speeches—he had declined dozens of "Texas" invitations—and a week of fishing and hunting at oilman Sid Richardson's San Jose Island.

"It is quite clear," the General noted in the letter to Carter, "that great changes in our economic and industrial life have forced government to intervene more intimately in our daily lives than was the

case a century ago. . . . The conditions of our life make us interde-
pendent," which has encouraged those leaning "toward paternalism
in government to insist that only through collectivism, with centralized control of all our affairs, can justice, equity, and efficiency be
maintained. You and I agree," he asserted, "this type of thinking is
completely false. . . . In our case, at least, we find that individual
freedom, all the basic rights of free speech, worship, self-government are the very core of our deepest desires and aspirations. The
universities must, therefore, point the way to perpetuation of these
and be alert in warning us against all the insidious ways in which
freedom can be lost."

Then, Eisenhower specifically explained, "My own belief is that
Columbia University has a faculty capable of taking the lead in the
study and analysis, from a national viewpoint, of these great social,
political, and economic problems. . . . I should like my friends to think
of Columbia and of the work to which I am personally dedicated. In
order to make progress, much is needed." During the fall he elaborated
on this message in his *Herald-Tribune* speech, and he would continue
to work on it throughout the next year; by the time he returned to
Texas in December, 1950, he had refined it in a fund-raising appeal
for the American Assembly, his conference program.[49]

Eisenhower reminded people when he arrived in San Antonio that
he was "a native Texan" and glad to be back. He had come to "sell
Columbia University"; while Texas had good colleges and universities, "people should keep in mind national institutions such as Columbia." Eisenhower had left social arrangements and private meetings for the trip in the hands of old friend and San Antonio rancher,
Hal Mangum. He went hunting one morning, and he met with prominent bankers, oilmen, and the King Ranch's Robert Kleberg, Jr.
Mangum invited H. J. "Jack" Porter, a Houston oilman and a Republican Party leader in the state, to meet the General and, in response
to a question, Porter recalled Eisenhower saying he had been "a
lifelong Republican . . . and that no man could refuse to do a service
for his country." That night Porter told his wife that Eisenhower would
be the 1952 Republican nominee for President.[50]

Five days later the President's speeches in Houston and Galveston
echoed his recent St. Andrew's talk and, according to newspapers,
President Truman had told "intimates" he believed that the General
would be a candidate for the 1952 Republican nomination. In Houston Eisenhower spoke at the annual Chamber of Commerce dinner

to 15,000 persons, and the next noon he addressed 1,800 persons at a combined meeting of luncheon clubs. In language reminiscent of his opening address at Columbia in September and of "champagne and caviar," he bluntly declared, "If all that Americans want is security, they can go to prison. They'll have enough to eat, a bed and a roof over their heads. But if an American wants to preserve his dignity and his equality as a human being, he must not bow his neck to any dictatorial government." Concluding, he reiterated that "we must not be tempted by paternalism so that we will give up our priceless birthright of freedom."[51]

The Eisenhowers then went down the coast to Richardson's San Jose Island, and others were left to respond or comment on his speeches. Reporters found Dean Carman in Chicago, who replied that, personally, he did not think the General had political ambitions; moreover, "there's not a word of truth in such rumors . . . that Eisenhower is unhappy at Columbia and that Columbia is unhappy with him." McCann wrote to the editor of the *Spectator*, "I deeply regret, however, that his talk before the St. Andrews' Society has in many quarters been grossly misunderstood." To another the President's assistant stated, "Please do not be misled by a few sentences from General Eisenhower's speeches, inaccurately quoted and snatched out of context." McCann would have agreed with columnist David Lawrence's assessment in the *Herald-Tribune* that Eisenhower's ambition "is an ambition that seeks the opportunity to become America's most useful citizen. . . . He is just trying to serve."[52]

The speeches, though, provoked considerable concern, as well, from supporters. A former executive director of the Republican National Committee told Bill Robinson, "For God's sake get your boy to close his trap and crawl into a hole for awhile. A few more speeches and he'll be up the creek without a bucket." Bruce Barton, the ex-Congressman and advertising executive who had done much to nominate Wendell Willkie for the Republicans in 1940, reminded Robinson that Willkie had talked himself out of the election: "I shan't draw any moral from this. . . ." Robinson, agreeing with both of them, noted that the General "feels very deeply that the present Administration is leading us into a dangerous area . . . he wants to do whatever he can to check it"; he would, though, "like to give up all speechmaking . . . until the timing of his protests might be more effective." The *Herald-Tribune* executive chose to place the blame, nonetheless, on Columbia's Trustees; he suggested that they were "using him in certain quarters as a preliminary build-up for raising some badly needed funds. That was the reason back of the reason for those two speeches in Texas."[53]

The handwritten warning from Milton Eisenhower conveyed greater urgency for the General. "No doubt you have read the enclosed"—the *Washington Evening Star* on the *Spectator* editorial— "as well as other criticisms. They are becoming numerous. Your Texas trip did appear, to the newspaper reader, to be a political trip." He reminded his brother that, "as a symbol and hero, you have been free of criticism. As a suspected politician, you will get plenty. I'm sure you haven't intended to give the impression of having become more receptive to a possible political future, but newspaper readers are bound to obtain such an impression." The Kansas State University President told the Columbia University President, "You don't need my advice—but I'd quit making speeches on everything but education."[54]

Eisenhower finally addressed, publicly and privately, on December 19 the issue of politics and his speeches. The General and Mrs. Eisenhower, following an afternoon Christmas tea at the School of General Studies, attended the traditional Yule Log ceremony in John Jay. With the *Spectator's* editorial, its publication of letters supporting and criticizing the paper, and its recent statement that Eisenhower had been "continuing his assault on 'illusory security' before Texas audiences" on the minds of those present, the General told 350 students, "I can't give you a sermon, because the chaplain is here. I can't talk about scholarly things; there are scholars present. Certainly, I'm not going to talk about politics." The *Times* reported that "a burst of handclapping and some whistling and footstamping" occurred, and then Columbia's President remarked, "A strange thing about that is that I never have."

To his brother, Eisenhower lamented that "everybody can enjoy 'freedom of speech' except me. . . . I am not allowed to open my mouth except for something so innocuous as sulphur and molasses for spring fever. I grow very, very weary of the whole business. I am about to blow up." He, nonetheless, recognized the soundness of Milton's advice: "I have already made up my mind to stop speaking entirely." Then, whining, he wrote, "I may even go to the extent of breaking tradition here and getting someone else to make the annual Commencement Address," and he supported McCann's opinion, concluding, "Incidentally, I have not yet seen a single one of my talks reported accurately." The criticism, however, had been so sharp and disconcerting that he soon asked Provost Kirk to handle all the University's public speaking engagements.[55]

Following the Yule Log ceremony, Eisenhower gave a dinner at the Faculty Club honoring the Shah of Iran and the opening of the University's Iranian Institute. During the fall he had called Kirk into his office and stated that the State Department had asked him to give a dinner for the Shah. Exploding, the General said, "Kirk, tell me why in hell I should give a dinner for some old, broken-down, oriental potentate." Kirk realized that Eisenhower "knew nothing about Iran so I said that the Shah was indeed an oriental potentate but that the rest of Ike's description did not fit." The Shah, Kirk added, "was young, very pro-Western and anti-Soviet, and that he was trying very hard to Westernize his country."

"Ike groaned," Kirk continued, and agreed to "give a stag dinner. . . . When I received my invitation I was horrified to read on it "BLACK TIE AND DECORATIONS." Kirk promptly informed Schulz that "only miniatures could be worn with black tie and that he would have endless phone calls about it," but Schulz replied that Eisenhower had so "insisted."[56]

The Eisenhowers remained in New York over the holidays. He kept his regular office appointments and had meetings with several Trustee Committees; in addition to the dinner for the Shah, he and McCann made an inspection trip to the Harrimans' Arden House. Christmas, importantly, provided the occasion for "a real family gathering" at 60 Morningside Drive. Mamie Eisenhower's parents came from Denver for a long visit, and Snyder noted that "this made it pleasant for Mamie because she didn't get out around the campus very much." John and Barbara and the grandchildren came down from West Point. They also returned for "quite a New Year's celebration," the General emphasized, "and we had lots of fun."[57]

The holidays also provided him with an opportunity to describe "the position in which I now find myself," and around New Year's he wrote at length in his *Diary*. He presented "cogent reasons why I should eschew this partisan field of citizenship efforts." They included his "obvious obligation" to veterans who "comprise BOTH Democrats and Republicans." Second, "I've always been a military officer instantly responsive to civil government, regardless of its political complexion." Third, "I accepted, after long urging, the Presidency of Columbia in the belief that in this post and with the help of these great faculties I could do more than anywhere else to further the cause to which I am devoted, the reawakening of intense interest in the basis of the American system." He believed that "even partial adherence to a specific party or any partial entry into the political field would demand from me an instant resignation from Columbia." Emphasizing his commitment to his Presidency, he added, "But here (in Columbia) is the place I THINK I can do more good for all—even if that most is a rather pitiful amount."

Addressing the political situation and the fact that "there is no doubt" where he stood on "the welfare state and the operation of a system of competitive enterprise," he listed the names of many who had offered to help him politically. Specifically, he mentioned "two memos, written by my two best friends in New York. . . . They take opposite sides" on whether he should "now associate himself definitely with the Republican party and participate in the ensuing struggles" during the fall Congressional elections. Without giving their names (Cliff Roberts and Bill Robinson) or positions in the *Diary*, he placed the memos in the back of the book. Both opposed the "Socialistic doctrines" of the Truman Administration. Roberts argued that Republican defeat in the 1950 Congressional elections "will give irresistible impetus to the further development of socialist doctrine which the Presidential election of 1952 may be too late to arrest. . . . The Republican Party desperately needs, first, leadership . . . second, a positive, progressive set of principles." Eisenhower, therefore, "should seriously consider joining the Republican Party at this time."

Robinson, equally worried that a "sweeping Democratic victory" would occur in 1950, did not agree with Roberts. He argued that if Eisenhower, "America's great untarnished hero," joined the Republicans "at this time" Democrats would "attack and discredit him at every turn." It would, furthermore, "undermine him with his faculty [at Columbia] which contains strong and leftish elements easily susceptible to sabotage" and "strong leftish elements in the student body could likewise be employed to harass and badger him and his administration." And, he warned persuasively, it might also harm Eisenhower's pet projects at Columbia. "Unfortunately, wealth frightens easily and potential gifts or grants to the University might be withheld" because of Eisenhower's alignment with or opposition to "politicians in power."

Eisenhower claimed that "why they happened to decide to write and give me their thoughts on this question, I do not know." Recent events, though, undoubtedly had prompted him to mention the memoranda in his New Year's *Diary* comments. Roberts and Robinson were addressing, after all, an issue which was political speculation throughout the country. The General concluded the entry by asserting that "the answer remains the same." Heeding Robinson's—and his brother's—advice, he decided to limit his public engagements. Perhaps, in the General's mind, his speeches had been misunderstood; in any event, they had been highly controversial and political. They had, moreover, as Robinson warned, provoked criticism at Columbia and encouraged questions about his leadership of the University. Consequently, he would not again address a non-University audience until early February.[58]

Eisenhower, nonetheless, remained busy. Initially, he had been working on and extensively revising "a rough outline and specific ideas" for the House Armed Services Committee's report on its investigation of unification and military strategy. Eisenhower had testified before it in October, and Chairman Carl Vinson requested his assistance. By early January the General's covering letter and long, confidential memorandum were ready for mailing. He attended a luncheon in honor of Kirk, given by Watson, at the Union Club. He went to several dinners downtown, including a black-tie affair for the Society of Older Graduates and a dinner given by investment banker William Burnham, at which he had made some remarks and then invited the host and three guests to the President's House for drinks. He launched a fund drive for the University's proposed $12,000,000 Riverside Engineering Center, and that evening he met with his committee at the Council on Foreign Relations. He attended services at Riverside Church with John D. Rockefeller, Jr., and expressed interest in exploring the "ways and means by which Columbia's connection with Riverside Church can be developed."[59] This may have prompted the story that Eisenhower, when asked to join Riverside Church, said he did not want to be committed to any one sect. But, he added—perhaps revealing his political astuteness— if he were to join any church, he would of course join Riverside.

On January 19 he left New York on an evening train for South Carolina and went on by private car to Augusta National, where he played golf for a week with Roberts, Robinson, Cities Service Company's president W. Alton "Pete" Jones, and several St. Louis friends. Then a military plane took him to an Air Force Base in Georgia, and he visited Edward Bermingham's plantation, Enon Farm. Describing Bermingham to Robert Woodruff, chairman of Coca-Cola's executive committee, as "one of Columbia's great supporters . . . I have a number of things I must talk over with him," Eisenhower stayed at Enon Farm, where they talked and hunted, for four days. On the 30th he traveled to Woodruff's Ichauway Plantation in Georgia, where he again went hunting. On February 2 a military plane took the General to meet Secretary Symington at Turner Air Force Base in Albany, Georgia; after lunch in the officer's dining room, they went to Washington on Lockheed's new Super Constellation; that evening another Air Force plane took the General to LaGuardia. Soon Eisenhower told Bermingham that "his schedule, since returning to New York," remained as busy as "the one I left behind me" at the start of his vacation. And, back less than a week, he wrote in his *Diary*, "General Snyder and I have decided. . . . We are reserving one full week out of each two months, to be completely blacked out of my calendar. Preferably I am to leave the city during the 'no work' week."[60]

Nothing, indeed, had changed his hectic schedule in New York from meetings, working luncheons, explaining Columbia and his programs in detailed letters to friends and potential supporters, and answering his correspondence. A note in his appointment book on January 31 indicated that he had received during the month "twenty-one hundred pieces of mail, or an average of one hundred letters" each working day. On Monday, the 6th, the Board of Trustees held its February meeting. On the 8th he met with Trustee Walter Fletcher, the Harrimans' lawyer who was working on the Arden House gift, and he wrote Averell Harriman, Truman's Special Representative in Europe, to arrange a meeting when returned to the States; he wrote Marcy Dodge in support of the Trustee Committee on Education's proposal to appoint Pegram as Special Adviser to the President; he thanked Bermingham for his hospitality and asked if he could be in New York in early March for a luncheon meeting with Eisenhower and Clarence Dillon, head of Dillon, Reed and Company, to discuss the General's proposal for an Institute of War and Peace Studies; at the *New York Times* building he had lunch with Sulzberger in connection with the Bicentennial; in the afternoon he left for New Haven, Connecticut, and at the *Yale Daily News* banquet he paid a tribute to Yale's retiring President, Charles Seymour.[61]

The next evening at the Waldorf-Astoria Eisenhower delivered his first major speech since returning from Texas. Supporting President Truman's decision to develop the hydrogen bomb, he declared, "I can't go along with those who believe we should hide the horror of the H-bomb in ignorance . . . faced as we are with a godless opponent, I do not believe we should bury our heads in the sand." Columbia, he hoped, would become the foremost scientific center and work for the country's defense and welfare. The *Times*, reporting that Eisenhower during his speech had expressed his praise of former President Herbert Hoover, observed that his "political beliefs have been a matter of question in recent months."[62]

The pace at Columbia continued. Eisenhower toured the School of Business with Dean Young, and at luncheon at the Men's Faculty Club the two had the opportunity to discuss his projects. At the Columbia College Alexander Hamilton dinner at the Ritz Carleton Hotel, Eisenhower presented the Alumni Award for distinguished public service to Major General William "Wild Bill" Donovan, a former varsity football quarterback and World War II's Office of Strategic Services leader. Speakers included Paul Hoffman of the Economic Cooperation Administration, who emphasized the need to speed up the integration of the European economy, and General Lucius Clay. Eisenhower also spoke at the second annual College Forum on Democracy, and the *Herald-Tribune* reported, "Jitters Decried by Eisenhower and Commager; General and Historian Tell Forum at Columbia that Red Fear Is Exaggerated." [63]

In an attempt to involve Eisenhower more closely with the College and offset mounting criticism, Dean Carman began making with Eisenhower unannounced visits to classes he thought the President would enjoy, among them British Constitutional Law and Elementary Economic Theory. Afterwards, Eisenhower talked with students and, according to the *Spectator,* said he had "a wonderful time" listening to the discussion between the instructor and students. "We can think of no better way for the President to become acquainted with the students," and the *Spectator* suggested "an even better idea . . . Ike teach a class himself." Yet it soon became known that after attending Charles Frankel's Contemporary Civilization class, Eisenhower told the professor at lunch, "I am astonished that those students didn't get angry at reading Karl Marx." Junior faculty, moreover, resented the disruption of their classes and some objected to his appearance on principle, one remarking, "Independence prevails here." Carman later acknowledged, "I can see how a younger man" would be upset. Dean Krout, employing a different tactic, took Eisenhower "to see the various departments of instruction." The General "showed an enormous interest . . . and I thought we had very successful conversations."[64]

During this spring Eisenhower also took pleasure in announcing the establishment of a nutrition center. "Hungry people must be fed before we will have peace in the world," and he emphasized the need to double the world's food supply. "During the last war we spent millions—literally millions—to develop packaged foods such as the 'ten-in-one' and 'C' and 'K' rations," he stated. "Now I am told by nutrition authorities that not one of these rations would keep a rat alive, if he had nothing else to eat, over a long period of time." In order to double the world food supply, "We need to assemble in one spot what is known about how to produce the maximum food value from a given piece of land," and he urged business leaders to join scientists and the Nutrition Foundation in Columbia's project.[65]

His close friend Swede Hazlett had written a long letter and, among other subjects, referred to reports that Columbia "completely bored" Eisenhower. The General immediately replied. Stressing how hard it was "to explain to my friends the difficulties in my present life," he asserted, "Actually, I believe that if a man were able to give his full or nearly full attention to such a job as this, he would find it completely absorbing. . . . Because I love to partake in or, at least, to listen to discussions on such subjects as economics, history, contemporary civilization, some branches of natural and physical science, public health and engineering, you can see that living with a distinguished faculty gives to me many wonderful hours that I could never have in any other environment." Admitting that his "loyalties to several different kinds of purposes lead me into a confusing, not to say almost nerve-wearing, kind of living" and could lead him to "express myself in tones of irritation and resentment," he wrote that "a chance listener could interpret some of these expressions as irritation with my 'apparently' sole preoccupation" of administering Columbia's affairs. (He did not mention that he had been called to testify that day before the House Military Appropriations Subcommittee in Washington.) The outbursts, he added, "are directed at myself for allowing confusion and uncertainty to arise. . . . If I were convinced that I had made a mistake in coming to Columbia, I am not so stupid as to fail to recognize the instant and obvious cure." He told Hazlett, "I am not only interested in the task, but I still believe it to offer a way in which I may render some service to the public at large."[66]

For him to continue to render service, however, administrative matters at Columbia required attention. Eisenhower already had agreed that Pegram, upon his retirement June 30, should become a Special Adviser to the President for one year, and the Trustees approved that at the March Meeting. No successor to Pegram had been found, and the Committee on Education noted that "some overlapping of function, particularly in the minds of the University family, between The Vice President and Provost" had evolved. The Committee recommended, consequently, that "a single official—in this price range—can, with suitable assistants, absorb the duties of both," and that Provost Kirk also become Vice President of the University.

The proposal did not require a revision of the Statutes, nor did it return to the structure under which the Provost would become Acting President. The Trustees adopted the recommendation at the April Meeting, and Kirk assumed his new duties on July 1, 1950.[67] With this issue settled, the Eisenhowers spent the second week of March at a club on the New Jersey shore, and the President looked ahead to delivering a major address outlining his Columbia programs which would render service to Americans.

"Tomorrow night," he wrote on his return to Morningside Heights, "I lecture (1 hr) on Peace. The donor of the money to support a yearly lecture on the subject insists that I deliver the first one!!" Leo Silver, a retired industrialist, had established the lecture in memory of his father, and Eisenhower noted "I could not allow an opportunity for a contribution of that sort to go by the board." McCann had been working on the speech and believed that "By early spring of 1950 Eisenhower was optimistic about his and the University's future," and that the speech would sum "up the Columbia record to date.[68]

Notes

1.   Dwight D. Eisenhower, *Diary*, June 4, 1949 (later entry after interruption), pp. 606-607; Eisenhower to Robert Bostwick Carney, June 21, 1949, pp. 651-57; Eisenhower to Louis Arthur Johnson, July 14, 1949, pp. 699-704; Eisenhower, *Diary*, July 17, 1949, p. 706, *The Papers of Dwight David Eisenhower*, vol. X (Baltimore, Md., 1984), *Columbia University*, ed. Louis Galambos, *PDDE* ; Dwight D. Eisenhower, *At Ease: Stories I Tell to Friends* (New York, 1967), p. 355.
2.   Eisenhower to Albert C. Jacobs, July 5, 1949, *PDDE*, X, 673-74; *New York Herald-Tribune*, July 6, 1949; *New York Times*, June 9, 1949, and Editorial, "The Role of

Education." President Truman promptly endorsed the NEA's report, June 10, 1949, ibid.; Ellen W. Schrecker, *No Ivory Tower: McCarthyism & The Universities* (New York, 1986), pp. 111-12.

3.   John Wood to Eisenhower, June 16, 1949, Central Archives, Columbia University (CACU); Eisenhower to Henry Steele Commager, June 16, 1949; Eisenhower to Wood, draft and letter, June 20, 1949, *PDDE*, X, 638-39, 646-49; *New York Times*, June 9, 19, 20, 21, 1949.

4.   Eisenhower to Ralph Waldo Gwinn, June 7, 1949, to Henry Merritt Wriston, June 12, 1949, and to Milton Stover Eisenhower, June 20, 1949, *PDDE*, X, 608-11, 628-29, 642-43; Milton Eisenhower to Eisenhower, July 1, 1949, Eisenhower MSS., Dwight D. Eisenhower Library (DDEL).

5.   *New York Times*, July 9, 1949.

6.   Eisenhower also wrote that Dewey "offered me the senatorship from New York State, but advised against my taking it." Eisenhower, *Diary*, Eisenhower's italics, July 7, 1949, *PDDE*, X, 677-79. The articles on his political interests in the *New Republic* and *Washington Times-Herald* are cited in fn. # 9, ibid., p. 640.

7.   Eisenhower "Memo to the Provost," June 24, 1949, ibid., pp. 660-61; Carman to Jacobs, July 14, 1949, Harry J. Carman MSS., Butler Library, Columbia University.

8.   Louis Hacker, Oral History Interview, May 15, 1975, OHDDEL; Albert C. Jacobs, "Memoirs," 1974; Eisenhower to Sulzberger, July 11, 1949, *PDDE*, X, 684-86.

9.   Jacobs to Jessup, June 23 and July 21, 1949, Philip C. Jessup MSS., Library of Congress (LC); Jacobs to Jessup, to Young B. Smith, and "Personal and Confidential Memorandum," July 14, 1949, CACU.

10.   Philip C. Jessup, personal interview, June 17, 1977, Norfolk, Ct; Jacobs to Pegram and Campbell, August 1, 1949; Jessup to Eisenhower with copy to Jacobs, August 1, 1949; Jacobs to Jessup and to M. Hartley Dodge, August 2, 1949; and Dodge to Frank Fackenthal, August 4, 1949, CACU; Eisenhower to Jessup, August 12, 1949, Eisenhower MSS., DDEL; Raymond J. Saulnier, personal interview, June 13, 1991, New York, N. Y.

11.   Jacobs to G. E. Kimball (same letter to other Professors), July 25, 1949; Jacobs, "Personal and Confidential Memorandum, July 14, 1949, CACU; Jacobs, "Memoirs"; Carman to Jacobs, August 11, 1949, Carman MSS.

12.   Jacobs to Eisenhower, September 29, 1949, CACU; Albert C. Jacobs, personal interview, February 5, 1965, Hartford, Ct.

13.   Eisenhower to Jacobs, August 9, 1949, *PDDE*, X, 713-14. See also Eisenhower to Jessup, August 12, 1949, Eisenhower MSS., DDEL.

14.   Jacobs, interview, February 5, 1965; Jacobs, personal interview, December 31, 1973, Ann Arbor, Mi; Jacobs to Carman, July 15, 1949, CACU; Schuyler Wallace to Jessup, August 11, 1949, Jessup MSS., LC.

15.   Jacobs, "Personal and Confidential Memorandum," August 15, 1949, CACU; Kevin McCann, personal interview, July 25, 1972, Gettysburg, Pa; Jacobs to Dodge (all Trustees), August 22, 1949; Dodge tel. to Fackenthal, August 23, 1949; Dodge to Fackenthal, August 19, 1949, CACU.

16.   Jacobs to Eisenhower, August 26 and 30, 1949, Eisenhower MSS., DDEL; Dodge to Fackenthal, August 25 and 28, 1949, CACU.

17.   Trustees of Columbia University in the City of New York, *Minutes*, October 3 and November 7, 1949, CACU; *Columbia Spectator*, October 4, 1949. The *Spectator*, not informed about the proposed amendments, described Kirk's position as defined by the March, 1949, Statutes.

18.   *Columbia Spectator*, September 26 and 29, 1949; *New York Times*, September 29, 1949; Memorandum for Dean Carman, September 13, 1949 (CACU).

19.   *Columbia Spectator*, September 30 and October 5, 1949; *New York Times*, October

5, 1949; Dean Millicent C. McIntosh to Eisenhower, October 10, 1949, Eisenhower MSS., DDEL.

20. McCann to Eisenhower, August 25, 1949, Eisenhower MSS., DDEL; *New York Herald-Tribune*, September 7, 1949; *New York Times*, September 6, 1949.

21. *U.S. News and World Report*, September 16 and October 7, 1949; Eisenhower, *Diary*, September 27, 1997, *PDDE*, X, 755-57; Robinson to Eisenhower, August 22, and September 6, 1949, and memorandum, August 29, 1949, William E. Robinson MSS., DDEL.

22. *New York Times*, October 9, 1949.

23. "Chronology," *PDDE*, XI, 1604-1607; Jacobs to McCann, September 22, 1949, with notations by McCann and Eisenhower, Eisenhower MSS., DDEL.

24. Jacobs, interview, February 5, 1965; Jacobs to Eisenhower, October 6, 1949, CACU; Eisenhower to Dodge, July 5, 1949, *PDDE*, X, 674-75; Douglas Black, personal interview, June 6, 1973, New York, N. Y.; Robert Harron, personal interview, February 5, 1965, Hartford, Ct; Eisenhower To the Trustees, May 1, 1950, *PDDE*, XI, 1094; *New York Times*, May 2, 1950; Smith to Jacobs, May 3, 1950, Albert C. Jacobs MSS., Bentley Library, University of Michigan; Davis memorandum, April 18, 1949 (CACU).

25. Ibid.; *New York Herald-Tribune*, October 9, 1949; *Columbia Spectator*, October 4 and 17, 1949; *New York Times*, October 15, 1949.

26. Editorial, "A Candle for Ike," *Columbia Spectator*, October 12, 1949.

27. Harry J. Carman, personal interview, December 1, 1961, New York, N. Y.; Mamie Eisenhower, personal interview, December 15, 1975, Gettysburg, Pa.

28. Jacobs, interview, February 5, 1965; Mamie Eisenhower, interview, December 15, 1975; Howard M. Snyder, "Summary of Year 1949," Snyder MSS., DDEL.

29. Roberts, Oral History Interview, September 12, 1968, COHP; Jacobs, interview, February 5, 1965; Mamie Eisenhower, interview, December 15, 1975; Bruce Wonnacott, personal interview, November 9, 1977, Middlebury, Vt; Ellis D. Slater, personal interview, September 1, 1972, Edgartown, Ma; Grayson Kirk, Oral History interview, November 11, 1985, COHP; Carman, interview, December 1, 1961; Lionel Trilling, personal interview, February 4, 1958, New York, N. Y.

30. George Warren to Schulz, July 7, 1949, and Schulz to Warren, July 11, 1949, Eisenhower MSS., DDEL; Pegram to McCann, July 18, 1949; Jacobs to Pegram, July 22 and August 4, 1949; Pegram to Jacobs, September 17, 1949, CACU. Edman's article, "America's Philosopher Attains an Alert 90," appeared in *New York Times Magazine*, October 16, 1949.

31. Jacques Barzun, personal interview, April 5, 1979, New York, N. Y.; Henry F. Graff, personal interview, January 30, 1958, New York, N. Y..

32. *Columbia Spectator*, October 21, 1949; *New York Times*, October 21, 1949; Fackenthal to Eisenhower, September 19, 1949, CACU; David B. Truman, personal interview, February 4, 1958, New York, N. Y.; Graff, interview, January 30, 1958. Eisenhower's calendar indicates that on October 22 he had played golf at the Deepdale Club, then "Dinner and bridge" before the Dewey celebration; presumably he delayed or interrupted the bridge game, which included Roberts and Robinson, to go to Teachers College. *PDDE*, XI, 1608-1609.

33. *Columbia Spectator*, October 17 and 19, 1949; *New York Times*, October 18, 1949; Nehru Dinner, October 17, 1949, Mamie Eisenhower MSS., DDEL; Jacobs, interview, February 5, 1965; Jacobs, "Memoirs," (1974).

34. Eisenhower to Helen Rogers Reid, June 10, 1949, and Eisenhower to Baruch, October 10, 1949, *PDDE*, X, 625-26, 773-74; Kevin McCann, *Man from Abilene* (New York, 1952), pp. 194-95; Eisenhower, *At Ease*, pp. 349-50.

35. *The New York Herald-Tribune*, October 25, 1949; *New York Times*, October 25, 1949; Helen Reid to Eisenhower, September 30 and October 28, 1949, Eisenhower

MSS., DDEL.

36. Eisenhower, *Diary*, October 14 and November 3, 1949, *PDDE*, X, 778-79, 808-809; ibid., XI, 1608-1609.

37. McCann to Eisenhower, August 12, 1949, Eisenhower MSS., DDEL; Ginzberg to author, May 4, 1999; Eisenhower to Deane Waldo Malott, November 8, 1949, and to W. Averell Harriman, November 30, 1949, *PDDE*, X, 819, 843-45; Pegram to colleagues (several senior faculty), September 30, 1949, CACU.

38. *New York Times*, October 29, 1949; Eisenhower to Grayson Kirk, October 31, 1949, *PDDE*, X, 802-804, and XI, 1610. Provost Jacobs, the day he left, informed Kirk that he had given Pegram "a long letter concerning the several appointments which must be made" with a copy for Kirk. Jacobs to Kirk, October 19, 1949. CACU. For the Trustee retirement issue, see Eisenhower to John Jackson, November 4, 1949, *PDDE*, X, 8125-16; Jacobs, "Memorandum," July 25, 1949, and Trustees, *Minutes*, November 7, 1949, CACU.

39. *Columbia Spectator*, November 21, 1949; *New York Times*, November 19, 1949; Eli Ginzberg, Oral History Interview, April 14, 1978, OHDDEL; Eisenhower, *Diary*, November 25, 1949, *PDDE*, X, 839-42.

40. "Chronology," *PDDE*, XI, 1611-14; Eisenhower to Lou Little, November 4, 1949, and to Edward Bermingham, November 15, 1949, ibid., X, 816-18, 825-26; *New York Times*, November 22, 1949; *New York Herald-Tribune*, November 29, 1949; *Columbia Spectator*, November 29 and 30, 1949. Medina had graduated from Columbia's School of Law and had been on the faculty until President Truman appointed him to the federal bench.

41. Ibid., November 11, 1949; Barzun, interview, April 5, 1979; "Chronology," *PDDE*, XI, 1607; *Columbia Spectator*, October 12, 1949; Grayson Kirk to author, March 13, 1992.

42. Douglas Black, personal interview, June 6, 1973, New York, N.Y.; Trustees, *Minutes*, December 5, 1949, CACU.

43. Jacobs, interview, February 5, 1965; Trilling, interview, February 4, 1958; Grayson Kirk, personal interview, May 15, 1973, New York, N. Y.; Barzun, interview, April 5, 1979; Carman, interview, December 1, 1961; Eli Ginzberg, personal interview, December 11, 1990, New York, N. Y.

44. Eisenhower, *Diary*, c. January 1, 1950, *PDDE*, XI, 882-89; Eisenhower, *At Ease*, pp. 349-50; McCann, interview, July 25, 1972; Clarence G. Lasby, *Eisenhower's Heart Attack: How Ike Beat Heart Disease and Held on to the Presidency* (Lawrence, Kans., 1997), p. 53.

45. Eisenhower, *At Ease*, p. 349; Eli Ginzberg, Oral History Interview, May 14, 1975, OHDDEL; McCann, interview, July 25, 1972; Black, interview, June 6, 1973; Adrienne Swift, telephone interview, December 5, 1993, Sarasota, Fl.

46. *Columbia Spectator*, December 8, 1949; *Newsweek*, November 28, 1949; McCann to Robert Frederiksen, December 7, 1949, Eisenhower MSS., DDEL; Kirk to Pegram, Davis, Campbell, and Rappleye, December 28, 1949, CACU.

47. *New York Times*, December 1, 1949; *New York World-Telegram*, December 1, 1949; Robert C. Harron, personal interview, February 5, 1965, Hartford, Ct.

48. *Washington Evening Star*, December 6, 1949; *New York World-Telegram*, December 6, 1949; "Student Daily Chides Eisenhower as Belittling 'Personal Security,'"*New York Times*, December 6, 1949. Frankel wrote in his *Memoirs*: "Neither Ike's eight years in the White House nor my forty-five at *The Times* would wipe away the memory of the Beer and Hot Dogs excitement." Max Frankel, *The Times of My Life and My Life with The Times* (New York, 1999), p. 105.

49. Eisenhower to Amon G. Carter, June 27, 1949, *PDDE*, X, 665-69. In his 1952 campaign biography McCann used most of the letter. *Man from Abilene*, pp. 186-91.

50. *Columbia Spectator*, December 6, 1949; Eisenhower to Hal Mangum, November 14, 1949, *PDDE*, X, 824-25; H. Jack Porter, Oral History Interview, 1969, COHP.

51. *New York Times*, December 9, 10 and 18, 1949; *PDDE*, XI, 851-52, fn #1.

52. *New York Times*, December 10, 1949; McCann to Robert Frederiksen, December 7, 1949, and to M. M. Andersen, December 17, 1949, Eisenhower MSS., DDEL; David Lawrence, "Today in Washington," January 18, 1950, *New York Herald-Tribune*.

53. Clarence Budington Kelland to Robinson, December 11 and reply December 13, 1949, and Bruce Barton to Robinson, December 9 and reply, December 13, 1949, Robinson MSS., DDEL.

54. Milton Eisenhower to Eisenhower, December 14, 1949, Eisenhower MSS., DDEL.

55. *New York Times*, December 20, 1949 and January 7, 1950; *Columbia Spectator*, December 12 and 15, 1949; Eisenhower to Milton Eisenhower, December 19, 1949; see also Eisenhower to Paul Carroll, December 21, 1949, *PDDE*, XI, 851-52, 860.

56. Kirk to author, January 16, 1997.

57. *Columbia Spectator*, December 15, 1949; Eisenhower to Paul Carroll, December 21, 1949, and to George Horkan, Jr., January 4, 1959, *PDDE*, XI, 860, 909-10; Snyder, "Summary of Year 1950," Snyder MSS., DDEL.

58. Eisenhower, *Diary*, c. January 1, 1950, *PDDE*, XI, 882-89; Peter Lyon, *Eisenhower: Portrait of the Hero* (Boston, 1974), pp. 405-406; The two memoranda are in the Robinson MSS., DDEL.

59. Eisenhower to Carl Vinson, January 3, 1950, to William Burnham, January 16, 1950, to John D. Rockefeller, Jr., January 18, 1950, *PDDE*, XI, 889-906, 930-31, 931-32; Kirk, July, 1987, COHP; *Columbia Spectator*, January 11, 1950.

60. Eisenhower to Robert Woodruff, January 11, 1959, to Stuart Symington, February 3, 1950, to Bermingham, February 8, 1950, *Diary*, February 7, 1950, and "Chronology," *PDDE*, XI, 924, 940-41, 957-59, 953-54, and 1620-21.

61. Eisenhower to Harriman, February 8; to Dodge, February 8, to Bermingham, February 8 and 10, to Dillon, February 6, 1950, *PDDE* XI, 950-51, 955-59, 961-62, 1621-22; *New York Times*, February 9, 1950. That same day the composer Richard Rodgers announced that Eisenhower had asked him to chair a committee to plan for a new arts center at the University. Ibid.

62. The occasion was the tenth annual Moles' Society Awards Dinner. Ibid., February 10, 1950.

63. "Chronology," *PDDE*, XI, 1622; *Columbia Spectator*, February 16, 1950; *New York Times*, February 17, 1950; *New York Herald-Tribune*, March 4, 1950.

64. Carman, interview, December 1, 1961; *Columbia Spectator,* February 23, and editorial, "Guest in the House," February 24, 1950; Graff, interview, June 13, 1991; Peter Gay, personal interview, March 24, 1958, New York, N.Y.; John A. Krout, personal interview, July 22, 1963, New York, N.Y.

65. *New York Times*, February 18, 1950.

66. Eisenhower to Hazlett, February 24, 1950, Eisenhower to George Mahon, February 13, 1950, *PDDE*, XI, 988-94, 970-71.

67. Trustees, *Minutes*, March 6 and April 3, 1950, CACU; Eisenhower to the Trustees, March 6, 1950, *PDDE*, XI, 1001-1003.

68. Eisenhower, *Diary*, March 22, 1950, ibid., 1023-24; Eisenhower, *At Ease*, p. 357; McCann, *Man from Abilene*, pp. 195-97.

7

Ike's Projects

Each of [these projects] will help Columbia University a little better to fulfill its purpose—the peace, freedom and good of America, and, therefore, of humanity.

—Dwight D. Eisenhower,
Gabriel Silver Lecture,
March 23, 1950

He was quite surprised and shocked to hear that Teachers College was not the most important school on campus, and we told him it was even worse than that. We had feelings about Teachers College, justified or not, which put it very low among the affilliated institutions. He just couldn't grasp it.

—Jacques Barzun
Personal Interview
April 5, 1979

"I come before you," General Eisenhower began the Gabriel Silver Inaugural Lecture in McMillin Theater, "as a witness of things that have happened and of the impressions those have made upon me." The donor had requested that Eisenhower deliver the first lecture, and the speech, "World Peace—A Balance Sheet" received front-page newspaper coverage and gave him the opportunity to describe his projects for Columbia. The General observed: "Until war is eliminated from international relations, unpreparedness for it is well nigh as criminal as war itself." America, he feared, had already disarmed more than "I, with deep concern for her *present* safety, could possibly advise, until we have certain knowledge that all nations, in concerted action, are doing likewise." He stressed that "international disarmament is essential to a stable, enduring peace" and added, "In a disarmed world—should it be attained—there must be an effective

223

United Nations, with a police force universally recognized and strong enough to earn universal respect."

Arguing that "All of us have come a long way in the past century" and since "the dark summer of 1940," he asked, "What then can be done now—by this University, by the United States, by the free peoples—to further the cause of peace?" His answer: Columbia University's purpose "can be epitomized in one phase—the good of humanity," and he outlined what Columbia proposed to do.

"We hope to build . . . a Nutrition Center" where "the world's scientists will find concentrated all the knowledge, the tools, the facilities that will enable them to devise better, more productive and more effective techniques for the use of physical resources and the satisfaction of man's physical needs." The University already had an International Affairs Institute where world leaders could find the information and data to "enable them to adjust the stresses and needs of one area to the strains and surpluses of another."

Eisenhower continued. "We hope to establish here a Chair for Peace, possibly an Institute . . . to study war as a tragic social phenomenon—its origins, its conduct, its impact, and particularly its disastrous consequences upon man's spiritual, intellectual and material progress." While millions had been donated "for research in the cancer of the individual body," it shocked him that "nothing similar has been done with respect to the most malignant cancer of the world body—war."

Similarly, the Conservation of Human Resources Project, he suggested, "will be of immeasurable benefit to all the world in furthering the dignity of man as a human being." He added. "Another hope is to conduct an exhaustive study into the ways and means of applying to every man's good, in today's intricate economy, *all* the resources of America, in such way as to maintain and enlarge every freedom that the individual has enjoyed under our system. There are other projects, under way or under discussion, that will take their places beside or even in front of these. Each of them," he concluded "will help Columbia University a little better to fulfill its purpose—the peace, freedom and good of America, and, therefore, of humanity."[1]

In the spring of 1950, President Eisenhower knew it would take time, great effort, and energetic fund-raising to accomplish these goals, which ranged from the Nutrition Center, the Conservation of Human Resources, and the Institute of War and Peace to the Citizenship Education Project and the American Assembly. He realized, also, that it would take the collaboration of the Columbia University community to fulfill his concept of Columbia's mission. Though the faculty did not share his focus and their criticism of his role as President continued, Eisenhower committed himself to the challenge of redirecting the University's goals.

That spring, as he pursued his projects, articles in two national magazines assessed his leadership of Columbia and provoked critical comment throughout the campus. In mid-April *Life* featured "Mr. President Eisenhower" with his picture on the cover and Butler Library in the background. McCann had suggested to Quentin Reynolds, a reporter who had covered the General during the war, that the time had come for "a portrait" of him "as the university president, no longer a five star general or supreme commander," and Eisenhower's assistant "sold" the General "on the idea." It was, Eisenhower recorded in his *Diary,* "a most flattering story." It also generated enormous publicity for "Ike," the civilian. "A couple of evenings ago," he wrote on April 27, "Gallup reported me running against Pres. Truman. Bad business! but nothing to do about it. I hope that Pres. is too philosophical to take real note of the 60-30 report against him." DeWitt Wallace, the *Reader's Digest* founder and editor, published a condensed version of the *Life* article during the summer, and he would later write the General, "You are the only *person* in sight who can give *real leadership* to this country."[2]

"From the start," Reynolds asserted, Eisenhower had expressed his "strong convictions" and, literally, solved problems overnight. When a retired professor told the new President that Columbia's graduate schools had "some of America's most exceptional physicists, mathematicians, chemists, and engineers," Eisenhower asked, "But are they exceptional Americans?" Then, according to Reynolds, "Eisenhower exploded, . . . 'Damn it, what good are exceptional physicists, unless they are exceptional Americans.'" In his Installation Address earlier that afternoon he had emphasized that institutions must contribute to advancing "democratic citizenship," or else it will fail. Echoing these convictions to the retired professor, Eisenhower asserted: "Yes, Professor, every man and woman who enters this university must leave it a better American, or we have failed in our main purpose."

Reynolds gave Eisenhower credit for making his office "accessible to faculty and students," though few agreed that it was. He stated, incorrectly, that a casual "luncheon conversation one day" with Eli Ginzberg and Dean Young prompted Eisenhower to start the human resources project, and that Young "managed to pry loose" General Snyder from the Surgeon General's office. When Eisenhower visited Teachers College, Reynolds continued, and heard Dean Russell exclaim that "too few Americans really understand what good citizenship means," Eisenhower enthusiastically endorsed a "Citizenship Education" project, obtained $450,000 from the Carnegie Corporation, and soon made Dean Russell the President of Teachers College. It had not been a long-distance telephone call from the General, as Reynolds stated, but one from Provost Jacobs which brought Professor Louis Hacker back from Oxford University to lead the School of General Studies. The journalist, of course, included the story of how Eisenhower kept Coach Lou Little for Columbia; moreover, he wrote that Snyder had ordered the General to take a three-week vacation the previous spring because of the General's exhaustion, and did not mention the General's serious illness. Finally, he emphasized that comments about Eisenhower at the Men's Faculty Club had "noticeably warmed with two years' acquaintance," and "90% of the undergraduate body is for Ike."[3]

The photograph of Ike in civilian clothes, with the title "Mr. President Eisenhower," on the front cover and the generous presentation of his leadership suggested a publicity campaign. Through McCann the University had encouraged the article, but it backfired badly on campus. Reynolds, the *Spectator* asserted, "gives a very picturesque account . . . a superficial picture," and he "reveals a flagrant lack of information." The college newspaper observed, "Concluding with the students' view of Ike, the writer depicted two years of the life of a Columbia University president as something very nice in the midst of the happy Columbia family." Few among the faculty questioned the *Spectator's* comments. Dean Ackerman saw an "astute political move," while an instructor asserted, "The *Life* article" with its silly stories "made people laugh sourly," and Ginzberg recalled that the article created "resentment, to put it mildly." Bob Harron, who had helped McCann gather material for Reynolds, acknowledged "the unfavorable faculty reaction" and admitted, "It was not good public relations."[4]

Then the *New Yorker's* Richard H. Rovere contributed the lead article, "The Second Eisenhower Boom," for *Harper's* in May. Writing that "Eisenhower's chances seem excellent" for the presidency in 1952, and "many think he is running hard right now," the journalist offered a scathing critique of the General's career. "Clearly Eisenhower has no qualifications worth discussing. . . . He is unintellectual and probably anti-intellectual." Only part of the article focused on his Columbia experience, which was "anything but a success. . . . There is intense hostility toward him on the part of the majority of both faculty and student body." Rovere added: "Columbia's disappointment in Eisenhower . . . stems not so much from any administrative ineptitude he has displayed as from his inattentiveness to the problems of administration. It isn't so much that he is a bad president as that he hardly ever functions as president." In conclusion, Rovere warned, "Eisenhower as President might find himself in the same state of unpreparedness in which he found himself when he was made president of Columbia." The *Spectator* described the article as "outstanding, . . . a full dimensional portrait. . . brilliant," and one which "revealed much insight and a full grasp of the question." Rovere had graduated from Columbia College and, when asked years later about his campus sources for the article, wrote, "I recall once talking with [Professor] Irwin Edman about it and finding it all quite funny."[5]

Yet, though Rovere acknowledged only one source, the criticisms of Eisenhower that winter and spring on Morningside Heights, and especially, those of the *Spectator*, illustrated for Provost Kirk "a feeling that was beginning to develop at Columbia." It reflected a sense that he was "using the University," and his "frequent absences" fed rumors. It was widely acknowledged that "He had alienated many people on the faculty by making speeches about the purpose of education being to develop citizens rather than to develop people intellectually." Specifically referring years later to Rovere's accusation of administrative "inattentiveness" by Eisenhower, Kirk stated, "I don't think that's an unfair comment." Adrienne Swift, secretary for Provost Jacobs and then Kirk, ruefully agreed. She reflected that Eisenhower had "no idea what was expected of him and without Jacobs he never could have survived and would have been lost." She added that "Eisenhower lost interest" after Jacobs left, and "he was off on projects . . . off on the American Assembly."[6]

His concentration during 1950 on his proposals, however, had consequences he never would have tolerated as Supreme Commander. According to Dean Krout, it "baffled and frustrated" him that "decisions could be made," and then "nothing is carried out." He would call Deans or administrative officers into his office, and "we'd agree on a program of action on a particular subject." A few weeks later, he would ask, "Whatever happened about that? We decided, didn't we? It was all understood by all of us. Has anything happened?" When he heard, "No, nothing's ever happened," he complained that "he didn't understand . . . academic life."[7] Yet his frustration partly resulted from his commitment to his particular mission at Columbia and his ensuing lack of attention to administrative matters; moreover, he had not found a chief of staff for his administrative structure.

Kirk feared criticism of the General from another source in early 1950. The *Spectator* reported, based upon a *Newsweek* account, that the Trustees were considering General Lucius Clay for the Dean of the Engineering School position, "despite some vigorous faculty opposition." Clay had been a guest at Columbia's Hamilton Day Dinner in mid-February, and Eisenhower talked with him about the position. "This was Eisenhower's idea," Kirk recalled, and the Provost worried "about campus reaction to another General at Columbia." Fortunately, he added, the position did not interest Clay. Eisenhower's *Diary* comments are interesting: "There is probably no more complicated business in the world than that of picking a new dean within a university. Faculties, including the retiring dean, feel an almost religious fervor in insisting upon acceptance of their particular views." The consequence, he added, "is complete confusion & I cannot see why Universities have followed such a custom! But I'll be d___ glad when we have a new dean of engineering and the fuss, fury & hysteria die down!!" During the spring he appointed John R. Dunning, a nuclear physicist at Columbia.[8]

He did, however, mention the mounting criticism in his *Diary*: "This week another article came out—this time in *Harper's*—which castigated me, on the ground that here the students & faculties hate me—and I return the sentiments with interest." Nonetheless, he continued, "If I could solve the money problems of the University I would not only regard this as almost an ideal place, but I'd have great opportunity & time for personal study. But its the nagging money problem that keeps me going always—including nights. And so I get tired out." Not surprisingly, he welcomed a letter from a retiring staff member, who wrote, "Columbia has been a more interesting and colorful place since you became its head." The letter showed, he recorded, "that not *all* old-timers resent the effort to bring Columbia and the world into closer, *cooperative,* effort.[9]

As if responding to charges of being away from Morningside Heights too much, he spent the entire spring in the city, with the exception of four days in Washington, a few day trips, and two weeks at Augusta National in mid-April. He was at Columbia when Senator Joe McCarthy accused Ambassador-at-Large Jessup of "unusual affinity . . . for Communist causes." Only a week earlier the Wisconsin Republican had announced his list of communist sympathizers in Wheeling, West Virginia. Jessup immediately returned from a fact-finding trip in Asia to respond to the charges, and he testified before the Senate Subcommittee. Eisenhower wrote "how much your University deplores the association of your name with the current loyalty investigation. . . . No one who has known you can for a moment question the depth or sincerity of your devotion to the principles of Americanism." The subcommittee's chairman read the Columbia President's letter into the record.

Jessup thanked the General right after the hearing. "Unless this attack was met and repulsed it might do very great harm to the United States," and he hoped Eisenhower could "spare me a few minutes to discuss" his plans. When they met in Low Memorial, Jessup asked that his leave of absence receive an indefinite extension, and Eisenhower agreed; Truman then announced that the Ambassador would continue in his position indefinitely. Years later Jessup commented that Eisenhower had written for the record, because "we had some contact, and he had a great respect for Acheson and knew that Acheson was a friend of mine and supporting me. . . the same with Marshall also. . . . I think those were the kind of things more than academic background." Whatever the reason, friendship and respect or academic freedom, Jessup added that during the fall of 1951 Eisenhower, as NATO Commander, again came to his defense.[10]

Eisenhower, himself, because of remarks he had made during the Silver Lecture, was invited to testify before a Senate Subcommittee. He told the Senators that in his speech on "international peace" he had argued that nations "would necessarily include universal disarmament as an inescapable step in reaching effective peace agreements." He had, though, cautioned against "precipitous or unilateral" American action "until all other countries, in coordination, are prepared to go along with us in implementation." He had indicated, he testified, that "because of my constant and deep concern for the safety of this country, I could not advise anything more in current reduction, and observed that in certain details we had probably gone below the line of reasonable safety." Eisenhower proceeded to provide his recollection of the Defense budget discussions in Washington the previous year, and he recommended a half-billion dollar increase in the proposed military budget. Secretary Johnson previously had denounced Eisenhower's statement that the government had disarmed too much; now, after the General's highly publicized testimony, President Truman declared that no disagreement existed; moreover, Johnson in a telephone conversation informed Eisenhower that he supported his recommendations.[11]

While in Washington Eisenhower, accompanied by Mamie, attended a dinner of alumni of the entire University on March 30 and suffered though perhaps his most embarrassing experience as President. It was "a big turn-out," Carman remembered, and Senator William Langer "gave the damnedest speech that ever a man could give. . . . He reminisced about Columbia College in his day" and told how boys from the country "had to be taken by the upperclassmen and taught their way" around the city. One evening "a couple of juniors" took him downtown to a brownstone. Trusting them, "he rang the bell" and they went into "a house of prostitution," where "this madam greeted them in a well furnished room . . . lined with books." One junior, surprised, asked the madam, "Well, how did you accumulate these?" "This small collection," she said, "I got those when I was an undergraduate at Barnard. Those over there, the little larger collection, I gathered those when I was a graduate student at Columbia University, and this collection, here, my very choice collection, I gathered those when I was doing post-graduate work at the Sorbonne." Whereupon the young man asked, "How come that you got into this line of endeavor?" The madam replied, "Just, lucky, I guess." The Columbia College Dean recalled, "I believe if Eisenhower had had a gun he would have shot him," and he noted that for "the Barnard people, this hasn't entirely died down" a decade later. "This was a terrible, terrible night, and Eisenhower got after me" and asked, "How do you. . . ?" Carman could only reply, "My dear fellow, I had nothing to do with it. I am as ashamed and humiliated as you."[12]

Between his Washington trip and his departure on April 9 in a special railroad car for two weeks at Augusta, Eisenhower and the Trustees ratified an agreement with Trinity Church to sell some extremely valuable property, known as the "Lower Estate" in downtown Manhattan. Columbia had been granted the property at the time of its founding but, as Eisenhower wrote in late 1949 to Trustee

Fleming, Rector of Trinity Church, the lands "may not be alienated for any greater term of time than sixty-three years" without the consent of Trinity Church. Eisenhower had asked for the removal of the restriction and, also, for the one stating in the grant of the "Lower Estate" that "the President forever for the time being shall be a member of and in Communion of the Church of England. I am informed," Eisenhower added, "that, although this provision is no longer a valid one, it might be a cloud on the title of this property." At the Trustees Meeting on April 3, 1950, it was reported that negotiations had been "successfully completed" and "a general release of these restrictions" for the "sum of One Dollar ($1) . . . has now been obtained" from Trinity Church. Columbia soon would sell the Lower Estate for over $100,000,000.[13]

During this period Eisenhower concentrated on what he considered the more important issues for Columbia, from its role in American society to its financial situation. He was playing golf in Georgia when the *Life* magazine article hit the newsstands and when Vice President Pegram awarded the Chilean President, Gabriel Gonzalez Videla, with an honorary degree at a Special Convocation in the Rotunda. The State Department, giving "Chile a clean bill of health on the question of freedom of the press," had suggested to Eisenhower the award, and Trustee Watson had thought it "very appropriate." During the ceremony, according to the *Spectator,* "a crowd of 3,000, including 100 vociferous pickets, kept vigil outside" and the caption over a front page photograph read, "'Viva Gonzalez' (The Butcher?)"[14]

Eisenhower had returned to Morningside Heights before the publication of Rovere's critical article and in time to address 1,400 persons at the annual Associated Press luncheon and confer an honorary degree on the Prime Minister of Pakistan. "Only an informed public opinion can win the peace," he told the newspaper editors, and he stated that universities shared the responsibility for the interpretation of the news in "this day of ideological conflict." The degree for the Prime Minister had been suggested, once again, by the Department of State, which had informed Eisenhower that the award "will go far to strengthen relations" and would be "eminently fitting if awarded by "an American university with the prestige enjoyed by Columbia." Kirk had disagreed in a handwritten note with Eisenhower's decision, but McCann informed the Provost that the Trustees had given the President a free hand in honoring the Pakistani and the ceremony was conducted in the Trustees Room. That same month Pakistan pledged $250,000, over ten years, for Pakistani Studies in the Near and Middle Eastern Institute.[15]

None of this, however, solved in Eisenhower's words "the money problems of the University," and he applied his belief in a decentralized structure to the Development Office after the departure of Vice President Davis. During the spring and early summer an advisory committee worked on arrangements and, with "things in a state of flux," Bob Harron asked Kirk about the "personnel and financial" prospects for the Office of Public Information. He asserted that his office, despite an inadequate staff and salaries, had done "a considerably better job in its field" than the Development Office, and that he knew of "no other University public relations organization which covers the scope of work that we do." While there were too many things "we can't get to," he mentioned the retirement rally for Dean Carman, which Eisenhower attended. The *Spectator* reported the surprise gathering with the headline, "1000 Students Flood Quadrangle To Honor Retiring Dean Carman: Development Drive Student Donations Received By Dean." The students, it added in an editorial, paid "tribute to one of the most beloved men ever to be associated with the Columbia community." Harron informed the Provost that the idea for the "spontaneous action of the students" was "born in our office." Under the new system "development activities" were decentralized, with programs having separate budgets and reporting to a coordinator, and Harron's office would report directly to Kirk. Harron's memorandum, though, had expressed his concern about spending "the rest of my working life at Columbia" and over the summer he accepted an offer from Jacobs to become Public Information Director at the University of Denver.[16]

Eisenhower, meanwhile, had appointed a "President's Committee" to "undertake a systematic assessment" of the University's "aims, organization and functions." Development planning, he noted, had not adequately considered "the relationship between an individual project and the overall requirements of the University." This acknowledged, implicitly, the problems posed by the fund-raising for his favorite projects. He asked for "a comprehensive statement of what we believe to be the proper and essential activities, given our history, our financial status, and our metropolitan setting, in which we should engage, and the aims and purposes which we should seek particularly to serve." And, in order to give himself more freedom to pursue his projects, he specifically listed matters to which Kirk "should give personal attention and supervision," as part of the Provost's responsibility for "the major portion of the University administrative load."[17]

During the weeks before Commencement he worked on a letter which would play a crucial role in his fund-raising efforts for his projects. He had met with Burnham in early April, before the investment banker traveled to Texas for several weeks to present the General's plans. Burnham concluded that Eisenhower should have a "good will" emissary and introduced him to L. F. McCollum, a Texas oilman and "a very patriotic and generous American." On May 8 the three had luncheon in New York. Eisenhower discussed his proposals and plans, and he told McCollum that he soon would write "of my hopes and purposes so far as Columbia University is concerned." McCollum informed Burnham that "he knew ten men who would give a million dollars to Columbia" and, moreover, that he now had "an entirely different conception" of Eisenhower's presidency.

The General finished what became known as the McCollum letter on May 31; it arrived as Eisenhower received more nationwide publicity. *Life* asked "What Has Ike Got?" and answered its question with three pages of photographs and the observation, "Rarely have Americans been so fond of a potential candidate of whose politics they know so little." Eisenhower had described his views to McCollum by declaring that "the chief responsibility of our educational institutions is to establish a sharper understanding of the American system, a sharper appreciation of its values and a more intense devotion to its fundamental purposes." The University, he added, had "an outstanding faculty capable of taking the initiative in the study and analysis, from a national viewpoint, of the great social, political and economic problems. . . . . The moral and intellectual strength of Columbia is a tremendous power for good in this country."[18]

Eisenhower proclaimed his commitment to "the American creed" in his Commencement Address on June 8 to 17,000 attendees and it was disseminated to thousands more through the media. The previous evening the Eisenhowers had given a formal dinner for a few Trustees and honorary degree recipients, including Federal Judge Medina, Economic Coordinator Administrator Paul Hoffman, Secretary-General Trygve Lie of the United Nations, Pastor Robert J. McCracken of Riverside Church, and former Provost Jacobs, with Eisenhower noting that this last degree "would be very fine gesture, with a good effect on the whole University family."

Some 8,100 graduates of the University's seventeen schools and colleges—including 3,750 World War II veterans—heard Eisenhower declare, "There is nothing wrong with America that the faith, love of freedom, intelligence and energy of her citizens cannot cure." Columbia's graduates, he insisted, had an opportunity to assist in making American leadership "a moral, intellectual, and material model for all time." He continued. "The Columbia family is dedicated to the driving out of ignorance, of the lies and half-truths of propaganda. The full truth, we believe, is the chief support of human freedom and of all eternal values."[19]

He had explained his projects in more detail to McCollum, and throughout the rest of 1950 they dominated Eisenhower's activities as President of Columbia; he continued to pursue these projects after he took a leave of absence and departed for NATO in early 1951. Specifically, he told McCollum that he planned "to initiate" when possible "a great conference center outside New York City"; a nutrition center; a "Peace Institute" to study "the causes, conduct and consequences of war"; a "Human resources" center; and "there are many others—both old and new in the sciences, the social sciences and humanities." Although he had already announced the establishment of the nutrition center, he was still seeking funds for it. He promised McCollum that the Texan would learn at their planning meeting the following week that "I have not even scratched the surface of what I believe can be done."[20]

His omission of the Citizenship Education Project, in this enumeration of his favorite proposals, can be easily explained. The program, under the direction of President Russell of Teachers College, had obtained a large grant from the Carnegie Corporation in 1949 and soon was working with high school systems in New York, Connecticut, New Jersey, and Pennsylvania to promote civic pride. In early 1949 Eisenhower, in spite of criticism about Teachers College and "pinkos," had hailed it as "one of the foundation stones of the American educational system" and asserted that "the first mission of our schools is to prepare our youth for effective citizenship in a free democracy." During the early months of the Korean War Eisenhower learned that Secretary of Defense Marshall had "the same worries we had in World War II" about young soldiers not understanding "our national history and concepts and . . . his own duties as a citizen." Eisenhower mentioned to Marshall the Citizenship project, arguing "We have made great progress and real success has been reported from the cities where pilot courses have been installed." The Defense Secretary expressed his interest, and within a few months the Citizenship Project collaborated with the Armed Forces on a training program. By 1952 the Carnegie Corporation had given or pledged $1,450,000 to the project, to Eisenhower's great pleasure, and by 1953 the project involved over 500 school systems in thirty-six states and over 100,000 pupils.[21]

West 120th Street, which separated Teachers College from the Columbia campus, long had been known as "the widest street in the world"; now, according to Quentin Reynolds in the *Life* article, Russell saw 120th Street, because of Eisenhower, "as probably the narrowest street in the world." In fact, Eisenhower's enthusiasm, Kirk noted, provoked considerable "grumbling" on the Columbia campus. "He was quite surprised and shocked to hear," Barzun declared, "that Teachers College was not the most important school on campus, and we told him it was even worse than that. We had feelings about Teachers College, justified or not, which put it very low among the affiliated institutions. He just couldn't grasp it." Kirk saw the citizenship program provoking "considerable disagreement between the President and a great many members of the faculty, because he had no hesitation in his public speeches to say that the primary goal of education was to create good citizens." This seemed, the Provost added, "to a great many faculty people a somewhat limited view of what higher education should accomplish." Eli Ginzberg stated the problem bluntly: "If there is anything to make the Columbia campus feel that its President is miscast, it is to get mixed up with Teachers College in some kind of a civics program." Not surprisingly, the gulf separating the two institutions may have become even wider. Such criticism, nonetheless, did not discourage Eisenhower. He followed the Citizenship Project from his NATO Headquarters in France and the "enthusiastic" response to the initial Armed Forces program, for example, delighted him.[22]

Viewing "war as a tragic social phenomenon," the former Supreme Commander had been pursuing his "Chair for Peace" proposal since the beginning of the year. In March, before the Silver Lecture, he wrote a three-page memorandum for Bermingham; he added the title in longhand "Professorship for Causes, Conduct and Impact of War, prepared by a brilliant Historian," and he included a handwritten cover letter providing salary estimates. Eisenhower hoped, Dean Krout emphasized, that the project "might contribute measurably toward an understanding of the gray zone between war and peace and toward more intelligent policy decisions affecting civilian-military relations." He worked closely with Bermingham and Clarence Dillon in raising money and defining the project, and by the spring of 1951 they had plans to launch the Institute of War and Peace Studies. Since Eisenhower was in France, Krout kept him informed and asked for the General's approval of plans and of the Director, Professor William T. R. Fox. The official announcement of the position came in December and stated that the project was one of several which Eisenhower regarded as comprising his "unique contribution" to Columbia. "We started out," Krout commented, "with the idea perhaps the institute would be a much broader and popularly based organization, I'm sure we had that in mind." Yet, perhaps because of Eisenhower's absence, the Institute, as Ginzberg observed, "never gets the money. . . . It doesn't come off." Consequently, "as it finally developed," Krout concluded, "it became really a research institute and properly so." Looking back on the project after a decade, he commented, "It seems to me that they have done a great deal of fine work."[23]

"The Conservation of Human Resources," Eisenhower wrote in *At Ease*, "had its beginnings"—as had his citizenship concern and "Chair for Peace" interest—"in my wartime realization that we had seriously neglected the full education and preparation of our young people to be vigorous and productive members of society." The wastage of manpower during the war had shocked the General and he had become personally interested in the problem, according to Snyder, "because of the shortages in personnel that he experienced in North Africa and later in Europe." Snyder estimated that "18 million men were screened for service. Almost two million, or one of every nine men aged eighteen to thirty-seven, were found to be either total illiterates, borderline illiterates, or so poorly educated that they could not read instructions or write a letter." When Eisenhower sought to examine the problem after the war, Snyder suggested that he meet with Ginzberg. That led not only to their long luncheon meeting at the Pentagon in early 1947 but to regular sessions after the General arrived on Morningside Heights; as Ginzberg recalled, "I saw him at least twice a week, frequently for an hour and a half or two hours in his office."[24]

By mid-December, 1948, Eisenhower and Ginzberg had prepared a letter for fifty-five business and public affairs leaders, and by the summer the professor had prepared final plans and they embarked on the initial fund-raising. Eisenhower told Dean Young, "You carry the ball. It's your job to go around with Eli now and call on these captains of industry and get the money." The first group of supporters, friends of the General, knew that Dean Young represented Eisenhower. During 1950 Young reported on the financial progress, and Ginzberg detailed "a threefold plan of attack" for the proposed five-year research study. This included examining "marginal and ineffective personnel in civilian and military life," the misuse of superior performers, and "a broad historical analysis of the major changes in the twentieth century of the attitudes of various groups toward their work."[25]

Ginzberg announced the Conservation of Human Resources Project, a five-year, $500,000 program, in December, 1950. After explaining that Eisenhower had taken "the leadership in initiating a comprehensive study" of manpower wastage, he described its two extremes: inadequate use of "poor performers" and "a failure to recognize and facilitate the development of the potentially talented." Soon, a series of important publications appeared representing, as Eisenhower asserted, "a unique achievement in cooperation between business, government, and our University." The first major one, *The Uneducated* (1953), studied illiteracy in America. Eisenhower, writing from the White House in 1953, was delighted that the project could make full use of Snyder's "rich experience in all phases of military-medical manpower problems" and that it was dedicated to the doctor. The *Negro Potential* (1956)—Eisenhower read the draft manuscript—showed, as Snyder observed, how "segregation in the Armed Services during World War II proved to be a seed-bed for frustration and emotional illness, particularly in the case of better educated Negroes from the North who developed intense hostility to what they considered a grossly unjust system."[26]

Eisenhower remained "directly interested in the project's outputs over the years," and Ginzberg dedicated the significant three-volume study, *The Ineffective Soldier* (1959) to the General. He had, after all, encouraged Ginzberg "to delve as deeply as possible into the reasons why one million young men were rejected for military service, and another three-quarters of a million were let out of the services prior to demobilization because they were adjudged to be emotionally unstable." Eisenhower had told Secretary Forrestal about the project in early 1949 and had arranged for Ginzberg's conversation with the Secretary, and their efforts had paid off, for the project "required the wholehearted cooperation of the Department of the Army and the Veterans Administration."

These volumes, the editors of Eisenhower's *Papers* have shown, answered the questions Eisenhower had asked in his December, 1948, letter to prospective supporters of the project. For Ginzberg and his associates, four basic conditions contributed to the waste of human resources: "unemployment; underemployment; inadequate training; and arbitrary employment barriers."

Moreover, "certain common denominators," the editors argued, "helped explain the failure of men to perform." They concluded: "Ginzberg's sweeping recommendations advocated a reevaluation of America's education policies, greater support for health services, and long-range plans for the improvement of personnel management." President Eisenhower's interest and commitment had been essential to the establishment of the Conservation of Human Resources Project, and he had good reason to emphasize in *At Ease* that his role in the project was "one of my proudest memories of life at Columbia."[27]

On June 6, 1950, the sixth anniversary of D-Day, Eisenhower took another step toward establishing the American Assembly, the conference center project which had received his greatest attention for months. McCollum, Burnham, and Young joined the General at 60 Morningside, and they planned a fund-raising luncheon which Burnham and McCollum would give at the University Club. The guests included Frank Abrams, chairman of Standard Oil of New Jersey; Clarence Francis, General Foods chairman; the presidents of Kennecott Copper, National City Bank of New York, and AT&T; and Bob Woodruff. Throughout the luncheon Eisenhower enthusiastically described his conference proposal.[28]

The following noon he departed for an extended fishing vacation in Canada and, during the last days of June, as he was planning the last details of his summer vacation, North Korea invaded South Korea. He traveled to Washington on the 28th, expecting to see his friends "engaged in the positive business of getting the troops, supplies, etc., that will be needed to settle the Korean mess. They seemed indecisive—which was natural in view of indecisiveness of political statements." Truman that day authorized General Douglas MacArthur to use available forces, and Eisenhower wrote, "This appeal having been made" for force, for [God's] sake, get ready!" He believed that "the United Nations . . . must be absolutely firm." The Eisenhowers spent the July 4th weekend, their thirty-fourth wedding anniversary, at 60 Morningside. On the 5th Eisenhower returned to Washington and, after appearing before a sub-committee of the Senate Foreign Relations Committee, he had lunch at Blair House with Truman, Marshall, Johnson, and the Chief of Naval Operations. The previous day American troops had engaged North Korean forces for the first time. He and Marshall "told the Pres. that his decision . . . must be *earnestly* supported." Yet, he thought that Johnson was complacent and "there seems no disposition to begin serious mobilizing. I *think* that it is possible that military advisers are too complacent when talking to H.S.T."[29]

His Minneapolis visit two days later received front-page attention. Though he emphasized he had come as President of Columbia, reporters sought the former Supreme Commander's views on the Korean crisis at a press conference and noted that he spoke "frankly and vigorously on the war picture." Eisenhower asserted that "a democracy must be very alert" and mentioned his conference proposal: "We believe that universities—and we want Columbia to take the lead—can be of more use to the world today." Harry Bullis, the General Mills chairman who had arranged the trip, had met the General through Burnham; Eisenhower had traveled to Minnesota with Burnham, Young, and McCann on the company's executive plane.

That evening Bullis gave a private reception and an informal dinner, during which the General discussed his plans for Columbia and, in a longhand letter, he hoped "I did not bore the assembly with my convictions and enthusiasm—I'm so devoted to this country, and want so much to do something about it, that I fear I grow garrulous." The guests were a who's who of Minneapolis and St. Paul industrialists, and he added, "I have tried to write each a personal note—hope I've missed none." Bullis already had written, "Like Julius Caesar, you came, you saw, you conquered." The General Mills executive declared: " You not only sold us on your Columbia project, but you made a sale of far greater potentialities—one that only you can close when the proper time comes."[30]

McCollum, meanwhile, had arranged a special trip for six very wealthy Texans to fly to New York for a luncheon with the General and Dean Young at Burnham's apartment. Burnham told Eisenhower that "Mc" realized the conference project required some $250,000 for "a flying start," and that the group knew it was "coming to assist you through aiding Columbia financially." The investment banker continued. "The idea about you yourself not asking directly for funds made sense to him, i.e. that you could not afford to be under obligations to anyone." Thus, Burnham suggested that Eisenhower adopt his "idea of yesterday and give 'Mc' and me a letter or something authorizing or requesting us to solicit funds for Columbia." The group, and he estimated their "total wealth over a billion," included Bob Kleberg, the president of the King Ranch who had offered to "devote time and money working for Columbia"; H. J. "Jack" Porter, who had met Eisenhower during the General's trip to Texas in December and actively supported the conference proposal; H. L. Hunt, founder of Hunt Oil, an ultra-conservative and ardent anti-communist; and three others. At the meeting, Young wrote, "We opened a drive for $500,000."[31]

Eisenhower, shortly after opening the University's fifty-first summer session, began his vacation with a trip to California and the Bohemian Grove before going to Denver for six weeks. He attended a luncheon to promote the American Assembly in San Francisco, given by the president of Standard Oil of California who soon sent $25,000 from his company to sponsor an American Assembly session. When McCollum brought another "Texas" group to Denver for luncheon with Eisenhower at the Cherry Hills Country Club, the guests contributed over $11,500 for the Assembly, and Porter personally handed Eisenhower a $10,000 check from Kleberg. The King Ranch president had liked the Columbia President's emphasis on "good citizenship" and the conference plan. With Eisenhower's "personal interest and guidance," Kleberg continued, the conferences might provide "some worthwhile answers to the vast and complicated problems with which our country is faced." The previous noon, ten top Phillips Petroleum executives met with him for luncheon; Chairman K. S. "Boots" Adams contributed $50,000 and, later, another $25,000.[32]

Several of McCollum's friends had asked the General specifically to "outline in writing the country's need for this [conference] program and the method of operation." Eisenhower replied in a long letter from Denver on September 12 that he had come "out of World War II" with "a profound conviction that America was in danger for two reasons. "The first was "The Communist threat from *without*," and the second, "The failure of most of us to remember that the basic values of democracy were won only through sacrifice and to recognize the *dangers of indifference and of ignorance.*" Emphasizing "that democracy could be destroyed by creeping paralysis from within," he added that, since America was "at war" in Korea, it was "even more important . . . that a greater effort be made to study these problems, in conjunction with the mess we face abroad."[33]

The Korean War, indeed, dramatically enhanced his appeal that summer. By early August American troops, badly outnumbered and lacking sufficient weapons, were forced to retreat to the southeastern corner of the Korean peninsula and had suffered over 7,500 casualties. Eisenhower had been dissatisfied with Secretary Johnson, and he was aware of the White House unhappiness which would lead to Johnson's resignation and General Marshall's appointment as Secretary of Defense in mid-September. "In the struggles that lie ahead," Eisenhower acknowledged, no one would assert that his assembly plan "will assure a fully successful outcome to the larger political, economic and military problems we face every day." But, he concluded his four-page letter, "better and more comprehensive studies . . . may *do something,* something that is vitally necessary. . . . This American Assembly . . . is action, not just words." Soon, he sent similar letters to Porter, friends, and a number of additional persons; Porter, meanwhile, had sent some 600 letters to solicit funds from Texans.

Throughout August Eisenhower kept his office calendar open, except for the fund-raising luncheons and several appointments concerning a major radio address in September, and he played golf regularly. He spent one morning talking about Columbia with Vice President Pegram and Dean Carman; both had retired, though they would remain active at Columbia. They were staying at the home of former Provost Jacobs, serving as consultants over the summer at the University of Denver. On the 23rd Jacobs awarded Eisenhower an honorary degree at the University's summer convocation.[34]

Before leaving Denver Eisenhower launched the "Crusade for Freedom" in a nationwide speech broadcast by the four major networks on Labor Day weekend to raise funds for the National Committee for a Free Europe. He had objected to a proposed draft and prepared one himself; after he made extensive changes on his revised draft, he read paragraphs over the telephone to the Deputy Secretary of Defense. "Eisenhower Opens Crusade for Freedom; His Charge," the *Denver Post* front-page headline read, "REDS PLOT TO ENSLAVE U.S." Underneath four photographs of Eisenhower at the podium, a two-column headline added, "General Urges 'Big Truth' to Fight 'Big Lie.'" Across the rest of the page came the headline, "BIG HOLE TORN IN U.S. LINE; 45-MILE FRONT PERILED." He called for the expansion of Radio Free Europe "to tell in vivid and convincing form . . . of our aspirations for peace, our hatred of war, our support of the United Nations, and our constant readiness to cooperate." The "Crusade for Freedom" speech received widespread coverage; Bullis enthusiastically praised it, and the talk unquestionably appealed to many of the General's American Assembly supporters. Eisenhower clearly saw a connection between his appeals for the "Crusade" and the Assembly.[35]

On the train trip back to New York, Eisenhower believed that the New York luncheons and his trips to Minnesota, California, and Colorado had provided sufficient financial support for the American Assembly; moreover, Young told him that Harriman had offered to contribute $200,000 by January and a total of $275,000 within five years for the rehabilitation and maintenance of Arden House. The Dean added that Harriman "feels very intensely that there is a greater need for the Conference Program than ever before," and he recommended that Eisenhower formally present his program to the Trustees.[36]

Eisenhower arrived back on Morningside Heights in time for the opening of the academic year. He greeted Columbia's Class of 1954—the University's Bicentennial Class—and urged that citizenship be taught in the classroom. At Barnard College's opening ceremonies, he described the "Crusade for Freedom" as a new method of "taking truth to all parts of the world." Soon Barnard students, and then Columbia College students, began a petition drive supporting the nationwide "Crusade for Freedom." At the University's formal opening exercises, the President reflected that "the new enrollees . . . were entering in a very uneasy period in the world's history." He told them, "Here at Columbia a whole convention of great minds is present which decidedly influence and determine the intellectual understanding that makes freedom secure and truth self-evident."[37]

The President's comments provided an appropriate introduction for Professor I. I. Rabi's keynote address. The renown physicist criticized the University of California's Board of Regents for demanding "loyalty oath" contracts. Thirty-nine professors had refused to sign the mandatory loyalty oath and had asserted that they were not communists; nonetheless, the University dismissed twenty-seven of them. At Columbia fifty faculty members, including Rabi, signed a formal protest, and the *Spectator* commended the Columbia professors and deans "for their courage and clear vision." In his speech the Nobel Prize winner condemned the California action as an example of national "moral hypochondria."[38]

The first time Rabi met Eisenhower, he was showing the President around Pupin Hall. The scientist "contradicted him flatly. He never forgot it, but gave me a lot of credit for it." When the Institute for Advanced Studies in Princeton offered Rabi an attractive position, the scientist could get no response from Low Memorial. For Rabi, who had seen Columbia lose Fermi and Urey, "nobody doing anything" was the nature of Columbia. Finally, he went to McCann, who arranged an appointment with Eisenhower, and he said, "Look, Mr. President, I don't know what's going on here. I have a definite offer. . . . People have expressed appreciation for my work at Columbia, which I appreciate, but this is a piece of paper, specific. I've had no answer to this." In *At Ease* Eisenhower recalled, "I stressed that, to the academic world, he symbolized pure science on Morningside Heights. His departure, I continued, would deprive the University of its chief drawing card." Eisenhower told Kirk to take care of Rabi; the Provost more than matched the offer; and, Eisenhower wrote, "Dr. Rabi delighted me . . . by agreeing to stay on."[39]

With the fall semester barely underway Eisenhower said that every student eligible to vote had a citizenship responsibility to register. In a special statement to the *Spectator* he asserted, "If ever there was a time to exercise your right to vote it is now. . . . A student must practice citizenship or he may lose it." It was a responsibility that accompanied individual rights, and he recalled that in 1948 not even half of the qualified electorate had voted. The plea, the *Spectator* declared, "has a fresh meaning today when democracy is going through a time of crisis. . . . We hope Columbia's voters, at least, will prove Ike isn't just wishfully thinking."[40]

Governor Dewey, as if he were responding to Eisenhower's plea for practicing citizenship, announced on the nationally televised program, "Meet the Press," that he supported Eisenhower for the 1952 Republican nomination for president. Dewey had assumed he would be asked the question on the program and had informed Eisenhower what he would say. The General merely replied "No comment" to the Governor. Eisenhower's office issued a statement that the General's convictions "have often been expressed" on how he could "best contribute something to the cause of freedom. They have not changed." He reiterated: "Here at Columbia University I have a task that would excite the pride and challenge the qualifications and strength of any man—I still believe that it offers to such an individual as myself rich opportunities for serving America."[41]

The *Spectator's* reporter saw the statement as "less firm than previous disavowals of political ambition," but the editorial, which noted that "Ike is very 'hot'" news, concluded, "We are willing to take President Eisenhower's words at their face value." The *Spectator* based its opinion on an exclusive interview Eisenhower had given the student newspaper on the second anniversary of his Installation, and before Dewey's comments. "I have no desire to go anywhere else if I can help do what I want here at Columbia. This is the place for me." Repeating, according to the paper, his assertions that education must "produce good Americans and good citizens," the University President said, "Underneath all of the individual's professional and technical skills must be a sense of values—an understanding that that kind of system which produces the *individual* with *freedom* is best." His comments, however, did not discourage speculation. A headline in *U.S. News and World Report* read, "Eisenhower Band Wagon Gets Going: General Far Out in front for '52 Nomination." Concluding that politicians rated his nomination and election chances "better than those of any other man in sight," it added that only a flat statement by him expressing his refusal to run or serve "can prevent his own nomination. . . . Anything less will cause skepticism."[42]

Eisenhower had not allowed the start of the academic year and the issue of presidential politics to distract from his focus on the conference plan, as he prepared for the October Trustees Meeting. Dean Young, in effect, expressed the General's thinking when he argued "the utmost importance that the Trustees" approve the plan in principle and accept Harriman's Arden House estate. "The American Assembly is more than a dream," he wrote and, "It comes from the same constructive group thinking that has developed the Citizenship Program at Teachers College, The Institute of War and Peace, the Graduate Business School's project on the Conservation of Human Resources, and the Nutrition Institute." Since many of the Trustees and leading citizens throughout the country had enthusiastically endorsed the project, "great pressure," he emphasized, existed "to initiate the program as rapidly as possible." On October 2 the Trustees formally approved the plan and accepted the Arden House estate and Harriman's funding for rehabilitation and maintenance, and Eisenhower proceeded to inform the University's Deans, Directors, and Department Executives.[43]

In what the General described as "the most important step I have taken as President of Columbia University," he announced the establishment of the American Assembly at a special Columbia Associates luncheon on October 18. He stated that Dean Young had agreed to serve as the administrator and that the Associates, a prominent alumni development group, offered to sponsor the proposal and to give all the support needed to bring the project to fruition. The members and many special guests constituted an impressive list, and they heard Eisenhower describe what he saw "not only as a great vision but something that can come into being instantly and effectively." The Associates suggested that contributions be sent directly to Eisenhower at his Columbia office, and Young indicated the first conference would occur in April, 1951.[44]

After the Associates luncheon he took the evening train to Pittsburgh and carried his message to alumni in western Pennsylvania and, then, spoke at the celebration of Founders Day at Carnegie Institute. He emphasized the need to defend freedom against "the announced purposes of Communist fanatics," while making sure not to "suffocate freedom in its own dwelling place." He stressed the need for universal military training, and he added that "post-service opportunities . . . should include appropriate educational help." The *Spectator* inferred that this was the first suggestion for the need of reviving the G. I. Bill since the draft had resumed. A *New York Herald-Tribune* editorial concluded, "A bold and imaginative appeal to rationality and informed good will, the assembly is a fine example of educational statesmanship."[45]

The General had agreed to present a series of awards at Columbia's Homecoming Weekend, and he returned from Pittsburgh the next day. That Saturday morning McCann called Bob Harron and said that Eisenhower wanted to see him—it was Harron's last day in the office before going to Denver. Describing Denver "as my favorite American city," Eisenhower said, "You are fortunate you are going out there to live. . . .You know sometimes I get quite sick and tired of the life I'm living, invited to dinner parties and so on where I feel that perhaps I must go for the University, but I know in my heart that the people just want me because they think that the name General Eisenhower adds a little bit." He continued: "I'm getting tired of being pawed over. Now, in an hour and a half I have to go up to Baker Field"—Homecoming Day— "and I have to be auctioned off to the class that has the biggest number of people present and I have got to eat lunch, a box lunch, with a lot of people I don't know and it is not pleasant." Then, he added, "Seven minutes before the end of the football game I have to go, the cops will come and get me and if we are losing people will think I am walking out on a losing football team." Harron could only comment, "General, this was just the result of being General Eisenhower and you just have to take it."

Harron finished what he had to do in his office and did not get to Baker Field until just before the game started. It was a perfect autumn afternoon, and 30,000 fans had arrived. Harron saw a friend, who was involved with planning the luncheon, and asked, "How did your Homecoming program go?" The friend replied, "Bob, it was just wonderful. General Eisenhower had the best time he ever imagined. How that man loves people!" As for the game, it was not even close when Eisenhower had to depart—Columbia lost, 34-0.[46]

The next evening he left for alumni appearances in Chicago, St, Louis, Indianapolis, Cincinnati, and Charleston—when he arrived in Chicago he had a message to call the President, who asked him to come to Washington after the alumni meetings. Before leaving Charleston on a military plane, the official silence had been broken and Eisenhower acknowledged his "duty as a soldier" to accept, if offered, the post of NATO Commander. Throughout his midwestern trip he had stressed the American Assembly and, as the *Alumni Magazine* noted, "press conferences were an important part of the trip." Neil McElroy, president of Proctor & Gamble, soon reported that after Eisenhower's Cincinnati visit he had "rounded up" $25,000.[47]

After the start of the Korean War, the question of NATO and the rearming of Germany became vital, and Truman wanted Eisenhower to become commander of the Atlantic Pact Defense Forces. The President and the Western allies believed that only Eisenhower could build the armed forces to defend Europe. The possibility had been "first mentioned *many months ago*," he wrote in a long *Diary* entry after the October meeting. "I am a soldier and am ready to respond" to orders, but the President "is particularly anxious that the matter" not be on "a cut and dried 'order and obey' basis." The General estimated, "I will be back in uniform in a short time. . . . It will, of course, be a wrench to give up the work I am so earnestly working on at Columbia." He did not see how he could give "a hard and fast estimate" for the length of service. "I am convinced," he wrote to a Denver oilman after seeing Truman, "that there is so much for us to do here in the interest of our country that I am anxious that the great work [the American Assembly] go ahead regardless of the location of my particular port of duty." In early November the *Spectator* reported that Eisenhower's Low Memorial office would make no appointments for him after January 5, 1951, and politicians speculated about the impact on the 1952 election.[48]

Eisenhower talked with his friends about the future of the American Assembly in the event he should be called back to duty. After golf and bridge with Cliff Roberts on November 2, he wrote "to make of record" what he had said. Arguing that "the concept of the American Assembly will increase in importance according to the duration and intensity of the tensions under which we live," he admitted that he must "depend upon my friends even more completely than I have in the past." Knowing that he could depend completely on "their loyalty and understanding," he added, "It will be a wonderful thing to know that all its adherents are more than ever determined upon its success." Indeed, they were. On the eve of his departure for an American Assembly trip to the southwest, Roberts surprised the Eisenhowers. "Their birthdays are within a month of each other, and we split the difference and had a birthday party for them at the Park Lane, and I asked about 40 people that they knew well, and we gave the General, as a birthday present, a number of contributions to get the American Assembly off the ground." A committee of solicitors—all friends and members of Augusta National—included, in addition to Roberts, "Pete" Jones, "Slats" Slater, Bill Robinson, Douglas Black, and Bob Woodruff, and they had raised $50,800. Eisenhower acknowledged each gift and, in thanking Roberts, wrote, "I never dreamed that the party would turn into such a fine thing for Columbia."[49]

"Today I start on a trip to Chicago, Dallas, Texas A&M, Houston, Oklahoma City, Chicago—Home," he recorded in his *Diary* on November 6. "I travel in interests of American Assembly. . . . It has appealed mightily to business men—and support, both moral and material has been fine." Emphasizing, parenthetically, "I personally never ask for a dollar," he added that "through my explanations to selected groups we've tagged, already, well over one hundred thousand." He proceeded to list specifically the major contributors and amounts given. "So I'm encouraged." Repeatedly, he stated throughout his Presidency that he would not ask people for money, and McCann asserted in *Man from Abilene* any such effort "might be interpreted by the prospect as a pistol at his head." Eisenhower, McCann continued, "simply did not have it in him to raise funds." Perhaps Eisenhower convinced himself—and McCann—that a difference existed between asking for money and explaining to people why they should contribute to his favorite projects, especially the American Assembly; perhaps he had persuaded himself that he was not raising money when he authorized personal emissaries to solicit funds in his name and knew how much was contributed.[50]

The trip proved successful. It began with a luncheon in Chicago for leading businessmen, given by Ed Bermingham, and ended in Texas with contributions of $10,000 from Amon Carter and $15,000 from Sid Richardson. Carter, president and publisher of the *Fort-Worth Star-Telegram,* and Richardson, a multimillionaire oilman, who the General had visited the previous December, were two of his oldest friends in Texas. Carter saw that this "great work you are carrying on" could "be a blessing to our country and humanity in general." Eisenhower spoke at the inauguration of the new president of Texas A&M University, which required military training. In addition to discussing the assembly plan, he asserted, "Until every young American comes to look upon prospective military service as a personal obligation to be cheerfully, efficiently and proudly performed . . . this nation will not be served well by her citizens who owe everything to her." Texas newspapers gave front-page attention to the General's visit and his American Assembly proposal. "Thoughtful citizens," the *Houston Post* concluded, "will find much nourishing food for reflection in Gen. Eisenhower's message."[51]

He continued his fund-raising "explanations." He traveled to Boston to promote his plan, and the *Boston Herald* saw the Assembly as "a fine complement to the New England tradition of free discussion in town meeting." Robert Cutler, president of the Old Colony Trust Company, in his words "invited a dozen gold-plated magnates" to meet Eisenhower, "who won them all to his side, for the American Assembly or anything else." During the overnight trip the General avoided all questions about politics and NATO.[52]

Perhaps the dinner arranged a week later by Clarence Dillon illustrated best Eisenhower's position that fall. Dillon invited prominent financiers in New York to give Eisenhower a chance to describe the Assembly, so that the Columbia Associates could go after the men for money. Actually, the General recorded in his *Diary*, since "everyone was in such a blue funk over the tragic news from Korea"—the Chinese Communists had launched a massive and devastating counter-offensive against MacArthur's forces—Dillon suggested he discuss "the Korean debacle." Eisenhower showed "some of the additional problems it imposed upon us as citizens. . . . And so, finally, I ended up arguing for the American Assembly idea!" He had the task, as he wrote to Bermingham, "of helping pick us all up from the 'mental floor,'" and people were looking to him for leadership. "In spite of the pall of gloom hanging over all of us," Eisenhower wrote in thanking Dillon for a "most interesting" evening, "for me is was also helpful."[53]

The critical Korean situation with the Chinese onslaught bothered the General and, because he was being called so often to testify, he worried about talking with General Gruenther, the Deputy Chief of Staff, and being briefed on military information which might be secret. That did not deter him from recalling, nonetheless, being puzzled by Washington's "seeming lack of urgency" following the North Korean invasion in June. He wanted to discuss with Gruenther, who would become his Chief of Staff at NATO, "what has happened—possibly what has not happened—since the Koreans' first attack and the decision was made to defend the territory south of the 38th parallel."[54]

Back on campus after Thanksgiving, Eisenhower accepted a long-standing invitation from Dean Hacker of the School of General Studies. Hacker directed an adult education program, as he recalled, "a second chance for persons who had not gone through educational careers in one jump, who had like myself been dropouts and then had decided to return." The program "fascinated" Eisenhower, and the two "became quite friendly." Eisenhower delivered an extemporaneous address to several hundred General Studies students, and in *At Ease* he remembered, "When I finished, I was astonished to find dozens of students on their feet, ready to ask questions." Admitting that he "had really been put through the wringer" by questions, he noted "there were no mean or loaded questions, none designed to trip up the old soldier; these people wanted to learn."[55]

The General Studies lecture began a busy period for him at Columbia. He attended the Trustees Meeting on December 4. He delivered a speech to freshmen as part of the Orientation Program, noting at the start, "If I read the papers correctly, you and I have something in common. All of us are subject to the draft." That afternoon he attended a War and Peace Institute organizing meeting, and for the evening he had accepted three dinners. "I'm *going to all 3, , . . .* What a Mess!" One was for alumni from the Engineering School and the other two involved people "active in helping the A.A.—" After describing "the Korean situation as tragic," he added in his *Diary*, "Something is terribly wrong—I feel that my hunch of last July 1 was right—but I was wrong when I supposed that both the Def. Depts. and the White House would heed the advice I gave on preparation." Three nights later he returned from a day trip to Fort Pickett, Virginia, and an American Assembly staff meeting in Washington in time to address two hundred graduate history students and, elaborating on his *Diary* entry, he called for an organization to study mobilization "exhaustively and carefully. . . . Only a few weeks ago we thought that the Korean War was over." At the College's fortieth annual Yule Log lighting, he commented that he might not be there the next year, for "I'm subject to the draft too." Apologizing for his humorless tone, he concluded, "I hope that each of us will have enough fortitude and courage to maintain this country and system."[56]

On December 11 Eisenhower, who knew that the announcement of his NATO appointment was imminent, attended the final meeting of his Aid to Europe committee at the Council on Foreign Relations. The group, acting on a suggestion from Henry Wriston, prepared a letter for Truman, and Eisenhower, who had met over the weekend with the JCS and Truman's Special Assistant, Harriman, wrote the initial draft that evening. It emphasized "the critical danger of defeat and the extinction of our treasured ideals." Though it underwent a number of revisions, the final letter stressed the dangers to national security, the need for a rapid military build up, and the stationing of American troops in Europe. Harriman, who had made some suggestions, then gave the group's letter to President Truman.[57]

On December 16 the General drafted a long letter to the President. He would, of course, accept "any military duty assigned me by you," but he also had "a personal and official duty" to express his views on the world situation. He saw a "great challenge to our survival," and he made a series of recommendations. He repeated that he would accept any military duty, including "the European Command that you have already requested me to assume." General Eisenhower concluded: "I am sure that you will perceive that I am not attempting to build up any advance alibis. I merely suggest to you that an entirely *different approach to the great crisis of our time might develop a wisdom in making certain changes in current programs.*" He never sent the letter, he wrote in a note at the bottom, because he "largely repeated" it over the telephone to Harriman, and in longhand he added, "Also given to H.S.T. verbally. He assured me that all these factors had been thoughtfully considered." In his *Diary* wrote, "I'm half way to Europe."[58]

Eisenhower had stated his terms; he had, in effect, issued an ultimatum similar to the ultimatum he had presented to Trustee Parkinson on the eve of his appointment as President of Columbia in 1947. This time President Truman had provided the assurances.

The next day the Eisenhowers left for Christmas in Denver with a stop at Heidelberg College in Ohio. Early in the year the College's President had asked Dean Krout, an alumnus, if Eisenhower would speak on the school's hundredth anniversary on November 11. Krout mentioned it to the General who, a week later, replied, "I've decided to go." In September, however, he said "I'm afraid I can't keep" the promise. "I'm going to be very honest with you. . . . I want to go down to Texas and shoot ducks and it'll cover the 11th of November and I can't make the trip." He added, "If you let me off my promise, I agree I'll get to Heidelberg College" before the end of 1950. The Dean, as the fall progressed, admitted "I wasn't sure."

Eisenhower had not forgotten, and he had told friends he wanted to see the small college which produced a John Krout. In early December he called Krout in and said, "We better make plans about that Tiffin trip if we're going to have it before the end of this year. I've got an idea." Mentioning that "Mamie and I are going" to Denver for Christmas, he suggested that his "special car would be attached to a train which went, if not to Tiffin at least near Tiffin, then we could be detached" and "go on the next day."

"We traveled from New York to Bucyrus, Ohio," Krout recalled, and were picked up by the college. "He had a wonderful time. He went over and had lunch in the commons with the students, he sang Christmas carols with them, and he spoke in Rickly Chapel and then drove back." That evening, back in the railroad car, Eisenhower said, "We've had such a wonderful day, let's sit around and talk now a while before you fellows go back to Tiffin." Just then someone arrived and said, "President Eisenhower, Washington has been trying to get you on the line all afternoon." He asked, "Where can I take a call," and was told, "Well, there's a little box down the line here, it's about a quarter of a mile, maybe an eighth of a mile. you can take the call right there." The General put the call through, and Truman asked him to take the NATO command.[59]

Columbia immediately granted Eisenhower an indefinite leave of absence and named Kirk, who would keep his titles, the top administrative officer. It was understood, Coykendall's statement asserted, "that General Eisenhower will resume his duties as President of the University immediately upon his military release." At a press conference in St. Louis Eisenhower, en route to Denver, said, "My personal aspirations are to get back to Columbia University." The *Spectator* emphasized on the front-page, "His great industry led him to succeed in his announced goal to make 'more and more people conscious of Columbia.'" Its editorial noted, "General Eisenhower must start from scratch in a desperate race for time. . . . The stakes are Western Europe and quite possibly all the democratic nations of the world." The *Spectator,* wondering "what the future holds for Columbia, declared: "there is no doubt that the University must strive to maintain the ideals which its President has been called upon to defend once again. With General Eisenhower go the hopes of the nation and free world."[60]

Eisenhower told Krout, twice, upon his return to Columbia after Christmas that "I hate to go and Mamie hates to go. We both have enjoyed it so much here at Columbia and we love 60 Morningside Drive. It's been a real home for us." The Eisenhowers, moreover, had just purchased their first home, a 179-acre farm near the Civil War battlefield at Gettysburg, for their retirement. Eisenhower told Roberts, "Of course I'm going . . . because Truman wants me to go," though he added that Mamie was just beginning to feel at home in New York. Mamie concurred, recalling, "We thoroughly enjoyed our stay at Columbia" and that she was not happy about going to Paris but Truman had asked them. Eisenhower, Ginzberg recalled, felt that Truman "was really putting a burden on him that he didn't want . . . that Truman was at the end of his rope in terms of finding someone to pull his chestnuts out of the fire. And that he leaned on him. . . he was not happy about it. . . . That is fact." Grayson Kirk, nonetheless, thought that "in all probability" Eisenhower "would not return to Morningside. I had felt that he had not been particularly comfortable in his position, and also he had been under a great deal of pressure from outside interests to get into national politics." He continued. "A combination of some discomfort at Morningside on his part" and various external pressures "made it unlikely in my judgment" that he would return and settle down.[61]

During his last days on Morningside Heights Eisenhower continued to push the American Assembly. When Robert Cutler declined to serve as Eisenhower's "personal representative" for the proposal, the Bostonian asserted that his enthusiasm for the Assembly had waned because of the Korean setback and his fear that the project would falter without Eisenhower's "constant, daily force to breathe life into it." Throughout the month the General had been writing letters on behalf of the Assembly, and on his last day in Low Memorial, December 31, he replied to Cutler that the Korean situation made it "more imperative than ever before to push the plan." He had tried "to reserve a day" to write "all those individuals who have jumped in so enthusiastically" on the Assembly, but "the calendar has defeated me." Consequently, he asked Burnham to thank personally the "many, many others" supporting the plan, and he extended invitations to visit him at NATO. He had, meanwhile, personally thanked the first eighty contributors, even some who had given only ten to twenty-five dollars.[62] On January 1, 1951, General Eisenhower left for briefings in Washington, and on the 6th he departed for Paris.

The General first conducted an exploratory trip of the Atlantic Pact nations, then he returned to Washington on January 31 and was met by President Truman at National Airport. After reporting to the President, he addressed a Joint Session of Congress at the Library of Congress and then delivered a radio and television broadcast to the nation. *Time,* which put him on the cover for the sixth time, reported that he had done what "Harry Truman could not do for himself. Ike appeared to have routed the calamity-howlers and the super-cautious. In the desolate winter of 1951," *Time* concluded, "the Western world heard a first, heart-warming note of spring."[63]

On the 4th of February he arrived back at 60 Morningside, and he told the Board that, after his inspection trip in Europe, he could not estimate the length of his assignment. Consequently, he proposed that his leave of absence begin on March 1, 1951, and that the President's house be closed. He added, according to the *Minutes,* that "you gentlemen cannot long afford to go on under the situation of having an 'absentee' President." They should "feel free" whenever they found it necessary, "to take steps to finds my successor." And, if necessary, he would also resign his position as Trustee. "You may consider, accordingly, that you have my resignation before you," as President and Trustee, "to be acted on at any time you desire."

He reminded the Trustees that they had sought a "public figure" to promote a new concept of the University, and he listed the projects, from the Citizenship Education Program and the Institute of War and Peace to the Conservation of Human Resources, "to which much of my attention and energy has been devoted." He specifically noted that the American Assembly had been "enthusiastically accepted" and had reached "the current financial and underwriting" goal. He continued. "My heart has been here very intensively" and, since he did not know when he would again attend a Board Meeting, he mentioned "a few ideas which I hold strongly." The country was entering "its decade of greatest trial" and "members of this great institution should be used to find out how it can adapt to the greater services of its country." Watson responded for the Trustees and emphasized that the President had given "great prestige to this whole institution." His NATO position, moreover, had "added greatly to the prestige of the University . . . to have you selected for the greatest job on the other side of the waters—if not the whole world."[64]

That evening the General, in uniform, and Mrs. Eisenhower said farewell to three hundred Trustees and faculty at a reception at the Faculty Club. In Dean Ackerman's opinion, the General "looked fit, healthy color and vigorous; she pale and . . . somewhat ashamed. Dr. Butler would have had reception in the Pres. House but Mrs. E. has not received any Univ. people in Pres. House." At six o'clock Coykendall called for attention, and Eisenhower, standing on a chair, said: "He had come to say Goodbye, that his profession was how to destroy the enemies of our country but he had learned at C.U. that a U. had an important role perhaps the most important role in carrying on the freedom we all believed in as our heritage." Eisenhower then stated that, as he contemplated his "future in Europe, . . . I will always have a warm spot in my heart for Columbia" and that he "hoped to return some day." Dean Ackerman concluded: "Rather perfunctory applause. Mrs. E. left. Gen. went around shaking hands and left also before the 6:30 deadline of the reception." That evening the Eisenhowers, accompanied by John and Barbara Eisenhower and their children, Roberts, Robinson, and Dr. and Mrs. Snyder flew to Puerto Rico for a long weekend. On the way back to New York, Eisenhower attended a dinner at Secretary of State Dean Acheson's on February 12 and a number of meetings the next day in connection with his NATO assignment.[65]

Just before the Eisenhowers sailed on the *Queen Elizabeth* on the 15th for France, he made a surprise appearance at the annual Alexander Hamilton dinner honoring Dean Carman "for distinguished public service." A spontaneous ovation greeted the President, who asserted that he could not miss such an important occasion. He emphasized that the "dirt farmer" Harry Carman's "selfless devotion and service" offered him his most memorable experience at the University. When Carman sent a photograph of the Dean listening to Eisenhower's presentation of the award, the General replied that even if he had had "to beg for a delay in the sailing of the *Queen Elizabeth*, I would not have missed it."[66]

Before he left Eisenhower assured friends that he would "continue my personal supervision of the Assembly," although his NATO assignment required him to delegate responsibility. The "world situation" convinced him of "even greater need" for the Assembly, and he paid careful attention to the fund-raising. He asked a few friends, including Clarence Francis, Chairman of General Foods, to serve "as my personal representatives" in securing corporate sponsorships and assisting Dean Young. The December, January, and February Trustees *Minutes* recorded the individual donors and the amount of the Assembly gifts, and Bermingham assured him that the Assembly would raise the necessary funds. Nonetheless, the General wanted Burnham, who had sent "special and intriguing gifts" for the Eisenhowers' room on the *Queen Elizabeth*, to write "our many mutual friends." Eisenhower suggested that Burnham's hint that his friends remember in their yearly gifts Columbia or, specifically, the Assembly should be delicate rather than of "the sledge hammer variety."[67]

Eisenhower also announced that Lewis W. Douglas, former Ambassador to Great Britain, had accepted the chairmanship of the Assembly's National Policy Board. Douglas, who said that he would appoint other board members soon, asserted that the sixty to eighty delegates to an Assembly conference would "bring a wide cross-section of American thinking to bear" on the conference's subject. The purpose was not "to tell the American people what they ought to do." He said that he and the General hoped that the delegates would "provide facts and factual interpretations of pertinent situations, so that the American citizen himself will be able to bring an enlightened judgment to bear upon problems that affect the nation."[68]

Eisenhower's conviction, enthusiasm, and charisma raised the funds for Columbia's American Assembly, and its organization proceeded so smoothly that the first conference was held in May, 1951. The topic, appropriately, was "The Relationship of the United States to Western Europe" and Eisenhower planned to return from NATO to participate. The initial Board members, in addition to Ambassador Douglas and Dean Young, represented business, labor, and agriculture. They included Bullis; McCollum; John Cowles of the *Minneapolis Morning Tribune;* Oveta Culp Hobby of the *Houston Post,* Robert Wood of Sears, Roebuck; former Postmaster General, James A. Farley; William Green of the American Federation of Labor; Allan B. Kline, president of the Farm Bureau Federation; Jacob S. Potofsky, president of the Amalgamated Clothing Workers of America; William C. Mullendore, president, Southern California Edison Co.; Dean William I. Myers of the New York State College of Agriculure, Cornell University; and Robert M. Hanes, president of Wachovia Bank & Trust Company, Winston-Salem. The Charter defined the purpose of the Assembly as "to arrive at and disseminate impartial and authoritative finds on questions of national and international importance, and thus stimulate the growth of informed opinion with a view to the preservation and strengthening of the democratic processes and principles of freedom."[69]

A few weeks before the scheduled conference, Eisenhower suddenly suggested that Young and Douglas consider postponing it until September. His reasoning was simple: a major foreign policy debate had centered on the Administration's proposal to send troops to Europe at the same time General MacArthur increasingly criticized Truman's failure to support a more aggressive policy in the Korean War. On April 4 a Senate resolution supported four U.S. divisions for NATO but added, as Eisenhower noted in his *Diary,* "It is the 'sense of the Senate' that Congress should be consulted." While Eisenhower saw this as "awkward," he realized it would be "absurd" for Truman to send soldiers "*if* American public opinion does *not* support reinforcement of Europe." Yet, he well understood that MacArthur's criticism complicated reaching "a union of hearts & minds . . . the indispensable formula for success" in Europe. "Any alternative promises little more than tragic failure." Thus, Eisenhower worried: "With all the free world in an uproar because people believe that MacA is trespassing on purely civilian functions . . . it becomes difficult . . . to preach this truth unendingly." In the process, the NATO concept could be damaged. Two days after this *Di-*

ary entry, Eisenhower learned that Truman had relieved MacArthur of all his commands. MacArthur's ouster provoked a political uproar, and in this situation Eisenhower believed that "no discussion or analysis" of America's European policy, such as the Assembly conference, could "attain an objective status in the public mind" and probably would contribute to "partisan warfare." This could damage "ultimate success in this great undertaking." Eisenhower stated that the decision to postpone the conference was for Douglas, Young, and the University to make, and they decided it was more important to hold it as scheduled.[70]

He informed Kirk, meanwhile, that he could not attend the May meeting. Certainly his friends, and specifically Roberts, did not want him to come home and face Congressional testimony over aid to Europe and become involved in the highly partisan debate over MacArthur's dismissal. When Roberts wrote, "If you are obliged to go to Washington you might as well be prepared to get into the overall policy argument, Eisenhower replied, "Your judgment is impeccable." Douglas would inform the conference's participants of the General's regrets and his enthusiastic support for the assembly.[71]

At the American Assembly dedication ceremonies in May, 1951, Harriman presented his family's Arden House Estate to Columbia University and expressed his "highest hopes" for this "1951 version of the old-fashioned town meeting." He saw Arden House as "a national meeting place" that would continue "this great experiment . . . so that our country, and our way of life can be strengthened. . . . That is our heritage." He urged its preservation "at all costs." The *New York Herald-Tribune's* caption over a prominent front-page photograph read, "Arden House Dedicated to 'Nation's Service' as Home of American Assembly," and its lead editorial saw "the beginning of an experiment which may have wide and fruitful significance." Anne O'Hare McCormick, Pulitzer Prize-winning correspondent for the *New York Times,* discussed her participation, and she praised Eisenhower for originating the conference and stressed its value for the American people.[72]

The opening session brought together two prominent foreign policy antagonists. Republican Senator Robert A. Taft of Ohio, who looked forward to capturing the Republican Party nomination for President in 1952, represented the "isolationist" forces in Congress, while Illinois Democrat Paul H. Douglas offered the "internationalist" position. Their comments provided the framework for the five days of discussions by eighty-five leaders of business, labor, government, and the professions. Taft bluntly declared his quarrel with the Truman Administration's policies. It was engaged in "a bitter and dangerous war" in Korea; yet, he emphasized, indirectly referring to the firing of MacArthur, that it refused "to fight that war with all the means at its command on the theory that we might incite Russia to start a third world war." On the other hand, "we have not hesitated to risk a third world war over and over again" in Europe. Douglas, however, argued that the fall of Europe to the communists had to be prevented, otherwise Russia would have an overwhelming advantage in population and an industrial potential almost equal to America's. After the opening sessions, the delegates met in smaller groups and, then, prepared a preliminary draft and final statement. The majority of the participants supported the defense of Western Europe and expressed confidence in the ability of the Western allies to "deter Soviet aggression or to meet it successfully whenever and wherever it emerges."[73]

The day after the dedication ceremonies Harriman wrote Eisenhower, on White House stationery, that the General had conveyed his expectation and enthusiasm for the important role the Assembly would play. Harriman's unwavering support demonstrated his conviction that Eisenhower was sincerely committed to the concept that the Assembly would be useful to the country in its forthcoming struggles, and his hopes would be fulfilled. Indeed, Arden House has taken great pride in introducing and developing the "conference-center concept." The American Assembly, Eisenhower recalled in 1967, had held "scores of meetings concerned with almost every aspect of human society. Throughout the years, its influence, although difficult to measure, has been far reaching beyond my dreams of almost two decades ago. Much of the time," he added, "I think its beginnings were my principal success as University President." The American Assembly "centered around this fact," Henry Wriston recalled, that Eisenhower believed "if you could get the academic and the businessman and the government man to sit down together, off the record," they could discuss without "inhibitions" major problems of policy. Wriston, who became president of the Assembly in the mid-1950s, declared that Eisenhower's idea brought "an extraordinarily distinguished group of people together and immured them up at Arden House." Harriman, looking back after twenty-five years, emphasized Eisenhower's "very fine motivations" and asserted his "tremendous satisfaction" that the American Assembly had been "remarkably successful."[74]

Harriman's important role, Eisenhower's commitment to democratic citizenship, and the success of the American Assembly seriously challenge assertions by several historians that Eisenhower had primarily partisan political ambitions in establishing the conference center. His idea for the Assembly can be traced back to World War II and questions from soldiers—"General, why am I here? Why is America in war? What is this stuff about Hitlerism and Americanism?"—and he had decided that "in the world of education I could do something." He had remained in the postwar period "deeply concerned with the problem of maintaining our country's democratic traditions" and stated, when he proposed the plan: "Today there is not a single place in the United States where a great subject can be discussed, analyzed, talked about by a group, a cross-section of America without prejudice or bias of some sort . . . so that we shall arrive at a somewhat saner and safer answer . . . for those who are coming immediately after us." The Assembly, Wriston reflected, "has worked out to do exactly what he set out to do." It soon had a list of over 4,000 individuals and organizations to which it sent conference papers and reports. What Eisenhower established at Arden House has had a long and influential history: the Assembly held its ninety-seventh conference in September, 2000, on "The Family."[75]

Eisenhower had met in his fund-raising for the American Assembly rich and influential persons throughout the country, and he maintained correspondence with these financial and political leaders, many of whom were Republicans. Since his arrival at Columbia he had emphasized themes of internationalism, personal liberty, democratic citizenship, the American way of life, non-partisanship, cooperation, and the danger of centralization and statism. In his St. Louis American Bar Association speech he had warned against the "ever-expanding Federal government" and proposed a path for America down "the middle of the road." As he stressed the need for service to his country and became associated with the term "middle way," he said what his audience wanted to hear, especially during the somber Korean War, and he was persuasive. As Phil Young recalled, if you wanted to meet Eisenhower you had to go to the fund-raising luncheons and dinners, and the General personally kept track of the contributors. In an era of increasing political partisanship and bitterness with Korea and McCarthyism, his listeners welcomed General Eisenhower's personal and seemingly non-partisan appeal and found it reassuring.[76]

While he succeeded in launching successfully his conference plan, his almost total concentration on the American Assembly during 1950 contributed to the resentments which had been building up against him on campus. His emphasis on "general education for citizenship" and the Citizenship Education Project at Teachers College appeared anti-intellectual to the academics on Morningside Heights. Other reasons included his frequent absences from the University and the dislike for a military man as President and, especially, for his military assistants in Low Memorial, who kept him inaccessible and had little sense of the academic world. Professor Lionel Trilling, who thought that Eisenhower's Installation Address had been impressive, "began to sense that he was no where in relation to the University and this gradually began to affect people." As time elapsed, Trilling gained the impression that Eisenhower was not interested in education at a large urban university. Douglas Black, the General's close friend and a knowledgeable Trustee, essentially concurred, commenting that Eisenhower "never had the feeling or understanding of Columbia."[77]

This negative reaction intensified as Eisenhower devoted more and more of his time and energies to the American Assembly, which was never an integral part of the University. Grayson Kirk saw the idea as "a naive or innocent approach to education. . . extremely simplistic." The intellectual did not view Eisenhower's concept as fitting within the purpose of a great university; indeed, as a former graduate school dean at Harvard observed, "Faculty members consider the teaching and training of new generations of graduate students as their highest calling." The General's efforts, according to economist Ginzberg, "added to the marginality of his administration." His fund-raising for the Assembly, moreover, did not help the University's overall financial plight and his appeals sounded more and more conservative to the Columbia faculty, especially as he associated during his trips with businessmen and Texas oilmen, many of whom were conservative. Years later Eisenhower acknowledged that "most on the faculties were against it and thought it was silly." The reaction, however, was more serious than that.[78]

For many at Columbia, the American Assembly came to illustrate, months before Eisenhower departed for NATO, his lack of interest in the University itself as well as the gap between him and the academic community. While he had been "the practical favorite of liberals" in America in 1948 and, according to historian Alonzo Hamby, many were willing to accept him as late as early 1952, liberals at Columbia often thought otherwise. They disliked his association with businessmen who opposed New Deal reforms; many, like political activist William E. Leuchtenburg, who received his Ph.D. under Commager and joined the history faculty in 1952, had lamented the postwar retreat from the New Deal. Increasingly, the intellectual at Columbia resented the General's association with the University. The *Life* cover story article, "Mr. President Eisenhower," suggested a publicity campaign and confirmed suspicions that he was using the University for his political interests. By the time he departed for NATO, the gap was growing wider, and few knew that the Trustees had refused to accept his resignation.[79]

Eisenhower did not return to the United States until November, when he made a brief visit. The enormity of the task facing him at NATO, the debate over the Mutual Security Program and providing military equipment for the NATO countries, and the controversy of the dismissal of MacArthur would keep him in Europe. Perhaps it was the prospect of such an extended absence from Columbia that caused him to rethink his position at the University. On the eve of the American Assembly dedication in May, when he realized he would not be returning to New York for it, he discussed in Paris with Trustee Black his fear that "many of the gains of the past 2 1/2 years will either be lost or, at best, not fully exploited" and that "my retention as the nominal President is working against Columbia." He repeated his thoughts—which included, once again, the possible title of Chancellor with reduced responsibilities for him—in letters to Trustees Sulzberger and Dodge and a conversation with Trustee Albert Redpath. In late June Coykendall and Black suggested that nothing should happen over the summer.[80]

Perhaps some of the uncertainty that summer, on the part of both Eisenhower and the Trustees, came from the possibility that Acting President Kirk might accept the Presidency of Rutgers University. One Sunday morning, when Eli Ginzberg was visiting the Eisenhowers, the General, while painting, said that Kirk had been offered the Rutgers job. He added, "Eli, I want you to go back and tell him for me that he should take it." Ginzberg recalled looking at Eisenhower and saying, "That's quite a message I'm supposed to bring." The General agreed, "Yes, you go back and tell him for me, he's supposed to take it." It was, Ginzberg remembered, "not ex-

actly the most pleasant message to be delivered. I delivered it."
Eisenhower knew that Black, and probably several other Trustees,
were not enthusiastic about Kirk and any change in titles would make
Kirk President, instead of Acting President; on the other hand, if
Kirk left, as Eisenhower suggested, there would be other possibilities. Kirk, nonetheless, decided to stay; Coykendall's telegram to
Eisenhower stated "no future commitment made with him except to
assist" him in every way. Thus, in September, Eisenhower withdrew
"every possible suggestion I have made" and agreed to keep the
status quo. Coykendall concurred and, informing Eisenhower that
the Trustees would give Kirk more assistance, added, "Please be at
ease about the whole thing and know that we now are at ease also."[81]

During 1951 General Eisenhower, on leave from Columbia, confronted the challenge of organizing NATO's forces to face the Soviet
threat in Europe. His personal dreams for the University, especially
the Conservation of Human Resources and the American Assembly,
were becoming a reality, but his relations were strained with the academic community. Yet the Trustees in February, 1951, had preferred
to give Eisenhower a leave of absence; they saw the leave as the
only alternative to another presidential search, and even the thought
of that was frightening.[82]

Notes

1.   Eisenhower, "World Peace—A Balance Sheet," Gabriel Silver Lecture, March 23,
      1950, Eisenhower MSS., Dwight D. Eisenhower Library, Abilene, Ks. (DDEL);
      Kevin McCann, *Man from Abilene* (New York: 1952), pp. 195-97; *Columbia Spec-
      tator*, March 24, 1950; *New York Times*, March 24, 1950.
2.   Quentin Reynolds, "Mr. President Eisenhower," *Life*, April 17, 1950, pp. 144-60;
      Kevin McCann, Oral History Interview, 1966, Columbia Oral History Project
      (COHP); Eisenhower, *Diary*, May 2, and April 27, 1950, The *Papers of Dwight
      David Eisenhower*, vol. XI (Baltimore, Md., 1984), *Columbia University*, ed. Louis
      Galambos, 1096-97, 1089 (*PDDE*); DeWitt Wallace to Eisenhower, October 30,
      1950, ibid.
3.   Reynolds, "Mr. President Eisenhower," *Life*, April 17, 1950, pp. 144-60.
4.   Carl W. Ackerman, April 21, 1950, Carl W. Ackerman MSS., Library of Congress
      (LC); Peter Gay, personal interview, March 24, 1958, New York, N.Y.; Eli Ginzberg,
      personal interview, December 11, 1990, New York, N. Y.; *Columbia Spectator*, April
      14, 1950; Robert C. Harron, personal interview, February 5, 1965, Hartford, Ct.
5.   Richard H. Rovere, "The Second Eisenhower Boom," *Harper's*, May, 1950, pp. 31-39;
      Columbia Spectator, May 5, 1950; Rovere to author, n.d. (1978), author's possession.
6.   Grayson L. Kirk, Oral History Interview, July 22, 1987, COHP; Adrienne Swift,
      telephone interview, Sarasota, Fl., December 5, 1993.
7.   John A. Krout, Oral History Interview, April 27, 1977, DDEL.
8.   *Columbia Spectator*, February 27, 1950; Eisenhower to Lucius DuBignon Clay,

March 21, 1950, and Clay to Eisenhower, March 23, 1950, *PDDE,* XI, 1021-22; Eisenhower, *Diary,* April 5, 1950, ibid.; Kirk, interview, July 22, 1987, COHP.

9.   Eisenhower, *Diary,* May 2 and June [?], 1950, *PDDE* XI, 1096-97, 1170; Mrs. Cecil P. Killien to Eisenhower, June 14, 1950, ibid.

10.   Eisenhower to Jessup, March 18, 1950, *PDDE,* XI, 1014; Jessup to Eisenhower, March 20, 1950, Eisenhower MSS., DDEL; Jessup, personal interview, June 17, 1977, Norfolk, Ct; David M. Oshinsky, *A Conspiracy So Immense* (New York, 1983), pp. 109, 122-25.

11.   To the Military Sub-Committee of the Appropriations Committee of the Senate, March 28, 1950, *PDDE,* 1041-48; *New York Times,* March 30, 1950; *Columbia Spectator,* March 30, 1950.

12.   Harry J. Carman, personal interview, December 1, 1961, New York, N.Y.

13.   Eisenhower to Fleming, November 29, 1949 (CACU). This significant letter is not in *PDDE*. The Trustees of Columbia University in the City of New York, *Minutes,* April 3, 1952, CACU. Trinity Church believed that the intent of the grant probably had been unconditional and that the provision about the President was not binding and had been so considered by the Trustees. *Vestry Minutes,* December 12, 1949, The Parish of Trinity Church in the City of New York.

14.   Eisenhower to Arthur Hays Sulzberger, March 20, 1950, *PDDE,* XI, 1017-19; *Columbia Spectator,* April 14 and 19, 1950.

15.   *New York Times,* April 25, 1950; Eisenhower to George Crews McGhee, April 24, 1950, *PDDE,* XI, 1078-79; *Columbia Spectator,* April 25 and May 9, 1950.

16.   Staff Meeting, May 16 and Kirk to Eisenhower, May 19, 1950; Minutes of Advisory Committee on Development, June 5, 1950; Harron, Memorandum for the Provost, May 23, 1950; Kirk to All Deans and Directors, June 28, 1950, CACU; *Columbia Spectator,* Headlines and Editorial, "Honoring the Dean," April 25, 1950.

17.   Eisenhower to George B. Pegram [letter to Deans and Directors], May 29, 1950; Minutes of Meeting, Advisory Committee on Development, June 5, 1950; Eisenhower to Kirk, June 13, 1950, CACU.

18.   William H. Burnham to Eisenhower, May 15, 1950, DDEL; Eisenhower to Leonard McCollum, May 31, 1950, *PDDE,* XI, 1144-48; "What Has Ike Got?" *Life,* June 5, 1950, pp. 32-34.

19.   *New York Times,* June 9, 1950; Eisenhower to Arthur Hays Sulzberger, February 10 and March 20, 1950, *PDDE,* XI, 693-94, 1017-18.

20.   Eisenhower to McCollum, May 31, 1950, *PDDE,* XI, 1144-48.

21.   Eisenhower to Alumni and Friends, February 3, 1949, *PDDE,* X, 462-65; Eisenhower to George Catlett Marshall, November 15, 1950, ibid., XI, 1423-24; Ibid., XII (Baltimore, Md., 1989), *NATO and the Campaign of 1952,* ed. Louis Galambos, 280-81; Russell to Eisenhower, March 30, 1951, DDEL; *Columbia Spectator,* February 6, 1951; Arthur Hays Sulzberger to Eisenhower, May 21, 1953, enclosing James Russell memorandum to Kirk, May 18, 1953, DDEL.

22.   Jacques Barzun, personal interview, April 5, 1979, New York, N.Y.; Kirk, interview, September 3, 1987, COHP; Eisenhower to Russell, March 9, 1951, *PDDE,* XII, 108-11; Ginzberg, interview, December 11, 1990; Reynolds, "Mr. President Eisenhower," *Life,* April 17, 1950, pp. 148-50.

23.   Eisenhower to Bermingham, March 10, 1950, *PDDE,* XI, 1010-11; Krout to author, June 1, 1960; Krout to Eisenhower, April 19, 1951, DDEL; Krout to Eisenhower, May 17, 1951, CACU; Press Release, December 1951, ibid.; Krout, interview, July 22, 1963; Ginzberg, interview, December 11, 1990.

24.   Dwight D. Eisenhower, *At Ease: Stories I Tell to Friends* (New York, 1967), pp. 350-51; Ginzberg, interview, December 11, 1990; Howard Snyder, "The Origin of

the Conservation Project," *Conservation of Human Resources* (New York, 1956), pp. 10-11; Snyder, "Conservation of Human Resources," *The Conservation of Human Resources* (New York, 1957), p. 12; Ginzberg, Oral History Interview, May 14, 1975, OHDDEL.

25. Ginzberg, "Final Plans for Research Project," July 1, 1949, CACU; Eisenhower to Philip Sporn, June 24, 1949, *PDDE*, X, 663-65; Ginzberg, May 14, 1975, OHDDEL; Young to Eisenhower, February 11 and August 4, 1950, DDEL; Eisenhower to Young, August 14, and to Carl Raymond Gray, Jr., December 14, 1950, *PDDE*, XI, 1277-78 and 1480-81; Ginzberg, *Science*, November 23, 1951.

26. *New York Times*, December 13, 1950; Press Release December 12, 1950, CACU; Eisenhower to Young, March 13, 1953, *PDDE*, XIV (Baltimore, Md., 1996), *The Presidency: The Middle Way*, ed. Louis Galambos, 99; Snyder, "Conservation of Human Resources," p. 11.

27. Ginzberg, interview, May 14, 1975, OHDDEL; Fn. #5, *PDDE*, XI, 1481.

28. Fn. 9, ibid., p. 1148.

29. Eisenhower to Kenneth William Dobson Strong, June 29, 1950, *PDDE*, XI, 1184-85; Eisenhower, *Diary*, June 30 and July 6, 1950, ibid.

30. *Minneapolis Morning Tribune*, June 8, 1950; Eisenhower to Bullis, July 11, 1950, *PDDE*, XI, 1218-19.

31. Burnham, Memorandum to Eisenhower, July 10, 1950, DDEL; Young to Walter D. Fletcher, August 4, 1950, "The American Assembly, 1950-59: General and Administrative Papers," vol. I, American Assembly, Columbia University (AACU).

32. Eisenhower to Krout, August 10, 1950, *PDDE*, XI, 1269-70; Eisenhower to Kleberg, August 14, 1950, ibid., 1273-74; The Trustees of Columbia University in the City of New York, *Minutes*, January 8, 1951, and February 4, 1952 (CACU).

33. Eisenhower to McCollum, September 12, 1950, *PDDE*, XI, 1305-10.

34. *New York Times*, August 24, 1950.

35. Eisenhower to Burnham, August 21, 1950, *PDDE*, XI, 1280-81; *Denver Post*, September 5, 1950; *New York Times*, September 5,1950; Eisenhower to Bullis, September 5, 1950, DDEL.

36. Schulz, Memorandum for General Eisenhower, September 8, 1950, DDEL.

37. *Columbia Spectator*, September 19 and October 17, 1950; *New York Times*, September 28, 1950.

38. *Columbia Spectator*, September 28, and Editorial, "Moral Hypochondria," September 28, 1950.

39. I. I. Rabi, Oral History Interview, January 26, 1985, COHP; Eisenhower, *At Ease*, pp. 347-48.

40. *Columbia Spectator*, October 13, and Editorial, "Wishful Thinking?" October 13, 1950.

41. *New York Times*, October 16 and 17, 1950; *Columbia Spectator*, October 17, and Editorial, "Your Move, Governor," October 17, 1950; Eisenhower, *Diary*, October 13, 1950, *PDDE*, XI, 1382-83.

42. *Columbia Spectator*, October 17, 1950; *U.S. News and World Report*, October 27, 1950.

43. Young to Eisenhower, October 2, 1950, and Eisenhower Memorandum to Deans, Directors, and University Executives, October 12, 1950, vol. 1, AACU. Eisenhower's telephone bill had been brought to Kirk's attention, and he noted that McCann assured him "the bill will be drastically reduced." Kirk to Richard Herpers, October 25, 1950, CACU.

44. Trustees of Columbia, *Minutes*, October 2, 1950, CACU; Columbia Associates Policy Committee, Meeting, October 4, 1950, and Eisenhower's Remarks, "The American Assembly," vol. 1, AACU; Columbia Associates Luncheon on the American Assembly Plan, October 18, 1950, ibid; *New York Times*, October 19, 1950;

Columbia Spectator, October 19, 1950. The previous evening Eisenhower had met with Porter, Burnham, and McCollum in Connecticut.

45. Editorial, "The American Assembly," *New York Herald-Tribune,* October 20, 1950; Editorial, "Ike's Address," *Columbia Spectator,* October 20, 1950.

46. *Columbia Spectator,* October 18, 1950; Robert C. Harron, personal interview, February 5, 1965, Hartford, Ct; *New York Times,* October 22, 1950.

47. "The American Assembly," vol. III, AACU; Eisenhower, *Diary,* October 28, 1950, *PDDE,* XI, 1388-92; McElroy to Eisenhower, November 24, 1950, ibid., 1443, n. 2; *New York Times,* October 28, 1950.

48. Eisenhower *Diary,* October 28, 1950, Eisenhower to Fred Manning, November 3, 1950, *PDDE,* XI, 1388-92; *New York Times,* October 29, 1950; *Columbia Spectator,* November 10, 1950; Cabell Phillips, "Eisenhower Encircled by Still More Mystery," *New York Times,* November 5, 1950.

49. Eisenhower to Roberts, November 6 and November 6, 1950, *PDDE,* XI, 1411-12, 1416-17; Clifford Roberts, Oral History Interview, September 12, 1968, COHP.

50. Eisenhower, *Diary,* November 6, 1950, *PDDE,* XI, 1408-11; McCann, *Man from Abilene,* pp. 184-85.

51. Eisenhower to Bermingham, November 18, 1950, DDEL; Eisenhower to Carter, November 29, 1950, and Eisenhower to Richardson, November 29, 1950, *PDDE,* XI, 1447-49; *Houston Post,* November 11, and editorial, "The Eisenhower Plan," November 11, 1950; *Dallas Morning News,* November 12, 1950.

52. Editorial, "Back to New England," *Boston Herald,* October 20, 1950; *Boston Daily Globe,* November 23, 1950; *Rochester Times Union,* October 18, 1966; "The American Assembly," vol. III, AACU.

53. Eisenhower, *Diary,* November 29, 1950, *PDDE,* XI, 1443-44; Eisenhower to Bermingham, December 12, 1950, DDEL; Eisenhower to Dillon,, November 29, 1950, *PDDE,* XI, 1447.

54. Eisenhower to Gruenther, November 30, 1950, *PDDE,* XI, 1450-51. The Tournament of Roses had invited Eisenhower to be grand marshal for the New Year's Day, 1951, parade, and on December 6 Eisenhower canceled his acceptance. Nts. #2-3, *PDDE,* XI, 1455.

55. Louis Hacker, Oral History Interview, May 17, 1975, OHDDEL; Hacker, personal interview, January 30, 1958, New York, N. Y.; *Columbia Spectator,* November 29, 1950; Eisenhower, *At Ease,* pp. 356-57.

56. *Columbia Spectator,* December 6, 8, and 14, 1950; Eisenhower, *Diary,* December 5, 1950, *PDDE,* XI, 1459-60.

57. See *PDDE,* XI, pp. 1464-67; Michael Wala, "An 'Education in Foreign Affairs for the Future President': The Council on Foreign Relations and Dwight D. Eisenhower," in *Reexamining the Eisenhower Presidency,* ed. Shirley Anne Warshaw (Westport, Ct.: 1993), pp. 9-10.

58. Eisenhower to Truman, and Eisenhower, *Diary,* December 16, 1950, *PDDE,* XI, 1490-93, 1495-96.

59. Krout Oral History, April 27, 1977, OHDDEL; Krout, interview, July 22, 1963; Note, *PDDE,* XI, 1498; Eisenhower, *At Ease,* p. 361.

60. *Columbia Spectator,* December 20, 1950, and editorial, "Call to Duty," ibid.

61. Krout, Oral History, April 27, 1977, OHDDEL; *Newsweek,* December 4, 1950; Roberts, Oral History, October 13, 1968, COHP; Mamie Eisenhower, personal interview, December 15, 1975, Gettysburg, Pa.; Ginzburg, Oral History, April 11, 1978; OHDDEL.; Kirk, Oral History, September 3, 1987, COHP.

62. Eisenhower to Cutler and to Burnham, December 31, 1950, *PDDE,* XI, 1477-78, 1517-18; Eisenhower to Burnham, December 31, 1950, DDEL; "The American Assembly," vol. III, AACU.

63. *Time*, February 12, 1951.
64. Trustees of Columbia, *Minutes,* February 8, 1951, and Eisenhower to Coykendall, February 7, 1950, CACU.
65. *Columbia Spectator,* February 9, 1950; "Eisenhower," February 9, 1950, Carl W. Ackerman MSS., Library of Congress; "Chronology," *PDDE*, XIII, 1540.
66. *Columbia Spectator,* February 16, 1950; Eisenhower to Carman, March 9, 1950, *PDDE,* XII, 111-12.
67. Eisenhower to Clarence Francis, January 4, 1951, and to Bermingham, February 8, 1951, *PDDE*, XII, 13-14, 43-44; Eisenhower to Burnham, February 16, 1951, DDEL; Trustees of Columbia, *Minutes,* December 8, 1950, January 8 and February 8, 1951, CACU.
68. Press Release, "The American Assembly," March 14, 1951, vol. IV, AACU; Columbia University; *Columbia Spectator*, March 14, 1951.
69. "The American Assembly," vols. II and IV, AACU.
70. Eisenhower to Young, April 27, 1951, and *Diary,* April 9, 1951, *PDDE*, XII, 246-47, 200-202.
71. Eisenhower to Kirk, April 28, 1951, and to Roberts, May 15, 1951, *PDDE,* XII, 247-48, 283.
72. Harriman, "Statement," and Young, "Remarks," May 21, 1951, "American Assembly," vol. II, AACU; *New York Herald-Tribune,* May 22, 1951, and editorial "The American Assembly," *New York Times,* May 28, 1951.
73. *New York Herald-Tribune,* May 22, 1951; *New York Times,* May 26, 1951.
74. Harriman to Eisenhower, May 22, 1951, DDEL; "The American Assembly," pamphlet (n.d.), AACU; Eisenhower, *At Ease,* p. 350; W. Averell Harriman, personal interview, October 13, 1977, Washington, D.C.; Henry Wriston, Oral History Interview, 1968, COHP; Phil Young, personal interview, June 15, 1977, Van Hornesville, N.Y.
75. Eisenhower, "American Assembly Luncheon Remarks," October 18, 1950, vol. II, AACU. For comments critical of Eisenhower and the Assembly, see Peter Lyon, *Eisenhower: Portrait of the Hero* (Boston, 1974), p. 407; Geoffery Perret, *Eisenhower* (New York: 1999), p. 383; Blanche Wiesen Cook, *The Declassified Eisenhower: A Divided Legacy* (New York, 1981), pp. 82-83; and Stephen E. Ambrose, *Eisenhower: Soldier, General of the Army, President-Elect, 1890-1952* (New York, 1983), p. 493.
76. *New York Times*, September 6, 1949; Young, interview, June 15, 1977.
77. Lionel Trilling, personal interview, February 4, 1958, New York, N.Y.; Douglas M. Black, personal interview, June 6, 1973, New York, N.Y.,
78. Grayson L. Kirk, Oral History Interview, May 12, 1975, OHDDEL; Ginzberg, interview, December 11, 1990; Henry Rosovsky, *The University: An Owner's Manual* (New York, 1990), p. 137; Eisenhower, Oral History Interview, 1967, COHP.
79. Alonzo L. Hamby, *Beyond the New Deal* (New York, 1973), pp. 229, 492; William E. Leuchtenburg, "Farewell to the New Deal: The Lingering of a Fable," *New Leader,* December 11, 1948, p. 5, cited by Alan Brinkley, *New Deal Liberalism in Recession and War* (New York, 1995), p. 265.
80. Eisenhower to Sulzberger, May 16 and June 18, 1951, to Dodge, June 6, 1951, to Black, June 21, 1951, and to Coykendall, July 9, 1951, *PDDE,* XII, 291-93, 361-63, 338-39, 373-74, and 410-11.
81. Ginzberg, Oral History, May 14, 1975, OHDDEL; Ginzberg, interview, December 11, 1990; Black, interview, June 6, 1973; Kevin McCann, personal interview, July 25, 1972 Gettysburg, Pa; Coykendall tel. to Eisenhower, August 16, 1951, DDEL; Eisenhower to Kirk, August 23, 1951, *PDDE,* XII, 484; Kirk, Oral History, September 3, 1987, COHP; Eisenhower to Coykendall and to Black, September 15, 1951, *PDDE,* XII, 542-44.
82. Black, interview, June 6, 1973.

8

Eisenhower, Columbia, and 1952

A young, ex-Columbia statistics professor—now with *The New York Times* . . . suggested we might get some good dope on Ike's regime at Columbia from the files of the *Spectator* and by interviewing a few Democratically-minded faculty members like Harry Carman, who had hair-raising stories about Ike's academic naiveté.

—Ken Hechler,
Working with Truman (1982)

On January 6, 1952, Eisenhower entered politics.

His agent in this endeavor was Senator Henry Cabot Lodge, who stated that he would enter the General's name in the New Hampshire primary as a Republican and that Eisenhower would stay in the race "to the finish." The Massachusetts Republican asserted in a letter to the Governor of New Hampshire that Eisenhower, during conversations with him at Columbia University, had told him he supported "enlightened Republican doctrine" and had a Republican "voting record." Lodge declared, moreover, that reporters could seek confirmation from Eisenhower at NATO Headquarters.[1]

"Come a-running for Christmas" to France, Eisenhower had told Bill Robinson and Cliff Roberts, and from December 23 until the 27th they discussed Eisenhower's political situation. "I am never going to get tangled up in any kind of political activity," he had told Robinson earlier, "unless forced to do so as the result of a genuine and deep conviction expressed by a very large segment of our people." As Stephen Ambrose has observed, the General declared his willingness to accept the Republican Party nomination, if it were given to him by acclamation, "but his friends knew that was impossible" because of Senator Taft's strong and determined campaign for convention delegates.[2] Yet Eisenhower had committed himself to the success of his NATO mission, and he could not see leaving Europe until late spring; moreover, Army regulations stated that members, while on active duty, only could "accept nomination for public office, provided such nomination is tendered without direct or *indirect* activity or solicitation on their part." During the extensive conversations over Christmas, according to Robinson, Eisenhower made "no objection to . . . a definite and unqualified statement . . . that while serving in a civilian capacity at Columbia" he had told Lodge about his voting record as a Republican. Eisenhower added that General Clay had "his complete confidence" and was "best qualified to act as an intermediary between me and the 'pros.'" Clay, thus, authorized Lodge's announcement. The Senator, however, during the press conference went beyond his instructions and referred reporters to the General's headquarters, and this "astonished" and angered Eisenhower. The General, consequently, was forced to issue a statement, and he reprimanded Clay in a "fiery" letter.[3]

Newspapers proclaimed Eisenhower's decision, and the *Spectator's* headline read "Ike Will Run on GOP Ticket If He Gets a 'Clear-Cut Call.'" It printed the General's press release, in which he acknowledged that Lodge had given "an accurate account of the general tenor of my political convictions and of my Republican voting record." He would neither seek the nomination nor "seek relief" from his NATO assignment; he would, though, accept "a clear-cut call to political duty," and he recognized the right of American citizens "to attempt to place" before him "a duty that would transcend my present responsibilities."[4]

The *Spectator's* editorial emphasized many earlier denials by Columbia's President of any political interest, from his Finder letter in 1948 through his statements after his controversial speeches in late 1949 and his reply to Governor Dewey's support in October, 1950. "They had the sound of sincere conviction" and, recently, the paper noted, he had stressed that any political involvement would jeopardize his NATO command. "Surely the General is not so naïve as to assume that he has not now done precisely that." The *Spectator* wondered if those who enthusiastically supported the news "know for whom and what they are plugging? A smile? The platitudes we have had from the General in his recent civilian years?" The American people "know so little" about him, and they should demand that "he abandon this coyness, if not outright arrogance" of awaiting a "draft." The *Spectator's* criticism opened the first round of an increasingly acrimonious controversy on Morningside Heights over

Eisenhower's candidacy for the Presidency. Sulzberger's *Times* immediately supported him in an editorial, "Eisenhower." Never had the paper endorsed a candidate so early in the campaign and without the nomination of an opponent, and the *Times'* unwavering position throughout the campaign would play a central role in that controversy at Columbia.[5]

The political opportunities Eisenhower had and rejected in the postwar years are well known, and perceptive books and articles on Eisenhower and the 1952 election can be found elsewhere. These accounts, however, either overlook or minimize the importance of his Columbia Presidency on his trip to 1600 Pennsylvania Avenue and the bitter dispute which erupted on the Morningside campus during the presidential campaign.[6] The friends Eisenhower made in New York as President of Columbia and the connections he established during his fund-raising for the American Assembly played a significant role in his decision to enter politics and in the struggle for the Republican Party nomination; moreover, the story of his Columbia years explains the depth and intensity of the opposition to him on Morningside Heights, as well as the controversy at the University during the campaign in 1952. This hostile reaction, indeed, may also explain, at least partially, the negative assessments of Eisenhower's Presidency of the United States for so many years.

Throughout 1951, from his departure for NATO until Lodge's announcement, Eisenhower stressed the American Assembly in his correspondence and, in the process, continued to expand his informal network. At NATO he worried increasingly about the dangers of inflation at home, and he proposed that the second Assembly topic be on that important and timely subject. He saw certain military programs as "expensive and driving us (along with a lot of political expenditures) straight toward inflation of an uncontrollable nature." Wanting an examination "into the economics of Nat'l security," he wrote in his *Diary,* "We will go broke and still have *inefficient* defenses." His letters to Bermingham, Roberts, and others reflected this concern about inflation, and he signed fund-raising letters for the Assembly which Dean Young had sent to him. In December Young announced that $1,119,000 had been given or pledged to the Assembly, and that the *Times,* the *Herald-Tribune,* and International Business Machines each had donated $25,000. Eisenhower, meanwhile, noticing that "the Assembly has no sponsoring group in the Pittsburgh area," gave Young a list of prominent individuals who had attended the Pittsburgh luncheon in 1950. Eisenhower knew that the inflation topic would appeal to the Assembly's major and potential donors. Telling "Boots" Adams "I can think of no more vital subject than Inflation," he asked the Phillips Petroleum Chairman for help "to put the Assembly on a sound five year basis." A few weeks later Young informed Eisenhower that the oil company had given $100,000 for a four-year period.[7]

During 1951, while Eisenhower was at NATO and the bitterly unpopular Korean War continued, his friends formed and, with the help of many Assembly supporters, financed "Citizens for Eisenhower." Years later, in a memorandum for Eisenhower, Robinson recalled that "the professional politicians control the delegates," and despite the Wendell Willkie nomination by the Republicans, a "freak, out of a [political] stalemate in 1940, there would be no chance to get the political pros to nominate an outsider and particularly a General." Thus, he wrote, "I (and there may have been others) conceived the idea of Citizens for Eisenhower. . . . The nomination was a political phenomenon—indeed a miracle." The *Herald-Tribune* executive continued. "Here is the spectacular fact that is so often lost sight of in the treatment of the era by current writers and commentators." Roberts, who had given a birthday party for the Eisenhowers before the General departed for NATO and with the "gang" had presented him with a large check for the American Assembly, played the major role in financing the Committee, and members of the "gang," including "Slats" Slater and "Pete" Jones helped, as did other Assembly contributors.[8]

In early November the Eisenhowers returned to the States for the first time since leaving Columbia, and reporters questioned him constantly about politics. A few days earlier Robinson had written for the *Herald-Tribune* a front-page editorial, "The Times and the Man," which asserted that Eisenhower was a "Republican by temper and disposition" and endorsed him for the 1952 Republican nomination; the previous evening Helen Reid had announced at the *Herald-Tribune's* Forum the newspaper's commitment to Eisenhower's candidacy, Eisenhower, "overwhelmed by the overgenerous estimate" in the editorial, also thanked Robinson for organizing a series of studies for him on major domestic issues. "You are really establishing a junior 'American Assembly,'" he wrote, "All of us will unquestionably profit a lot from the results"—Roberts and Jones financed the studies.[9]

The Eisenhowers arrived in Washington on November 4, after a brief visit in Kentucky with John and Barbara Eisenhower, who were expecting their third child. The General had lunch with President Truman, a meeting with NATO representatives, and a press conference, and the trip gave the Eisenhowers an opportunity to see a number of friends, including General Clay and Kevin McCann. In June McCann had left the General's staff at NATO and accepted the Presidency of The Defiance College in Ohio. In August, Douglas Black suggested that he write a survey of the General's career, but he had "put the manuscript aside" when the college year opened; now, in November, he resumed work on the biography.[10]

They stopped briefly in New York on the way back to France. The General stayed on his plane at LaGuardia Airport. While Mamie Eisenhower went to 60 Morningside to get a few things from their house, he met with his political advisers for three hours. Robinson, Roberts, and Milton Eisenhower joined Eisenhower on the plane, and Doug Black and Young arrived a little later. Milton had warned his brother that Taft's nomination, without a good opponent, seemed likely and many believed "this would be calamitous" for the party and for the nation. If the choice in 1952 were between Truman and Taft, Milton argued, "any personal sacrifice . . . is wholly justified."[11]

"That deep-seated sense of duty which was drilled into you," Milton told his brother, "must be causing you to suffer much anguish." The General, before officially assuming his NATO assignment, secretly had tried to obtain Taft's support for the collective security concept and the Atlantic alliance at a private and unannounced meeting. If Taft agreed, the General was prepared to issue an unequivocal statement making "any political future for me thereafter . . . impossible." He asked the Senator, "Would you, and your associates in the Congress, agree that collective security is necessary for all of us in Western Europe—and will you support this idea as a bi-partisan policy." Taft's answers, however, seemed to be "playing politics" and desiring to cut "the President, or the Presidency, down to size." Taft's failure to say "yes" on collective security was "distressing" and, after the meeting, Eisenhower called in his assistants and tore up his prepared statement. During 1951 his unhappiness with Republican criticism of Truman's NATO policy prompted him to write in his *Diary* that several Senators, including Taft and McCarthy, "are disciples of hate—hate and curse anything that belongs to the administration."[12]

Eisenhower's friends on the airplane that afternoon knew well Eisenhower's passionate opposition to Taft's isolationism. They decided to form a small advisory group, which Eisenhower wanted to be "completely independent of whatever political group might organize itself around the ideas of forcing me into the political picture." In addition to the visitors at LaGuardia, Roberts soon proposed for the group Jones, Slater, and several others who also had contributed to the American Assembly. Eisenhower quickly replied from NATO that he trusted these people "implicitly." He acknowledged, meanwhile, that "things are moving much faster than we had anticipated."[13]

Eisenhower may have been referring to rumors that Truman had offered to support the General on the Democratic ticket in 1952. Arthur Krock, an influential *New York Times* journalist, reported that at the luncheon with Eisenhower the President had repeated his 1945 Potsdam offer and "guaranteed" the General's nomination as a Democrat. Eisenhower replied that Truman knew he was a "Republican"; when Truman persisted, Eisenhower declared that on domestic issues his differences with the Democrats were far too great. Krock stated that his story came from "a highly placed northern Democrat," and he added that "vehement and august denials would be forthcoming." They were, from both Truman and Eisenhower; years later in his *Memoirs* Krock identified Supreme Court Justice William O. Douglas as the source and wrote that Eisenhower "obliquely" affirmed the story. The *Spectator* bitterly criticized Eisenhower's failure to mention Columbia, "the only Presidency that didn't creep into the volumes of newsprint" during his visit. The Trustees had granted him a leave to lead NATO "with the clear understanding" he would return "immediately upon his military release." Eisenhower, the student paper concluded, has "broken the bargain."[14]

As the political tempo increased that fall, the pressures on Eisenhower grew. Prominent Democrats, worried about their party's prospects in 1952, argued that Republican Party regulars did not share the General's commitment to NATO and the defense of Europe. Eisenhower's political friends in the Republican Party, on the other hand, insisted that they had to have an active candidate and that Taft might be too far ahead, while Taft's supporters asserted that the General's foreign and domestic views placed him outside the Republican Party. For these reasons in early December Senator Lodge, who had been selected by a number of politicians to lead the

Eisenhower-for-President campaign, told the General that he had to come home and campaign for the nomination. Eisenhower recoiled at this insistence by the "political engineers." If he did not energetically seek delegates, he wrote Roberts, "I am told the whole effort is hopeless"; yet, to do so, he added, "would be a dereliction of duty." In his *Diary* he emphasized "the impropriety—almost the illegality—of any pre-convention activity as long as I'm on this job. . . . I cannot in good conscience quit here." Then, after writing "Hurrah," he emphasized he was telling Lodge that the Senator must "stop the whole thing, now." Eisenhower, nonetheless, in the same letter to Roberts authorized his friend to arrange the advisory group's first meeting, and he asserted that a Christmas visit by Roberts and Robinson would be "wonderful!"[15]

Just before leaving New York, Robinson attended Jones' Christmas party and sat with Slater and Herbert Brownell, who had been Dewey's political manager. As Robinson tried to convince him to organize convention delegates for Eisenhower, Brownell replied, "I'm through with politics and I am very happy. . . . Not only have I never met him—I have never even seen him." Robinson persisted and said he would guarantee expenses for the visit with the General— Brownell would take the trip in early 1952 and it would lead to his vital role in the campaign. Slater, commenting on his friend's Christmas plans with the Eisenhowers, noted that this was when Robinson got "Eisenhower—with many misgivings from Mamie—to agree to run" provided that there was sufficient popular demand.[16]

While waiting for his friends to arrive in Paris, Eisenhower received a handwritten letter from the President. Although Truman expressed his desire to return to Missouri, he emphasized, "I must keep the isolationists out of the White House." He knew that Eisenhower shared this vital concern, and he asked what the General intended to do. "My own position," he wrote, "is in the balance."[17]

Eisenhower did not answer the President's letter until January 1, and by that time he had reached important decisions with Robinson and Roberts and they had returned to New York. Initially, Eisenhower told his friends that he had a mission to fulfill at NATO, but Roberts emphasized that the General's statements had been confusing and he had to be fair to his supporters on the "fence." Eisenhower's advisers insisted that if his supporters were to continue their efforts, they had to have a definite commitment that he would run. "He quickly saw the point," Roberts recalled. He agreed not to take himself out of the race and acquiesced in the decision that Lodge would announce the General's Republican voting record; he insisted, however, on staying at NATO. Robinson, after weighing at length the advantages and disadvantages of an active candidacy, finally agreed. "There is more to be gained than lost by staying on the job in Europe." Then, wanting to explain carefully the military regulations and that Eisenhower would "consider a call to political service," they prepared the letter Lodge would send to New Hampshire Governor Sherman Adams that would enable Eisenhower to be entered in the presidential primary.[18]

Thus, when Eisenhower replied to Truman, he carefully watched his words; nonetheless, he consciously misled the President. He reminded Truman that "a conviction of duty" had put him "again on military duty and in a foreign country!" He saw "no duty to seek a political nomination" while on "a project of the utmost importance"— it would, moreover, violate Army regulations. Consequently, he concluded that the possibility of being "drawn into political activity is so remote as to be negligible." The last weekend in December he also wrote Sulzberger, who had told him that the *Times* would support Truman in a race against Taft. Without telling the Columbia Trustee about Lodge's forthcoming announcement, he insisted "my own feelings and instinct" opposed "any thought of political office" and involved "the hope of a quiet, stable family life for Mamie and me." He had, he insisted, a "great desire to return to Columbia and pick up where I left off."[19]

In spite of the political pressures, he remained determined to control his alternatives. He had settled on a "predetermined course of action," and any "slight modification," he informed Robinson, would come "only on the advice of some such group as one composed of you, Cliff, Pete Jones, Clay, Milton, and Slats." Yet, important events, from Truman's budget proposal to former President Hoover's campaign to bring "American troops . . . home" from Europe and a huge Madison Square Garden rally by his supporters, were beyond his control. The budget contemplated a huge deficit, and Eisenhower expressed his great alarm in a long *Diary* entry. Even making "allowances" for the costs of the Korean war—"we did the right thing in defying and opposing the Communist advance into Southern Korea"—he saw this budget as leading to "unconscionable inflation" and "internal deterioration." Then, a few days later, he responded to Hoover's speech by emphasizing in a letter the need to combat the "false doctrine of isolationism." Perhaps it is not surprising that Eisenhower, who noted "Our times are tumultuous," should be "deeply touched and most highly complimented" by some 15,000 supporters giving a "Serenade to Ike" at an enormously successful, late-night celebration at Madison Square Garden. Well-known aviator Jacqueline Cochran immediately flew to France with the film of the rally, and viewing it "developed into a real emotional experience for Mamie and me. . . . Clearly to be seen is the mass longing of America for some kind of reasonable solution for her nagging, persistent and almost terrifying problems."[20]

In his January statement Eisenhower had asserted he would not campaign for the nomination; by mid-February, however, he admitted that "my attitude has undergone a quite significant change" since watching the Madison Square Garden movie and listening to his close advisers. Unlike the party professionals, who insisted he had to start campaigning by March, his friends were urging a non-partisan appearance during a brief spring visit home—possibly appearing at the opening of the American Assembly meeting in May—and, then, a vigorous campaign for uncommitted delegates during the weeks before the convention. Meanwhile, Eisenhower had asked Robinson if he would fly to Paris on a day's notice for the weekend: the General decided to discuss with Robinson "my hope of obtaining . . . the services of Kevin McCann." The Defiance College President, however, was hesitant about leaving, even to respond to a call from the General for a few weeks, since he had committed himself to raise quickly "some twenty-five thousand dollars" for the college. Eisenhower, though "reluctant to ask anyone specifically for help," wanted McCann's assistance so much that he was willing to suggest that his "warmest friends" resolve the difficulty. Robinson, upon his return to the States, met several times with McCann, and soon Roberts promised Defiance $15,000, with Jones offering to contribute anonymously "any part or all" of it; Roberts, moreover, paid McCann's expenses. Eisenhower's trusted assistant took a leave from Defiance to handle the political correspondence and keep it from interfering with NATO business; he rejoined Eisenhower in mid-February and stayed for many months.[21]

Robinson also was working with McCann on "getting together material which represented [Eisenhower's] political philosophy" in time for the critical New Hampshire primary with Taft on March 11. Over the winter McCann had been preparing *Man from Abilene,* based on the General's letters, occasional *Diary* entries, and public speeches—while visiting in Paris over Christmas Robinson had been told by Eisenhower that it was all right to take "notes and quotes" from personal correspondence for McCann's use. (Doug Black's Doubleday would publish *Man from Abilene* in May; earlier, it had issued a fifty-cent edition of *Crusade in Europe*, and the Woolworth Stores initially ordered 139,000 copies of the first printing of 570,000.) By mid-February Robinson had enough material to publish, "almost overnight," a paperback, "Eisenhower's Creed," and it was reduced "to a series of articles for newspaper syndication" by the *Herald-Tribune*. Robinson visited every editor in New Hampshire by car and placed the articles "with four of the seven regional daily papers" and many of the weeklies, and he thought they were "especially effective." A week before the election he described for Eisenhower his "second safari" to the state and "the views of newspaper publishers and editors." He emphasized that Governor Sherman Adams and his organization for Eisenhower had "done a good job," though Taft had made "some real gains." Robinson added that the *Herald-Tribune* planned "a prominent editorial" explaining why the General "cannot come home to engage in this campaign, and why you should not."[22]

Eisenhower's personal popularity, as well as Taft's harsh attacks on the General, brought a heavy voter turn out in New Hampshire, in spite of snow and rain, and he won all fourteen Republican delegates and over 50 percent of the presidential-preference ballots. His "astonishing" victory had exceeded Robinson's prediction, and he told reporters, "Any American who would have that many other Americans pay him that compliment would be proud or he would not be an American." Earlier, he had asked his "previously-designated group of friends" to give him their assessment of the results. The majority believed that "with proper organization from here on" he had "an even chance for the nomination, even though your duty in Europe" prevented a return before the convention. They agreed that his "sense of duty" should govern his decision; if he could return before the convention his "availability for direction, advice and consultation would also be a great boon to the movement." While New Hampshire did not prompt him to change his plans, after the primary he mentioned to Phil Young the "faint possibility that, at the last minute, I might be able to join in a session of your next Assembly meeting.[23]

Eisenhower's friends in Minnesota, whom he had cultivated through the American Assembly, meanwhile, presented a problem for the Eisenhower organization. The party professionals did not want him in the Minnesota primary, which came a week after New Hamsphire's and was expected to be an easy victory for favorite son and former governor Harold Stassen. For the same reason, Taft had decided not to run. Eisenhower's friend Brad Mintener, however, thought that the General should enter the primary. A vice president of Pillsbury Mills, he had visited Eisenhower after the war in Washington and had stayed at 60 Morningside and taken Eisenhower to the theater; moreover, he had attended the American Assembly fundraising dinner in Minneapolis shortly after the start of the Korean War. In August, 1951, he had told the General in Paris, "I think you ought to be the President of the United States," and added that he was going home to organize "Minnesotans for Eisenhower." Shortly after Lodge's announcement, Mintener mentioned his efforts for the Minnesota primary, and Eisenhower replied that the executive's "conscience" had to be his guide and "I have every confidence in you as a team player." Mintener interpreted this as not being told to stop, and he filed a petition for a slate of Eisenhower delegates. The Minnesota Supreme Court, however, in an extraordinary session, decided 4-3 in favor of a challenge from the Stassen campaign that Mintener's group had not compiled with a technicality and removed the Eisenhower slate from the ballot.[24]

"Now, this was the greatest thing that ever happened to Eisenhower," Mintener recalled, "and biggest political mistake that Stassen ever made." Encouraged by Eisenhower's strong showing in New Hampshire, Mintener obtained a ruling on Friday, the 14th, that write-in votes would be counted, and that "the name can be written in any way so that the election judges can identify the person for whom the write-in voters vote." Eisenhower's supporters over the weekend—without any assistance from the national organization and with no time to raise funds—launched a dramatic write-in campaign by using the telephone, newspapers, radio, and television to encourage people to call five people and tell them to write-in Eisenhower's name and call five more people. Any write-in effort faces difficult odds, and election day brought bad weather throughout the state for the primary. Yet, by mid-morning newspapers started reporting "they're running out of pencils here, and there's a tremendous flock to the polls." By noon Mintener heard "They're running out of ballots," and he called the Attorney-General, who ruled that pieces of paper would count, and he recalled then cabling Eisenhower: "It looks as though, in the worst blizzard in Minnesota's winter, between 100 and 125 thousand people are going through this blizzard to write your name on the ballot. I hope you consider this a second call to duty."[25]

"Write-In Vote Called Political Miracle" read the *Minneapolis Morning Tribune.* Stassen, with his name printed on the ballot, had received 129,000 votes and won all the delegates, but Eisenhower "astonishingly" had some 107,000 voters write in his name with spelling from "Eisonhauer, Eausonhower, Ineshower, or just Ike." The *Times'* Arthur Krock considered the write-in for Eisenhower "qualitatively the most spontaneous outburst in the history of political preference in this country." The successful campaign can be partially attributed to the General's American Assembly efforts and associates. Mintener's determination to demonstrate the state's enthusiasm for Eisenhower had led the effort; moreover, Harry Bullis and John Cowles, two prominent Minnesotans, served on the American Assembly's original National Policy Board and ardently supported his candidacy. Bullis, the General Mills chairman, had attended Board meetings and was the Eisenhower National Committee's financial representative in the state, and Cowles' *Minneapolis Star and Tribune* played an important role "in an eleventh-hour write-in challenge." The *Tribune*'s lead editorial declared it "An Amazing Vote." These Minnesotans for Eisenhower, buoyed by their success, began efforts to maintain momentum and pressure Stassen's delegates to switch to Eisenhower at the convention.[26]

The activity of over 100,000 write-in voters forced Eisenhower to admit that "the mounting numbers of my fellow citizens who are voting to make me the Republican nominee are forcing me to reexamine my personal position and past decisions." The professionals, who also had opposed the Madison Square Garden rally, had argued, Eisenhower recalled, that Mintener's write-in campaign was "doomed to miserable failure and would have a depressing effect." While the professionals had been unsuccessfully urging Eisenhower to return home to campaign, Eisenhower's friends and voters in Minnesota had a far greater impact on his thinking that he "could not much longer remain actively in command" at NATO. As Slats Slater later recorded, Eisenhower's associates "drew courage" from his "strong advocates" in Minnesota.[27]

On April 2, 1952, he wrote President Truman, who on March 29 had announced he would "not be a candidate for reelection." As Alonzo Hamby has observed, the President faced Eisenhower's candidacy and was "seriously battered" by "Korea and McCarthyism." The General requested relief as Supreme Commander "on or about June 1st," and he requested that the public announcement come after the completion of NATO's "first comprehensive Command Post Exercise" on April 11. In a press release on the 12th he stated that he would resign from the Army, if nominated in July, and that he would go to Abilene for the dedication of the Eisenhower Foundation on June 4th. Earlier he had admitted to Roberts, "When I once cut myself off from the income and perquisites of military life . . . I shall have to have some kind of help." He worried, moreover, about how he could keep the services of Colonel Schulz and Master Sergeants Mooney and Dry, for without their presence "I could not possibly carry the load that each day brings to me." Roberts told him that during the campaign the National Committee would pay any "Headquarters expense," and he would cover "everything that might be called personal."[28]

The Columbia Trustees expressed their support. Only days after the Minnesota primary and over a week before Eisenhower's letter to Truman, they informed him that "the President's home is ready." This "quite agreeably surprised" Eisenhower, Roberts recalled, especially since "he should feel at perfect liberty to entertain anyone that he wished to entertain there until he had officially resigned and severed his connection with Columbia," and that if he returned home he could continue in his "present status." It was, he added, "very much of a plus to have Columbia as a base, rather than to have no home at all."[29]

After a farewell tour of NATO countries, General and Mrs. Eisenhower, General Snyder, and Eisenhower's personal staff left Paris on May 31. They arrived in Washington late the following afternoon, and the General went to the White House for a briefing with Truman. On June 2nd, the President awarded him the Distinguished Service Medal, and he retired from active service on the 3rd and left for Kansas; on June 6 the Eisenhowers returned to Columbia and their home at 60 Morningside. By this time, Taft had more than recovered from New Hampshire and Minnesota, and a crucial struggle for delegates was underway in Texas, where the Taft forces controlled the small Republican Party in the Democratic state.

Eisenhower's earlier trips to Texas and activities on behalf of the American Assembly paid even greater dividends than they had in Minnesota. Porter, who had started energetically raising money for the Assembly in 1950, during 1951 led the Eisenhower challengers to the Taft-dominated party in Texas. He had strong and influential support from prominent American Assembly associates. Sid Richardson, a long-time friend of Eisenhower's, had made a significant contribution to the Assembly; "Mc" McCollum, a National Advisory Board member, had been one of the most enthusiastic advocates for the Assembly and arranged an advisory committee for Porter; and Oveta Culp Hobby, another active Board member and World War II Director of the Women's Army Corps, was executive vice president of the *Houston Post*, and she used her newspaper and television station to partisan advantage.[30]

During the early months of 1952 the struggle for Texas' thirty-eight delegates became bitter. The Taft forces, knowing that any Democrat or Independent was likely to vote for Eisenhower, sought to limit voting on the precinct level to Republicans; on the other hand, Porter argued that a Texan could "vote Republican one day, Democratic the next," and Hobby's *Post* published front-page editorials for Eisenhower and distributed over 400,000 political primers. Since Texas had a complicated process for choosing delegates, and it started on the precinct level, the *Post* and its television station delivered voting instructions and declared that "every qualified voter has an obligation." The *Dallas Morning News* also published precinct locations, and the *Post* warned that Eisenhower's "nomination at Chicago may depend on Texas' delegation."[31]

Hobby's *Post* assigned a reporter to each of the state's 185 precinct conventions on May 3, and they witnessed unprecedented numbers voting for Eisenhower. The newspaper celebrated the "Ike Landslide" with a picture of a "jubilant" Porter. The Taft forces, outnumbered at the county level, held their own meetings, and they regained control of the party by the state convention on May 27 and selected a pro-Taft delegation. The *Post* had followed the story closely and issued a "Plea to Taft for Fair Play." It called the Taft-dominated state executive committee's actions "a farcical demonstration of political piracy," and it predicted that the Eisenhower forces, even though they represented the majority of the voters at both the precinct and county levels, would have to hold their own meeting. They did, and they chose a rival delegation.[32]

"SUPPORTERS OF IKE STAGE BOLT," the *Post* declared, "Hold Own Session, Vow Fight, Victory at Chicago," and the ensuing fight over the contested Texas delegation became a *cause célèbre*. It quickly received national attention. Washington columnist Joseph Alsop had attended the state convention and wrote two articles about the "Taft 'Steal.'" They appeared on the *Houston Post's* front-page, and Alsop reported, "This steal has been accomplished by a system of rigging as grossly dishonest, as namedly anti-democratic, as arrogantly careless of majority rule, as can be found in the long and often sordid annals of American politics." The campaign slogans in Texas against Eisenhower included "Reds, New Dealers Use Ike In Plot To Hold Power" and "Ike Coddled Communists While President Of Columbia University." Throughout this period the *Post* focused daily on the need for "Fair Play," "the voice of the people," and the "Taft 'Steal,'" and Senator Taft, needing delegates, did nothing to separate himself from the controversy. The *Post* eagerly looked forward to Eisenhower's previously scheduled visit on June 21 to Dension, Texas, where he had been born. His trip—less than two weeks before Chicago—received enormous publicity, and that evening in Dallas in a nationally broadcast speech he stressed that the Republican Party had been betrayed by the Old Guard's "Steal." In this case, he asserted, "The rustlers stole the Texas birthright instead of Texas steers." The *Denver Post* declared, "Ike's first fire-breathing speech."[33]

In mid-June Eisenhower had set up his pre-convention headquarters in Denver, and he returned to the Mile High City after his Texas trip. Herbert Parmet has argued that the General, in his up-hill battle against Taft, sought to present himself "as a political amateur devoid of glib theories but, in contrast to his opponent, a sincere, plain-talking American." Yet, as the Chicago convention approached, estimates gave the Senator over one hundred more delegates than the General had; moreover, Taft controlled the party machinery, especially the national committee and the important Committee on Credentials, which would decide the contested delegates, half of whom were from Texas. Furthermore, General Douglas MacArthur, a Taft supporter, had been chosen to deliver the keynote address. Perhaps with these obstacles to his nomination in mind, Eisenhower told Al Jacobs just before his departure for Chicago, "Al, if I'm fortunate enough not to be nominated, I will, after three months' vacation, return to Columbia."[34]

In Chicago the Eisenhower campaign exploited "Taft's 'Steal'" and skillfully used the issue at the Convention. "The truth of the matter," Roberts emphasized, "was that he only had a fighting chance and a slim one at that to get the nomination," and Taft and Texas gave an opportunity. "If we hadn't been able to get the public to believe that there had been some unfair practices on the part of the Taft managers" in Texas, Roberts recalled, "we never would have been able to get some of the rulings that we did get" at the convention. Brownell, who played a major role in the campaign, had attended the controversial Texas convention and said, "The Taft forces are now convinced that he cannot win the nomination—so now they are out to steal it." Lodge, who called it "scandalous and shameful," spurned any compromise by the Taft forces. Any agreement on the contested Texas delegates, he knew, would eliminate the moral issue for the Eisenhower forces, and he wanted a floor vote on the "Fair Play Amendment" for contested delegates. Roberts added that "the hue and cry was such that the Taft crowd finally had to allow it to be held publicly, and the proceedings didn't help Taft at all." And, once Eisenhower's managers got the issue to the floor, Lodge had lined up the votes—it was, Ambrose has emphasized, Lodge's "finest hour." Soon, the Porter group became the official Texas delegation, and Taft had been hurt badly. For the first time, Eisenhower surged ahead in the delegate count. Although Minnesota's Stassen furtively hoped that an anti-Eisenhower coalition would emerge with him as the leader, his state's delegation contained strong support for Eisenhower, especially in the wake of the primary, and began to split. When Eisenhower fell only nine votes short of the nomination on the first ballot, the General's advocates in the Minnesota delegation prompted it to switch and make him the Republican Party nominee.[35]

Eisenhower, as President of Columbia, had energetically campaigned during 1949 and 1950 to establish the American Assembly and, in the process, he also had cultivated many valuable friendships and created an informal, and influential, organization. His Assembly associates in Texas and Minnesota had contributed to his victory in Chicago, and it is conceivable that he would not have defeated Taft without their support. Yet, his devotion to the Assembly concept, from his travels and his fund-raising with corporate executives and oilmen, as well as the constant political speculation, had increased the resentments against him on the Columbia campus in the months before he left for his NATO assignment. Then, upon his return to the States he had spent a week at Columbia in June, and the constant political activity at 60 Morningside quickly rekindled many of these sentiments. Although he attended a Trustees Meeting while in New York he spent most of his time on his campaign. He met at the house with Dewey, Lodge, Adams, Clay, and Brownell, among others, and received at least fifteen state delegations to the Chicago convention; he also spent an afternoon at Blind Brook with two golfing foursomes, including Roberts, Robinson, Slater, and Jones. It had been essential, Roberts commented, to get key people to meet Eisenhower before the convention, and his Columbia home offered a better place than a hotel.[36]

While the faculties of Columbia University could be expected to oppose in 1952 any Republican nominee, the depth of the opposition to Eisenhower had deep roots. As Peter Gay, an Instructor in Government at the College, noted a few years later, "You started with considerable anti-Eisenhower sentiment on campus." This position hardened with the nomination by the Democrats of an attractive candidate, Governor Adlai Stevenson of Illinois, and the conservative additions to Eisenhower's campaign, from Vice Presidential nominee Richard M. Nixon to Senator Joseph McCarthy. The intensity of the criticism increased when Eisenhower on September 12 welcomed Senator Taft to the President's House at 60 Morningside for breakfast. Taft, so far, had not asked his followers to work for Eisenhower, and the General needed their support in the presidential campaign. The Senator's previously prepared statement, however, represented his policies: it emphasized the importance of "liberty against creeping socialization in every domestic field," while asserting only "differences of degree" existed in foreign policy. After Taft left 60 Morningside he read his statement to reporters and encouraged his supporters to work for Eisenhower, who subsequently made no clarifying comment about the Senator's statement. Only three days earlier Eisenhower had been embraced in Indiana by Republican Senator William Jenner, an ardent anti-internationalist and staunch supporter of Senator McCarthy; now, after Taft's statement, Stevenson declared, "Taft lost the nomination but won the nominee."[37]

A sharp, negative reaction occurred at Columbia, and overnight the meeting became known as "The Surrender at Morningside Heights." Taft "represented a good deal of what was unacceptable to the University faculty people," Economics Professor Raymond Saulnier has recalled, "and to have Eisenhower sit down and make peace was, of course, a surrender." An agreement with Taft was bad enough, but to have it happen at the President's House was even worse. Many on Morningside Heights saw it as an embarrassment for them and the University. The "Surrender" opened the political campaign on campus, and the controversy quickly became acrimonious.[38]

The same issue of the *New York Times* contained a letter from Instructor Gay protesting the *Times'* editorial position in the presidential race. Gay has recalled it being the first letter in the paper urging a switch to Stevenson; the letter, also, was the first public expression of a growing sentiment at Columbia in favor of the Democratic nominee. Furthermore, with the "Surrender" and Gay's letter, Columbia became indirectly associated with partisan politics. Gay agreed on the importance of defeating Taft and the isolationists in the Republican Party, and he saw the paper's early endorsement of Eisenhower as a "defensive" move; now, however, with Taft out, he asked if "a continued endorsement" of Eisenhower was "wise." On issues from federal control of tidelands oil to McCarthy and Jenner, Gay emphasized that the *Times* agreed with Stevenson. "What can we expect," he asserted, from Eisenhower "who talks of a 'crusade' and is at the same time unwilling to reject the most miserable segments of his own party? . . . How much more courageous would it be if it admitted," Gay asked, that "what the *New York Times* stands for is Governor Stevenson?" The frustration on campus with the *Times* continued to grow because Sulzberger, owner and publisher of the newspaper, was a Columbia alumnus and Trustee, and for Professor David Truman that helped explain the *Times'* inconsistency.[39]

Sulzberger, in fact, in May had informed Eisenhower, "There are, of course, no loose threads left so far as the *Times'* support of your candidacy. Whatever can be done will be done." In mid-August the publisher advised him, "If you would cut yourself loose affirmatively from McCarthy, I think the heart of the world would rise up to you." He worried, moreover, that Eisenhower did not have advisers who were "men with clear heads and high ideals and the ability to express those ideals in glowing prose" and who could "keep him up with the events that are moving so rapidly." Ten days later the two met, although time did not permit Sulzberger to mention one thing "which strikes me as being quite important." In Europe, he wrote after their conversation, "you were surrounded by a most loyal and devoted group of newspapermen"; now, "you no longer seem to be at ease with the newspapermen. . . . That, I think, is unfortunate."

And, returning to the problem of McCarthy, the publisher took issue with Eisenhower's position that the Senator "deserved credit for having awakened the country to some of its security problems." Sulzberger enclosed a recent *Times'* editorial, "Loyalty in Government," and expressed his distress that no one had furnished Eisenhower with "this editorial or with the facts on which it was based." Sulzberger might have enclosed another recent editorial, in which the *Times* bluntly asserted "General Eisenhower has disappointed many of his friends and supporters, this newspaper among them, for his failure to state unequivocally that he will not support" McCarthy. Not surprisingly, the *Times'* continued endorsement of Eisenhower provided a forum for both the anti-Eisenhower and pro-Stevenson followers on Morningside Heights.[40]

The pace quickened as soon as classes resumed, and reaction produced further reaction. In late September the *Spectator* reported that Allan Nevins, acting as honorary chairman, was forming a committee of faculty members for Stevenson. Nevins later recalled that he and Stevenson had been good friends for years "with a close personal devotion" and, in this respect, the Stevenson movement was not just a spontaneous outburst against Eisenhower during the campaign. Joseph Campbell, in fact, remembered that George Walker Mullins, Professor Emeritus of Mathematics, and Noel Thomas Dowling, Harlan Fiske Stone Professor of Constitutional Law, had mentioned to him at the Century Association in February their interest in a Stevenson-Fulbright ticket, or the reverse, for the Democrats. During the fall, however, the Stevenson movement on campus almost immediately took an anti-Eisenhower emphasis. Nevins, whose stated initial desire had been to assist Stevenson, knew the contemptuous attitude toward Eisenhower on Morningside Heights and might have foreseen the consequences.[41]

On Wednesday, October 1, over one hundred professors and instructors met in a packed classroom on the top floor of Hamilton Hall and formed the "Columbia Faculty Volunteers for Stevenson." This meant, the *Spectator* emphasized, "a large segment of the Columbia faculty had gone on record as opposing" Eisenhower. The group chose Nevins as permanent chairman and elected to the Executive Committee Justus Buchler, Associate Professor of Philosophy; Oscar J. Campbell, Professor Emeritus of English; Irwin Edman; Peter Gay; Richard Hofstadter; and David Truman. Nevins told his colleagues, "No one in the country [is] as well qualified for the Presidency as Adlai Stevenson" and that he looked forward to a "really a great Presidency. . . . Not since the days of Woodrow Wilson has a candidate run a campaign on such a high level." As the meeting continued, Charles Frankel suggested a subtitle for the committee: "Keep Ike for Columbia or don't let them take him away" and, according to the *Spectator,* it "evoked loud laughter." Then it was suggested that the committee buy a full-page advertisement in the *Times* to endorse Stevenson and protest the paper's editorial position. The faculty chose Hofstadter to prepare a draft statement and Gay to solicit the estimated $3,500 cost. The session concluded with plans for three members to speak the next day at an all-College meeting of Students for Stevenson.[42]

"Three Professors Blast Eisenhower," the *Spectator* reported, "Stevenson Backers Jam Into Harkness to Hear Speakers." Edman noted the "simple, stupid integrity" of the Republicans and their right-wing's "playing with phantom hysteria." Referring to Eisenhower and that "many of us here feel that our loss is the country's loss," he stated, "The General has now almost shrunk to normal human size and after he shares the platform with Senator Joe McCarthy, he will become even smaller." Stevenson's intellect and wit, Edman added, offered an incisive way to comment on these "absurdities, incongruities, and stupidities." Oscar Campbell observed that Eisenhower has been "trained in a narrow, military manner and is therefore necessarily uninformed." The *Spectator,* meanwhile, described Eisenhower's campaign as "The Great Disenchantment" in a front-page editorial and called the University's President "a plodding, orthodox, unimaginative thinker" who was once "the hope of millions of liberals." The next day it endorsed Stevenson. Grayson Kirk, the University's Acting Head, promptly declared that "Columbia believes in the freedom of speech and of the press" and that the *Spectator's* policies did not represent official University policy or views.[43]

The vice chairman of the Columbia Alumni for Eisenhower, however, thought otherwise, and he attacked the *Spectator* for "journalistic sensationalism" and "taking advantage of the greater news possibilities" by endorsing Stevenson. Columbia's alumni, Dr. Millard C. Faught argued, seemed "overwhelmingly for Eisenhower," and he prepared for mailing a brochure describing Eisenhower's work at the University. National Chairmen of the organization included Dean Carman and Trustee Black. When Eisenhower heard in mid-September that the group was being formed, he wrote Carman, "It is mighty good to know that so many Columbia Alumni all over the country are actively working in behalf of the things in which you and I believe." In his statement Faught emphasized that the alumni "represent a more thoughtful and mature view of the campaign" and were increasing their efforts on behalf of Eisenhower.[44]

The Eisenhower brochure, as well as the Taft episode, according to Truman, encouraged faculty members who normally refrained from public comment to become politically active for Stevenson. Initially, the Taft episode provided a double shock: they strongly opposed the Senator's foreign and domestic policies and, second, it occurred on Columbia property. Then the Alumni Association published an eight-page brochure exalting Columbia's experience under Eisenhower. Quotations ranged from references to his "brief but dynamic role," "his accomplishments were absolutely phenomenal," his "active and successful part in raising funds," to the suggestion that "he chose key personnel for the academic staff." The Alumni Association sent the pamphlet to 15,000 alumni, and the Stevenson people considered this a direct exploitation of the University's name. Even if Eisenhower tried not to use Columbia's name, his supporters appeared to do so.[45]

On October 5 Nevins and Professor Richard Morris, a colleague in the History Department, issued a "stinging criticism" of a political expense fund for Senator Richard M. Nixon, the Republican Vice Presidential nominee. The statement's twenty-three signers, according to the *Times*, included some of Columbia's best known professors. Nixon recently had explained the fund in his famous "Checkers Speech," and Nevins asserted that the Senator made "so essentially dishonest and emotional an appeal that he confused a great many people as to the issues involved." While Stevenson, it subsequently had been learned, had funds which were distributed to state employees in Illinois for meritorious service, and both funds were apparently legal, Nevins criticized Nixon for setting a "vicious example" and defending himself with "a blatantly emotional and cheap appeal to the sympathies of Americans." Moreover, Nixon knew who the contributors to the fund for his political expenses were, and it "opened the way to a sense of obligation to private interests." Stevenson, on the other hand, had no knowledge of the donors; while his fund was objectionable, the professors saw nothing reprehensible. "This is not a point of partisan politics," Nevins said. "It is a point of public morals."[46] For the Stevenson people Nixon and the fund analysis were, inevitably, associated with McCarthy and witch-hunting on campus.

The mounting political activity and, specifically, the *Spectator's* endorsement of Stevenson, prompted Bob Harron to inform Kirk hours before the Trustees Meeting of "vigorously stated suggestions" on campus to curb the *Spectator*. "The Trustees," he hoped, "will not think of taking any action, while the campaign is still on, which might even faintly be related to the matter of the *Spectator* and politics." Kirk in pencil "noted" receipt of Harron's memo.[47]

Criticism of the professors immediately came from the President of the Association of the Alumni of Columbia College, James M. Blackwell, in a letter to Kirk. He "excused" the editors of the *Spectator* for endorsing Stevenson because of "their age and inexperience," but the professors have "no such justification." He questioned their "sincerity" and "the airing of their personal prejudices," and he declared, "There is no urgent call for the analysis of Nixon's motives by twenty-three nondescript citizens—it is only when these citizens are teachers at Columbia that their names have significance." Blackwell trusted that "individual officials and students of the University will refrain from using Columbia's name" during the rest of the campaign. Kirk stated that he had no reply for Blackwell's letter, except to repeat Columbia's commitment to freedom of speech and the press.[48] Members on each side believed that the other exploited their association with Columbia in criticizing or supporting President Eisenhower and, therefore, that they had to clarify their position.

Four days later the *New York Daily News* reported that nine of the twenty-three professors had links with communist front associations, and it emphasized that the names, which included J. Bartlett Brebner, Henry Steele Commager, Irwin Edman, Robert Merton, and Mark Van Doren, were in the House's Un-American Activities Committee files. The *Spectator*—its headline stating, "Link Nine Professors To Communist Fronts"—called the article "one of the most irresponsible pieces." The *"News* didn't even bother to interview the professors" and "most of the professors never heard of the 'subversive' organizations to which they are linked." The *News* "smeared" the professors and "attempts to bluff into silence those who would otherwise speak out. As far as Columbia is concerned, it won't work." Taking the opportunity to wade into the controversy, Republican Governor Earl Warren of California voiced his displeasure over the Republican ticket and received nationwide attention when he declared, "The University which Ike heads has more Reds than any other in the country." These accusations prompted Dean Carman, the influential Eisenhower supporter on campus, to defend his colleagues who "are not Red and Columbia is not a Red institution."[49] Yet, with the prominence of Senator McCarthy and McCarthyism in the campaign, the accusation of "Red" and communist affiliations only intensified the response on Morningside Heights. Many an academic, who had been silent during the initial controversy on campus, now defended his colleagues; moreover, he became even more apprehensive about an Eisenhower-Nixon election and the re-election of McCarthy.

Edman's warning about Eisenhower and McCarthy, meanwhile, became a reality for the foes of the Senator. Eisenhower had spent the last weekend of September at 60 Morningside preparing for a campaign trip which would take him to Wisconsin and a platform appearance with the Senator. Interestingly, he invited to the President's House Sulzberger and the managing editor of the *Times* for a discussion of his dilemma. As much as Eisenhower opposed McCarthy's methods, the question was what would he say in Wisconsin? McCarthy, after all, had bitterly denounced General Marshall for disloyalty. Eisenhower saw an occasion "to pay a personal tribute to Marshall—right in McCarthy's backyard," and his speech writers prepared a strong paragraph which stressed Marshall's "singular selflessness and the profoundest patriotism." In Peoria, on the way to Wisconsin, Eisenhower and McCarthy met alone and, "in red hot anger" Eisenhower refused to delete the paragraph. The next morning they met on the train, and Eisenhower told McCarthy "being booed doesn't bother me" but, as the train approached Milwaukee, the party professionals persuaded Eisenhower to drop the critical passage. They argued that party unity and winning the election was more important than defending General Marshall in McCarthy's home state. The press, though, had received the original text; the speech, however, as delivered by Eisenhower, endorsed the McCarthy crusade.[50]

The reaction was sharp. The *Times'* editorial the next morning, "An Unhappy Day," asserted it was neither "a happy day for General Eisenhower . . . nor was it a happy day for many supporters." The newspaper "deeply regretted" the endorsement of McCarthy. Even Eisenhower's friends and supporters on Morningside Heights were deeply distressed. Dean Kenneth Johnson of the School of Social Work wrote Eisenhower, "To say that you and McCarthy agree in your 'aims' but not in your 'methods' is tantamount to saying that the end justifies the means. . . . Brother, you are wrong—dead wrong—when you ally yourself with him." John Krout sadly regretted that "Eisenhower's failure to take a firm stand . . . was disquieting to a great many of his close friends and staunch supporters" at Columbia. His refusal to praise Marshall and repudiate McCarthy became one of the low points in a nasty campaign and, coming after the Taft "Surrender" and the Nixon fund affair, it reinforced the belief among many on Morningside Heights that the General's "crusade" had little morality or integrity.[51]

In response to the McCarthy challenge, three Harvard professors, Archibald MacLeish, Arthur M. Schlesinger, Jr., and Mark DeWolfe Howe, launched a nationwide campaign on October 9 to raise funds for his defeat and Jenner's. They sent five thousand letters to faculty members at colleges and universities, and the Columbia and Harvard faculty, also enthusiastic for Stevenson, exchanged ideas and information about McCarthy's re-election campaign and the presidential race. Jenner called the campaign a smear: "These pink boys and the campus theorists of the *Harvard Crimson* are doing their best to defeat any man who stands up and fights for America." In a letter to the *Times* Schlesinger, denying a charge that he belonged to a communist front organization, wrote, "General Eisenhower watches the progress of the disease with evident contentment. How much longer does the *Times* think that the General will remain immune?" That same day the *Times* published a letter from thirty-one persons, including Columbia's Commager, Nevins, Hofstadter, Rogers, and Reinhold Niebuhr, also protesting the paper's position.[52]

The Nevins group, which now included 175 faculty and staff members, had approved Hofstadter's draft statement for the advertisement in the *Times*. They discussed several changes in the text and, when a reference to Eisenhower as a "hero of the war" was considered, Lionel Trilling noted, "A hero of war is all that we can admire him for." Gay, meanwhile, had appointed captains all over the campus to raise money for the ad, and he later recalled that they needed $4,600 and received over $6,000. This enabled them to pay for the ad and mail off-prints. The National Stevenson organization did not assist, and the only outside contributors were friends of the faculty; a great proportion of the contributions were $5 or less.

The group's official name concerned Trilling, who wanted to be absolutely accurate for the ad. The word "staff" was the pivot point and meant that Gay, as an Instructor, was on the "Staff" of Columbia, whereas "Faculty" included those with a professorial appointment. Finally, they settled on "The Volunteers for Stevenson on the Columbia University Faculties and Staff." But, as the campaign escalated at Columbia during the next week, their proper use of "staff," Gay remarked, "involved part of our political stupidity." Nevins sent a copy of the statement to the administration and expressed his regrets "about the embarrassment this is causing," but the University's Acting Head insisted, "From my point of view this is an ill-advised project which will be a source of difficulty and embarrassment to the University." In a letter to Sulzberger, Kirk added, "I am most unhappy about the proposed advertisement. . . . I have done all I could through the route of persuasion. . . . I have failed completely. . . . It is an unfortunate thing which will embarrass the University." He concluded, "We are in for it, and I for one will be delighted when November 4 arrives." On his suggestion the University's top officers agreed not to be drawn into the campus dispute or have their names publicly connected with either organization. Kirk, Gay acknowledged, "behaved himself very well."[53]

Trouble arose when Dean Ackerman, who had contributed for the ad, wanted to be on the list, and his name would appear at the top. The administration asked the group to remove his name, and Hofstadter believed that Kirk's recommendation should be honored. Paul Seabury, an Instructor in Government, conveyed the message to Ackerman, who agreed. Seabury then suggested that the Dean write a personal letter to the *Times*, supporting Stevenson. The *Times*, he added, "would be very pleased to have you do so."[54]

Ackerman sent a telegram, and it received two columns on the front-page of the *Times*, with the headline, "Dean, for Stevenson, Charges Columbia Gag; Kirk Denies It." And, not surprisingly, his newspaper connections meant that his remarks received extensive coverage. "The election of Governor Stevenson is of paramount importance to education," he asserted in a telegram to Joseph Pulitzer of the *St. Louis Post-Dispatch*, which had endorsed the Democrat. Emphasizing that "officers of the University, including myself, have been urged to remain silent," he declared, "I do not intend to remain silent as long as General Eisenhower is free and unrestricted in his use of the University's name and property for campaign purposes." Specifically, he charged that the University, by allowing Eisenhower to use 60 Morningside, was "inadvertently subsidizing" his campaign. Eisenhower's Columbia supporters "have sought by their use of powerful vehicles of public information," he continued, "to give the impression that the University community" solidly supports Eisenhower, "whereas there is tremendous support for Governor Stevenson." Being told to be silent "on political issues," the Dean concluded, "is not academic freedom." Edman promptly told Ackerman that his statement pleased "any number of people around here" and would help the forthcoming ad in the *Times*.[55]

Kirk promptly stated: "The acting administration has tried scrupulously to avoid partisanship in the election. "He added that he had suggested that "the administrative leaders of this University . . . refrain from public expression of their personal preferences." Ackerman's telegram, in fact, upset some members of the Stevenson group; Truman called it "imprudent." In a thoughtful letter on October 13 William T. De Bary, a Chinese and Japanese scholar, protested both the solicitation on campus for the Stevenson ad and the Alumni for Eisenhower, "which started this misuse of Columbia's name for political purposes." Since neither group worked through "the existing channels of political activity," the consequences of their actions "can only be to exploit the prestige of an educational institution dedicated to an impartial search for truth." But, by the time the letter appeared, it was lost in the next round of the escalating controversy.[56]

The next day, for the second morning in a row, the Columbia battle over its President's candidacy received a two-column spread on the front-page of the *Times*. The headline read, "Columbia Faculty Split by Politics; 2 Groups Back Presidential Rivals," and the article described the group supporting Eisenhower and the full-page Stevenson ad. Both groups, the *Times* reported, emphasized that they were not speaking for the University, and both asserted that they could have obtained more signatures; neither list contained the name of a top administrative official.[57]

Dean Carman, Emeritus and no longer an officer, asserted at a press conference that the statement supporting Eisenhower, and signed by thirty-one faculty and staff members, was issued in reply to the Stevenson group. Emphasizing that "General Eisenhower is unusually well qualified to provide the leadership that the country sorely needs in this distressing hour," Carman stressed the importance of change in Washington and the preservation of a two-party system, "the foundation and effective guaranty of democracy in our Republic."[58]

It was the hostility to Eisenhower, Carman bluntly stated, that drove them to escalate the battle. The mild-mannered and highly respected Dean recalled, "It got to the point where I thought it was hatred almost on Lindsay Rogers' part and there were others. . . . This atmosphere I thought ought not to go unchallenged . . . . Honest differences didn't go to this extreme. The opposition was terribly strong in certain parts of the campus . . . and it was pretty tough going around here for a person who tried to keep his integrity and be fair minded. Some of the fellows just went overboard." Meanwhile, "Steve" Saulnier, who had not had any contact with Eisenhower at Columbia, was appalled when he read the announcement of the Nevins group opposing Eisenhower, and he said to himself, "God Almighty, isn't there anybody on the University campus who will say a good word for this man?" He called Dean Young and suggested getting "a group together who would say something supportive for the man," and Eisenhower's friend surprised him by saying, "Well, why don't you call Harry Carman." He did, and Carman told him, "Well, Steve, write something, do a piece, we'll issue a statement, get people to sign it."[59]

Carman liked the draft, and they started getting signatures. "We had a hell of a time," Saulnier remembered, and one colleague looked at him as if "I had been asking him to support some criminal." Somehow, Bill Robinson had seen the statement, and the dozen or so signatures, and told Saulnier, "This is fine, I'm sure these are all very fine people and scholars but nobody will recognize them. . . . Can't you get somebody?" Carman thought he could get Lou Little, and Robinson exclaimed, "Oh, that would be great." They got a few others, as well as some "service people who were willing to sign." It was, Saulnier added, "a universal statement in that sense."[60]

When Carman heard that the Stevenson ad would be running soon in the *Times,* he told Saulnier they should release their statement, even if it had only thirty-one names. The list included, besides Carman and Saulnier, French Professor Justin O'Brien, Professor of History John Wuorinen, Law Professors Willis L. M. Reese and John Hanna, Lou Little, several professors from the Medical School, and the Director of Columbia University Press; many of the signers, they emphasized, in the past had "voted for Democratic platforms." Saulnier thought that Robinson had engaged a public relations group to promote the statement; in any event, Saulnier recalled, "I was so exhilarated because we had got to the front-page at no cost." Later,

Carman sadly commented, "Even two of my very dear friends among the younger men in the College and Graduate School couldn't believe that Harry Carman was lending his name and support to this man. They thought that there must be some mistake." They went to Margaret Carman, and she assured them that the Dean supported Eisenhower. "Some of them," he regretted a decade later, "have never forgiven me for it."[61]

The Volunteers for Stevenson on the Columbia University Faculties and Staff declared their support in a full-page ad the same day. It contained the signatures of 324 persons and their reasons for supporting the Democratic nominee. They had carefully checked the names, and Gay recalled, "I would defend at least 315 of the 324 names." Stevenson, the ad stated, gave promise of a great presidency. "He opposes Communism and McCarthyism"; he had successfully fought corruption in Illinois, whereas Nixon failed to recognize the moral issue in his "dramatic monologue insulting to the intelligence." The signers considered Eisenhower wrong on most of the crucial issues and concluded, "We regret that General Eisenhower, by leaning indiscriminately on its most undesirable elements, has thrown away his magnificent opportunity" to rehabilitate his party. The hour "is too critical . . . to entrust our destinies and our children's destinies to a soldier who has served his country well in war but has not mastered the arts of civilian statecraft."[62]

The Stevenson ad had a tremendous impact. Comments flooded the campus from universities all over the country, and copies of the ad appeared at many other institutions, including the University of Michigan and the University of California at Berkeley—occasionally the text was used in its entirety with the committee's permission. While the Stevenson leaders sought to involve the University as little as possible, the association of the advertisement and Columbia, and Eisenhower and Columbia, could not be ignored. If Eisenhower were not the President of Columbia, the ad, if there had been one, would have been easily dismissed and prominent newspapers would not have given the story widespread publicity. Yet, he was Columbia's President and, as the *Nation* observed, "Republicans can take little comfort from this landslide for Stevenson in the 'constituency' where Eisenhower has had his first experience as a civilian executive."[63]

While it is impossible to determine to what extent the advertisement's statements represented a rationalization of the opposition to Eisenhower at Columbia, the ad and its ensuing publicity drove Eisenhower supporters on campus to prepare their own advertisement. It intensified their determination to disprove the ad's impression that the Stevenson group had greater strength at Eisenhower's University. They would have agreed with Gay's recollection: "The intellectuals here are overwhelmingly Democratic or at least anti-Republican," except for the professional schools. Many of the Eisenhower supporters, moreover, understood the sentiment of colleagues that the achievements of the New Deal and Fair Deal periods might be threatened in a Republican administration dominated by a Taft and a McCarthy. A strike on campus during the spring of 1952, moreover, had received sympathetic support, and Kirk's handling of the affair generally had been resented by the faculty. A taste of bitterness remained after the strike, according to Gay, and contributed to the atmosphere that fall. The Eisenhower advocates had little quarrel with these arguments and concerns, but they resented the hostility at Columbia toward Eisenhower.[64]

Led by James Dohr and Howell Inghram, both Professors of Accounting, they published their Eisenhower advertisement, containing 714 signatures, in both the *Times* and the *New York Herald-Tribune* on October 23, one week after the Stevenson ad and several days after the *Spectator* reported that 414 of 603 faculty members in a survey supported the Democratic nominee. Robinson, learning that the Eisenhower supporters planned an ad in the *Times,* offered them a reduced rate for an ad in the *Herald-Tribune.* Dohr, who evidently gave much of the money and had important help from Inghram, remembered the Stevenson group as "a bunch of left-wingers" and questioned the purported 8:3 ratio in favor of the Democrat. "We didn't believe that and found some 700 pro-Ike names connected with Columbia University, and we said the real ratio was 2:1 for Eisenhower." Dohr reiterated the charge that the accusation Columbia did not like Eisenhower meant something in the eyes of the public—that day, in fact, the *Spectator* published a "thank you" letter from Stevenson, saying "the special circumstances lend piquancy to your endorsement." Dohr concluded, "I think they pulled a fast one. People flocked to our office as they resented the implications of the Nevins group." Edward Le Comte, who had returned to Columbia to teach in the English Department, found the Stevenson ad "in deplorable taste." In effect, it stated, "We who have experienced Eisenhower as President are against him 99 to 1." That was, he thought, "to mix up two utterly different positions," and he signed the counter-ad.[65]

For several days Peter Gay had heard rumors of an Eisenhower ad in the *Herald-Tribune,* and he purchased the early edition when it appeared on the newsstand around eight o'clock on October 22. He immediately went to Hofstadter's apartment, and "We looked at all these strange names. Some, like Carman's, were familiar, and perhaps two dozen were recognized as teachers." Hofstadter then recognized the name of the superintendent at 35 Claremont Avenue. They talked with him and, finding out that the Eisenhower group had not solicited money, they concluded that it must have come from outside the community and that many of the signers were economically dependent upon the University. Gay and Hofstadter proceeded to consult the *Columbia University Directory.* They discovered names of bookstore clerks and secretaries and decided to analyze the entire list. They found the word "staff" used loosely, in contrast to Trilling's determination for accuracy. By then it was eleven o'clock, and they went and purchased the city edition of the *Times.*

A two-column front-page story reported, "Election of Eisenhower Is Urged by 714 on the Faculty of Columbia," and Gay immediately called the *Times* and asked for a correction. The *Times,* delighted with the opportunity for a good story and a scoop on the *Herald-Tribune,* requested the names of those protesting. By this time Paul Seabury had arrived at the Hofstadters' and over the telephone Justus Buchler agreed to allow the use of his name on any statement. Gay, serving as spokesman for the four, recontacted the *Times.*

Consequently, the late city edition contained a long, overlapping article. Gay charged the Eisenhower group with "deliberate misrepresentation intended to mislead the readers of the advertisement and the article." The composition of the list, he argued, should be labeled clearly. For example, he challenged putting "dieticians, building superintendents, stenographers and students, including non-matriculated students at the School of General Studies" in a group described by the ad as "faculties and staff." Only 259 names, he added, were in the same category as the signers of the Stevenson ad. The Eisenhower people, thus, should have used the words "Columbia University Employees."[66]

Considerable bitterness developed among the Stevenson supporters on campus. Historian William E. Leuchtenburg, recalling "the battle of the ads," has written, "When we said that the people on the Ike ad did not count, we met the rejoinder that that was curiously elitist doctrine from those who claimed to be advocates of the common man." Truman emphasized that the Eisenhower names were a distinct caste from part of the University. "Custodians and superintendents of apartments were told to give their signatures or else." As enmity mounted, a story circulated that an apartment doorman, who had signed the Eisenhower ad, had had a frontal lobotomy. When Trilling saw his English Department colleague Le Comte, he hissed, "Republican!" and Edman similarly "stabbed" the younger scholar, who had been his "once-promising protégé."[67]

Soon, Edman commented, "We applaud the expression of political views by any or all members of our Columbia community, but we deplore the illicit use of their names to misrepresent the trend of faculty opinion." The Stevenson committee had checked the Eisenhower list, he asserted, and he gave the following results. Faculty or administrative officials accounted for 259 names but 455 names were in no way connected with teaching or academic functions. Of this last group, he added, students accounted for 89 names, the University employed 138, and 228 did not appear in any official *Columbia University Directory*. As Gay tersely noted, "The quality of the two advertisements was quite different." The *Spectator*, emphasizing that spokesmen for the Eisenhower group "steadfastly refuse to answer questions about the signers," asserted, "This is the second surrender of principles at Morningside; let there be no more."[68]

Two days after the Eisenhower ad, the General appeared at Baker Field for Homecoming before the Columbia-Army football game. "Whatever happens to me in the future," he assured the alumni during the pre-game celebration, "I shall never sever the last tie that binds me to this institution." When he was asked whether he favored Columbia or Army, he replied, "I'm rooting for Columbia. The cadets may express displeasure at this." He added, "But even though I played on the cadet team, this memory is not as close to me as Columbia. As long as I am allowed to stay here, I'm going to be on the Columbia side." Thirty-one thousand fans attended the game, and Eisenhower had to leave at half-time for a campaign speech in Harlem. "As he left his box he ran across the field," Bob Harron recalled, "and saluted the Army Corps and, then, turned and ran toward the 218th Street exit. This was a great moment that afternoon." He missed an exciting finish, with a touchdown pass in the last minute Columbia tied the game, 14-14, against the favored Cadets.[69]

A week later Paul Seabury called Gay and told him that Eisenhower was going to attend services at St. Paul's Chapel, and Gay decided to go. Eisenhower sat up front; Mamie, who arrived later, sat in the pew next to Gay—he was wearing a Stevenson button, and he removed it.[70]

Gay's gesture symbolized the ending of the bitterly contested activities on campus. The fervor and intensity, which badly strained friendships, had been building up for over a month and reached their peak in late October with the Eisenhower ads and the counter charges by the Stevenson group. The frustrations of the Eisenhower years at Columbia had been unleashed and received nationwide publicity. Such a level of activity, as academic work and commitments piled up during the semester, could hardly be maintained, especially as Eisenhower's election became ever more likely. And the day after the Eisenhower ad, and the day before he returned to Columbia for Homecoming, the World War II hero had pledged, "I shall go to Korea." This "electrifying announcement," Ambrose has concluded, "practically guaranteed" his election. On campus Edman and Inghram exchanged charges of "misrepresentation," but the dispute degenerated into an emotional display of numbers which had no relative meaning. The *Spectator* acknowledged that "the battle of the advertisements is now over, and happily so"; it added, though, "What is of concern are the petty and downright dishonest methods used by the Eisenhower supporters." Even a rival alumni group, formed under the chairmanship of Arthur Garfield Hays, the head of the American Civil Liberties Union, "to combat the incorrect impression that Columbia alumni unanimously support the Republican candidate," seemed to attract little attention.[71]

After the Eisenhower ad, according to Truman, the Stevenson group tried to discourage letters to the *New York Times*. "Things were getting petty enough as it was"; the *Times,* moreover, had "Reaffirmed" its choice for Eisenhower the day of the advertisement and was unlikely to change. "We have openly disagreed," the editorial declared, "with some of his positions," from his "wrongly" endorsing McCarthy to his failure "to indicate disapproval" of Nixon's fund. The editorial found no fault, however, with his effort to work with Taft and argued that he had not "surrendered" collective security and bipartisan cooperation in foreign policy. Yet, in the *Times'* newsroom, "a hotbed of Stevenson support," according to a recent history of the paper, "reporters correctly assumed" that Mrs. Sulzberger "disagreed with her husband and her own paper." *Newsweek*, indeed, claimed that the *Times'* editorial board was split and wondered whether the weight would remain "on the Eisenhower side of the scale." CBS news broadcaster Eric Sevareid, *Newsweek* added, had reported that only three of the eight members of the *Times'* editorial board supported Eisenhower.[72]

The *Times* remained firm. On November 1st Sulzberger's paper asserted in "Campaign Rumors" that there will be "no switch" in its endorsement. "No member of the editorial staff of this newspaper is ever requested—in fact he would not be permitted—to write any editorial which was not a true and faithful expression of his own opinion." Sulzberger subsequently admitted that tremendous pressure was exerted on the paper right up to the election, and he believed that a shift would have made a difference. He added that if he had been for Stevenson, he would have switched the paper's position. He remained adamant; after the election he told Gay that the *Times'* main reason had been opposition to Taft and isolationism. According to his Columbia colleague Doug Black, he kept the *Times* for Eisenhower against the will of the editorial board: they all preferred Stevenson, as did Mrs. Sulzberger, a Barnard Trustee.[73]

Eisenhower scored a tremendous personal victory in the election, and on November 15th he resigned as President of Columbia University, effective January 19, 1953. His decision to resign his position as a permanent Trustee, however, stunned many; after all, he had stated, as recently as Homecoming, that he would never sever that tie. On January 5, 1953, the Trustees elected him President and Trustee Emeritus. They also named Kirk the fourteenth President of Columbia. As Doug Black recalled, "Why go through all over again what we went through from 1945 to 1947. . . . Grayson had it made, I don't think he was any more prepared for it than Ike." The next morning Eisenhower, who was staying at 60 Morningside until he left for Washington on the 18th, walked up the steps in front of Low Memorial and in his former offices congratulated Kirk. Later, in a message to the University's 150,000 living alumni he wrote, "Serving as your President has been a high honor and a rewarding experience." He thanked those "who had worked for his election" and those "who so loyally and energetically supported Governor Stevenson."[74]

While preparing to leave Columbia Eisenhower admitted to John Krout that he had been hurt by the controversy during the campaign. "John, I can't understand why Allan Nevins was so vigorous in opposition to me." Nevins' brother, General Arthur Nevins, after all, was a very close personal friend who had worked with Eisenhower on *Crusade in Europe* and managed the Eisenhowers' farm in Gettysburg. Moreover, ironically, the historian had been at 60 Morningside "many times"—one of the few faculty members entertained there—and he and Eisenhower had enjoyed discussing history, especially the importance of military history. The General, furthermore, had attended with Nevins a luncheon which would lead to the founding of *American Heritage* a few years later. "I think he was more hurt by Allan Nevins' name than anything else," McCann recalled. "I know that it hurt him. . . . The others, he just shrugged it off." Nevins, for his part, reflected a few years later, "All my experiences with Ike were favorable." He added that he worried about what he had initiated in 1952: "Perhaps it was not in the best taste for us, but, after all, we were citizens first and faculty second."[75]

On January 16 Eisenhower said "Farewell" to Columbia, and the *Times* published on the front page a large picture of him, standing in front of Alma Mater on the steps of Low Memorial and waving to students and faculty. That noon the Institute of War and Peace Studies had given a luncheon for him at the Faculty Club, with Krout describing the University's efforts to support the project. The question, though, for a while had been whether the faculties, especially after the acrimonious campaign, would arrange a farewell reception for Eisenhower. As Carman remembered, people wondered "what would be done? Would there be any gesture one way or the other? Well, Lindsay Rogers said it would be wonderful to get up a big affair and get him there and tell him to his face how glad we were he was going, that it was a terrible mistake he was ever brought here. Well, that didn't go over."

Dean Carman added, "Columbia College, the boys, the student body, to their credit without any prompting from anybody came to me." They told him what they planned to do for a farewell from all University students in the Rotunda. They expected over a thousand students, arranged for the band to play, for cheers led by the cheerleaders and songs by the Columbia Kingsmen, and short speeches, including one by Eisenhower. The *Spectator* predicted, "All who attend—and all should attend—will have a memorable occasion to look back on." During the ceremony twelve hundred students heard Eisenhower mention campaign criticism of his earlier remarks that a person could find security in prison. "Look for opportunity rather than security," he urged. "Let minimum security rest under you as a floor for your feet. Don't ever let it build a ceiling over your head." The students presented him with a bronze replica of the Columbia Lion, and Public Relations Director Harron thought the President was "very deeply moved."[76]

Meanwhile, Professor James Angell, chairman of the Graduate Faculties Committee on Instruction, had gone to the former Dean of the College: "Well, we've decided something has to be done," and a faculty reception was planned for Eisenhower in Mcmillin Theater after the ceremony in the Rotunda. "But," Angell added, "I can't find a damn person to do it." Carman asked, "What about yourself?" and received a quick reply: "Nope, I won't, I won't." "God knows," Carman emphasized, "my basic interest was not in the Graduate Schools," though he had regularly taught a graduate course; nonetheless, the introduction for Eisenhower was left for him to deliver. "One of the hardest things I ever had to do. I knew that my colleagues were saying 'How in hell can Harry Carman stand up there and say those things.'" The distinguished Mark Van Doren, for example, had said about the campaign and its results, "I felt as if God had gone to sleep." Henry Graff, who had signed the Stevenson ad, helped his colleague and friend prepare the introduction and "persuaded him not to talk about the Eisenhower team, an irritant to the Stevenson supporter."[77]

Eisenhower, himself, however, addressed the campaign controversy on Morningside Heights. "My mind went back to those people among you who had the terrible decision to make, who didn't want me as President of the United States but were faced with the alternative of bringing me back as President of Columbia. The reason I bring this up," he told the assembled faculties, "is to pay my respects to those individuals." Emphasizing his support for "the rights and freedom of the individual and his right to express his honest conviction, no matter what it may be," he concluded, "If that individual happens to be wise enough to entertain many justifiable doubts as to my capacity for occupying some of these major positions, I should say there is on my part a temptation to respect him very highly."[78]

"Eisenhower went out of the way after the campaign to thank both sides," Nevins recalled. "He showed a great magnanimity" that afternoon. "The atmosphere was a warm and good one," Harron observed, while Carman thought "It was an excellent atmosphere. It was wonderful—the hard part was before." That evening Eisenhower, in his last function at Columbia, attended a testimonial dinner for Young B. Smith, who had resigned as Dean of the Law School. Smith had worked hard for Eisenhower during the campaign and, while collecting money at the last minute for the Eisenhower ad, had suffered a heart attack. Two thousand dinner guests heard Eisenhower pay tribute to the Dean's advice and wise counsel during his Presidency of Columbia, thus bringing his career at Columbia to an end.[79] Four days later Dwight D. Eisenhower became the thirty-fourth President of the United States.

Notes

1. *New York Times,* January 7, 1952.
2. William E. Robinson, Memorandum, December 29, 1951, Robinson MSS., Dwight D. Eisenhower Library (DDEL), Abilene, Ks.; Eisenhower to Robinson, October 31, 1951, *The Papers of Dwight David Eisenhower, NATO and the Campaign of 1952* , ed. Louis Galambos (Baltimore, Md., 1989), XII, 670-73 (*PDDE*); Stephen E. Ambrose, *Eisenhower: Soldier, General of the Army, President-Elect, 1890-1952* (New York, 1983), p. 518.
3. Eisenhower to Clay, December 27, 1951, *PDDE,* XII, 817-18; Lucius D. Clay, Oral History Interview, 1967, Columbia Oral History Project (COHP); Jean Edward Smith, *Lucius D. Clay: An American Life* (New York, 1990), pp. 589-90. Robinson had talked with Lodge before the press conference and had thought that the Senator could handle the questions. Robinson to Eisenhower, January 15, 1952, Robinson MSS., DDEL.
4. *Columbia Spectator,* January 8, 1952; *New York Times,* January 8, 1952; Editorial, "Straight to Victory," *New York Herald-Tribune,* January 8, 1952.
5. Editorial, "Politician Ike," *Columbia Spectator,* January 8, 1952; Editorial, "Eisenhower," *New York Times,* January 7, 1952; Susan E. Tifft and Alex S. Jones, *The Trust: The Private and Powerful Family Behind the New York Times* (Boston, 1999), p. 260.
6. For example, see Ambrose, *Eisenhower,* Chapters 25-27; Herbert S. Parmet, *Eisenhower and the American Crusades* (New York, 1972), Chapters 10-18; John Robert Greene, *The Crusade: The Presidential Election of 1952* (Lanham, Md., 1985); and Barton J. Bernstein, "Election of 1952," *The Coming to Power: Critical Presidential Elections in American History,* ed. Arthur M. Schlesinger, Jr. (New York, 1971), pp. 385-436.
7. Eisenhower, *Diary,* October 18, 1951, *PDDE,* XII, 650-52; Eisenhower to Edward Bermingham and to Clifford Roberts, November 1, 1951, and to K. S. Adams, November 20, 1951 and January 15, 1952, Eisenhower MSS. DDEL; *Columbia Spectator,* December 13, 1951; Eisenhower to Young, November 10 and November 20, 1951, and Young to Eisenhower, January 11, 1952, "The American Assembly," 1950-59: General and Administrative Papers, vol. I, American Assembly, Columbia University (AACU).
8. Robinson, "Stray Notes on pre-nomination 1951-52," Robinson MSS., DDEL.
9. Editorial, "The Times and the Man," *New York Herald-Tribune,* October 25, 1951; Eisenhower to Robinson, October 31 and October 31, 1951, *PDDE,* XII, 669-73.

10. Fn. #3, *PDDE,* XII, 675; McCann gave the book's royalties to The Defiance College scholarship fund. Kevin McCann, *Man from Abilene: Dwight David Eisenhower, A Story of Leadership* (New York, 1952), pp. 7-8.

11. Eisenhower to Roberts, November 8, 1951, *PDDE,* XII, 690-93; Milton Eisenhower to Eisenhower, October 20, 1951, Eisenhower MSS., DDEL.

12. Ibid.; Dwight D. Eisenhower, *The White House Years: Mandate for Change, 1953-1956* (New York, 1963), pp. 13-14; Dwight D. Eisenhower, *At Ease: Stories I Tell to Friends* (New York, 1967), pp. 371-72; Ambrose, *Eisenhower,* pp. 498-99; Eisenhower, *Diary,* June 14, 1951, *PDDE,* XII, 354-55.

13. Eisenhower to Robinson, November 8, 1951, and to Roberts, November 8 and 24, 1951, *PDDE,* XII, 690-93, 729-30.

14. *New York Times,* November 8 and 9, 1951; Arthur Krock, *Memoirs: Sixty Years on the Firing Line* (New York, 1968), pp. 267-69; Editorial, "Ike for President," *Columbia Spectator,* November 14, 1951. Eisenhower promptly wrote Sulzberger: "The story is completely without foundation," but he did not send the letter. November 10, 1951, *PDDE,* XII, 701. On April 2, 1958, Krock wrote the author that he had "an affidavit from him which not only supports what I wrote but amplifies it."

15. Eisenhower to Roberts, December 8, 1951, and *Diary,* December 11, 1951, *PDDE,* XII, 763-65, 772-73.

16. Ellis D. Slater "Diary," December 20 1951, *The Ike I Knew,* (n.p., 1980), p. 14

17. Dwight D. Eisenhower, *The White House Years: Mandate for Change, 1953-56* (New York, 1963), p. 19; Eisenhower to Truman, January 1, 1952, *PDDE,* XII, 830-31.

18. Robinson, Memorandum, December 29, 1951, Robinson MSS., DDEL; Clifford Roberts, interview, October 13, 1968, COHP; David Owen, *The Making of the Masters: Clifford Roberts, Augusta National, and Golf's Most Prestigious Tournament* (New York, 1999), p. 174.

19. Eisenhower to Truman, January 1, 1952, and to Sulzberger, December 29, 1951, *PDDE,* XII, 830-31, 825-26.

20. Eisenhower to Robinson, January 19, 1952, to Clay, February 9, 1952, to Young, February 11, 1952, and *Diary,* January 22, February 11, and 12, 1952, *PDDE,* XII, 890-92, 896-902, 962-65, 970-72; Jacqueline Cochran, Oral History Interview, 1969, COHP.

21. Eisenhower to Clay, February 20, 1952, to Roberts, February 1, 1952, and to Robinson, February 9, 1952, *PDDE,* pp. 997-1000, 940-42, 961; Roberts, interview, December 11, 1968, COHP; Kevin McCann, Oral History Interview, 1966, ibid.

22. Robinson to Eisenhower, March 3, 1952, and Robinson, "How the Paperback— 'The Eisenhower Creed' came to be Published," October 25, 1965, Robinson MSS., DDEL; Douglas Black to Eisenhower, March 10, 1952, DDEL. Robinson soon heard that Eisenhower was "a bit angry at this unauthorized publication of your quotes." He wrote: "I was always fearful that you would be very angry with me for having done this without your permission. But by this time we'd kind of gotten accustomed to doing things without your permission." Ibid.

23. Eisenhower to Adams, tel., March 12, 1952, *PDDE,* XIII, 1059-60; *New York Times,* March 12, 1952; Robinson to Eisenhower, March 14, 1952, Robinson MSS., DDEL; Eisenhower to Young, March 15, 1952, DDEL. When the second American Assembly met in May, many thought that Eisenhower would return dramatically from Europe just for the conference. Raymond J. Saulnier, personal interview, June 13, 1991, New York, N. Y.

24. Bradshaw Mintener, Oral History Interview, August 5, 1968, COHP; Eisenhower to Mintener, January 21, 1952, *PDDE,* XIII, 894-96.

25. Mintener, Interview, August 5, 1968, COHP; *Minneapolis Morning Tribune,* March 14, 1952; Greene, *Crusade,* pp. 82-83.

26. *Minneapolis Morning Tribune,* March 19, 20 and 21, 1950; Editorial, "Eisenhower in the Primary: An Amazing Vote," ibid.; Eisenhower to Mintener, March 20, 1952, *PDDE,* XIII, 1097; *New York Times,* March 21, 1952; Greene, *Crusade,* p. 84.

27. *New York Times,* March 21, 1952; Eisenhower, *Mandate for Change,* p. 22; Slater, *The Ike I Knew,* p. 21.

28. Alonzo Hamby, *Man of the People: A Life of Harry S. Truman* (New York, 1995), p. 600; Eisenhower to Truman, April 2, and to Roberts April 1 and 4, 1952, *PDDE,* XIII, 1154-56, 1150-51, 1163-64; *New York Times,* April 13, 1952.

29. Frederick Coykendall to Eisenhower, March 24, 1952, Central Archives, Columbia University (CACU); Roberts, interview, August 3, 1969, COHP.

30. H. J. Porter, Oral History Interview, 1969, COHP. Mrs. Hobby's husband was a former Governor of Texas and had been president of the newspaper since 1924.

31. *Houston Post,* May 1, 2, and 3, 1952; *Dallas Morning News,* May 2, 3, 1952; Parmet, *Eisenhower,* p. 76.

32. *Houston Post,* May 4-7 and May 26-28, 1952; Parmet, *Eisenhower,* pp. 76-77; Greene, *Crusade,* pp. 92-93.

33. *Houston Post,* May 28-30 and June 22-23, 1952; Parmet, *Eisenhower,* p. 77; Greene, *Crusade,* pp. 93-94. See also *Dallas Morning News,* May 28-29 and June 22-23, 1952; *Denver Post,* June 22, 1952.

34. Parmet, *Eisenhower,* pp. 70-71, 73-74; Albert C. Jacobs to author, March 10, 1958.

35. Roberts, interview, August 3, 1969, COHP; James T. Patterson, *Mr. Republican: A Biography of Robert A. Taft* (Boston, 1972), p. 542; Greene, *Crusade,* pp. 94, 114-15; Parmet, *Eisenhower,* pp. 83-101; Ambrose, *Eisenhower,* pp. 539-41. Taft, according to Patterson, in failing to disavow his supporters' tactics, "lent himself to one of the more clumsy grabs for delegates in recent American history." *Mr. Republican,* p. 543.

36. "Chronology," *PDDE,* XIII, 1609-10; Roberts, interview, August 3, 1969, COHP.

37. Peter Gay, personal interview, March 24, 1958, New York, N. Y.;*New York Times,* September 13, 1952; Parmet, *Eisenhower,* pp. 128-30; Patterson, *Mr. Republican,* pp. 577-78. Yet Eisenhower, Ambrose has concluded, was "the real winner," since it helped "with the Old Guard more than it hurt with the independents." Ambrose, *Eisenhower,* pp. 552-53.

38. Saulnier, interview, June 13, 1991.

39. *New York Times,* September 13, 1952; Gay, interview, March 24, 1958; David Truman, personal interview, February 4, 1958, New York, N.Y.

40. Arthur Hays Sulzberger to Eisenhower, May 13, August 18 and 28, 1952, Eisenhower MSS., DDEL; Editorials, "Loyalty in Government" and "McCarthy as a Symbol," *New York Times,* August 18 and 24, 1952.

41. *Columbia Spectator,* September 26, 1952; Allan Nevins, personal interview, March 14, 1958, New York, N.Y.; Joseph Campbell, personal interview, March 11, 1958, Washington, D.C.

42. *Columbia Spectator,* October 2, 1952; Gay, interview, March 24, 1958; *New York Times,* October 2, 1952. A newcomer to the faculty, historian William E. Leuchtenburg, has recalled "Nevins saying that Stevenson was the greatest figure since Wilson, a remark that led me to wonder what he thought of FDR." Leuchtenburg to author, March 15, 1993.

43. *Columbia Spectator,* October 3, and editorials, "The Great Disenchantment," October 1, and "Why Stevenson?" October 2, 1952; Grayson Kirk, statement, October 2, 1952, CACU; *New York Times,* October 3, 1952.

44. *Columbia Spectator,* October 3, 1952; *New York Times,* October 2, 1952; Eisenhower to Carman, September 18, 1952, *PDDE,* XIII, 1355-56.

45. Truman, interview, February 4, 1958; "Mr. President of Columbia University," a

brochure prepared by the National Committee of Columbia Alumni for Eisenhower (New York, 1952).

46. *New York Times,* October 6, 1952; *Columbia Spectator,* October 6, 1952.
47. Robert Harron to Kirk, October 6, 1952, CACU.
48. *New York Times,* October 8, 1952; *Columbia Spectator,* October 8 and 9, 1952.
49. Ibid., October 10 and 15, and Editorial, "It Won't Work," October 10, 1952.
50. Tifft and Jones, *The Trust,* p. 261; Ambrose, *Eisenhower,* pp. 563-66; David M. Oshinsky, *A Conspiracy So Immense: The World of Joe McCarthy* (New York, 1983), pp. 234-38. McCann, who overheard the General's Peoria conversation with McCarthy, recalled that "Eisenhower just tore the hide off Joe McCarthy. . . . It was the only time I heard him use profane language." McCann, interview, July 25, 1972.
51. Editorial, "An Unhappy Day," *New York Times,* October 4, 1952; Eisenhower to Kenneth Johnson, October 16, 1952, *PDDE,* XIII, 1384-87. John A. Krout, personal interview, July 22, 1963, New York, N.Y. For Eisenhower's defense two days later, see Eisenhower to Harold Stassen, October 5, 1952, *PDDE.,* XIII, 1372-74.
52. *New York Times,* October 10 and 11, 1952; Henry F. Graff, personal interview, January 30, 1958, New York, N.Y.; David B. Truman, personal interview, February 4, 1958, New York, N.Y. On Sunday, October 12, Eisenhower was in Denver, taking a break from the campaign, and that morning he asked Jacobs if he would spend the entire afternoon driving around the Colorado countryside. Jacobs, unfortunately, left no notes, except to write: "I have never had a closer heart-to-heart talk with him. Around six o'clock he dropped me at our home." Besides the campaign, they undoubtedly discussed Columbia and Jacobs' decision to inform the University of Denver Trustees the next day that he had accepted the Presidency of Trinity College in Hartford, Connecticut. In the fall of 1954 Eisenhower would travel to Trinity for a Special Convocation and honorary degree. Jacobs, "Memoirs," 1974, 1974; Jacobs, Oral History Interview, 1968, COHP.
53. Gay, interview, March 24, 1958; *Columbia Spectator,* October 9, 1952; Nevins to John Krout, October 11, 1952, and Kirk to Nevins, October 13, and to Sulzberger, October 14, 1952, CACU; Krout, interview, January 30, 1958, and July 22, 1963.
54. "Presidential Campaign, 1952," Memorandum, October 13, 1952, Carl W. Ackerman MSS., Library of Congress (LC).
55. *New York Times,* October 15, 1952; Gay, interview, March 24, 1958; "Presidential Campaign, 1952," telephone message, October 15, 1952, Ackerman MSS., LC.
56. Kirk, statement, October 14, 1952, CACU; Truman, interview, February 4, 1958; *New York Times,* October 17, 1952.
57. *New York Times,* October 16, 1952; *Columbia Spectator,* October 16, 1952.
58. Ibid.
59. Carman, interview, December 1, 1961; Raymond J. Saulnier, personal interview, June 13, 1991, New York, N.Y.
60. Ibid.
61. Saulnier, interview, June 13, 1991; Carman, interview, December 1, 1961; *New York Times,* October 16, 1952; *Columbia Spectator,* October 16, 1952.
62. *New York Times,* October 16, 1952; *Columbia Spectator,* October 16, 1952.
63. Truman, interview, February 4, 1958; Graff, interview, January 30, 1958; Gay, interview, March 24, 1958; *Nation,* October 25, 1952.
64. Harry J. Carman, personal interview, December 1, 1961, New York, N.Y.; Gay, interview, March 24, 1958; Truman, interview, February 4, 1958, New York, N.Y.; Nevins, interview, March 14, 1958.
65. *New York Times,* October 23, 1952; *New York Herald-Tribune,* October 23, 1952. According to the *Columbia Spectator,* the ads cost $4,500 and $3,500, respectively.

October 23, 1952. James Dohr, personal interview, February 24, 1958, New York, N.Y.; Carman, interview, December 1, 1961; Edward Le Comte, "Dinner With Butler and Eisenhower: A Columbia Memoir," *Commentary,* January, 1986, p. 62.

66. Gay, interview, March 24, 1958; *New York Times,* October 23, 1952.
67. Leuchtenburg to author, March 15, 1993; Truman, interview, February 4, 1958; Le Comte, "Dinner With Butler and Eisenhower," *Commentary,* January , 1986, p. 62.
68. *Columbia Spectator,* October 30, and editorial, "What's in a Number?" October 29, 1952; Gay, interview, March 24, 1958.
69. *Columbia Spectator,* October 27, 1952; Robert Harron, personal interview, December 1, 1961, New York, N.Y.
70. Gay, "Conversation," April 8, 1999, Middlebury, Vt.
71. *New York Times,* November 2 and 3, 1952; Ambrose, *Eisenhower,* pp. 569; *Columbia Spectator*, October 27, and editorial, "What's in a Number?" October 29, 1952.
72. Truman, interview, February 4, 1958; Editorial, "A Choice Reaffirmed," *New York Times,* October 23, 1952; Tifft and Jones, *The Trust,* p. 262; *Newsweek,* October 27, 1952.
73. Editorial, "Campaign Rumors," *New York Times,* November 1, 1952; Arthur H. Sulzberger, personal interview, April March 27, 1958, New York, N.Y.; Gay, "Conversation," April 8, 1999; Douglas Black, personal interview, June 6, 1973, New York, N.Y.
74. Eisenhower to Coykendall, November 15, 1952, *PDDE,* XIII, 1432-33; *Columbia Spectator,* November 18, 1952 and January 6, 7, and 9, 1953; Black, interview, June 6, 1973; *New York Times,* January 11, 1953. Harron had called Eisenhower's office and suggested that he congratulate Kirk. Harron, interview, February 5, 1965.
75. Krout, interview, July 22, 1963; Allan Nevins, personal interview, March 14, 1958, New York, N.Y.; McCann, interview, July 25, 1972.
76. Carman, interview, December 1, 1961; *Columbia Spectator,* January 13, and editorial, "Ike's Last Stand," January 13, 1953; Robert C. Harron, personal interview, December 1, 1961, New York, N.Y.
77. Carman, interview, December 1, 1961; Le Comte, "Dinner With Butler and Eisenhower," *Commentary,* January, 1986, p. 62; Graff, interview, June 13, 1991.
78. Eisenhower, "Farewell Speech," McMillin Theater, January 16, 1953, Eisenhower Files, Columbiana, Columbia University. It was widely noted that Mamie Eisenhower did not attend either ceremony.
79. Nevins, interview, March 14, 1958; Harron, interview, December 1, 1961; Carman, interview, December 1, 1961; *New York Times,* January 17, 1953.

9

Eisenhower and Columbia

Supervising the management of a vast endowment that included one of
the largest real estate empires in New York; administering an economic
enterprise that employed more maintenance people, to mention just
one category, than most colleges had students; satisfying the demand
for speeches, alumni appearances, ceremonial functions; correcting an
appalling deficit that threatened academic standards, salary scales, and
Columbia's traditional objective of excellence—all these, as ravenous
of energy as they were of time, fast became a moat against communica-
tion with the young men and women.

—Dwight D. Eisenhower,
At Ease (1967)

His great industry led him to succeed in his announced goal to make
'more and more people conscious of Columbia.'

—*Columbia Spectator,*
December 20, 1950

General Eisenhower arrived at Columbia University in the spring
of 1948, and the large, complex urban institution represented the
polar opposite from his preference, as he later wrote, for "a small
school in a rural setting." He remembered that General Lee had become a college president after the Civil War and enjoyed living among
students. "In such a place, where friendly ties with students and faculty could easily be developed," General Eisenhower thought he
could "share with them the lessons in hindsight from a reasonably
full life." As Henry Wriston, a university president for years, recalled,
Trustee Watson "persuaded him that at Columbia he could see lots
of students." There were, Wriston continued, "some misapprehensions, both on his part and on [Watson's and Parkinson's]. I know
this story because Mr. Eisenhower told it to me, and also Thomas J.
Watson, Sr., told it to me, and the two dovetailed exactly. . . . They
decided they wanted Eisenhower . . . and they did what we used to

call in fraternity language 'hot box him.'" And, according to Wriston, he found "a wall of deans between him and the students, except for special occasions," and discovered that the Trustees wanted him to raise money. "He remarked to me rather plaintively one day, 'I have never been pushed around so much since I was a shavetail.'"[1]

Thus began Eisenhower's controversial Presidency of Columbia. The General had lived in Abilene, Panama, Washington, Manila, London, and Paris, and was one of the most famous men in the world—few had seen as much of the world and had known as many of its leaders. He had been, however, a career army officer and did not have the normal qualifications for the presidency of a major university when he arrived in the greatest city in the world. Yet, as Kevin McCann wrote, "No man as alert and as mentally sharp as he could have lived as long as he in those places without developing a cosmopolitan frame of reference that, I think, is also essential for the direction of a great university." No person with Eisenhower's experience, regardless of what happened during his years at Columbia, could be called a "hayseed," as he was in 1969 by Columbia's distinguished sociologist Robert Merton.[2]

To Columbia, a University which had been static for at least the last ten to fifteen years under the ailing Presidency of Nicholas Murray Butler, Eisenhower brought his charisma, confidence, and proven leadership ability. While he perhaps had seen himself after World War II relaxing and writing at a small liberal arts college, his enormous energy and his ambition, as well as his commitment to "democratic citizenship" and strengthening institutions to serve American values, infused his activities at Columbia. Indeed, his views would not have found a similar outlet at a small college; Columbia offered him a forum and widespread publicity for his beliefs, and he was able to propound on his mission. While he had other opportunities, some with enormous economic benefits, he saw in the field of education an opportunity to address concerns, which had come out of World War II, and to articulate his belief in the American system.

His speeches, from his Installation Address to the Inaugural Silver Lecture, received front-page attention and brought renewed interest in Columbia. Three talks, extemporaneous and often overlooked, conveyed his commitment and explained why he had accepted the Columbia Presidency. Throughout the war soldiers had asked him why were they fighting and about Nazism and Hitler; moreover, he had been shocked about the shortage in fighting personnel and the enormous waste of manpower. At the Jewish Theological Seminary, two weeks before his Installation, he declared that "the ancient Jewish leaders" have given us "inalienable rights and none can take them away," as the Nazi dictators had wanted people to believe. "These rights can never be destroyed" and, he concluded, "all the free world is the seed of Abraham, Moses, and the ancient kings." At Columbia College's First Forum on Democracy on February 12, 1949—he had flown in from the Pentagon that morning—he talked about the meaning of Lincoln's birthday. Worrying about "a kind of dictatorship that can come about through a creeping paralysis of thought" in America, he declared "I believe it is things such as this, that we must watch today if we are going to be true to the standards that Lincoln gave to all of us." Then, at Barnard College's opening convocation in 1949 he asserted that schools in Germany before World War II had bred "fanatical devotion to wickedness," and he hoped that "fine privately endowed institutions" would "establish the standards" so that "we are in no danger of any such thing." These speeches did not provide intellectual and scholastic leadership for the faculty of a prominent university, but they expressed values which a democratic society and institutions of learning should hold dear.

Eisenhower repeatedly stressed the "mission of America," and he firmly believed that Columbia had a responsibility to further that mission. In writing to Arthur Sulzberger, Chairman of the University's Bicentennial Committee, he emphasized that the concepts "we are dealing with in our Bicentennial, namely, freedom and free access to knowledge," were "basic to the American system."[3] He had no doubt that the programs he proposed would contribute to society and the strengthening of American values and institutions and, moreover, that they would bring a greater awareness of Columbia. The Citizenship Education Program, for him, had a constructive impact on American youth and promoted his concept of "democratic citizenship." The Institute of War and Peace came from his hatred of war and it soon began producing important research studies. The Conservation of Human Resources, now the Eisenhower Center for the Conservation of Human Resources, continues its series of significant publications under the leadership of Eli Ginzberg. The American Assembly, to which he devoted considerable attention and energy, became an important think tank which, by definition, would not produce immediate results. It, too, continues, and it conducts major conferences regularly at Arden House. These projects expressed for him his view on Columbia's mission. He saw the University's role as providing service and general education, not the training of scholars and professionals.

His views were not shared by academics at the elite Eastern universities and, certainly, not by most of the professors in the liberal arts at Columbia College and the University's Graduate Faculties. They did not see his favorite projects contributing to the academic life of Columbia. "The faculty were not there to propagandize the American way of life," according to Steve Saulnier, "they were there to do studies . . . and there were a lot of people in the University who felt there were other ways to organize the world, along lines other than we were following." One professor told biographer John Gunther in 1951, "As a general he was accustomed to obedience and unity. He may not have understood that the essence of a university is intellectual warfare. He needed far greater knowledge of the intellectual life of the community." Eisenhower, the professor added, never was a leader at Columbia. He had, of course, been called back to Washington by President Truman soon after his arrival and, two months later, he become ill; moreover, his subsequent trips on behalf of the American Assembly made him, in the minds of some, an absentee President. "The Columbia faculty," a commentator recently observed, "became infamous—they still are infamous—for mocking, not his absences nor his dislike for fund-raising, but rather his intellectual unsuitability for the job." There was, Peter Gay acknowledged, "considerable anti-Eisenhower sentiment."[4]

Eisenhower's passion for playing bridge and golf with the "gang" and for painting, as well as stories about his lack of interest in academic affairs and his reading habits, added to the impression that Columbia's President was unintellectual and, moreover, uninterested in the pursuits of the University. Perhaps because he lacked academic credentials, he remained uncomfortable with faculty groups. Gunther's comment, moreover, resonated: "The coarse joke was heard, when he became president of Columbia, that he was the first president in the history of that institution who had never read a book." Grayson Kirk reinforced that belief when he recalled that in the afternoon he would find Eisenhower "reading a Western novel at his clean desk." Eisenhower, Ambrose has emphasized, "could not 'lose' himself in a book, a concert, or a masterpiece, but he did 'lose' himself when he was on a trout stream, painting, playing golf or bridge."[5]

An afternoon of golf at Deepdale or Blind Brook, or a vacation at Augusta National, became even more important for him after his illness in 1949, and after golf he was ready for an evening of bridge. A few years later in the White House, a bridge hand Eisenhower played with Oswald Jacoby, one of the game's greatest players, against Chief Justice Fred Vinson and Air Force Secretary Harold Talbott, was the only one to be published in *Time,* at least until the 1980s. His non-academic hobbies, as well as his failure to preside over University Council Meetings and his initial reluctance to attend the celebrations honoring John Dewey, for example, were widely noted on campus and weakened his leadership of the University.[6]

These opinions about Eisenhower and Columbia prompted journalist Rovere to emphasize at the time the "intense hostility" toward the President "on the part of the majority of both faculty and student body." Two decades after Eisenhower's election as President of the United States, Herbert Parmet concluded, "Eisenhower and the super-intellectual climate of Columbia were not compatible." Recently, Geoffrey Perret declared, "The faculty's scorn was based not so much on what it saw of Eisenhower as what it heard" and, similarly, "Eisenhower never really knew what was happening at Columbia." *New York Times* correspondent Max Frankel, looking back fifty years to his days at the *Columbia Spectator,* has recalled, "Like General of the Army Dwight D. Eisenhower . . . I picked Columbia for essentially unworthy reasons. And like Ike, I exploited the place shamelessly."[7]

Not surprisingly, writers and historians have ignored or forgotten that Eisenhower and Columbia had experienced a dynamic relationship during his first months as President. With a burst of activity, he changed the atmosphere on campus. He became an eloquent spokesman for Columbia University in New York and across the nation. The University entered an exciting era with the impressive Installation festivities, some 35,000 persons flocking to see him at Baker Field for Homecoming and subsequent football games, the publication of his widely hailed wartime memoirs, *Crusade in Europe,* and his extemporaneous talks on Morningside Heights which impressed faculty and students. At the annual History Department dinner that fall Eisenhower, provoked by comments about Churchill's "soft underbelly of Europe" proposal, gave "with not a single hesitation a superb lecture" on the history of military campaigns in the Balkans, Jacques Barzun recalled fifty years later: "It was a stunning performance, and from a man reputed to be without learning or readiness of speech. No one who heard him ever forgot it."[8] Eisenhower's presence invigorated the University, and Columbia benefited from his immense popularity. Nothing similar had happened on the Morningside Heights campus since the onset of the Great Depression.

Eisenhower quickly acknowledged the University's pressing problems. Soon after his arrival he told College alumni that the University needed money and asked "Why should $170,000,000 scare us?" At a stag dinner for Trustees at 60 Morningside Drive he discussed the importance of a development program and emphasized the necessity of reorganizing the administration. He then asked Provost Jacobs, before leaving for his summer vacation, to have a reorganization proposal ready for the Trustees upon his return. Eisenhower had found in Jacobs, his chief of staff, the person with whom he could work closely and confidently, and he believed that he could proceed with a decentralized plan. His hectic and demanding schedule that fall, as well as his willingness to accept non-Columbia engagements, emphasized further the need for action strengthening the structure of the administration; then, during November he learned that he probably would be called back to military duty to advise the Secretary of Defense at the Pentagon for a period of some weeks.

It was at this time that he wrote the Trustees, suggesting that they name him, in effect, Chancellor, and name Provost Jacobs the President. With his administrative skills and staff experience, Eisenhower may have sensed, after only a few months at Columbia, the best way to define his role at the University. Such a proposal, ironically, would have recognized by University Statute the unofficial arrangement that Watson and Parkinson had offered the General in 1947. They had told him he would not have to worry about "curriculum, or faculty, or any of that sort of thing." Furthermore, Watson then told Jacobs that he had the responsibility for the internal administration of the University. But, when the press broke the news in early December that Eisenhower would go to Washington for two or three months in early 1949, the Trustees had not yet acted and appeared not to know what to do. A change in the General's title, suddenly announced under circumstances of his departure for an indefinite period, might convey the impression that the General would not return to Columbia; once again, it appeared better to the Trustees to do nothing than send an unsettling message. Columbia's spokesman denied that even an official "leave" was necessary.

On January 20 Eisenhower departed from Columbia in time for President Truman's Inauguration, and he still planned to spend a few days a week in New York. By early February, however, the controversy over the defense budget and the intense inter-service rivalry precluded him from keeping even his reduced commitments at Columbia. He and the Trustees decided that the Provost should be recognized, according to statute, as Eisenhower's "'alter ego' and successor" during the General's absences. Accordingly, in March the Trustees adopted a reorganization proposal. It decentralized the administration by creating four vice presidents (Education, Development, Business Affairs, and Medical School), who reported to the Provost; yet, as long as President Eisenhower was absent, the Provost had to assume presidential responsibilities as well his own. And, no sooner than the statutes had been approved, and while the University's budget crisis continued with little successful fund-raising by the Development Office, Eisenhower suffered a serious illness in mid-March and did not return to New York until mid-May. A few weeks later Jacobs resigned, thereby disrupting the effective administrative arrangement which had evolved during Eisenhower's first academic year.

During his first weeks back on Morningside Heights Eisenhower was determined to protect his schedule. His illness had finally forced him to admit, as Clarence Lasby has written, "that he had been careless in exceeding his limits."[9] He decided to sever his consulting trips to the Pentagon; although Secretary Johnson wanted him to serve as Chairman of the Joint Chiefs of Staff, their differences over the defense budget were too great. In July he left for an extended vacation in Colorado, and he gave Jacobs the responsibility of recommending four or five major appointments, including his successor as Provost. Eisenhower also had on his mind a major speech he had agreed to deliver before the American Bar Association over Labor Day weekend. That speech, known by his "middle of the road" phrase, received nationwide publicity and revived suspicions that he was interested in presidential politics. (The subtitle for his published papers for his first term in the White House would be *The Presidency: The Middle Way.*)

When Eisenhower returned from Colorado in mid-September, 1949, the atmosphere on campus and the framework of his presidency had changed drastically from the previous fall. The tremendous sense of excitement and anticipation had vanished from throughout the campus. He had been away most of the year, and that limited his opportunity to provide leadership. Moreover, he soon discovered, as Eli Ginzberg has emphasized, that he did not have the same chief of staff association with the new Provost, Grayson Kirk. The economist added that on more than one occasion, once Eisenhower "made the wrong selection, he was very inept in getting out of it." Yet, Ginzberg continued, Kirk did "more and more of the paper stuff," permitting Eisenhower to withdraw for "his off campus" projects. Eisenhower, indeed, may have been relieved that he did not have a Provost who insisted on his involvement in day-to-day matters and academic activities. Kirk, for his part, concluded that Eisenhower was not "particularly comfortable in his position" as President. "While I saw a great deal of him," Kirk recalled, "he had been too long in the military to have lost a feeling of hierarchy when he came to Columbia. Our relationship was hardly on a basis of intimacy, shall we say."[10]

Ironically, perhaps the major weakness of his Presidency of Columbia was in the area of his greatest strength. During World War II, he had "led one of the most complex endeavors in human history: the invasion of France and the campaign in Europe that culminated with the defeat of Nazi Germany" and, Fred Greenstein recently added, "No other chief executive has entered the White House with his organizational experience, and none has put comparable effort into structuring his presidency." Yet once his initial reorganization plan at Columbia unraveled, he did not carefully seek to rework it. And, although Greenstein asserted that "Eisenhower gave careful thought to finding the right incumbents for the right roles," he was unable to do that in the academic community and restructure his administration at Columbia.[11]

That fall, consequently, saw the convergence in Eisenhower's mind of two transformative conclusions. First came the realization that he had a different working relationship with the Provost and, second, was his growing conviction that he had to follow new paths in order to fulfill his goals for Columbia. He had proclaimed that the University had the responsibility to educate better citizens; he discovered, however, that the academic community, especially the graduate and professional schools, did not share his vision for Columbia. "Eisenhower turned to the American Assembly," according to Kirk, "after he realized that the University simply could not be made to concentrate upon citizenship training as he had hoped, and rather naively thought, it could." With his ardent sense of mission, Eisenhower pursued his "hopes and dreams" for Columbia rather independently and, in the process, he showed less and less interest and involvement in administrative and academic details. Eisenhower, after all, had informed Parkinson, when he accepted the Presidency, that his internal leadership would be along only "broad and liberal lines," and that he would promote "basic concepts of education in a democracy." The General now committed himself, increasingly, to building new vehicles for his crusade. "The chief responsibility of our educational institutions," he asserted, "is to establish a sharper understanding of the American system, a sharper appreciation of its values and a more intense devotion to its fundamental purposes," and he saw Columbia as a great University capable of advancing the cause of "democratic citizenship."[12]

Eisenhower elaborated on his ideas and plans for Columbia in a number of prominent speeches throughout the academic year. He specifically outlined what he saw as Columbia's purpose for "the good of humanity" in the Inaugural Silver Lecture on peace. He concentrated on his own proposals, from the fall of 1949 until his departure for NATO. These projects, whether the American Assembly or the Institute for War and Peace, were not integral to Columbia's academic programs and purpose. In this respect, Jacobs suggested, "he never envisaged what Columbia was" and, as Lionel Trilling recalled, "I began to sense that he was nowhere in relation to the University." His close friend, Trustee and publisher Douglas Black added that Eisenhower "never had the feeling or understanding of Columbia." As Kirk emphasized, by not attending important academic events, such as the University Council meetings, Eisenhower "destroyed his leadership with the faculty." Thus, while his favorite projects were becoming a reality during 1950, his last active year, the gap between him and the academic community at Columbia was widening, and it spread rapidly when he became a presidential candidate in 1952 yet continued to reside at 60 Morningside Drive.

During the campaign Eisenhower's critics on Morningside Heights charged that he had used Columbia as a stepping stone for his presidential ambitions. Initially, though he never repeated General William Tecumseh Sherman's famous statement, "I will not accept if nominated and will not serve if elected," as Robert Harron, Columbia's spokesman, recalled, "He didn't slam the door."[13] Still Eisenhower remained determined not to enter politics in 1948, even though public opinion polls emphasized his great popularity and several close friends, including Tom Watson, harbored presidential ambitions for him. His decision made it unlikely he would ever be a candidate. Nearly everyone assumed that summer that Governor Dewey would defeat President Truman and run for re-election in 1952.

Truman's amazing victory in 1948 thrust the General back into the political spotlight, and Eisenhower's speeches, especially on behalf of the American Assembly, came to sound more and more political, especially as he associated throughout the country with businessmen and Texas oilmen. They enjoyed being courted by the World War II hero, and they liked and were reassured by his opposition to "paternalistic and collectivistic ideas which, if adopted, will accomplish the lessening of individual rights and opportunities and finally the collapse of self-government." Historian Robert Griffith has argued thoughtfully that Eisenhower developed during these years a concept of corporate liberalism. Yet his Columbia speeches and analytic and clear letters seem essentially to reflect the values of small town America and plans for his projects, as well as his commitment to internationalism, rather than any well developed political philosophy. His domestic political ideology was, as the editor of the *Eisenhower Papers* has added, largely that "of the heartland in which Eisenhower had grown up."[14]

In spite of the views of some of his new and wealthy friends, from whom he was soliciting funds, he maintained his "moderately conservative" position. They expressed to him their dislike of his defense of Philip Jessup against charges of communist subversion and, when Jessup was again attacked by McCarthy, Eisenhower, though at NATO, again supported the diplomat. "Ike was very kind in responding," the Ambassador recalled, "and helping to do anything he could." Eisenhower's "middle of the road" speech, which criticized "the unfettered power of concentrated wealth" and implied no undoing of the New Deal, displeased Republican conservatives. His commitment to internationalism, moreover, and acceptance of President Truman's request that he lead NATO in the defense of Western Europe alienated ardent nationalists and isolationists. Nor could they be comfortable with Eisenhower's speech to the English Speaking Union in London on July 3, 1951. On this occasion he stressed, as he recalled in *At Ease,* his "conviction that European unity was both possible and necessary to the full achievement of its destiny," and in his talk to a thousand persons he envisioned the United States and

Great Britain as "joined together in purpose and growing determination" to achieve European unity.[15]

Indeed, his leave from Columbia for the NATO assignment easily could have removed him from political consideration. Back on active duty in the army, he lost the freedom and the opportunity he had as a civilian and as President of Columbia to speak on controversial public issues. Moreover, because of his commitment to NATO, he had told Taft that he would stay out of politics if the Senator endorsed collective security. Taft refused and, as Greensntein has emphasized, "Ohio's isolationist-leaning Senator" became "the almost certain GOP choice." Eisenhower, nonetheless, throughout 1951 indicated from his NATO Headquarters that he would only get "tangled up" in politics if there were a genuine draft. He would accept the Republican nomination, Stephen Ambrose has observed, if it were given to him by acclamation.[16] This was reminiscent of when he had given an ultimatum to Watson and Parkinson in 1947 and to Truman in 1950; on both occasions he received the assurances he sought. Senator Taft's strong and determined pursuit for convention delegates, however, made such a nomination of Eisenhower impossible in 1952.

The General finally recognized that he could not continue at NATO and also receive the Republican Party nomination. While he had demonstrated his diplomatic skills during World War II, he had been the Supreme Commander and the Allies had a common goal in defeating Nazi Germany. Columbia may have served as a reminder to the General that the civilian world worked differently. According to a story that circulated around Morningside Heights, Eisenhower once stated, "The University has decided to do so and so." A senior faculty member, supposedly, stood up and replied, "You don't understand, General Eisenhower, the faculty *is* the University."[17]

He knew that to block Taft and isolationism he had to begin to fight for the presidential nomination, and he demonstrated unflinching confidence in his ability to lead the nation. In this respect, his Columbia career, and the associations he had made during his travels to sell the American Assembly and the University, played a vital role. He had successfully formed an influential grass-roots organization, which contributed significantly to his nomination at Chicago. Yet, one could argue, if he had had the White House in mind when he left for NATO and throughout 1951, McCann undoubtedly would have remained on his staff, instead of departing to become a college president and, then, being called back to Paris a few months later. Eisenhower came perilously close to waiting too long to enter the race. In retrospect, his election as President was inevitable, but his nomination by the Republicans was not; he would have lost at the convention without the rallying of last minute enthusiastic support in several states and crucial mistakes by his opponent's campaign.

Eisenhower believed, even before the Korean War, that he could do the job. In 1949, after a long conversation with Governor Dewey, he recorded in his *Diary*, "I wish I [did]¹⁸ could merely say what Sherman said. But how can I know *today* what the situation of this country will be 4 years from now—& whether I'll believe I could do something about it better than most others could. It all seems unreal & forced to me—but I'm not egotistical enough to give any kind of an irrevocable, arbitrary answer at this moment." These musings were brought to bear on his decision in April, 1952, to leave NATO and come home in early June, to campaign aggressively for the nomination, and to win the election.¹⁹

*   *   *

He won the election, after assuring that under his leadership, in his words, "NATO had become a vital and intercontinental institution, a historic fact," but how does one assess his career at Columbia? His Presidency had started in dramatic fashion, but in early 1949 his return to the Pentagon and illness took him away for five months and deprived his leadership of any continuity; second, he left for NATO at the end of 1950. (If he had lost the 1952 election and then returned to Columbia, that would have been an additional two-year absence.) Columbia was a complicated University, and "Eisenhower was not there long enough effectively to adjust himself to the situation," Jacobs observed. "How well he would have adjusted himself, had he had a consecutive uninterrupted period is something I have never been able fully to gauge."²⁰

General Eisenhower, moreover, was accustomed to operating through subordinates and this, too, influenced the relationship between the University and its President. McCann and Schulz controlled his appointments, and they arrived on Morningside Heights, as Dean Smith observed, with "the erroneous idea that at a university the Deans were most important, like Colonels, and the faculty were like Lieutenants and instructors like privates" and required less attention. McCann's and Schulz's failure "to understand the faculty accounted for most of the President's problems," Jacobs reflected, and because of their presence in Low Memorial Eisenhower "never" would have won the faculty. "They didn't have the knowledge of things academic," Carman added, and "I put part of the difficulty which President Eisenhower encountered here right squarely on their doorstep." According to Kirk, Schulz kept the faculty away, "sometimes with disastrous consequences" and faculty members often left the office "feeling terribly disgruntled." Helen King, who worked for a short time in the office with McCann and Schulz and then moved to the Provost's Office, recalled, "I'm not sure now whether I instigated the change or Schulz did. But Schulz made it convenient. . . . I think he hated me worse than I did him, because I had only the University at heart." Years later, Mamie Eisenhower stated that after the General's death she learned that Schulz had caused her husband "a lot of harm" at Columbia; McCann, also, subsequently acknowledged the conflict between Schulz and the faculty. "The fault was on both sides. The faculty didn't try to learn Eisenhower." McCann suggested that Jacobs "could have told Schulz bluntly to stay out of faculty-president relations"; nonetheless, he continued, "some of the faculty were just naturally hostile to Dwight Eisenhower. With them he had absolutely no creditibility."[21]

While McCann "after awhile learned" to work better with the faculty, according to Carman, in the eyes of the academic community he and Schulz appeared indistinguishable in blocking access to Eisenhower. One evening at a cocktail party in honor of McCann and his wife Ruth, Mark Van Doren served as toastmaster. After proposing a toast to Mrs. McCann, he said, "To Kevin McCann, the third best President of Columbia University in all its history." As far as Van Doren was concerned, McCann admitted, "I was the academic man in that office," not Eisenhower. Yet, it was not only Van Doren who stressed McCann's role. "There is no doubt in my mind," his Columbia College colleague Carman declared, "that Kevin McCann exercised a great deal of influence over the General in all things." Perhaps the President, with enormous demands on his time and his extensive correspondence, never understood the problems caused by his front office; Kirk wondered if he even knew about it. In any event, the animosity on campus toward Eisenhower's assistants grew and increasingly harmed his reputation within the University.[22]

Of far greater importance in assessing Eisenhower at Columbia was the failure of Watson and Parkinson and, ultimately, the Trustees to inform Columbia University of their arrangement with the General. This misunderstanding contributed to the marginality of his Presidency. They had no authority to offer the terms they did to Eisenhower, and he specifically accepted the position on those conditions; the Trustees proceeded to confirm and reconfirm these terms before he arrived on campus. The Chairman, Coykendall, who may have been the weak link, did not even know about the special arrangement for nearly six months. The Board of Trustees never officially discussed the implications of the arrangement, nor did it explain it to the faculty. In no way could such a Presidency provide the necessary leadership for Columbia, and the Trustees, in hiding their understanding with Eisenhower from the faculty and students, did a disservice both to him and the University.

The Columbia community, for its part, expected a President who provided both internal and external leadership and who would energetically raise badly needed funds for the University. These expectations were not fulfilled and resulted in mounting criticism of his Presidency. Only a few knew that he did not have the responsibility for an active, internal leadership, and his lack of comfort with faculty groups and activities became apparent quickly when he participated in academic events. And, on occasion, he lost his temper, as he did at the rehearsal for the Cabot Moors awards—for Ginzberg, "Eisenhower had the shortest fuse of almost anybody I've ever known." Carman, reflecting "on this non-enjoyment in getting into things academic," stated that Eisenhower "didn't know, it was ignorance, he didn't understand." Moreover, as Kirk added, many assumed, "He's bound to bring in a great deal of money." Although Watson and Parkinson undoubtedly thought that Eisenhower's name alone, without effort on his part, would raise funds for Columbia, it did not; he neither successfully raised large sums for the University nor established an effective development program.[23]

No assessment can overlook the thoughtful comments made by Carman during a long conversation a decade after Eisenhower's departure from Columbia. Among the faculties no one enjoyed more widespread respect and popularity than the former Dean of the College; no faculty member had been closer to Eisenhower throughout the President's tenure, and they shared a highly valued and loyal friendship. "I think that had he not had the interruptions and if he had nothing other than the University on his mind and then if he had sense enough to have waited on some people . . . or even with members of the faculty and tried to get from them their ideas," it would have been a start. Then, if he had "let it be known that he was going to lean over backwards to see that something could be done to strengthen the University along those lines, both as far as things physical, which meant buildings and equipment, and particularly had he emphasized the importance of scholarly personnel. . . . had he done this and made headway, as I think he might have, you would have had a different story to tell." Carman added, "The great difficulty which the man had, I'll say to my dying day, was he just didn't have the know how."[24]

Eisenhower had seen in Columbia, however, an opportunity to express fervently held convictions, and he had explicitly stated from the beginning that his role was not to administer the University. He knew that with his determination to express his views—and he had the ambition and energy to do so—he was not suited or inclined after his World War II responsibilities and Pentagon duties to undertake what Carman had seen as necessary for a successful Presidency of Columbia. He had not realized what he was getting into at Columbia; nonetheless, with his personal commitment and self-discipline he became far more involved that first year than he ever anticipated, and certainly more than his critics ever acknowledged. He had an amazingly strenuous schedule, and wherever he traveled he brought attention to Columbia. He provided the external leadership he had promised Watson and Parkinson and, as he relentlessly pursued his projects, he had confidence he was doing his job; though he knew he had critics, he could sarcastically dismiss them in his *Diary*. While he sought to modernize the University's structure, his absences and personnel changes prevented the reorganization from functioning smoothly. Not until he departed for NATO, on official leave from the University, and Kirk became Acting President was Columbia's leadership officially and clearly in the hands of one person.

Dean Ackerman, echoing the criticisms of Eisenhower at Columbia, argued that the University "survived" him. Yet, it may be more accurate to contend, as Eli Ginzberg has asserted, that he survived Columbia. "The last years of Butler," Jessup painfully remembered, "were very sad and tragic." For this reason, according to Ginzberg, "The story of Ike at Columbia is really the story of the disorganization of Columbia. . . . The dynamics" of the two-year search for Butler's successor, "are absolutely a crucial piece of this story. The state of disrepair of the University. . . the administrative morass, incompetent Trustees, lack of planning are a big piece of the story," Ginzberg continued. "Nobody other than Ike would have not blown it conspicuously." The fact, he concluded, that Eisenhower "doesn't really become bloodied by pulling some terrific blunders is only an indication of how sophisticated a guy he is." Eisenhower, as Parmet recently wrote, was "far more complicated" than Columbia's Merton imagined.[25]

The "hayseed" view of Eisenhower at Columbia, as well as of his Presidency in Washington, persisted on Morningside Heights for years; indeed, a commentator recently declared, the opinion ranged between "burning resentment and comic relief." For Trilling, the General aroused "contempt," not hostility. "It was very easy to make fun of Eisenhower," Rabi reflected, "since nobody was fighting back." One summer, after Eisenhower assumed the Presidency of the United States, a box arrived at Carmen's office containing "little sculptured figures of the Presidents of the United States, lovely things." James Shenton and Bernard Wishy, colleagues in the History Department, "opened that box, and when we came back in the fall on the edge of the shelves they had arranged each President, not in chronological order but as to their qualifications and the contributions they had made." They had done, Carman remarked, "a remarkably good job." They had not included Eisenhower, however, and they left a statement: "We didn't put the present President in the list because we think it is unfair yet to make a judgment. However, were we to make a judgment on what he has done to date, we would have to put him down along with Mr. Grant."[26]

Carman's colleagues continued to remind him into the 1960s of how little they thought of Eisenhower at Columbia and of his Presidency of the United States. Although a Democrat, he had supported Eisenhower in 1952, but only one or two members of his department had agreed with him. The Stevenson supporters among the Americanists, besides the well-known scholars Nevins, Hofstadter, Morris, and Commager, included the prominent or soon-to-be prominent Lawrence A. Cremin, David H. Donald, Henry F. Graff, William E. Leuchtenburg, Dumas Malone, Walter P. Metzger, James Shenton and Harold Syrett. These historians would be among the nation's leading interpreters of the American past for years to come. In *Anti-Intellectualism in American Life,* for example, Hofstadter stressed Eisenhower's "conventional" mind and "fumbling inarticulateness," whereas he described Stevenson as "a politician of uncommon mind and style" who had a "flair for the apt phrase." Leuchtenburg declared that "Eisenhower vented his hostility toward the public power projects Roosevelt had fostered" and "surrounded himself with men who abhorred the age of Roosevelt." Eisenhower left, the historian added, "an accumulation of unsolved social problems that would overwhelm his successors in the 1960's."[27]

In 1983 Arthur Schlesinger, Jr., asserted that "a tone of condescension was set, at least among intellectuals," during Eisenhower's White House years. "The notion of a genial, indolent man of pied syntax and platitudinous conviction, fleeing from public policy to bridge, golf and westerns, undoubtedly influenced the historians and political scientists who, in my father's poll of 1962, rated him twenty-second among American presidents"—among the ten worst. Yet the critical assessment of Eisenhower, as Schlesinger well knew, already had existed on Morningside Heights during his Columbia Presidency.[28]

Ironically, a signer of the Stevenson campaign ad, which emphasized that Eisenhower had not "mastered the arts of civilian statecraft," would play a major role in the rehabilitation of Eisenhower. In 1964 Donald, who had won the Pulitzer Prize for biography in 1961 and was a member of the History Department at Johns Hopkins, went to the University's President, Milton Eisenhower. He recommended that the publication of the General's papers, as soon as possible, would enhance his reputation. Milton Eisenhower arranged for his brother to meet with Donald and him, and General Eisenhower enthusiastically endorsed the historian's idea. The first five volumes, which covered World War II, appeared as soon as 1970 and by the end of the decade Johns Hopkins Press had published four additional volumes running through his Chief of Staff assignment; moreover, his papers were becoming available at the Eisenhower Library. Soon, a reassessment of Eisenhower was underway, leading to "Eisenhower revisionism" and, as Ambrose has observed, "American historians began to discover that Eisenhower was not the lazy, ineffective, simpleminded 'chairman of the board,' a nice guy with a big grin and an empty head, that they had thought he was." At the time of Donald's suggestion, historians had agreed with the prediction of Shenton and Wishy; by 1982 a new poll ranked Eisenhower ninth.[29]

Eisenhower "revisionism" has not examined his career as President of Columbia, 1948-1953, and these years were far more than an interlude between World War II and the White House. This project, based extensively on contemporary sources and access to Columbia's

Central Archives, began long before "Eisenhower revisionism"; it, though, has benefited likewise from the publication of his papers and the availability of material at the Dwight D. Eisenhower Library.

*   *   *

A visit to Butler Library offers a striking insight into Eisenhower at Columbia. The Library, the center of learning on campus, was named after Eisenhower's predecessor in 1946, a year before the General's appointment. Inside the modest entrance is a large, double stairway which rises to each end of Butler Library's main floor. The visitor, climbing the western side, sees at the top of the stairway a large portrait of Eisenhower in a black academic gown with burgundy trim. On the table in front of him are several books, and the only visible title is "School of General Studies." Undoubtedly not a coincidence. Like the citizenship initiatives, the School's adult education program "fascinated" Eisenhower. General Studies offered a second chance for persons, like Dean Hacker, who had been dropouts and for those with "thwarted or broken educational careers." It gave an opportunity to an Army nurse, partially disabled during the war, who graduated in 1950 at the age of fifty on the G.I. Bill. "I like what you are doing," Eisenhower told Hacker. "Keep on seeing me and telling me what's going on." General Studies students were part-time, older, and commuters; Hacker and Ruth McCann organized a place where they could meet, called "the attic," and the General would stop by, and occasionally Mamie joined him. "He did get around," McCann sighed, "although he does not get any credit for it." One evening he gave a lecture for Hacker at General Studies, sketching "some of the major aspects of war, from its historical beginnings to the tactics and weapons we employed in World War II," and he speculated "about the prospects of future wars now that the atomic bomb existed." The General, the Dean proudly noted, "signed all of the diplomas." Hacker, a widower, married the Army nurse in 1953, and he enjoyed telling her, "You have two fascinating names on your diploma—one was to become President of the United States and the other was to be your husband."[30]

The portrait helps explain why Eisenhower believed in and committed himself to Columbia, which he saw as an academic forum from which he could best articulate and promote his views on contemporary American society. General education, whether it be for adults or college students, or citizenship education for youth; a conference center where important and divisive issues could be discussed; and programs for the study of war and of human resources all assumed a central place in his academic mission. As Eisenhower sought to establish his projects for Columbia, he experienced a world far different than the military with its chain of command and army orders. Initially, he learned, according to Wriston, that the Columbia "faculty was labeled 'Red,' particularly the Teachers College faculty, and he set out in the most industrious way . . . and intelligent way to take that label off them." Second, his work on Morningside Heights, his meetings and speeches in New York City, and his fund-raising trips introduced him to civilian life. It opened new vistas and horizons for him, according to Phil Young, his close associate who worked with him for the American Assembly. If he had become Chancellor of Columbia, with a President responsible for academic and administrative leadership, he could have pursued his projects and sense of mission while widely advertising the University, and he would not have received much of the subsequent criticism. The story of his Columbia tenure might have been considerably different.[31]

Eisenhower succeeded in raising funds for his favorite projects, not for the University's academic programs, though the money, whether from his friends in Texas or Minnesota, would not otherwise have gone to Columbia. Dean Young admitted that Columbia got prestige, not cash, from the American Assembly, but he emphasized that this brought important recognition to Columbia. Did it, though, in the long run lay a foundation for future development programs? In one important instance, the answer was "Yes." Twenty-five years after Eisenhower left Columbia, the University received a $12,000,000 bequest from the estate of alumnus Percy Hudson and his wife, Vida. During the 1930s Hudson, because of "pacifism and radicalism among students," had removed the University from his will. Eisenhower had written Hudson in 1951: "The long-range security of the American people and the free nations rests squarely on American technology and science, and such an institution as the Columbia School of Engineering can contribute to the advancement of American know-how in both pure and applied science." Soon, Eisenhower and Hudson met, and the alumnus proceeded to arrange a new trust agreement unbeknownst to Columbia.[32]

While his projects may have had an intangible financial benefit for the University, they had no impact on the institution's regular academic programs. He had not seen himself as providing educational leadership for the University, and he never assumed that he could. "Eisenhower could think like a civilian," Wriston astutely observed, "but he didn't think like a professor. He didn't think like an intellectual, and he never was a great reader." Doug Black observed that the American Assembly and the Institute of War and Peace "aren't major achievements" and concluded, "I wish I could be more affirmative about it. . . . Maybe there isn't too much to be affirmative about." Milton Eisenhower noted that, while his brother had "sound educational values," he was "without experience with faculty, students, and a university" in his pursuit to achieve institutional objectives. Accordingly, "his influence on the total educational effort was not substantial." [33]

In spite of his lack of academic leadership, his Presidency was significant in the history of Columbia. Any person succeeding Nicholas Murray Butler would have faced a most difficult challenge, even if Columbia had been in better shape than it was in the immediate postwar years. Barzun perceptively described "a transition of a rather negative kind." When President Grayson Kirk "got hold of four or five of us and said what we have got to do is bring this whole place together again and modernize every operation, we perhaps had less resistance because people had seen what inaction produced, drifting." Barzun continued. "We had to sit down and see how the University ran, how it could be run better and that was a slogging job that took a half dozen years." Kirk, himself, saw the interregnum after Butler including the Eisenhower years and lasting until 1953; thus, it made his Presidency more difficult.[34]

Yet if Eisenhower's Presidency were a transition, it contributed immensely to the University's reputation. Eisenhower undoubtedly made the job easier for his successor. One of the world's great figures had come to an institution which had seemingly little interest or excitement for years. With Eisenhower's arrival, glamour and prestige returned to Columbia after a long absence; he gave a new breath of life to the University, and throughout the postwar period he remained America's most popular and respected leader. His name, his speeches and travels, and the programs he initiated brought widespread publicity to Columbia, as did the enormous political interest in him. All this greatly enhanced the University's profile. Kirk did not automatically face a comparison to Nicholas Murray Butler, and he benefited from the hostility to Eisenhower on campus during the 1952 campaign; moreover, by the time he became President the country was entering a period of prosperity and economic expansion. Fund-raising became easier, and Kirk did not have the serious budget crisis of the postwar years.

*   *   *

Eisenhower did not accept the Columbia position with the Presidency of the United States in mind. Columbia offered him an excellent forum from which to articulate his views and to initiate programs which reflected his concerns for contemporary American society, and he took advantage of it. Columbia, thus, played a significant role in the General's education as a civilian; it not only gave him a chance to express his political views, it helped prepare him for the White House. "His years at Columbia were important in the history of that institution and crucial in his career," the editor of the *Eisenhower Papers* has written. "At Columbia he broadened and sharpened his ideas about the political present and future of the United States." Highly disciplined, energetic, conscientious, and hard-working, his activities and his extensive correspondence demonstrated his commitment to democratic citizenship. He enjoyed the opportunity he had at Columbia, and Mamie Eisenhower declared, "He was doing what he wanted to do and was terribly interested in it." One hot day, while walking down the steps in front of Low Memorial and glancing toward Butler Library, "the factory yard appearance" of the campus and "116th Street crowded with parked cars and traffic" distressed Eisenhower. "This was," he recalled, "the physical center and heart of the University. It should be a green oasis." His proposal to close 116th Street and make it "a pleasant mall" took time—he had left for the White House "before the dream became a reality" and dramatically enhanced the beauty of the campus. At Columbia, "I found the work fun—or would have," he continued, "if only I could have concentrated without the distraction of other demands." Still, Columbia was, Mamie Eisenhower added, "one of the very happiest periods" and, when he was dying, she kept the news of the 1968 Columbia disturbances from him.[35]

The demands and constraints Eisenhower faced in the White House, from the Cold War and national security requirements to partisan politics, including McCarthyism, limited his opportunities to pursue goals similar to those he had at Columbia. In the nuclear world of the 1950s he quickly obtained an armistice in the Korean War, and he "waged peace" for eight years. General Andrew Goodpaster, his staff secretary and close confidant at the White House, has written that Eisenhower saw as "a crucial part of his duty . . . the obligation to promote among his fellow citizens . . . responsibility, seriousness, and restraint." Echoes from Columbia could be heard in proposals, ranging from his Atoms-for-Peace Plan to educational exchanges and, as he recalled, "a broad-scale People to People program." In his "Farewell Address" in January, 1961— "The Military Industrial Complex" speech—Eisenhower emphasized the theme he long had considered essential for a democratic society, the need for "an alert and knowledgeable citizenry." As General Colin Powell has concluded, the speech was "a moment worthy of the man from Abilene who so fervently believed in the basic tenets of a democratic society."[36]

Dwight Eisenhower, one of the notable personages of the twentieth century, had a dramatic impact on Columbia, and his appointment was a publicity coup for the University. With his charisma, ambition, and energy he put Columbia on the front page of the nation's newspapers and in the widely circulated news magazines. The postwar era, from demobilization of veterans to the emergence of the Cold War, was a strenuous, hectic and demanding period for the General and Columbia, and both grew from the association. It has been asserted that Eisenhower and Columbia were "not compatible," yet when he arrived on Morningside Heights in 1948 and throughout his first half-year, they complemented one another. Whatever he did and wherever he went, "Ike" was headline news and Columbia benefited. The *Columbia Spectator*, a vociferous critic of Eisenhower, declared on the eve of his departure for NATO, "His great industry led him to succeed in his announced goal to make 'more and more people conscious of Columbia.'" He did this as he pursued his crusade for Columbia, and on his terms he succeeded. As America's most popular and respected person, General Eisenhower brought Columbia's name to people who had not known what or where Columbia was. It is conceivable, moreover, that without the associations he made while selling Columbia and his projects—his "crusade"—he would not have been nominated for President in 1952. His Presidency of Columbia cannot be dismissed nor can it be called "all wrong all around" for either him or the University. Eisenhower paved the way for Columbia's reemergence as a preeminent institution, and his Columbia tenure played a vital role during his appearance on the world stage for two decades.

Notes

1. Dwight D. Eisenhower, *At Ease: Stories I Tell to Friends* (New York, 1967), p.336; Henry Wriston, Oral History interview, 1968, Columbia Oral History Project (COHP).
2. Albert C. Jacobs, Oral History Interview, 1968, COHP; Kevin McCann to author, March 3, 1958; Herbert Parmet, review of *Eisenhower*, by Geoffrey Perret, *New Leader*, November 1-15, 1999, p. 15.
3. Eisenhower to Arthur Hays Sulzberger, December 8, 1950, pp. 1463-64, *The Papers of Dwight David Eisenhower*, vol. XI (Baltimore, Md., 1984), *Columbia University*, ed. Louis Galambos (*PDDE*).
4. Raymond J. Saulnier, personal interview, June 13, 1991, New York, N.Y.; John Gunther, *Eisenhower: The Man and the Symbol* (New York, 1951), pp. 93-94; Sue Zschoche, "The Making of Presidents," comments at "The Presidents Eisenhower Conference," Kansas State University, October 2, 1998; Peter Gay, personal interview, March 24, 1958, New York, N.Y.
5. Gunther, *Eisenhower*, p. 24; Grayson Kirk, Oral History Interview, January 14, 1987, COHP; Stephen E. Ambrose, *Eisenhower: The President* (New York, 1984), p. 28. "His entire bent of mind—this is my firm opinion," McCann argued, "despite all contrary assertions, and I have known him much more intimately than those who criticize him—has been definitely bookish." McCann to author, March 3, 1958.
6. Alan Truscott, "Presidential Savvy," *New York Times,* March 20, 1983.
7. Richard H. Rovere, "The Second Eisenhower Boom," *Harper's Magazine* (May, 1950), p. 33; Herbert S. Parmet, *Eisenhower and the American Crusades* (New York, 1972), p. 15; Geoffrey Perret, *Eisenhower,* (New York, 1999), pp. 382-83; Max Frankel, *The Times of My Life and My Life with the Times* (New York, 1999), p. 93.
8. Jacques Barzun, "Reminiscences of the Columbia History Department," *Columbia* (Winter, 2000), p. 34.
9. Clarence G. Lasby, *Eisenhower's Heart Attack: How Ike Beat Heart Disease and Held on to the Presidency* (Lawrence, Kans., 1997), p. 50.
10. Eli Ginzberg, personal interview, December 11, 1990, New York, N.Y.; Grayson L. Kirk, Oral History Interview, January 14 and September 3, 1987, COHP.
11. Fred I. Greenstein, The Presidential Difference:Leadership Style from FDR to Clinton (New York, 2000), pp. 46, 55.
12. Grayson L. Kirk to author, January 3, 1993; Eisenhower to Leonard McCollum, May 31, 1950, *PDDE,* XI, 1144-48.
13. Robert C. Harron, personal interview, December 1, 1961, New York, N.Y.
14. Eisenhower to McCollum, May 31, 1950, *PDDE,* XI, 1144-48; Robert Griffith, "Dwight D. Eisenhower and the Corporate Commonwealth," *American Historical Review,* 87 (February, 1982), 87-123; Galambos, "Introduction, *PDDE,* X, xxi.
15. Ibid.; For H. L. Hunt's criticism of Communist sympathizers and Jessup in letters to Eisenhower, see PDDE, XI, 925-36, 961-62; Philip Jessup, personal interview, June 17, 1977, Norfolk, Ct.; *New York Times,* September 6, 1949, and July 4, 1951; Eisenhower, *At Ease,* pp. 376-77; McCann, interview, July 25, 1972.
16. Greenstein, *Presidential Difference*, p. 47; Stephen E. Ambrose, *Eisenhower: Soldier, General of the Army, President-Elect, 1890-1952* (New York, 1983), p. 518.
17. Kirk, interview, January 14, 1987, COHP. The faculty member may have been I. I. Rabi.
18. The "did" was crossed out in the original *Diary* entry.

19. Eisenhower, *Diary,* July 7, 1949, *PDDE,* X, 677-79.
20. Dwight D. Eisenhower, *At Ease: Stories I Tell to Friends* (New York, 1967), p. 377; Albert C. Jacobs, personal interview, February 5, 1965, Hartford, Ct.
21. Young B. Smith, personal interview, February 4, 1958, New York, N.Y.; Albert C. Jacobs to author, March 10, 1958; Jacobs, interview, February 5, 1965; Harry J. Carman, personal interview, December 1, 1961, New York, N.Y.; Kirk, interview, January 14, 1987, COHP; Helen King, Oral History Interview, May 12, 1975, Dwight D. Eisenhower Library (OHDDEL); Mamie D. Eisenhower, personal interview, December 15, 1975, Gettysburg, Pa.; Kevin McCann, personal interview, July 25, 1972, Gettysburg, Pa.
22. Carman, personal interview, January 30, 1958, New York, N.Y., and December 1, 1961; McCann, interview, July 25, 1972; Kirk, interview, January 14, 1987, COHP.
23. Eli Ginzberg, Oral History Interview, May 14, 1975, OHDDEL; Harry J. Carman, personal interview, December 1, 1961, New York, N.Y.; Kirk, interview, January 14, 1987, COHP.
24. Carman, interview, December 1, 1961.
25. Carl W. Ackerman, personal interview, March 24, 1958, New York, N.Y.; Ginzberg, interview, December 11, 1990; Jessup, interview, June 17, 1977; Parmet, review of *Eisenhower,* by Perret, *New Leader,* November 1-15, 1999, p. 15.
26. Zschoche, "The Making of Presidents," comments, October 2, 1998; Lionel Trilling, personal interview, February 4, 1958, New York, N.Y.; Rabi, interview, January 26, 1985, COHP; Carman, interview, December 1, 1961.
27. *New York Times,* October 16, 1952; Richard Hofstadter, *Anti-Intellectualism in American Life* (New York, 1963), pp. 3-4, 21-22; William E. Leuchtenburg, *In the Shadow of FDR: From Harry Truman to Ronald Reagan* (Ithaca, N.Y., 1983), pp. 54-55; Leuchtenburg, *A Troubled Feast: American Society Since 1945,* updated edition (Boston, 1983), p. 91; Steve Neal, "Why We Were Right to Like Ike," *American Heritage,* 37 (December, 1985), pp. 49-64.
28. Arthur M. Schlesinger, Jr., "The Ike Age Revisited," *Reviews in American History*, XI (March, 1983) 2. For the 1962 poll, see Arthur M. Schlesinger, "Our Presidents: A Rating by 75 Historians," *New York Times Magazine,* July 29, 1962, pp. 12, 40-41.
29. Ambrose, *Eisenhower*, pp. 653-54; David H. Donald, personal interview, July 30, 1990, Cambridge, Mass.; Louis Galambos, Daun Van Ee, and Elizabeth Hughes, "Eisenhower's First Presidency," *Columbia* (February, 1985), p. 12; Steve Neal, "Our Best and Worst Presidents, *Chicago Tribune Magazine,* January 10, 1982, pp. 9-11.
30. The painting by Elio Christo-Leveanu was finished in 1950. Louis M. Hacker, Oral History Interview, May 15, 1975, OHDDEL; McCann, interview, July 25, 1972; Eisenhower, *At Ease,* 356-57.
31. Phil Young, personal interview, June 15, 1977, Van Hornesville, N.Y.; Wriston, interview, 1968, COHP.
32. Young, interview, June 15, 1977; *New York Times,* April 12, 1978.
33. Milton Eisenhower, personal interview, July 26, 1972, Baltimore, Md. ; Wriston, interview, 1968, COHP; Douglas Black, personal interview, June 6, 1973, New York, N.Y.
34. Jacques Barzun, personal interview, April 5, 1979, New York, N.Y.; Grayson Kirk, personal interview, May 15, 1973, New York, N.Y.
35. Galambos, "Introduction," *PDDE,* X, xxiii; Mamie D. Eisenhower, personal interview, December 15, 1975, Gettysburg, Pa.
36. Andrew J. Goodpaster, "Foreword," *Eisenhower: A Centenary Assessment,* ed. Gunter Bischof and Stephen E. Ambrose (Baton Rouge, La., 1995), p. xix; Dwight D. Eisenhower, *The White House Years: Waging Peace, 1956-1961* (New York, 1965), pp. 392, 410-11, 614-16; Colin Powell, "Eisenhower:Warrior and President," The History Channel, June 6, 2000.

Bibliography

This study relies heavily on unpublished sources, the published papers of Dwight D. Eisenhower, two contemporary newspapers, and personal correspondence. Initially, personal interviews by the author, by the Columbia Oral History Project, Butler Library (COHP), and by the Dwight D. Eisenhower Library in Abilene, Kansas (OHDDEL) contributed valuable material. The paper could not have been written without material in the Central Archives of Columbia University in Low Memorial Library (CACU) and the Eisenhower Papers at the Eisenhower Library (DDEL). The primary files at the Eisenhower Library are "pre-Presidential, 1916-52." When this material has appeared in *The Papers of Dwight David Eisenhower* (*PDDE*) I have cited the published papers. The *Eisenhower Papers*, to date, include seventeen volumes, 1941-1957, and volumes VIII-XII were the important ones for the study. The newspapers are the *New York Times* and the *Columbia Daily Spectator;* I have also used newspaper clippings in files at the Eisenhower Library and selected newspapers and magazines at the Library of Congress and on microfilm.

Primary Sources

Additional Manuscript Collections

Carl W. Ackerman Papers, Library of Congress (LC), Washington, D.C.
American Assembly Papers, American Assembly, Columbia University (AACU) Interchurch Center, New York.
Edward J. Birmingham Papers, DDEL.
Harry J. Carman Papers, Butler Library, Columbia University
Dwight D. Eisenhower Files, Columbiana, Columbia University.
Mamie D. Eisenhower Papers, DDEL.
Albert C. Jacobs Papers, Bentley Historical Library, Michigan Historical Collections, Ann Arbor, Mi.
Philip C. Jessup Papers, LC.
William E. Robinson Papers, DDEL.

Hopward M. Snyder, M.D., Papers, DDEL.
Lewis L. Strauss Papers, Herbert C. Hoover Library, West Branch, IA.
Vestry Minutes, The Parish of Trinity Church in the City of New York.
Ann Whitman File, DDEL.

Additional Unpublished Material

Ackerman, Carl W. "The Story of General Eisenhower." LC.
Ayers, Harry Morgan. "Recollections of June 21, 1947." Eisenhower Files, Columbiana.
Columbia University. Installation of Dwight David Eisenhower As Thirteenth President. October 12, 1948.
Jacobs, Albert C. "Memoirs." Unpublished, 1974. Personal Possession.
Jewish Theological Seminary of America. "Convocation." September 28, 1948. New York.
Murrow, Edward R. "With the News." October 12, 1948. DDEL.
Stebenne, David L. "Thomas J. Watson and the Business-Government Relationship, 1933-1956." Forthcoming.
Zschoche, Sue. "The Making of Presidents: Who Have Universities Sought as Leaders and Why?" The Presidents Eisenhower Conference, October 2, 1998, Kansas State University.

Personal Correspondence

Joseph Campbell. February 4, 1964; November 21, 1981; February 21, 1982.
Milton S. Eisenhower. January 28, 1982.
Barbara Foltz. November 21, 1995.
Henry F. Graff. April 14, 1998.
Eli Ginzberg. April 4, 1991; May 4, 1999.
Albert C. Jacobs. March 10, 1958.
Grayson L. Kirk. March 3, 1992; January 3, 1993; January 16, 1997.
Arthur Krock. April 2, 1958.
John A. Krout. June 1, 1960.
William E. Leuchtenburg. March 15, 1993.
Kevin McCann. March 3, 1958; June 26, 1963; December 16, 1964.
Richard H. Rovere. c. April, 1978.
Philip Young. March 5, 1982.
Aaron Warner. March 20, 1996.

Personal Interviews

Carl W. Ackerman. March 24, 1958. New York, N.Y.
Jacques Barzun. April 5, 1979. New York, N.Y.
Douglas M. Black. June 6, 1973. New York, N.Y.
Joseph Campbell. March 11, 1958, and February 25, 1964. Washington, D.C.
Harry J, Carman. January 30, 1958, and December 1, 1961. New York, N.Y.
James Dohr. February 24, 1958. New York, N.Y.
David H. Donald. July 30, 1990. Cambridge, Ma.

Mamie D. Eisenhower. December 15, 1975. Gettysburg, Pa.
Milton S. Eisenhower. July 26, 1972. Baltimore, Md.
Peter Gay. February 24, 1958, New York, N.Y., and April 8, 1999. Middlebury, Vt.
Eli Ginzberg. March 14, 1958, and December 11, 1990. New York, N.Y.
Henry F. Graff. January 30, 1958, and June 13, 1991. New York, N.Y.
Louis M. Hacker. January 30, 1958. New York, N.Y.
W. Averell Harriman. October 13, 1977. Washington, D.C.
Robert C. Harron. April 10, 1958, and December 1, 1961. New York, N.Y.
R. Gordon Hoxie. November 10, 1978, and June 9, 1995. New York, N.Y.
Albert C. Jacobs. February 5, 1965, Hartford, Ct., and December 31, 1973. Ann
    Arbor, Mi.
Loretta B. Jacobs. October 2, 1979. Edgartown, Ma.
Philip C. Jessup. June 17, 1977. Norwalk, Ct.
Robert L. Johnson. March 3, 1958. Philadelphia, Pa.
Grayson L. Kirk. May 12, 1975. New York, N.Y.
John A. Krout. January 30, 1958. New York, N.Y.
Kevin McCann. July 25, 1973. Gettysburg, Pa.
Clifford Nelson. September 16, 1993. Middlebury, Vt.
Allan Nevins. March 14, 1958. New York, N.Y.
Raymond J. Saulnier. June 13, 1991. New York, N.Y.
Robert L. Schulz. March 11, 1958. Washington, D.C.
Ellis D. Slater. September 1, 1972. Edgartown, Mass.
Young B. Smith. February 4, 1958. New York, N.Y.
Arthur H. Sulzberger. March 27, 1958. New York, N.Y.
Adrienne Swift. December 5, 1993 (telephone conversation). Sarasota, Fl.
Lionel Trilling. February 4, 1958. New York, N.Y.
David B. Truman. February 4, 1958. New York, N.Y.
Bruce Wonnacott. November 11, 1977. Middlebury, Vt.
Philip Young. June 15, 1977. Van Hornesville, N.Y.

Columbia Oral History Project Interviews

Douglas M. Black. 1967.
Herbert Brownell. 1967-68.
Lucius D. Clay. 1967.
Jacqueline Cochrane. 1968-73.
Dwight D. Eisenhower. 1967.
Luther H. Evans. 1970.
Frank D. Fackenthal. 1956.
Albert C. Jacobs. 1968.
Grayson L. Kirk. 1985-87.
Sigurd S. Larmon. 1970.
Kevin McCann. 1966.
Bradshaw Mintener. 1968.
Arthur Nevins. 1970.
I. I. Rabi. 1983.
Clifford Roberts. 1969-72.

Lindsay Rogers. 1958.
Richard H. Rovere. 1968.
Raymond J. Saulnier. 1967.
Robert L. Schulz. 1968.
Ellis D. Slater. 1970.
Harry J. Wriston. 1968.

Dwight D. Eisenhower Library Oral History Interviews

Eli Ginzberg, 1975-78.
Louis M. Hacker, 1975.
Joe Ingraham, 1972.
Helen S. King, 1975.
Grayson L. Kirk, 1975.
John A. Krout, 1977.
Jack H. Porter, 1972, 1975.

Secondary Sources

Books

Ambrose, Stephen E. *Eisenhower: Soldier, General of the Army, President-Elect, 1890-1952*. New York, 1983.
_____. *Eisenhower: The President*. New York, 1984.
_____, and Immerman, Richard H. *Milton S. Eisenhower: Educational Statesman*. Baltimore, Md., 1983.
Bender, Thomas. *New York Intellect: A History of Intellectual Life in New York City, from 1750 to the Beginnings of Our Own Time*. New York, 1987.
Bischof, Gunter, and Ambrose, Stephen E., eds. *Eisenhower: A Centenary Assessment*. Baton Rouge, La., 1995.
Brinkley, Alan. *New Deal Liberalism in Recession and War*. New York, 1995.
Bush, Vannevar. *Pieces of Action*. New York, 1970.
Childs, Marquis. *Eisenhower, Captive Hero: A Critical Study of the General and the President*. New York, 1958.
Columbian, 1949. Baltimore, Md., 1950.
Conant, James Bryant. *My Several Lives: Memoirs of a Social Inventor*. New York, 1970.
Coon, Horace. *Columbia: Colossus on the Hudson*. New York, 1947.
Cook, Blanche Wiesen. *The Declassified Eisenhower: A Divided Legacy*. New York, 1981.
Cremin, Lawrence A. *American Education: The Metropolitan Experience, 1876-1980*. New York, 1988.
_____. ; Shannon, David A.; and Townsend, Mary Evelyn. *A History of Teachers College, Columbia University*. New York, 1954.
David, Lester, and David, Irene. *The Story of the General and His Lady*. New York, 1981.
Davis, Kenneth S. *Soldier of Democracy: A Biography of Dwight Eisenhower*. New York, 1945.

Dolkart, Andrew S. *Morningside Heights: A History of Its Architecture & Development.* New York, 1998.

Doyle, William. *Inside the Oval Office: The White House Tapes from FDR to Clinton.* New York, 1999.

Eisenhower, Dwight D. *At Ease: Stories I Tell to Friends.* New York, 1967.

_____. *Crusade in Europe.* New York, 1948.

_____. *The Eisenhower Diaries.* Edited by Robert H. Ferrell. New York,1981.

_____. *Mandate for Change: 1953-1956.* New York, 1963.

_____. *The Papers of Dwight David Eisenhower.* Baltimore, Md., 1970-. vols. I-V, *The War Years,* edited by Alferd D. Chandler, Jr. (1970); vol. VI, *Occupation, 1945,* edited by Alfred D. Chandler, Jr., and Louis Galambos (1978); vols. VII-IX, *The Chief of Staff,* edited by Louis Galambos (1978); vols. X-XI, *Columbia University,* edited by Louis Galambos (1984); vols. XII-XIII, *NATO and the Campaign of 1952,* edited by Louis Galambos (1989); vols. XIV-XVII, *The President: The Middle Way,* edited by Louis Galambos (1996).

_____. *Waging Peace: 1956-61.* New York, 1965.

Eisenhower, John S.D. *Strictly Personal.* New York, 1974.

Eisenhower, Milton S. *The President Is Calling.* New York, 1974.

Eisenhower, Susan. *Mrs. Ike: Memories and Reflections on The Life of Mamie Eisenhower.* New York, 1996.

Forrestal, James. *The Forrestal Diaries.* Edited by Walter Millis. New York, 1951.

Frankel, Max. *The Times of My Life and My Life with The Times.* New York, 1999.

Ginzberg, Eli. *Human Resources: The Wealth of a Nation.* New York, 1958.

_____. *The Ineffective Soldier: Lessons for Management and the Nation.* New York, 1959.

Greene, John Robert. *The Crusade: The Presidential Election of 1952.* Lanham, Md., 1985.

Greenstein, Fred I. *The Presidential Difference: Leadership Style from FDR to Clinton.* New York, 2000.

Griffith, Robert, ed. *Ike's Letters to a Friend: 1941-1958.* Lawrence, KS. 1984.

Gunther, John. *Eisenhower: The Man and the Symbol.* New York, 1951.

Hamby, Alonzo L. *Beyond the New Deal.* New York, 1973.

_____. *Man of the People: A Life of Harry S. Truman.* New York, 1995.

Hechler, Ken. *Working with Truman: A Personal Memoir of the White House Years.* New York, 1982.

Hofstadter, Richard. *Anti-Intellectualism in American Life.* New York,1963.

_____. *The Progressive Historians: Turner, Beard, Parrington.* New York, 1970.

Jumonville, Neil. *Henry Steele Commager: Midcentury Liberalism and the History of the Present.* Chapel Hill, N.C., 1999.

Krock, Arthur. *Memoirs: Sixty Years on the Firing Line.* New York, 1968.

Kluger, Richard. *The Paper: The Life and Death of the New York Herald Tribune.* New York, 1986.

Lasby, Clarence G. *Eisenhower's Heart Attack: How Ike Beat Heart Disease and Held on to the Presidency.* Lawrence, 1997.

Leuchtenburg, William E. *A Troubled Feast: American Society.* Updated Edition. Boston, 1983.

_____. *In the Shadow of FDR: From Harry Truman to Ronald Reagan.* Ithaca, N.Y., 1983.

Lyon, Peter. *Eisenhower: Portrait of the Hero.* Boston, 1974.

Marrin, Albert. *Nicholas Murray Butler.* New York, 1976.

McCann, Kevin. *Man from Abilene.* New York, 1952.

Neal, Steve. *The Eisenhowers: Reluctant Dynasty.* New York, 1978.

Oshinsky, David M. *A Conspiracy So Immense: The World of Joe McCarthy.* New York, 1983.

Owen, David. *The Making of the Masters: Clifford Roberts, Augusta National, and Golf's Most Prestigious Tournament.* New York, 1999.

Parmet, Herbert S. *Eisenhower and the American Crusades.* New York, 1972.

Patterson, James T. *Mr. Republican: A Biography of Robert A. Taft.* Boston, 1972.

Perret, Geoffrey. *Eisenhower.* New York, 1999.

Rosovsky, Henry. *The University: An Owner's Manual.* New York, 1990.

Schrecker, Ellen W. *No Ivory Tower: McCarthyism & The Universities.* New York, 1986.

Slater, Ellis D. *The Ike I Knew.* Baltimore, Md., 1980.

Smith, Jean Edward. *Lucius D. Clay: An American Life.* New York, 1990.

Smith, Richard Norton. *Thomas E. Dewey and His Times.* New York, 1982.

Taylor, Allan, ed. *What Eisenhower Thinks.* New York, 1952.

Taylor, Maxwell D. *Swords and Plowshares.* New York, 1972.

Tifft, Susan, and Jones, Alex S. *The Trust: The Private and Powerful Family Behind the New York Times.* New York, 1999.

Troy, Gil. *Affairs of State: The Rise and Rejection of the Presidential Couple Since World War II.* New York, 1997.

Tugwell, Rexford. *To the Lesser Heights of Morningside: A Memoir.* Philadelphia, 1982.

Warshaw, Shirley Anne, ed. *Reexamining the Eisenhower Presidency.* Westport, Ct., 1992.

Watson, Thomas J., Jr., and Petre, Peter. *Father, Son & Co.: My Life at IBM and Beyond.* New York, 1990

Wechsler, Harold S. *The Qualified Student: A History of Selective College Admission in America.* New York, 1977.

Articles

Ambrose, Stephen E. "Eisenhower's Legacy." In Gunter Bischof and Stephen E. Ambrose, ed., *Eisenhower: A Centenary Assessment.* Baton Rouge, La., 1995, 246-56.

_____. "The Ike Age." *The New Republic,* May 9, 1981.

Barzun, Jacques. "Reminiscences of the Columbia History Department." *Columbia* (Winter, 2000), 24-34.

Berger, Meyer. "Rich Color and Solemn Pageantry of Middle Ages Greet Eisenhower." *New York Times,* October 13, 1948.

Bernstein, Barton. J. "Election of 1952." In *History of American Presidential*

Elections: 1789-1968, vol. IV., edited by Arthur M. Schlesinger, Jr. New York, 1971.

Boyer, R. O. "Drive, Drive, Drive." *New Yorker,* October 9, 1948.

Brandt, Joseph August. "Poison in the Ivy." *Saturday Review of Literature,* January 13, 1945, 5-7.

Brinkley, Alan. "A President for Certain Seasons." *Wilson Quarterly,* XIV (Spring, 1990), 110-19.

Carmichael, O. C. "What Makes a Good College President." *New York Times Magazine,* September 7, 1947.

Childs, Marquis. "Why Eisenhower Said No." *Collier's,* August 28, 1948, 14-15.

Deutsch, Monroe Emanuel. "Choosing College Presidents." *School and Society,* October 25, 1947, 308-309.

Davis, Kenneth S. "Ike and I: A Personal Remembrance." *The American Scholar,* 55 (Winter, 1985-86), 55-74.

"Dwight Eisenhower: 1890-1969." *Time,* April 4, 1969.

Eisenhower, Dwight D. "An Open Letter to American Students." *Reader's Digest* 53 (October, 1948), 1-5.

_____. "An Open Letter to Parents." *Reader's Digest* 54 (February, 1949), 11-14.

_____. "Lincoln Had the Proper Attitude toward Power: Service to Others and the True Meaning of Liberty." *Vital Speeches of the Day* 15, no. 8 (1949), 335-36.

_____. "Mental Health: Key to World Peace." *Cosmopolitan* 125, no. 2 (August, 1948), 35, 91.

Fine, Benjamin. "Education in Review." *New York Times,* October 10, 1948.

Freeman, Ira Henry. "Eisenhower of Columbia." *New York Times Magazine,* November 7, 1948.

Galambos, Louis; Van Ee, Daun; and Hughes, Elizabeth. "Eisenhower's First Presidency." *Columbia* (February, 1985), 12-18.

Ginzberg, Eli. "Conservation of Human Resources." *Science,* November 23, 1951, 3.

Goldhamer, Joan D. "General Eisenhower in Academe: A Clash of Perspectives and a Study Supressed." *Journal of the History of the Behavioral Sciences* 33 (Summer, 1997), 241-59.

Goodpaster, Andrew J. "Foreword." In *Eisenhower: A Centenary Assessment.,* edited by Gunter Bischof & Stephen E. Ambrose, xv-xx. Baton Rouge, La., 1995.

Greenstein, Fred. "Eisenhower's Leadership Style." In *Eisenhower: A Centenary Assessment,* edited by Gunter Bischof & Stephen E. Ambrose, 55-63. Baton Rouge, La., 1995.

Griffith, Robert. "Dwight D. Eisenhower and the Corporate Commonwealth." *American Historical Review* 87 (February, 1982), 87-123.

Hatch, Alden. "The Prexy Plan of General Ike." *Collier's,* September 13, 1947, 11+.

Hoxie, R. Gordon. "Dwight David Eisenhower: Bicentennial Considerations." *Presidential Studies Quarterly,* XX (Spring, 1990), 253-64.

_____. "Eisenhower and Presidential Leadership." *Presidential Studies Quarterly,* XIII (Fall, 1983), 589-612.

Le Comte, Edward. "Dinner with Butler and Eisenhower: A Columbia Memoir." *Commentary,* January 1986.

McAuliffe, Mary S. "Commentary/Eisenhower, the President." *Journal of American History* 68 (December, 1981), 625-32.

Neal, Steve. "Our Best and Worst Presidents." *Chicago Tribune Magazine,* January 10, 1982.

_____. "Why We Were Right to Like IKE." *American Heritage* 36 (December, 1985), 49-64.

Nevins, Allan. "University City With in the City." *New York Times,* June 6, 1948.

O'Donnell, Francis. "Ike's Other Presidency." *Humanities* 2 (October,1981), 4-5.

Parmet, Herbert S. Review of *Eisenhower* by Geoffrey Perret. *New Leader,* November 1-15, 1999, 14-15.

Phillips, Cabell. "Eisenhower Encircled by Still More Mystery." *NewYork Times,* November 5, 1950.

Pogue, Forrest C. "Genesis of *The Supreme Command."* In *Eisenhower: A Centenary Assessment.,* edited by Gunter Bischof and Stephen E. Ambrose, 19-39. Baton Rouge, La., 1995.

Porter, Russell. "Eisenhower Takes Office At Columbia: Stresses Freedom." *New York Times,* October 13, 1948.

Reynolds, Quentin. "Mr. President Eisenhower." *Life,* April 17, 1950, 144-60.

Rogers, Lindsay. "Reflections on Writing Biography of Public Men." *Political Science Quarterly* 88 (December, 1973), 25-33.

Rosenthal, Michael. "Nicholas Murray Butler: Captain of Erudition." *Columbia Library Columns* XLIV (Autumn, 1995), 5-11.

Rovere, Richard H. "The Second Eisenhower Boom." *Harper's,* May 1950, 31-39.

Schlesinger, Arthur M., Jr. "The Ike Age Revisited." *Reviews in American History* XI (March, 1983), 1-11.

Schlesinger, Arthur M. "Our Presidents: A Rating by 75 Historians." *New York Times Magazine,* July 29,1962, pp. 12, 40-41.

Snyder, Howard M. "Conservation of Human Resources." *Conservation of Human Resources.* New York, 1957.

_____. "The Origins of the Conservation Project." *Conservation of Human Resources.* New York, 1956.

Truscott, Alan. "Presidential Savvy." *New York Times,* March 20, 1983.

Wala, Michael. "An 'Education in Foreign Affairs for the Future President': The Council on Foreign Relations and Dwight D. Eisenhower." In *Reexamining the Eisenhower Presidency,* edited by Shirley Anne Warshaw, 1-15. Westport, Ct., 1992.

"What Has Ike Got?" *Life,* June 5, 1950.

Zinsser, William. "Columbia Confronts Eisenhower With a Complex, Difficult Job." *New York Herald-Tribune,* June 6, 1948.

Television Programs

"Eisenhower," *The American Experience*, PBS Video, 1993.

"Eisenhower:Warrior and President." The History Channel, 2000.

Index